The
Imaginary Witness

The
Imaginary Witness

The Critical Theory of
Herbert Marcuse

Morton Schoolman

New York University Press
1984

Library of Congress Cataloging in Publication Data

Schoolman, Morton.
    The imaginary witness.

    Bibliography: p.
    Includes index.
    1. Marcuse, Herbert, 1898-1979. 2. Social sciences
—Philosophy. 3. Political science. 4. Civilization,
Modern. 5. Marcuse, Herbert, 1898-1979. —Biography.
I. Title.
H61.M4234S36   300'.1   80-640
ISBN 0-8147-7833-X

Printed in the United States of America

For Maureen
and
Ethan and Rachel

Contents

Four

Civilization Without Discontents I:
Domination—Political or Technological?   131

Concluding Remarks

Preface

Few figures in contemporary social theory have been as controversial as Herbert Marcuse. While he lived, his thought most often was celebrated and attacked, embraced and dismissed with a passion blinding adequate and reasoned consideration. Marcuse was constantly on the defensive against his accusers and supporters, who both frequently attributed views to him that he did not hold. Seldom was *criticism* forthcoming.

Certainly prejudice can be held responsible, though not exclusively, for the misinterpretations of Marcuse's social thought. The explosive era in which he became highly visible and the nature of Marcuse's work are implicated as well. Rooted in the Germanic tradition extending from Hegel through Marx, Dilthey, Weber, Husserl, Heidegger, Lukacs, Freud, and the Frankfurt School, and at all times creatively assimilating the ideas of these and other members of that tradition, Marcuse's work is difficult and, as has been alleged, sometimes painfully so. Beyond the obvious problems, such difficulty in style as well as in substance has antagonized many readers while beguiling others and hence has led to the greatest misunderstandings. Also, Marcuse was never shy about engaging in polemics. In fact, he looked upon the polemic as an indispensable tool for social theory, all the more so, he believed, the greater the extent to which the critical perspectives of theory appeared to be disarmed by the powers of ideology. Consequently, Marcuse's argument often was hidden behind his ostensible argument, a discursive tactic adapted to a political cause but unfortunately sacrificing clarity of meaning and actually harming the cause that ultimately depended upon arguments clearly presented. And by virtue of his polemics, on few occasions his positions encouraged discussion and debate of the sort that allowed the issues with which he was feverishly occupied to be advanced to another and perhaps more promising level of discussion. His arguments, and particularly those on the most pressing matters, often shut down debate. Moreover, characteristic of Marcuse's polemical style was an unwavering confidence that encouraged his readers to pass over problematic areas and perplexing questions and to take sides—to become, in effect, disciples or opponents. Refusing to do so, from either side one nevertheless seemed to be allied with the other. Not least important, the turbulent period of the 1960s, in which Marcuse's social theory first became widely known, and the political events with which it became associated help to explain why criticism lagged far behind extreme reactions to his work.

None of these factors now pose obstacles to comprehending the richness, complexity, and significance of Marcuse's thought. During the past decade there has been a groundswell of interest in the Frankfurt School, its history and heritage, and in those who have developed critical theory by overcoming its formative isolation in the Germanic tradition through an appropriation of other traditions of thought, particularly British analytic philosophy, once narrowly considered to be hostile to critical theory. Publications, formal meetings, and informal discussions in the academic community, additions to graduate and undergraduate curriculums in colleges and universities, and changing perspectives in many disciplines within the social sciences and humanities are indications that critical theory and its tradition are becoming increasingly accessible and ever more influential. As a result, the intellectual climate is favorable to a renewed consideration of Marcuse's social theory. And not only the intellectual but the political climate, too, has altered. For the present, at least, Marcuse's arguments, especially those shrouded in polemics, can be evaluated properly in an atmosphere perhaps no less politicized, but certainly less polarized, than that of the last decade.

In the short time since his death there has been a flourish of activity marking the beginnings of a reconsideration of Marcuse's social theory. One of the two primary aims of *The Imaginary Witness* is to facilitate such investigations by providing the first systematic and comprehensive exposition and interpretation of Marcuse's entire life's work. Its second objective is a critical analysis internal to Marcuse's social theory in the sense that it attempts to discover the conceptual limits of his theoretical framework, to account for the origins of these limits, and to demonstrate how his arguments are shaped within and by this framework and what highly important considerations it necessarily excludes. But the critical analysis has been made sympathetically. The account that I offer for what I contend to be his errors implicitly serves to extricate Marcuse from the harsh indictments that have been leveled in the past. It is my wish that the critique be received in this spirit.

There is one phase of Marcuse's work to which I am particularly sympathetic. Criticism is focused largely upon Marcuse's thought as it took shape after 1933. But before the nightmarish shock of that year produced a dramatic turn in Marcuse's thinking, his early work had constituted a significant project that ought to be pursued by contemporary social theory, though not necessarily in the same manner in which it was first conceived by Marcuse. Although there is not a single aspect of Marcuse's thought that has not been of fascination to me, perhaps more than anything else the ambitions and humanism of his early writings provided inspiration for this study.

For two reasons I have not attempted to analyze extensively the development of Marcuse's social theory in relation to that of Max Horkheimer, Theodor Adorno, and the other members of the Frankfurt School. To the extent to which this task is necessary and, I believe, possible, it has been accomplished ably and admirably by Martin Jay in *The Dialectical Imagination: A History of the Frankfurt School and the Institute for Social Research, 1923–1950* (Boston: Little, Brown, 1973). Second, Marcuse's thought now seems to me to be distinctive in so many respects that drawing attention to views similarly held by his Frankfurt School colleagues would obscure his originality. I am aware that this last point requires demonstration. But the comparative and historical investigation such an effort entails would lead far beyond the limits of this study and the powers of its author—both exhausted by the task of comprehensively and critically examining Marcuse's life work.

Although this study was in part inspired by the need not only for a comprehensive evaluation of Marcuse's social thought but also for a reevaluation of the majority of his arguments already examined in the secondary literature, many of the critical essays on Marcuse are clearly excellent. Because my study has assumed a course quite different from any taken by earlier investigations, to avoid the awkwardness of frequently interrupting discussions to summarize and entertain criticisms by others of particular aspects of Marcuse's work, I have chosen to respond to critical arguments at an implicit level of analysis. For the reader's consideration I have appended my bibliography of nearly all the critical literature on Marcuse published in several languages up to 1979.

Whenever possible I have used English translations of Marcuse's works. On those occasions when translations were not satisfactory I have not hesitated to introduce necessary changes. Each such case has been indicated. In my translations I have rendered the German texts as literally as possible without primary regard for stylistic considerations.

During the three years spent writing this book and the prior years devoted to its conception, I have accumulated substantial intellectual debts, which, though I can never begin to repay, I am very happy and eager to acknowledge.

My indebtedness is heaviest to William Connolly and Martin Jay. Both provided sound advice, invaluable criticism, and the kindness and friendship that gave me much needed support and encouragement during all stages of this manuscript. They have established the highest standards for their own work, which I have tried to adopt as a model of excellence.

Susan Buck-Morss and Paul Piccone read earlier drafts of certain chapters and offered comments that proved extremely useful. Ted Norton devoted long hours to discussing Marcuse's work with me; his understanding of complex issues and keen insights improved this book considerably. Jean Elshtain drew my attention to significant aspects of psychoanalytic theory, which gave depth to my critical analysis of Marcuse's interpretation of Freud. Although brief, discussions with William Leiss, C. B. Macpherson, and Stanley Aronowitz left a deep impression on me that is reflected in arguments in the text. Over the years there has never been a moment when my friends Jeff Tullis and George Alkalay were not willing to extend a helping hand and to give of their time and energy to offer suggestions. For their generosity and thoughtfulness I am very grateful. Guy Dodge, Duncan Smith, Dan Brock, Eric Nordlinger, Helen Feldstein, and Susan Marsh were valued teachers during my years as a doctoral candidate at Brown University; each in a different and important way contributed to my examination of various problems. Knut Tarnowski's translations of many of the darker passages of Marcuse's early writings, to which I have deferred in the text on several occasions, and his knowledge of German philosophy have improved my understanding as well as my own translations of Marcuse's early work. I am grateful to the senior members of the Department of Government, the Mellon-Fellowship Committee, and, in particular, Dean Alfred Fuchs for professional assistance and financial support during my years teaching at Bowdoin College. Several graduate students at the University of Massachusetts, particularly Bradley Klein, Joe Martin, Terry Aladjem, Judy Epstein, Christine DiStefano, and Preston Smith, either read and commented extensively on various chapters or offered their views on points of mutual interest. Their comments were always challenging and forced me to present my ideas with greater clarity.

To Colin Jones, Director of the New York University Press, I want to express my gratitude for the great care he has exercised with this project, for his professional counsel, for his patience and understanding, and for his judicious refusal to spare the rod when it would have spoiled the child.

To Deborah Broder I am grateful for a flawless preparation of the final two drafts of this entire manuscript. For her remarkable industry, initiative, tolerance of long hours spent at the typewriter and in libraries doing research and checking and rechecking references, and thoughtful criticisms of content as well as form, she is deserving of a sense of pride equal only to the pride of authorship.

Last, and most important, to my wife, Maureen, I am truly indebted for the many sacrifices she has made on behalf of this work and for the love and understanding that allayed my intellectual doubts and anxieties and restored my confidence on the many occasions it failed.

ONE

Early Writings, Early Hopes

We can no more reduce dialectics to reification than we can reduce it to any other isolated category, however polemical. The cause of human suffering, meanwhile, will be glossed over rather than denounced in the lament about reification.

Theodor W. Adorno, *Negative Dialectics*

MORE THAN a half century stands between our time and that of Herbert Marcuse's first published essay in 1928. Yet it and the works produced at an almost furious pace during the next five years are extremely significant for contemporary social theory and politics. This is a strong claim, all the more so because Marcuse's early writings are not well known. How is it that a substantial and quite important body of literature by such a controversial figure has received negligible interest in comparison to the critical attention shown his later works? Several reasons can be offered in explanation.

First, the "project," as I shall refer to it, that so intensely occupied Marcuse during this early period nevertheless was short-lived, lasting from 1928 to 1933. Without ever being executed— and I use the term "executed" because the finished project was to include a practical as well as a theoretical dimension—it ends abruptly, dramatically, and prematurely in the wake of fascism. Throughout the early writings the project consistently appears in outline, as is even suggested by the words "contribution," "foundation," "on the problem," and "problematic," used in the titles of many of Marcuse's early essays. Such words indicate theoretical beginnings and serve to qualify the objectives of Marcuse's

1

undertakings. From time to time the project is given depth, but it seems clear that Marcuse is always *aiming* at depth, as though the real work would follow once the outline had been completed. The skeletal nature of the project may make it difficult to grasp its essential purpose.

Next, the arguments of these first published works, particularly those written between 1928 and 1931, are saturated with the most complex terminology and appear to be repetitive, confusing, and obscure. As such, they are readily open to misunderstanding and are easy targets for criticism.

Third, the essays of this period implicate Marcuse in ontology, a mode of philosophical inquiry that close examination of the arguments indicates was characteristic only of the earliest writings, once again those published from 1928 to 1931. The conservative features of the ontological view, which appears to be shared by the works of this entire period, may have prompted many of those who otherwise would have been interested in Marcuse's early project hastily to pass it by.

Last, against their neglect any critical attempt to rehabilitate the project of these essays must contend with Marcuse's abandonment of his early work. And while it is also true that Marcuse looked back upon his early period as characterized by a painful mistake he believed he later rectified—the attention he had given to Heidegger's philosophy—it would be a more serious error to explain the fate of his project and to evaluate all the works belonging to it according to Marcuse's judgment of its specifically Heideggerian elements.[1] Marcuse did not abandon his project because it contained flaws that derived from his studies with Heidegger. Indeed, as will be shown, there are quite promising works of this early period that fall within the framework of his project but break completely with its Heideggerian dimensions. Once the terrible pressures of fascism are brought to the surface and related to the development of Marcuse's thought, as they will be in the following chapter, it will become evident that without first hesitating to reflect upon and salvage its most promising and progressive aspects, Marcuse moved too hurriedly to discard the entire project of his early period.

While the task of this chapter is to explore Marcuse's early writings, the purpose is not merely to describe youthful concerns that he shortly abandoned. Although these concerns are extremely interesting in themselves and must be included in any serious study of Marcuse's critical theory, they are examined in the belief that from the standpoint of our own time the early period is the most important in Marcuse's life work. The grounds for this conviction will be indicated at the chapter's close, though they will become apparent much earlier, and the reasoning behind it informs the arguments of each of the following chapters. In the concluding remarks of this study I will suggest why Marcuse's early writings and early hopes may be important to an era more than a half century older.

Lordship and Bondage

HEIDEGGER AND HISTORICITY

Several years before his death in July 1979, Marcuse reported in an interview that he had returned to the University of Freiburg "to work" with Martin Heidegger after reading *Being and Time* in 1927, the year of its publication.[2] Beyond this interesting though ultimately insignificant biographical detail, Marcuse tells us little about the precise impact of Heidegger's philosophy on his own thinking and certainly nothing about his personal relationship with Heidegger as it may have developed during the next five or six years. Nor does Marcuse discuss these matters elsewhere. After studying the early essays, which in any event is the correct approach to weighing the impact of Heidegger's thought on Marcuse, it will become clear that Marcuse's bare description of the attraction held by Heidegger's philosophy accurately portrays the extent of the Heideggerian influence.

> I must say frankly that during this time, let's say from 1928 to 1932, there were relatively few reservations and relatively few criticisms on my part. I would rather say on our part, because Heidegger at that time was not a personal problem, not even philosophically, but a problem of a large part of the generation that studied in Germany after the First World War. We saw in Heidegger what we had first seen in Husserl, a new beginning, the first radical attempt to put philosophy on really concrete foundations—philosophy concerned with the human existence, the human condition, and not with merely abstract ideas and principles . . . I was very much interested in [the social aspect of Heidegger's philosophy, its implications for

political and social life and action] during that stage, at the same time I wrote articles of Marxist analysis for the then theoretical organ of the German Socialists, *Die Gesellschaft*. So I certainly was interested, and I first, like all the others, believed there could be some combination between existentialism and Marxism, precisely because of their insistence on concrete analysis of the actual human existence, human beings and their world.[3]

Marcuse's recollection provides an insight into the nature of his relationship to Heidegger during this early period. It suggests that it was not the principles of Heidegger's thought per se that drew him to Freiburg, but that Heidegger's philosophy addressed a particular problem and filled a void that, as we shall see, was created by Marxism. From the outset, Heidegger was to be received favorably only to the degree that he contributed to solving that problem and eliminating the void, in effect, to the degree that his philosophy made a definite contribution to Marxist theory and practice. Consequently, "working" with Heidegger does not necessarily imply either that Marcuse invested his intellectual energies in the same issues for the same purposes or that he had become a disciple of Heidegger's or even had adopted without qualification a few of his ideas, categories, and so forth. And if Marcuse expressed few reservations and made few criticisms of Heidegger's thought during this period, it is not difficult to understand why. From Marcuse's early writings it can be seen that he borrowed little from Heidegger — in fact, no more than an inspiration and a general focus. Proof of this claim lies in the swiftness with which Marcuse cast off the Heideggerian truss. It took but a single event to persuade Marcuse of what the first essays of this early period occasionally indicate he had known all along; namely, that what existentialism offered Marxism was already implicit in Marxist theory. When, in 1932, Marcuse turns to an examination of the newly published *Economic and Philosophic Manuscripts*,[4] we find him developing the same theoretical project through Marx's thought that he had elaborated through Heidegger's. This time, however, Heidegger is no longer present because he is no longer needed to contribute what had been there from the beginning.

But in 1928 the publication of Marx's *Paris Manuscripts* is several years away, and before that event will occur and introduce a new coherence to Marcuse's project, Heidegger's existentialism suffices as a timely theoretical support for the problem with which Marcuse is concerned. Marcuse's problem, and one that in some form is as central to all versions of neo-Marxism as it had been to Marx and Engels since the midpoint of the nineteenth century, is the division between Marxist theory and practice precipitated by the increasing extent to which the social relations of capitalism have become "reified." During this period Marcuse defines the problem primarily according to the terms of Georg Lukács's *History and Class Consciousness*, although Lukács is not referred to specifically. Marcuse's solution to this problem, however, or rather the direction that he proposes should be taken toward discovering a solution, departs from Lukács in a decisive way. And it is only in this context of a possible solution to the schism between theory and practice that Marcuse defines his position explicitly in opposition to Lukács.

Marxism's fundamental commitment, Marcuse stresses, is to radical action, to the revolutionary transformation of the material conditions of human existence as they are present under capitalism. Its historical goal is a socialist society, a "new reality" that establishes the possibility for the "total man." The agents charged with the task of revolutionary change are historically conscious individuals bound together in their needs and interests through their class association.[5]

Marxism, however, finds itself in a predicament because the practical, revolutionary function attributed to the proletariat by Marxist theory has been obstructed by the complete assimilation of each individual's thought and action to the requirements of capitalist productivity. Consciousness, Marxism claims, is wholly absorbed by the norms and rules governing the day-to-day operations of a commodity producing system and is not sufficiently free to take that first step toward a consideration of what are essential human values, much less free to aspire to those more complex insights into the social, economic, and political structure of capitalism that could possibly mature into a distinctively socialist consciousness. This is not Marcuse's position, however, as will begin to become clear in his description of the process of "reification" in these terms.

The historical situation in which "today's" existence stands . . . is determined in its structure by the structure of capitalist society in the stage of high capitalism, i.e., organized capitalism and imperialism. These concepts [high capitalism, i.e., organized capitalism and imperialism], which outline the situation, in this case not only refer to political or economic states of affairs but focus on the existential determinations (*existenzielle Bestimmtheiten*) of contemporary human existence (*Daseins*). A form of existence has become a reality that is definitely and uniquely capitalist. The economic system has drawn all areas into the process of "reification" (*Verdinglichung*) . . . The modes of "being with others" (*Miteinander-seins*) are emptied of all essential content and are ruled from outside by "alien" laws. Fellow men are primarily economic subjects or economic objects, professional colleagues, citizens, members of the same "society." The essential relationships of friendship, love, of every authentic community of persons, are confined to the small circle of life which remains left over from busy-ness (*Geschäftigkeit*).[6]

Those things which are encountered in this world are from the beginning referred to as "goods," as things that one must use not in order to fulfill necessities of human existence (*Daseins*) but rather to keep busy or to occupy an otherwise idle (*leerlaufende*) existence, to the extent that they actually do become "necessities." Thus, ever more modes of existence are used up only in order to support "industriousness" ("*Betrieb*").[7]

Instead of having a suitable mode of existing in terms of managing their affairs, men become economic "subjects and objects" and function in the service of the commodity economy, which has become an autonomous "affair" . . . They stand in the service of their tools and more and more forms of existence are being used up for the purpose of maintaining the "functioning" of these tools.[8]

These passages are outstanding for two important reasons. First, they constitute most of Marcuse's consideration of the reification of social relations during his early period. The fact that Marcuse's other discussions do not extend this analysis and, as can be seen, his presentation of reification is obviously elementary already defines both the nature of the problem confronting Marxism and its seriousness as he understands them at this time. Certainly, one could not help but be struck by the extremely brief attention paid to reification in these early essays in contrast to the all-encompassing place given to its advanced formulation, "technological rationality," in Marcuse's later writings. It would be an exaggeration, in other words, to infer from Marcuse's straightforward analysis of social relations as commodity relations that he views capitalism as having attained much more than a higher stage of development. "High capitalism," though a substantially more durable structure than capitalism during its previous stages, is not a qualitatively "new form of control," an essentially altered social structure. It is not, to put it simply, a "one-dimensional society," a society without opposition.

Second, these passages are instructive about Marcuse's relationship to Heidegger's philosophy. While it is apparent that the theoretical summary of reification is based upon Lukács's work,[9] the conceptual framework is extended to include Heideggerian terms such as "human existence" (*Dasein*), "existential determinations" (*existenzielle Bestimmtheiten*), and modes of "being with others" (*Miteinander-seins*). Behind Marcuse's idiomatic mixtures, so to speak, I believe there is a definite purpose. Through Heidegger Marcuse is softening the meaning assigned to reification by Lukács. Instead of referring to an impenetrable and ironlike ideological veil that prevents the individual from ever discerning the social, or class, dimensions of exchange relations, reification now connotes a somewhat less harsh form of domination—one that is an orderly, rhythmic, habituating existence that occupies the individual's intellectual and physical powers. Without interruption, Marcuse is arguing, consciousness is persistently distracted by everyday routines and incidental concerns that surround the individual. Occupation has become preoccupation.

But this "forfeiture," as Heidegger called it, of the individual's creative abilities through surrender to mundane affairs is still submission to the organized, rationalized, alien affairs of capitalism. To express this point differently, what is given an ontological status by Heidegger is interpreted by Marcuse in materialist terms through Lukács's framework. With the aid of Heidegger's concepts, however, Marcuse has begun very gently to pry the individual loose from the tightly secured ideological moorings erected by Lukács's theory of reification. Although capital invades and subjects to its rule the social forms of human existence, the existential inclination or fundamental human striving toward these forms endures because it is an essential attribute of each individual. Basic dispositions toward love, friendship, and community are increasingly denied and limited as their areas of expression are annexed by a commodity economy. Yet, as these inclinations constitute the individual, it not only remains possible but also is necessary to speak of an individual living apart from and against the reified world of affairs, even though this individual now views this world in fetishized terms. Within the extended framework the individual is understood to be *constrained* to view the world ideologically but not *determined* to do so. And constraints can be shattered.

On both of these accounts a conclusion can be drawn, albeit quite tentatively at this stage. In Marcuse's estimation reification is not the crucial issue for theoretical inquiry. What is to be decisive in the historical situation that Marcuse is investigating are not the factors that inhibit radical action and a critical perspective of the society.

What, then, are the decisive factors? Marcuse does not pose this question explicitly. But by way of calling attention to particular inadequacies in Marxist theory, Marcuse asks, "does the theoretical basis from which Marxism derives its truth, i.e., the necessity for the historical [revolutionary] activity that it addresses and comprehends, come from a full grasp of the phenomenon of historicity?"[10] "Historicity"—there is, perhaps, no more important concept in Marcuse's first writings. It expresses the inspiration and incorporates the general focus provided by Heidegger, both of which were noted earlier. By identifying factors that dispose the individual to action, the conception of historicity begins to chart progress toward the formation of a socialist consciousness. In spite of social relations of domination, the theory of historicity maintains, the enslaved individual, the "bondsman" in Hegel's terms, possesses attitudes toward existence that potentially undermine the perpetuation of domination as much as they actually support it. Historicity thus offers the possibility of envisioning an end to the Marxist dilemma. The individual may be heavily burdened by the mystifications of ideology, but at a deeper level of existence he is simultaneously disposed to a radically different and unfettered social experience. Before discussing specific existential characteristics that historicity makes visible, precisely what does Marcuse mean by historicity and why is there a question as to whether Marxism grasps this phenomenon completely?

The clearest definition of historicity to be found in Marcuse's early essays sharply outlines its conceptual properties. "All determinations of radical action," Marcuse explains, "join together in their basic determination [of radical action] as *historicity*" (*flies-*

*sen zusammen in ihrer Grundbestimmtheit als Geschichtlich-
keit*).[11] Marcuse is quite certain, then, about the properties of
historicity. Historicity pertains to factors that determine radical
action. This point brings us directly to the thrust of Marcuse's
theory of historicity. There is one factor, one determination of
radical action especially, that has prompted Marcuse to ask
whether Marxism fully comprehends the phenomenon of historicity. At one and the same moment, Marcuse departs from Lukács and shifts the focus of Marxism from theoretical to existential, abstract to concrete determinations of action. Expressing
his agreement with the theorist Siegfried Marck, Marcuse argues
that "the weak point in Lukács's dialectic" is "the concept of
'correct class consciousness.' "[12]

> This notion is (as the conception of class consciousness has been on
> the whole) a violation of the dimension of historicity, a fixation
> "outside" of what happens from whence an artificially abstract con-
> nection with history must be produced.[13]

The importance of Marcuse's statement cannot be overemphasized. If "correct class consciousness" is the measure of radical opposition, then those who have not achieved this level of
political and theoretical knowledge, who do not understand the
social system from the "class standpoint," are necessarily judged
to be disinclined to radical politics. To put this point more succinctly, those who are not class conscious are victims of a "men-
dacious," or false, consciousness and accordingly support the
social order without the least qualification. Class consciousness
allows no conceptual space for consideration of individuals
whose thought, language, and behavior reveal a tendency toward
radical political activity. Insofar as class is strictly defined as the
sole determinant of radical action, tendencies, dispositions, or
inclinations to radical practice are excluded from the outset.

Marxism's theoretical basis, therefore, does not permit an adequate grasp of the phenomenon of historicity. By narrowing the
determinants of radical activity to the factor of class, it reduces
radicalism to an abstraction. Theory must then fail to discover a
solution to the problem of reification because the problem is approached from an initial misconception. Marxist theory, in other
words, cannot solve the dilemma of how a totally alienated subject, an individual who views the society exclusively from the

perspective of ideological principles in which he is believed to be immersed, can come to know of his objective, class function. Marcuse, on the other hand, insists upon apprehending the subject not from the theoretical position of class but from the existential situation of the living, concrete individual.

> The meaning of philosophizing, though not completed in the "individual person" (*Einzelnen*), can be fulfilled only through each individual person *and thus has its basis in the existence of each individual person*. The concreteness of philosophy, in the existence of each individual person, must never be relegated to an abstract subject, to a "one," for this would mean relegating decisive responsibility to some arbitrary universality.[14]

And by focusing on the concretely existing individual, Marcuse has not simply indicated a way to crash through the barriers of ideology, to move toward a solution to the problem of reification. In effect, he has redefined the problem of reification and shown it to be a false problem as Marxism conceives it. For if the individual is at all disposed to radical activity, then he is not the pillar of support for society that the concept of correct class consciousness implies that he is.

Marcuse has neither jettisoned Marx's theory of revolution nor abandoned the proletariat as the agent of historical transformation. What he has done is to break open the rich terrain lying between the radical individual whose action springs from a conscious identification with his class and the individual who appears antagonistic to such radical action only because his behavior is not informed by his class interest. In one sense Marcuse has radicalized Marxism. Although Marcuse's ordinary working-class individuals are less radical than they must become to fulfill their historical task, they are also more radical in their everyday conduct than Marxist theory recognizes. Hence we can understand why Marcuse's new radicalism is based upon Heidegger's philosophy. It is through emphasis on the individual in his "public, daily existence"[15] that Heidegger's thought opens the way to a new, concrete science. In another sense, of course, Marcuse's unorthodox approach does not radicalize Marxist theory but returns to the original intentions of Marx's method. In support of his project, Marcuse at one point recalls the suppositions Marx set forth in the first pages of *The German Ideology*.

The premises from which we begin are not arbitrary ones, not dog-
mas, but real premises from which abstraction can be made only in
the imagination. They are the real individuals, their activity and
the material conditions under which they live, both those which
they find already existing and those produced by their activity.[16]

In keeping with Marx, Marcuse argues that "every genuine
method permits its approach to be guided by the manner in
which its object is given."[17]

"Concrete philosophy" is the form of investigation that emerges
from Marcuse's theory of historicity. It is distinguished from all
other aspects of Marx's theory and from subsequent versions of
Marxism, such as Lukács's, that have encouraged a disregard of
the individual. For Marcuse, the premises of concrete philosophy
are identical to those of historical materialism. These premises
are simply ordinary people, the "objects" that are to provide the
guidelines for any theoretical discussion of political practice.

Now, what are the determinants of action for each individual?
Action, first of all, has an "existential" basis. It is determined
"existentially." Existential action, Marcuse appears to be saying
in his early essays, is action that arises from existence and that
has existence as its goal. For example, in *The German Ideology*,
Marcuse suggests, Marx interpreted the activities of material
production and reproduction as categories of existential action.
To be precise, both are types of existential, "practical" action —
practical in the sense that they insure survival and arise in response to the problem of satisfying basic needs; existential in the
sense that they are rooted essentially in the very structure of existence because man must always produce to meet human needs
and reproduce the means of production.

Yet it is not existential action that intends mere existence as its
goal that is of primary interest to Marcuse. He is searching for
modes of existential action that project definite forms of existence. It is here that Heidegger's philosophy becomes especially
pertinent. For the average individual, Marcuse explains, life's
possibilities and the decisions about which possibilities are to be
seized and made reality are preordained. The great majority of
people submit unreflectively to the values and aspirations of the
public consensus. At all times and in all his purposes the individual bends under the weight of social pressures. But the plight of
the ordinary individual, which stands out in the typical features

of commonplace existence, covers over the deeper layers of human need. It is these deeper layers that Marcuse reclaims for social theory.

> At the very bottom of existence there remains, however obscure, an understanding of its uniqueness. Existence is always concerned for its own being, and this existentially conceived concern is regarded as the true being of existence (*eigentliche Sein des Daseins*). In spite of all thrownness and forfeiture, in this concern [for existence] lies the possibility to comprehend true being (*das eigene Sein zu ergreifen*) and to break forth from untrue to true existence (*aus der uneigentlichen in die eigentliche Existenz durchzudringen*).[18]

Marcuse is arguing that no way of life, regardless of its uniformity, can totally suppress an awareness on the individual's part of the singular character of his personal existence, of the manifold though intensely private recognitions of his difference from others. Marcuse is alluding to that uncomfortable awareness of not belonging, of feeling alien in one's surroundings without knowing why or without knowing of alternatives to them. And in the individual's anxious insights into his detachment from the existence apparently acceptable to others is embedded a care for one's *own* existence, a concern expressed through fears about the possible sacrifice of life implied in purely privatized discontents. Within this care and concern lies an as yet unarticulated desire to make public that which is private, to create space for the unnamed but no less real human potentialities. Within the deeper layers of human existence is contained the need and, most important, the secret ambition to change the world. The disposition to radical action, to change, reshape, and freely to create existence, surfaces as an existential attitude. Or, as Marcuse expresses it precisely, this disposition, this "concern," is part of the "true being of human existence" (*eigentliche Sein des Daseins*).[19] As part of man's very being, Marcuse's existential inclinations to definite sorts of action are reduced to an ontological foundation. As a priori elements of an experience defined as concern, they precede this experience and make it possible. We shall soon see, however, that Heidegger's ontological foundation for a radical disposition is later discarded when Marcuse further develops his theory of historicity through an interpretation of Hegel and Marx.

Marcuse's analysis thus expands the conceptual boundaries of historicity. In so doing it adds not only philosophical but also political dimensions to Marxist theory. From the Marxist notion of historicity the conclusion is reached that the non-class conscious individual is allied with the status quo, whereas Marcuse's inquiry discerns in the same individual vague attitudes of a generalized disaffection — generalized in the sense that the individual is no more disaffected from one society than he would be from another but is equally disaffected from all forms of existence. Of course, such a radically disposed individual is not a radical individual. Rather, one who has deeper inclinations to radical activity is an individual who has become uneasy about principles he has long held to be true, skeptical about the validity of popular beliefs, uncertain about the legitimacy of established political norms. This is an unstable individual whose hazy insights must be developed from an implicit to an explicit level of understanding. And a well-defined political position can supersede a vague existential disposition only if the individual is engaged in political discourse. Consequently, Marcuse's focus on the existential determinations of radical action seems to suppose or entail liberal practices *because* he embraces radical politics — not the practices of liberalism, in other words, that seek some intermediate point between a simple preservation of the social order in its prevailing form and its radical transformation, but a liberal politics that serves as a stepping-stone toward radical action. This obviously controversial point will be returned to in the final section of this chapter.

The foregoing analysis considered the central arguments Marcuse presented in three early essays: "Contributions to a Phenomenology of Historical Materialism" (1928), "Concrete Philosophy" (1929), and "On the Problem of the Dialectic" (1930, 1931). Taken together, these essays constitute his most concentrated effort during the first four years of this early period to define a new project that compensates for the inadequacies of Marxist theory. As it stands, the project is clearly in outline form. While Marcuse's criticisms of Marxism are persuasive, he has provided little in the way of systematic analysis of existential characteristics that could become candidates for determinations of radical action. But the elaborate design of the project perhaps excuses Marcuse's lack of rigor during these years. And if these essays appear confused and repetitious, such difficulties arise because Marcuse's discursive style reflects his newly proposed analytical method. Frequently returning to the same arguments, concepts, and themes, Marcuse is attempting to draw out their deeper meanings and implications in a fashion resembling that of his probing of the individual's experience to discover attitudes not visible at first.

By way of brief review, a few points in particular should be stressed. While Marcuse's project adopts Heidegger's concrete approach, Marcuse does not want the existential dimensions of social life to be embraced at the expense of a decisive aspect of Marxist theory. Existential analysis must recognize the ideological constraints on thought and action. It must not forget that the individual's dispositions to radical action are precarious because they are deeply buried beneath the weight of ideological pressures that can prevent their entering conscious awareness, much less their being acted upon. Concrete philosophy must comprehend these dispositions as they could develop in relation to the dynamics of organized social structures, in order to push beyond *dispositions* to radical action to radical action itself. At the same time Marxism must become concrete. It must cease to view the world through theoretical categories that suppress knowledge of the broad range of characteristics that prove the individual to be active, concerned, intentional, and reflective, that is, in embryo the subject that the truth of Marxist theory rests upon. These points are summarized in Marcuse's own concise proposal for a new theoretical project.

> Thus, on the one hand, we demand that Heidegger's phenomenology of human existence be driven to dialetical concreteness so that it can be fulfilled in a phenomenology of concrete existence and of the historically concrete act demanded of it. And, on the other hand, the dialectical method of knowing must go the other way and become phenomenological so to incorporate concreteness in a complete account of its object. In the analysis of the given, it must not simply locate it historically, or indicate its roots in a historical situation of human existence. It must also ask whether the given is thereby exhausted, or whether it contains an authentic meaning which, although not ahistorical, it endures through all historicity. Although this question may seem superfluous in relation to actual historical action, it becomes unavoidable if [action] is to actually arise out of knowledge. Only a unification of both methods, a dialectical phenomenology as a method of continuous and radical concreteness, can do justice to the historicity of human existence.[20]

It is important to be clear about the developmental lines of Marcuse's early writings. The three essays mentioned above and which span the years 1928 to 1931 not only launch Marcuse's project and outline its basic features but also complete the project's outline insofar as it is to be understood as a theoretical framework integrating Marx and Heidegger. Several additional essays published during these four years incorporate the theoretical standpoint of Marcuse's project as it has been described. The problems considered in these essays shall be examined in this chapter's closing section. The first step was to present Marcuse's project as he outlined it. With this task accomplished, the discussion can turn now to works after 1931 that conform to the established outline of the project but also mark a shift away from its explicitly Heideggerian dimensions.

HEGEL AND HISTORICITY

Hegel's Ontology and the Foundation of a Theory of Historicity, appearing in 1932, is Marcuse's first published book and the first indication that he is distancing his thought from Heidegger's.[21] But a reader of this text will search in vain for the usual signs of an author's breaking with his past views. At no time, for example, does Marcuse express dissatisfaction with Heidegger's philosophy, nor does he explicitly pose any problem that is then shown to be artfully managed by Hegel rather than Heidegger, and so on. In fact, Marcuse's study of Hegel continues to bear the imprint of Heidegger, though superficially, in two ways. Appended to the introduction is a generous acknowledgment in which Marcuse expresses his indebtedness to Heidegger's philosophy for any contribution that *Hegel's Ontology* may have made to clarifying and developing the issues examined.[22] Second, Marcuse's terms are frequently Heideggerian and Hegel is occasionally said to have addressed questions that are recognizably those raised by Heidegger. To illustrate, at one point Marcuse remarks in passing that a particular conception of Hegel's "stands under the question as to the meaning of being (*der Frage nach dem Sein*), ultimately under the question as to the true meaning of the being of existence" (*nach dem eigentlichsten Sein des Seienden*).[23]

If Marcuse is dissociating his thought from Heidegger's and is about to pursue an independent direction, how are these connections to be explained? Why the acknowledgment, the similarities in terminology, and the assimilation of Hegel's concepts to Heidegger's investigations? As the title of Marcuse's book indicates, historicity is to be a focal point of theoretical inquiry. So Marcuse is continuing to explore territory mapped by Heidegger. Yet, this broadly based continuity in Marcuse's work should not obscure the possibility that through his return to the philosophical origins of the concept of historicity in Hegel's system, Marcuse may be rethinking and revising its meaning. Actually, we will find that this is exactly the case in *Hegel's Ontology*. Here the shift away from Heidegger's conception of historicity is gradual though quite noticeable nevertheless. For this reason it is understandable that the trappings of Heidegger's philosophy would be carried over from the earlier essays into Marcuse's new work. After *Hegel's Ontology* Marcuse's essays on Marx make explicit what was implicit within the former study. A break with Heidegger anticipated by the shift characterizing Marcuse's first study on Hegel crystallizes in the subsequent writings on the *Economic and Philosophic Manuscripts*.

Marcuse's study is divided into two parts. An analysis of Hegel's *Logic* forms the content of the first, though other works, particularly *Faith and Knowledge* and *Difference between Fichte's and Schelling's System of Philosophy*, are considered briefly and to the extent that they contribute to Marcuse's exposition of the *Logic*. The second section briefly examines Hegel's *Early Theological Writings* and the *Jena Logic*, proceeds to an extensive discussion of the *Phenomenology of Mind*, and is completed with a short chapter on the relationship between Hegel and Dilthey. The internal structure and complexity of *Hegel's Ontology* makes it impossible to trace the finely detailed steps in the development of its argument. And such an approach would be necessary largely for the purpose of evaluating the correctness of Marcuse's interpretation of Hegel's philosophy. Within the present context a description of the decisive claims made in *Hegel's Ontology* in relation to Marcuse's early essays must suffice. Marcuse's extremely short chapter on Dilthey shows how the latter's philosophy is rooted in that of Hegel. It adds nothing to an understanding of Marcuse's early work that is not already acquired from an exposition of the major arguments of *Hegel's Ontology*. For this reason it will be passed over. In the next section, however, there will be an opportunity briefly to consider the significance of a particular feature of Dilthey's philosophy for Marcuse's social theory.

In *Hegel's Ontology* Marcuse is concerned with three essential aspects of Hegel's philosophy: the concept of life (*der Begriff des Lebens*) and its ontological status (*der Seinsbegriff des Lebens*), the conception of motion, or movement (*Bewegung; Bewegtheit*), as an ontological dimension of all existence (*Sein als Bewegtheit*), and their bearing on the theory of historicity. According to Marcuse's interpretation, although Hegel intended none of these aspects to be more fundamental than any other, there is a tendency in his philosophy away from an ontological characterization of human existence toward a strictly historical conceptualization. Marcuse never denies that Hegel ultimately subsumed history under ontology. On the contrary, Marcuse clearly considers ontology to be the organizing principle of Hegel's view of history. By drawing out and upon this tendency, however, Marcuse wants to express a tension between ontology and history inherent in Hegel's philosophy and finally to separate the two—but without losing the advantages offered by an ontological foundation.

Everything that exists is in motion, meaning that all things are in the process of becoming something else. That which is true or essential about any particular thing is not its apparent form of existence but its movement toward another state. Being, by nature, is endless movement, and the structural dynamics of this process, the essential properties of being, are represented by the categories of Hegel's *Logic*. These categories are also categories of thought. Hence, movement is not random and directionless but assumes a necessary course prescribed by the activity of thought as it reflects on the states it achieves. Developing through the various contradictions peculiar to each stage of existence, thought comprehends its basic characteristic as motion, that is, as movement indistinguishable from reflection. Marcuse's purpose is to establish that the author of existence is an active and dynamic subject, a reflective subject, that reflection is continual movement from one stage to another, and that each stage, though originally authored by the subject, places limitations upon the subsequent stage to which the subject can aspire.

Marcuse's explication, however, is not a demonstration of this process as purely ontological but in fact opposes all such interpretations of the *Logic*. Marcuse insists that this process is constituted by the relations of living individuals (*lebendigen Individuums*). It is living human existence (*lebendiges Dasein*), first and foremost a living process (*Lebensprozess*). Precisely this point, Marcuse argues, is established by Hegel's concept of life. Life is basically the struggle of the individual with his world to insure self-subsistence. Accordingly, all of the individual's capacities and activities, together with everything that lies outside the individual, enter into and define this struggle. The significance of this concept for Marcuse begins to become clear. The concept of life focuses attention directly on the subject, and as it does so all that is known about life becomes unified, that is, becomes an integral part of a coherent concept of the individual. From the standpoint of life, *absolutely* nothing about or around the subject can be excluded from its concept. Life, which is not merely the life *of* the subject but *is* the subject, possesses a diversity from which arises the essential characteristic of movement. Life, subjectivity, and movement are assimilated.

Through Hegel's concept of life Marcuse finds a more satisfactory vehicle for a theory of the active and dynamic subject than a strictly ontological conception of subjectivity would yield. By rooting the dialectic of the individual's development in the process of life, the subject is no longer moved from the outside, as is the case when movement is given a purely ontological foundation, that is, one independent of human existence. As life the subject is movement. The process of movement ceases to be ahistorical with history its manifestation. Movement, or action, is as much historical as ontological. Or, if movement is ontological it is so precisely because of the constitution of life.

In this transition from a purely ontological to an ontological-historical conceptualization of movement, ontology is not cast off. Because it pertains to the entirety of existence, to being, the process of life (history) remains an ontological process. Consequently, although he recognizes that it was Hegel's intention to abolish the distinction between ontology and history, and that for this reason the *Logic* must be defended against the accusation that it is simply a transcendental system, Marcuse's point is that ontology and history cannot be drawn together without sustaining a tension between the two dimensions. Ontology cannot provide a universal and objective foundation for the characteristics of subjectivity without in some sense turning the subject into a result of something prior to it. Although life (history) is supposed to affirm the autonomy of the individual, the subject is dissipated in the objectivity of life's absolute structure. As long as movement, or action, necessarily unfolds in the context of a life (history) of struggle, the concept of life restricts freedom to particular forms of action. History cannot be a true realm of freedom. Compromised by an *essential* structure of life as struggle, history (as freedom) exists in tension with ontology (the concept of life that reduces history to freedom *within* the limits of struggle). If the freedom of the individual is to be preserved, theory must go further than a shift from ontology to an ontological-historical position. Interpreted in light of Hegel's attempt to abolish the distinction between ontology and history, to establish in unqualified terms the freedom of the individual and freedom as an absolute fact of existence, the tension sustained by this position yields a tendency toward a new historical conception of the subject—the theory of historicity. Marcuse draws out this tendency, severs the tie between history and ontology, and emphasizes the former to the exclusion of the latter but without sacrificing the certain guarantees of an active and dynamic subject provided by an ontology. How does he manage this?

Marcuse now turns to consider Hegel's *Jena Logic*, the *Early Theological Writings*, and the *Phenomenology of Mind*. Written after these works, the *Logic* distills and formalizes their arguments, he argues, particularly those of the latter two. A richer, more explicitly historical conception is therefore to be found in the *Logic's* philosophical predecessors. Of the earlier texts, the *Phenomenology* is the most significant for it is Marcuse's interpretation of the master and slave relation that charts the greatest progress toward eliminating the need for an ontological foundation for the theory of historicity.

Marcuse's analysis of the master and slave relation reproduces its basic features as they are laid out in the *Phenomenology of Mind*.[24] In the context of Marcuse's broader argument, however, a few of these features receive emphasis. The first is that the slave initially accepts the relationship of domination as legitimate. Because there are no other norms available to the servant to spur a different understanding, the relation is understood strictly in terms of its regulative principles. The authority of the master is believed to be valid by the slave and his function of servitude is thought to be proper. Mastery and servitude become the universal principles shaping all attitudes and practices of each of the participants. But no sooner does the slave actually begin to serve the master than his labor causes him to reflect upon his previously unquestioned attitude of deference. Through labor, the servant learns, a mastery over the world is achieved that is denied to the lord, who lives off the labor of others. The second feature that is stressed, therefore, is that by the very fact of forced labor the slave acquires an insight that challenges the validity of the principles that define his position of subordination. It is the servant who is truly independent and upon whom the master is really dependent. And the independence of the slave established by means of his labor can be developed further only by going beyond the relation of domination.

With the introduction of the relation of lordship and bondage, instead of life in general, as in the *Logic*, the issue is now a specific way of life, life with a definite structure. By virtue of the dynamics arising from the structure of this relation, life as a blind struggle for self-subsistence comes to an end. An awareness is bred that struggle is not a brute fact of existence, that much of it results from the coercive structure of life, and that there can be freedom from struggle and coercion if the structural relation is altered. In other words, what has occurred is a disposition to radical activity. Furthermore, the disposition, that is, the slave's insight into his independence and its limits within the relation of domination, is a theoretical activity—self-consciousness—that springs from a practical activity—labor. Knowledge of the essential character of social relations has a historical content. It occurs only but—and here is the crucial point—necessarily, inevitably, through the dynamics of organized social structures.

Marcuse's analysis of lordship and bondage is designed to show that a theory of an active, developing subject, of a subject in motion, can dispense with ontology. A concept of a reflective subject need not be rooted in an ontological foundation, whether it be transcendental or ontological-historical. Rather, an individual becomes capable of a radical sort of knowing, of a reflection that aims at transcending historical conditions, as the practices of social life in which he is engaged unfold. Marcuse acknowledges, of course, that Hegel compromises the notion of a subject developing through practical activity with the *Phenomenology's* concept of "absolute knowledge." According to Marcuse, in the

Phenomenology Hegel is thus left with a double or dichotomous foundation for a theory of the subject, which he later attempts to resolve into a single foundation in the *Logic* by abolishing the distinction between ontology and history. As we have seen, though, Marcuse proves Hegel's resolution to be fragile by demonstrating through an examination of the *Logic's* concept of life that a tension is sustained between history and ontology. Marcuse has presented an argument of great importance. Whereas in the *Logic* the historical dimensions of subjectivity never quite escape an ontological casing, in the *Phenomenology* the development of the subject is grounded securely in history before it is dissolved into ontology.

Marcuse's argument has another, albeit implicit, goal besides the analysis and appropriation of the historical dimension of Hegel's theory of subjectivity. With his interpretation of lordship and bondage historicity has been given a new basis, one that corrects Heidegger's theory of historicity. With Heidegger, the determinations of radical action are existential givens, the a priori elements of experience that precede the individual's activity and make it possible. With Hegel, on the other hand, dispositions to radical action do not precede but are *created through* and for that reason alone are embedded in the practices of the subject. In Hegel's philosophy the theory of historicity achieves a level of concreteness that Heidegger fails to achieve. Important implications follow from this basic difference. Hegel's subject is freer. Characteristics of the subject involved in shaping the world in which the individual lives and his relation to that world are constantly changing, or evolving. Individuals author not only their existence but also the subjective and objective determinants of that existence. Furthermore, Heidegger's existential determinations of activity are too generalized or abstract to be meaningfully related to the structural dynamics of the practices that express the existential determinants. Hegel's subject, however, can engage in no practical activity without a corresponding level of theoretical self-consciousness, a knowledge intimately tied to the structure of those practices and the structure of social life of which they are a part. Hegel integrates theoretical and practical activity to a far greater extent than does Heidegger.

The significance of this last point, to be revisited shortly, cannot be overemphasized. Only when the integration of theoretical and practical activity—praxis—is given its due place in Marcuse's writings can his position on the relationship between ontology and history, his dissociation from Heidegger, and his theory of historicity be fully understood. And it is not difficult to decide about its place. With the interpretation of Hegel's relation of lordship and bondage, Marcuse implicitly has made praxis the theoretical centerpiece of his project. If there could be any doubt that lordship and bondage constitute the turning point in the development of Marcuse's theory of historicity, it should be removed by the two essays that soon followed *Hegel's Ontology*.

MARX AND HISTORICITY

An extensive critical exposition of Marx's 1844 *Economic and Philosophic Manuscripts*, "The Foundation of Historical Materialism" was published in 1932, the year that saw the complete German edition of the *Paris Manuscripts*. Marcuse's argument is that Marx's *Manuscripts* force a reconsideration of the origins and meaning of historical materialism and "scientific socialism." Marx's theory is improperly understood if its basis is thought to be economic. Marx, Marcuse is claiming, did not intend a theory of historical or economic determinism, nor would Marx have approved of any politics rooted in such a theory. Historical materialism is not crude historicism. It is not, in other words, a theory that maintains that history develops according to rigid economic laws that establish socialism as its necessary and inevitable outcome. Marx's theory, in fact, has a philosophical foundation that opposes all such interpretations of materialism. This foundation is set forth most clearly in his *Manuscripts*. It is also a foundation that proves the origins of Marx's theory to lie deep within Hegel's *Phenomenology of Mind*. Marx's theory, like Hegel's philosophy, is a theory of revolutionary praxis.

Marx's conception of labor is the philosophical foundation that Marcuse explicates. Actually, it is within the context of an analysis of alienated labor and private property in the *Manuscripts* that Marcuse demonstrates that labor *as such* is the central category of Marx's theory. While the contextual aspects of Marcuse's exposition are interesting, they are important primarily for a lucid account of Marx's notion of alienation and are not controversial. Without loss to this discussion they will be introduced only to the extent that they bear on the meaning Marcuse attributes to the concept of labor per se.

Man's nature—his faculties, abilities, capacities, character, personality, needs, and wants—is literally his own "work." Whenever an individual labors upon something, for example, whether this something is an idea or a material thing, the individual is shaping and developing himself, that is, increasing his knowledge or sharpening his skills at the same time as he is shaping and developing the object of his labor. In a very definite sense, through labor man takes himself as his own object, the object of the social activity of labor. His nature, therefore, is not finished, or given before labor but is a social creation. Human nature is always social nature. It can thus be said that through labor man brings into reality what was previously only potentiality. Potentiality becomes objective. Labor is the process of object-ification. History, as the history of all forms of the social activity of labor, is nothing less than the history of man making himself. As Marcuse explains, we "are no longer dealing with an abstract human essence which remains equally valid at every stage of concrete history, but with an essence which can be defined in *history* and *only* in history."[25]

But though human nature is historical nature, this does not mean that what has become of man historically is his true nature. Historically the activity of labor has been organized into relations of domination. Under capitalism all aspects of the labor process—what is to be produced, how production is to be organized, and what is to be done with the fruits of human labor—are determined by social relations based upon private property. Labor, objectification, or the creation of man by man is in every way unfree or alienated; the essence of man is an alienated essence. The ideologies of capitalism, however, conceal the unfree, alienated character of human labor. Having come to understand the organization of production in ideological terms, the individual views the process of production and the social and political relations of society as natural rather than as the result of a particular social formation of private property. Social relations are reified. Ideology masks the fact that it is society, its social and economic structure, that determines all aspects of the labor process and the ultimate product of labor: man.

Once again, the question arises of whether it is possible for the individual to penetrate the illusions fostered by ideology, or does he forever remain the helpless victim of reification? Regardless of the extent of reification, Marcuse answers, through his labor the individual learns that labor is much more than the exchange of labor power for wages, that is, more than the means to satisfy basic needs. Labor, it is quickly learned, is either a satisfying experience or a frustrating one, an expression of abilities or a denial of personal resources. Labor is not a perfunctory task that can be performed and then forgotten because as an intimate part of life it affects every thought, action, and relation. Labor is in every sense social, not natural. No individual can work without becoming concerned about what factors—social, economic, and political—influence the activity of labor. Through the activity of labor a decisive issue is forced upon the individual: what is the relationship between labor and the larger society? Marcuse expresses the dynamics of this connection in this way.

> We know that objectification is essentially a social activity and that it is precisely in his objects and in his labor on them that man recognizes himself as a social being. The *insight* (*Einsicht*) into objectification, which penetrates (*durchbrechende*) reification, is the *insight* (*Einsicht*) into society as the subject [determining factor] of objectification.[26]

Marcuse thus returns us to Hegel's relation of lordship and bondage. Labor, as a practical activity, facilitates reflection, or "insight," a theoretical activity that penetrates the ideological framework manufactured by capitalism. It is important to emphasize that Marcuse has made no claims for this theoretical consciousness other than calling it "insight" or "recognition" (*Einsicht; Erkenntnis*), insight into (or recognition of) the fact that society determines "how and through what man and his objective world *as social relations* have become what they are," and "insight into the historical-social situation of man."[27] And it is not the owners of the means of production who are capable of this insight, but the producers.

> We know that the abolition (*Aufhebung*) of alienation (*Entfremdung*) (a state in which both master *and* servant find themselves, although not in the same way) can be based only on the penetration (*Durchbrechung*) of reification, i.e., on the practical insight (*Erkenntnis*) into the activity of objectification in its historical-social situation. Since it is only in *labor* and in the objects *of his labor* that man can really come to recognize (*Erkenntnis*) himself, others, and

the objective world in their historical-social situation, the master, as *non*worker, cannot come to this insight. Since what is actually a specific human activity appears to him as a material and objective state of affairs, the worker has an (as it were) irreducible advantage over him. He is the real factor of transformation; the destruction of reification can be *his* work only. The master can come to this penetrating insight (*durchbrechende Erkenntnis*) only if he becomes a worker, which, however, would mean abolishing (*aufhebt*) his own essence.[28]

Looking back upon *Hegel's Ontology* in light of this interpretation of Marx's concept of labor in "The Foundation of Historical Materialism," we see that the former work is clearly a turning point in the development of Marcuse's social theory. The master-slave relation has been carried forward from the study on Hegel and now figures prominently as the conceptual apparatus through which Marcuse analyzes relations of domination under capitalism and uncovers a prospective means to their destruction. The theoretical insights produced by the practical activity of labor in themselves do not alter the relations of domination. Marcuse, it must be emphasized, is not speaking in these very important passages of the actual destruction or abolition of alienation, reification, and the social relations from which this condition arises. On the contrary, Marcuse is speaking of a *cognitive* act, of an act of *understanding*, of the impulse *upon* which the act of abolition, of social revolution, is eventually to be based. Marcuse's entire discussion of insight and recognition through the activity of labor is an answer to this question that he first posed: "To what extent can cognition (*Erkenntnis*), the recognition of objectification as something social, become the real impulse for the abolition (*Aufhebung*) of all reification?"[29] His answer, as we have seen, is that such cognition, recognition, or insight occurs through the practice of labor to the extent that the individual actually penetrates reification, or pierces the veil of ideology.

Theoretical insights are indicative of the individual's disposition to entertain alternatives to and to change the prevailing social structure. Marcuse has thus presented an argument for the existence of an insightful, reflective individual who, although inclined to radical action, does not spontaneously or necessarily engage in radical politics. With Marcuse's concept of praxis there is no automatic, inevitable transition from one society or stage of history to another. Marcuse's theory of historicity guarantees a reflective individual but offers no "scientific" guarantee of how such a person would act. By explicating the philosophical foundation of Marx's theory, Marcuse has thus revealed its hostility to historical determinism.[30]

It is not difficult to understand why Marcuse began "The Foundation of Historical Materialism" by declaring that "the publication of the *Economic and Philosophic Manuscripts* written by Marx in 1844 became a crucial event in the history of Marxist studies." How could Marcuse have made any other judgment? Earlier he had argued for a synthesis of Heidegger and Marx, phenomenology and materialism. Marcuse's aim was a Marxist theory more sensitive to, or more in touch with, the individual's rich and complex dispositions to action than the notion of correct class consciousness allowed Marxism to be. Then, with the publication of the *Paris Manuscripts*, Marcuse discovered that Heidegger's contribution, in other words, that which he had believed to be missing from Marxism, had always been present in Marx's theory and waiting to be developed. Radical action, as remote as the radical consciousness atrophied by the ideological paralysis of class interests, suddenly appeared potentially as near as the ordinary individual's thought and action.

The publication of the *Manuscripts* was an event not only in Marxist studies. For Marcuse it was an event of personal significance as well. Marcuse must have recognized immediately that with his exposition of lordship and bondage in *Hegel's Ontology* he had anticipated the implications of Marx's concept of labor in the *Manuscripts*. In the study of Hegel he had moved toward a theory of historicity that implied a break with Heidegger. What began with Hegel was then completed with Marx. In "The Foundation of Historical Materialism" Marcuse went far beyond Heidegger's notion of the individual's generalized concern for existence, for such a diffuse awareness cannot easily be tied, if it can be tied at all, to an understanding of specific social structures of domination. On the other hand, the praxis of labor, its practical and theoretical dynamics, draws together the simple fact of labor and the complex social structural factors that organize the labor process. Theoretical and practical activity are tightly integrated. By rooting historicity in a praxis of labor rather than in a praxis of existential determinants of radical action, Marcuse clearly dissociates his work from Heidegger's existential ontology.[31] Where does this theory of historicity leave Marcuse with respect to the ontological dimensions of Hegel's system?

One answer to this question, and the one that is the most correct, is contained in "The Foundation of Historical Materialism," as well as in the second of the essays written after *Hegel's Ontology*: "On the Philosophical Foundation of the Concept of Labor in Economics," published in 1933, marks the close of Marcuse's early period. But the central argument of the 1933 article also suggests another answer that should be considered first because it could serve as a ground for dismissing Marcuse's project.

The concept of labor, Marcuse argues in this essay, must be rescued from the science of economics. Economics defines labor narrowly as *economic* activity, activity that is directly involved in the production of material goods. Politics, art, and intellectual effort in general do not meet this strict criterion for labor. Whatever characteristics other than material production are found to be associated with labor cannot therefore be attributed to noneconomic forms of activity.

Against the specialized conception of labor in economics, Marcuse expands the concept of labor to include all forms of human activity. In that way, labor can be related to all modes of social existence. Marcuse destroys the artificial economic boundaries of labor by giving it a philosophical foundation. More than simply economic activity, all labor has in common the property of "doing" (*tun*). What Marcuse means is that all activity is labor insofar as labor is understood as the act of objectification, as the struggle to realize human potentialities and to impart to the world molded by labor a distinctively human form. Through Marcuse's philosophical foundation an answer to our question is provided. Embracing all activities in every form of social existence, and pertaining to the very nature of "being" human, labor becomes an ontological category. Marcuse's foundation appears to draw him back into Hegel's ontological framework. Man seems fated to be forever *homo faber*, a being whose relation to the world is governed by the need to transform it into an expression of human potentiality, to view it instrumentally as the vehicle of self-development and self-creation (objectification). World and nature exist only to be dominated.

But this interpretation of the 1933 essay stands only if the true theoretical significance of labor as Marcuse understands it is lost sight of. For Marcuse the emphasis is not on labor as objectification but on labor as *praxis*, the practical activity that gives rise to reflective activity. This argument, made in "The Foundation of Historical Materialism," is retained in "The Concept of Labor." And now, in this second essay, with all activities conceived as forms of labor, all activities become reflective activities. Labor — no matter how it is organized, regardless of what it produces, and in spite of the particular kind of practice that it is — can never be reduced to a single end. It could never become just instrumental activity; as reflective activity labor contains the possibility for changing any commitment to a definite end or goal. When Marcuse asserts, therefore, that every "historical community . . . is constituted upon the basic relation of *lordship* and *bondage*,"[32] he does not mean that all social relations are inseparably bound to some relation of domination by or of human labor, nor does he mean that progress can be made only as progress in and through the domination of men and nature. On the contrary, Marcuse is arguing that in all possible practices of all possible societies are rooted the dynamics of praxis. Arising from social practices are new concepts that challenge the norms by which those activities are customarily understood. Arising from all practical activities, in other words, are reflective activities that can transcend all relations of domination, any so-called givens, or any apparently natural obstacles to human growth and development be they ideological or ontological.

The Historical Tasks of Philosophy

Durchbrechung — "penetration" or, literally, "breakthrough." I have selected the former translation because it more accurately conveys the theoretical significance of labor as it is explicated by Marcuse in his discussions of Hegel and Marx. The reflective activities, or basic insights, that he associates with labor weaken but do not, as the term "breakthrough" may suggest, abolish the ideological yoke that holds the individual mentally captive. The newly acquired insight is a radical or critical perspective in the sense that the individual has an altered view of the social system, its goals, values, and organizational principles. The limits of lordship and bondage have been surpassed.

But while "penetration" means that the individual can transcend the limits of ideology, he does not transcend the limits of experience. Marcuse's theory of historicity is no idealism or transcendental philosophy that allows the individual to become completely independent of social existence, his thought and action to be unconditioned by social factors. For the sake of clarifying the precise character of Marcuse's radically disposed individual, this point should be emphasized. Within capitalist society all individuals share a context of meaning that can be construed broadly as the ideology of exchange relations. Ideology shapes or mediates each aspect of everyday experience. Consequently, the shared ideological context of meaning is also a shared experience of domination. At the same time, because this shared context of meaning is structured according to class relations, the burden of production falls predominantly upon a single class. As we have seen, it is labor that generates the insights that transcend the limits of domination established by the universality of exchange. But the insights gained through labor do not *displace* ideological beliefs. The norms rooted in the experience of domination mediated by ideology continue to influence thought and action, while insights arising from the experience of labor challenge that influence. Within the individual, ideology and critical insight compete. Members of the working class, therefore, view the society dichotomously or ambiguously.

Society, in other words, cannot impose its ideology heteronomously, but neither is the individual autonomous. Marcuse sees this as a position taken by Marxist theory. Marx, Marcuse explains, did not understand man to be either self-determining or determined by society but rather a "concrete historical life in a concrete historical world. Neither man nor world is an autonomous power that then would have to be brought into some relation with each other after the fact."[33] Marcuse's position, and one that is implicit in Marx's, is that with respect to the dominant ideology the individual is *semi-autonomous*. Because there are insights obtained through labor, to some degree the individual must be independent of ideological thought. By "insight," it should be recalled, Marcuse meant a primitive understanding that labor has a social character, that social factors are intimately related to how the individual and society develop and have become what they are, and that the individual has no real control over these factors. Insight is an understanding preliminary to real knowledge of the structure and operation of the social system. Lacking certainty, insight is a disposition to real knowledge and to the action based upon it but in itself is not sufficient ground for action. As an important measure of independence and autonomy, insight strongly suggests an individual who is poised somewhat delicately or precariously between extremes — between obedience to long held beliefs and their rejection, between fealty to society and disaffection, between being completely integrated into the ideological fabric of society and being completely free from it. Insight connotes the formation of new ideas and attitudes whose further development and expression are *constrained* by the pressures of an ideological framework that has been the basis of the individual's identity within the social system and that has conditioned the meaning of his every personal and social relation. In short, the insightful individual is also an ambivalent individual. A decisive question can now be posed. How can a radical disposition escape the constraints of ideology and become the standpoint from which the individual begins to think and act? Or, put differently, how does insight become knowledge?

Marcuse's response answers not only this question but also a second question that arises from a problem directly related to the fate of the ambivalent individual. Before considering Marcuse's answer, it is therefore appropriate to define this problem and to pose the question it raises.

From his interpretation of Hegel's relation of lordship and bondage and his examination of Marx's concept of labor, it seems evident that for Marcuse the ideas of all individuals within a society originate within that social order. Certain of the ideas, the rules laid down by the master or the ideological principles of capitalism, are shared by all of society's members. Other ideas, specifically insights acquired through labor and belonging to a particular class, are critical of these shared ideological meanings. Generally, all thinking is conditioned or limited by the meanings created within the particular social context and by its social structure, that is, division of labor. When the issue is then raised, on what grounds is capitalism to be judged, Marcuse's view is that standards of critical evaluation are to be found already formed within capitalist society.

This point is decisive, of course, for it carries two very important implications. First, there is no danger that the ideological principles of capitalism would serve as the final basis for determining its rationality. The rationality of capitalism would always be challenged from within by the insights of working-class individuals, which are inevitable expressions of the system's structural arrangements. Second, since critical standards of rationality are internal to capitalism, there is no need to resort to transcendental conceptions of right, the good, or other such universals. In fact, since Marcuse's theory of historicity maintains that all meaning, including standards of truth and validity, are formed within a historical, social context, his theory excludes a transcendental foundation for criteria of rationality.

By maintaining that conceptual meaning, in particular, criteria of rationality, that is, concepts of truth and falsity or of right and wrong, is always defined within a social context, Marcuse has explicitly followed not only Hegel (as he is interpreted in *Hegel's Ontology*) and Marx but Wilhelm Dilthey as well. Dilthey's view that all meaning is formed within and is relative to a social context is endorsed by Marcuse. Dilthey, Marcuse explains, understood that

> all the [social] structures and [cultural] forms of [historical-societal] reality . . . have been produced by a definite historical life. *And only as such products in the concrete coherence of the respective life do they have existence and meaning.*[34]

Marcuse's agreement with Dilthey that meaning cannot be decided on some universal, objective basis independent of social life brings us directly to the new problem. Within capitalism there are two fundamentally opposing views — the ideology of the bourgeoisie and the ideals of the working class, capitalist institutions and socialist aspirations. Each is false from the standpoint of the other. But if meaning or, in this case, rationality is internal to a way of life and both views, as the perspectives of its major social classes, are internal to the *capitalist* way of life, are not principles of capitalism and socialism equally rational? On one occasion Marcuse characterizes the problem in very similar terms.

> If Marxist theory is only the formulation of a particular standpoint under which a particular class necessarily experiences and interprets reality, can Marxism then on the whole still meaningfully lay claim to being a "true" theory? And then, is not the analysis of capitalist society and the theory of proletarian revolution based upon it nothing more than a one-sided representation of this reality, a historically unique perspective? From its perspective, does not the capitalist bourgeoisie have an equal claim to truth and falsehood?[35]

Marcuse's definition of this problem is familiar. It does, in fact, appear within an essay devoted to Karl Mannheim's *Ideology and Utopia*. Mannheim's challenge to Marxism, according to Marcuse, is for Marxist theory to demonstrate that the claims it makes for socialism are more rational than the truth that capitalism claims for its principles if, as is also an implication of Dilthey's theory of meaning, what is true and false is relative to the social and historical situations of particular social groups.

At this point, the question raised by this problem can now be considered along with the question posed earlier. First, how can a radical disposition escape the constraints of ideology and become the standpoint from which the individual begins to think and act? And second, how can the claims for socialism be proven to be more rational than claims to the contrary? Marcuse responds to both of these questions with a single answer — both fall within the domain of philosophy, as we shall now see.

Social science makes an important contribution to the question of rationality. Through the social sciences, by which Marcuse means the study of political economy, it is learned that capitalism is not a fixed, unchanging social order. As a society based upon a particular form of private property, it is burdened with contradictions that threaten not only its stability but also its very existence. By introducing a variety of institutional modifications these contradictions can be managed and stability preserved, though the threat continues so long as the changes do not include the elimination of private property. But the change to a higher order of capitalism does not exhaust the possibilities for social transformation. Social science proves, Marcuse argues, that the "future nature of the class society is determined and worked out in extremely different ways."[36] Its future is not un-ambiguous.[37] Social science can discover its developmental tend-encies, possible alternatives to the established order, possible his-torical solutions to the contradictions of capitalism. Marcuse cites approvingly sociologist Hans Freyer's description of these tendencies: "These are, first, the Marxist tendencies; second, the solution of a state-socialism; and, finally, a new one that bases itself on 'folk characteristics' rather than on orders of class or state."[38] The contribution made by social science is thus one of clarification, for the final decision about the rationality of the al-ternatives—capitalism, Marxist socialism, state-socialism, and National Socialism—must take into account the social tenden-cies that would constitute opposition to the formation of a ra-tional society. The question of truth is tied to the question of its practical realization, to political struggle.

But the importance of social science lies equally in what it can-not know as in what it knows. While the social sciences are able to clarify tendencies, it is not within their capacities to determine the outcome of history, that is, to predict with certainty which of the competing alternatives will supersede the others. This limita-tion of social science derives from the ambiguity of the future, that is, from the fact that the beliefs and attitudes of individuals are ambivalent, uncertain, and hence unpredictable. Because the future is indefinite, because the outcomes of history are final-ly the choices (though not necessarily the free choices) made by the members of society whose choices cannot be known in ad-vance, social science cannot provide historical laws whose causal necessity eliminates the problem of deciding which of the tend-encies or alternatives are rational. By virtue of this important limitation of social science, the task of determining the truth passes to philosophy.

Marcuse goes only so far as to say that the difficult task of de-termining the truth belongs wholly to philosophy. But for Mar-cuse this is already to define the means by which the truth can be known, for philosophy is reason, reflection on its every principle and on every assumption of social life. Beyond this, any attempt to conceive unquestionable universal truths would be to compro-mise the nature of philosophy as an essentially reflective enter-prise. Consequently, the certainty that Marcuse denies to social science he denies to philosophy as well. No claim to truth by philosophy and no justification for any such claim is ever exempt from further consideration. And it is precisely because philosophy is constant reflection on every position attained, or because philosophy knows that the work of reason is never completed, that through an act of *volition* it must finally *decide* on a rational position!

But the philosopher's activity is completed neither in the activity of reflection nor in the act of deciding truth, for "truths are not grasped in the work of knowledge in order to be laid on ice and preserved somewhere in abstraction. In the knowledge of truth lies the demand for its appropriation."[39] "Practice," Marcuse asserts, "must be taken back into the innermost task of philosophy."[40] The practice that Marcuse demands of philosophy is political practice. Philosophy must reach out to the individual and engage him in political discourse; it must

> encourage movements that go in the direction of truth and hinder those that lead to decaying modes of existence. Thus, the noblest desideratum of all philosophizing, namely, the unity of theory and practice, can become reality.[41]

Marcuse has proposed a political but not a revolutionary political act for the philosopher. There is no doubt, of course, that the goal of politics is the radical transformation of society and that Marcuse's philosopher becomes involved in politics with that eventual end in mind. Yet, what comes through implicitly in these early writings is a concern with the practice of political discourse. Through dialogue an effort is made to engage not a radical individual but an individual who at some level of thought and action is disposed to radical activity. It is precisely this radical *disposition* that makes discourse — and only discourse — a practical and political possibility. It was the theory of historicity that established the existence of such a radically disposed individual, and Marcuse's earlier point will be recalled that "any genuine methodology permits its approach to be directed by the manner in which its object is given." The concretely existing subject defines the guidelines of practice. Where the individual is not revolutionary, not class conscious, but ambivalent in attitude and uncertain in belief, politics turns into pedagogy, practice into philosophical discourse, and insight into knowledge. The radical act, the class act, does not occur spontaneously; it does not precede but must follow reflection and the political discourse through which reflection acquires a true understanding of the social order. Through discourse initiated by philosophy radical dispositions can escape the constraints of ideology. It is no surprise that in a discussion of the practical function of philosophy, Marcuse points to the philosopher who celebrated the critical function of political discourse.

> Socrates still had the possibility of addressing the individual person in the marketplace and of philosophizing with him because the individual person still existed within the society of the Athenian city-state.[42]

Marcuse's theory of historicity seeks to prove that the individual still exists in modern capitalism. This individual, and the theory that lifted the theoretical shadows that concealed him from view, are the early hopes of Marcuse's early writings.

Marcuse's project placed the Marxist theory of revolution on a new foundation. Reification had prevented the emergence of a class conscious proletariat. Ideology was not so effective, however, that it could paralyze the faculties of individuals whose insights, no matter how primitive, were the embryos of an understanding of the social system in class terms. While theoretically class remained the vehicle of revolution, its practical significance depended upon another theory that would recognize the individual as a viable political unit. Marcuse's project, his theory of historicity, constituted this recognition. But although the project is fascinating and compelling in its arguments for a critical disposition that prevails in and against ideological hegemony, ultimately it offers no more than an abstract theoretical outline of the individual's capacities for radical thought and action and the barest proposals for engaging such a person in the affairs of politics. Nevertheless, the project is no less important for these shortcomings. At the close of this early period in 1933, Marcuse's work had placed him in a position to develop his project through a theoretical and practical immersion in the social existence of the individual subject. Marcuse had recommended this next move when he declared that philosophy can reach the individual in his existence only if it does not conceive of him as an abstract subject but conceives of him in the fullness of his unique historical determination. This means that philosophy has to reach and grasp, *along with the individual person*, his . . . societal being . . . The philosopher must know that he has not only the right but the obligation to engage himself in the concrete needs of existence . . . Thus, public practice stands at the end of every genuine concrete philosophy. Hence the accusation and defense of Socrates, and his death in prison; hence Plato's political activity in Syracuse; hence Kierkegaard's struggle with the national church.[43]

Does Marcuse perhaps have a definite purpose in mind for selecting these particular examples? Is he not arguing implicitly for a particular approach to politics in modern capitalist society? If so, it is important to add that according to the norms of modern democratic capitalism, the political activities of Socrates, Plato, and Kierkegaard to which Marcuse refers would be considered a radicalized liberal politics. Here lies the significance of Marcuse's project — its theoretical recognition of the individual and the politics that it entails.

Marcuse's project never develops beyond its theoretical outline. The question is why? The answer, I believe, is revealed by the stage that the project had reached by 1933 in relation to an event of that year. As of that time Marcuse's theory conceived only abstractly of the individual as capable of critical insight, disposed to radical activity, though inclined by the pressures of reification to view his society in ideological terms. Not yet having passed beyond this abstract theoretical phase, the expectation would be that the future political allegiance of the individual would continue to follow the line of least ideological resistance. Now comes a crucial point. If, before further investigating and before engaging the individual in his concrete social existence, as Marcuse declared philosophy must, a political event of such barbarity occurred that all established political and traditional cultural forms of opposition appeared to have been swept into a torrent of ideology, the danger could arise that Marcuse would discard his project and abandon the individual, whom he could no longer regard as a potential source of antagonism and change. And this project would be discarded and the individual abandoned prematurely. For under the impact of such a terrible event the truth of concrete philosophy would be obscured — that the individual believed to have succumbed to ideology along with all other forms of opposition is actually *disposed* to resistance and that such a disposition is meaningful only when politically engaged!

Fascism was that political event and, as will be shown in the following chapter, did eventually lead to Marcuse's abandonment of the individual. It will also become apparent that the theoretical project that established the existence of the individual is entirely absent after 1933. Hegel's relation of lordship and bondage and Marx's concept of labor, the central elements of the theory of historicity and praxis, which proved the individual to be a theoretical as well as a practical subject, have been discarded. In the wake of fascism the hopes of Marcuse's early years, which bore the promise of the years to come, are lost.

Notes

1. "Heidegger's Politics: An Interview with Herbert Marcuse by Frederick Olafson," *Graduate Faculty Philosophy Journal*, 6, 1 (New York: 1977), p. 29. This interview was taken from the transcript of a film presented at a conference on the philosophy of Martin Heidegger sponsored by the Department of Philosophy, University of California, San Diego, May 4, 1974. As this part of the interview clearly indicates, it was specifically the Heideggerian dimensions of his early work that Marcuse later rejected. Marcuse judges these aspects of his project by saying that he "soon realized that Heidegger's concreteness was to a great extent a phony, false concreteness, and that in fact his philosophy was just as abstract and just as removed from reality, even avoiding reality, as the philosophies which at that time had dominated German universities, namely a rather dry brand of neo-Kantianism, neo-Hegelianism, neo-Idealism, but also positivism." (What Marcuse means by concreteness will be explained shortly.) Marcuse does not say *how* soon this rejection occurred. One cannot determine from this statement, in other words, whether he rejected Heidegger before the early period ended in 1933 or afterward. I will argue in this chapter that the break with Heidegger took place *before* 1933, although implicitly. But though I will show that Marcuse departed from Heidegger before this early period concluded, I will also argue that the entire early project, that is, not only the work that incorporated Heidegger's philosophy but also the much more promising work that broke with

Heidegger while continuing the project through interpretations of Hegel and Marx was abandoned after 1933 in the wake of fascism. Since it is my contention that Marcuse's early project should be taken seriously by contemporary social theory but, as the chapter will indicate, I am also sympathetic to Marcuse's reasons for rejecting Heidegger, I thus want to emphasize that the significance of Marcuse's entire project should be evaluated neither in light of his rejection of its specifically Heideggerian aspects nor in terms of his abandonment of the entire project. It must be stressed as well that Marcuse's rejection of the Heideggerian dimensions of his early work should not be construed as an explanation for his abandonment of the entire project.

One additional point deserves mention. On other, though little known, occasions Marcuse also expressed hostility toward Heidegger. In an article published in 1965, for instance, Marcuse praised "the anti-metaphysical structure of the English language for constituting a limit," in fact, "an agreeable limit to a broader reception of Heidegger" in the United States. See "Der Einfluss der deutschen Emigration auf das amerikanische Geistesleben: Philosophie und Soziologie," *Jahrbuch fur Amerikastudien*, 10 (Heidelberg: Carl Winter Universitätsverlag, 1965), p. 29.

2. "Heidegger's Politics," p. 28.

3. Ibid., pp. 28-29.

4. In *Karl Marx: Early Writings* (New York: McGraw-Hill, 1964), p. xvii, T. B. Bottomore reports that Marx's *Economic and Philosophic Manuscripts* were first published in a complete and accurate version by the Marx-Engels Institute (now the Institute of Marxism-Leninism) in Karl Marx and Friedrich Engels, *Historisch-kritische Gesamtausgabe* (MEGA) (Berlin: Marx-Engels Verlag, 1932). This edition prompted Marcuse's essay on Marx's *Manuscripts*, which is to be considered later in this chapter.

5. Herbert Marcuse, "Contributions to a Phenomenology of Historical Materialism," *Telos*, 4 (St. Louis: 1969), p. 5; originally published as "Beiträge zu einer Phänomenologie des Historischen Materialismus," *Philosophische Hefte*, 1, 1 (Berlin: 1928), pp. 45-68.

6. Herbert Marcuse, "Über konkrete Philosophie," *Archiv für Sozialwissenschaft und Sozialpolitik*, 62 (Tubingen: 1929), pp. 118-119. Resorting to a play on words I have translated *Geschäftigkeit* as "busyness" to capture both its Marxist element ("business") and its Heideggerian dimension (the activity of being busy). Either "business" or "activity" alone would fail to convey the meaning of Marcuse's argument.

7. Ibid., p. 119.

8. Ibid., p. 120.

9. Consider the chapter entitled "Reification and the Consciousness

of the Proletariat" in Georg Lukács's *History and Class Consciousness* (Cambridge: MIT Press, 1975), pp. 83-222.

   10. "Contributions to a Phenomenology of Historical Materialism," p. 3 (translation changed).

   11. Ibid., p. 7 (translation changed).

   12. Herbert Marcuse, "On the Problem of the Dialectic," *Telos*, 27 (St. Louis: 1976), p. 24; originally published as "Zum Problem der Dialektik" (part 1), *Die Gesellschaft*, 7 (part 1), 1 (Berlin: 1930), pp. 15-30. This article is a critical essay on Siegfried Marck's *Die Dialektik in der Philosophie der Gegenwart* (Tübingen: J. C. B. Mohr, 1929), the first half volume, and though favorable to Marck also develops the problem of the dialectic beyond the author's framework. Marcuse reviews the second half volume of Marck's study (1931) in "Zum Problem der Dialektik" (part 2), *Die Gesellschaft*, 8 (part 2), 12 (Berlin: 1931), pp. 541-557; also translated in *Telos*, 27 (St. Louis: 1976), pp. 24-39.

   13. Ibid., p. 24.

   14. "Über konkrete Philosophie," pp. 125-126.

   15. Ibid., p. 124.

   16. Herbert Marcuse, "Transzendentaler Marxismus?" *Die Gesellschaft*, 7 (part 2), 10 (Berlin: 1930), pp. 323-324.

   17. Ibid., p. 323.

   18. "Contributions to a Phenomenology of Historical Materialism," p. 14 (translation changed).

   19. Ibid.

   20. Ibid., p. 22.

   21. Herbert Marcuse, *Hegels Ontologie und die Grundlegung einer Theorie der Geschichtlichkeit* (Frankfurt: V. Klosterman, 1932). I have used the third edition, published in 1975 by Klosterman; it is unchanged except for its omission of *Grundlegung* from the title, which now reads *Hegels Ontologie und die Theorie der Geschichtlichkeit*.

   22. Ibid., p. 8. "Whatever this work contributes to a clarification and development of the problems is indebted to the philosophical work of Martin Heidegger. Let this be emphasized in place of all particular acknowledgements."

   23. Ibid., p. 282.

   24. Ibid., pp. 283-299, in particular.

   25. Herbert Marcuse, "The Foundation of Historical Materialism," *Studies in Critical Philosophy* (Boston: Beacon, 1973), p. 28; originally published as "Neue Quellen zur Grundlegung des Historischen Materialismus," *Die Gesellschaft*, 9 (part 2), 8 (Berlin: 1932), pp. 136-174.

   26. Ibid., p. 34 (italics added and translation changed).

27. Ibid., pp. 34–35.

28. Ibid., p. 39 (translation changed).

29. Ibid., p. 34.

30. In an earlier article Marcuse had argued that the concrete dialectic of historical materialism eliminates "causality and teleology" from Marx's theory. See Herbert Marcuse, "Besprechung von Karl Vorländer: *Karl Marx, sein Leben und sein Werk*," *Die Gesellschaft*, 6 (part 2), 8 (Berlin: 1929), p. 188.

31. In "The Struggle against Liberalism in the Totalitarian View of the State" (1934), published the year following the Nazi assumption of power, Marcuse argued that "genuine historicity presupposes a cognitive relation of existence to the forces of history and, derived from it, the theoretical and practical *critique* of these forces." *Negations: Essays in Critical Theory* (Boston: Beacon, 1968), p. 34; originally published as "Der Kampf gegen den Liberalismus in der totalitären Staatsauffasung," *Zeitschrift für Sozialforschung* 3, 2 (Paris: 1934), pp. 161–195. Failing to integrate theory and practice, Heidegger's theory of historicity is not "genuine" in the sense indicated by Marcuse. In this passage Marcuse is, in fact, clearly alluding to Heidegger. In the context in which the statement appears, Marcuse is indicting existentialism for extolling the man who acts without first reflecting on the meaning or consequences of his action. Such an individual, in Marcuse's view, is fascistic, as is the theory that turns unreflected action into a virtue. Without an adequate cognitive dimension, a theory of historicity, such as Heidegger's, is precisely this sort of existentialism. In this 1934 indictment Marcuse may be looking back upon his early period and engaging in self-criticism for at one time having become entangled in a theory of historicity that does not sufficiently integrate theoretical and practical activity. Marcuse was already on the path to this particular critique of Heidegger when the latter's missing cognitive element, as we have seen, was secured by rooting the theory of historicity in Hegel and Marx.

32. Herbert Marcuse, "On the Philosophical Foundation of the Concept of Labor in Economics," *Telos*, 16 (St. Louis: 1973), p. 34 (translation changed); originally published as "Über die philosophischen Grundlagen des wirtschaftswissenschaftlichen Arbeitsbegriffs," *Archiv für Sozialwissenschaft und Sozialpolitik*, 69 (Tübingen: 1933), pp. 257–292.

33. Herbert Marcuse, "Zur Kritik der Soziologie," *Die Gesellschaft*, 8 (part 2), 9 (Berlin: 1931), p. 277.

34. Herbert Marcuse, "Das Problem der geschichtlichen Wirklichkeit: Wilhelm Dilthey," *Die Gesellschaft*, 8 (part 1), 4 (Berlin: 1931), p. 361.

35. Herbert Marcuse, "Zur Wahrheitsproblematik der soziologischen Methode: Karl Mannheim, *Ideologie und Utopie*," *Die Gesellschaft*, 6 (part 2), 10 (Berlin: 1929), p. 359.

36. Herbert Marcuse, "Zur Auseinandersetzung mit Hans Freyers *Soziologie als Wirklichkeitswissenschaft*," *Philosophische Hefte*, 3, 1-2 (Berlin: 1931), p. 86.

37. Ibid.

38. Ibid.

39. "Über konkrete Philosophie," p. 112.

40. "Wilhelm Dilthey," p. 367.

41. Über konkrete Philosophie," p. 121.

42. Ibid., p. 126.

43. Ibid., p. 127 (italics added).

TWO

Fascism, Rationalism, and the Abandonment of the Individual

> If in the development of the State itself, periods are necessitated which impel the soul of nobler natures to seek refuge from the Present in ideal regions—in order to find in them that harmony with itself which it can no longer enjoy in the discordant real world, where the reflective intelligence attacks all that is holy and deep, which had been spontaneously in-wrought into the religion, laws and manners of nations, and brings them down and attenuates them to abstract godless generalities—Thought will be compelled to become Thinking Reason, with the view of effecting in its own element, the restoration of its principles from the ruin to which they had been brought.
>
> Hegel, *The Philosophy of History*

FOLLOWING THE Nazi assumption of power in 1933, Marcuse initially fled to Geneva to escape the dangers of fascism and then, little more than a year later, left Switzerland to seek refuge in America.[1] Fascism, too, was that period in the development of the state that forced Marcuse to seek refuge for theory in an ideal region.[2] There its principles would be saved from certain ruin and their critical disposition restored. Contrary to Hegel, however, in the midst of crisis Thought may not easily become Thinking Reason. It may not, in other words, be within the power of reflection to effect a restoration of theoretical principles. The impact of crisis on the reflective capacity may be dramatic, indeed crippling, and yet opaque. Such is the tragedy of Marcuse. Though he avoided the immediate perils of fascism, it was to leave its impression on his every work. In that one sense, at least, there was to be no escaping the Fascist horrors. In a way that never became apparent to Marcuse, their memory was seared deeply, grotesquely, into the structure of his thought.

Within the historical context of fascism, for a period of roughly eight years, the theoretical project that absorbs all of Marcuse's intellectual energies from 1941 onward begins to take shape. The eight years prior to that date should be viewed primarily as years of transition. At the outset they are marked not only by the Nazi rise to power but also by Marcuse's association with the Frankfurt Institute for Social Research. At the conclusion of this period *Reason and Revolution* is published, which among other tasks summarized Marcuse's conception of "critical theory" as it developed since 1933.[3] During the interim, Marcuse wrote a series of essays in which the ambitions informing his earlier, pre-Frankfurt work were discarded. It is as though a sudden, sweeping, and brutal purge of Marcuse's intellectual history has occurred. Essentially, these essays are theoretical fragments. Examined together they show that a new project is being formulated. And there is barely an element of that project as it was carried out after 1941 that is not present in some form during this transitional stage.

With these brief introductory remarks I have defined the twofold objective of this chapter. Expository analysis will focus on the central concerns of Marcuse's critical theory, as he understands them and as they unfold between 1933 and 1941. Fascism is the nucleus of these concerns and each will be studied and appraised in relation to it. Of interest here, it must be emphasized, is Marcuse's explicit design, his deliberate theoretical response to the emergence of the authoritarian state and society. At the same time, through this analysis the contours of Marcuse's future work will be brought to the surface. Second, I will step outside Marcuse's examination of fascism and its related issues to a different consideration of the effect of fascism on his theoretical development. Attention here will be paid to the manner in which fascism shaped Marcuse's critical theory, an influence of which he nevertheless remained unaware. To a significant extent, Marcuse and his social theory became the victims of that crisis he attempted to escape and to comprehend.

Marcuse's writings, and those of other theorists belonging to the Frankfurt School, are widely held to be unusually and perhaps unnecessarily difficult, often obscure, and occasionally impenetrable. Whatever the merits of these claims as they pertain to the entirety of Marcuse's work, the essays written during this transitional period are very clear not only with regard to style but also with respect to the questions posed, the straightforwardness of analysis, and the conclusions drawn. Furthermore, none of the ambiguity characterizing many of Marcuse's later efforts is present. On the contrary, Marcuse's positions are stated with directness, free of even irony and sarcasm. The steady clarity and sobriety of this period may be the result of fascism, as though this particular crisis lent a certain transparency to the complex theoretical problems to which it gave rise and with which Marcuse became occupied. Nevertheless, the clarity Marcuse's theory does achieve during this period of his work will, in the final analysis, prove to be illusory for it conceals a deeper and dark set of implications.

Authoritarian State

Marcuse's examinations concentrate on the tendencies and relations peculiar to liberal, democratic, capitalist societies. His analytical purpose is to identify the economic and ideological factors in liberal capitalism out of which grew the authoritarian state. Although National Socialism is the immediate form of Fascist totalitarianism Marcuse considers, it is apparent that his real target is the authoritarian state as a social formation potentially heir to all liberal capitalist societies.[4] There is, in other words, common to all variations of liberal capitalism a foundation that contains the seeds of fascism.

Economic factors are of singular importance to Marcuse's analysis. Private property, the individual entrepreneur's ownership of the means of material production, is the fundamental principle of liberal capitalism. As a basic right its preservation and protection are guaranteed. But private ownership is also liberalism's irrational element. Because this configuration is by nature prone to instabilities such as unemployment and inflation, its preservation constantly endangers the social order. If economic contradictions become so pronounced that an economic crisis threatens, liberalism's commitment to the safeguarding of property rights permits state power recourse to authoritarian measures of control. Such measures would be directed especially against political organizations that, representing the interests and needs of those classes suffering from the impoverishment brought in the wake of crisis, attempt to exercise their liberal freedoms to alter the conditions of social existence. For this reason, in the event of crisis the rational elements of liberalism, say, freedom of speech, press, and assembly, are suspended by the state. Fascism expresses the inner logic of liberal capitalism or, as Marcuse argues in "The Struggle against Liberalism in the Totalitarian View of the State," "the turn from the liberalist to the total-authoritarian state occurs within the framework of a single social order."[5]

Sharing fundamental economic principles, fascism and liberalism are consequently consistent with one another. This identity of interests is hidden from view, however, because fascism openly struggles against liberalism. Through its attacks on liberalism, and among other examples Marcuse notes the attack on the liberal practice of sacrificing the nation and the state to conflicts of interest between particular social groups, fascism derives political support for its claims to a superior social organization. But the liberalism that it opposes is far more a creation of Fascist ideology than an accurate portrayal of liberalist doctrines. Historically, for instance, liberal states have rescued the national interest from conflicting groups placing their own interests above it. Fascism transforms liberalism into an abstract world view and does so to disguise what it holds in common with liberalism: private property. Fascism's struggle against liberalism is more a diversionary tactic to conceal its deeper commitment to basic liberal capitalist norms than the laying of an alternative foundation for society.

Marcuse's intention, then, is to pass behind the deceptive appearance of radical differences between fascism and liberalism and to reveal their essential agreement. According to Marcuse, on two accounts specifically this agreement extends beyond the simple protection of private property interests to ideological norms that serve to perpetuate a social order rooted in the institution of private property. These are liberalism's "naturalistic interpretation of society" and "liberalistic rationalism."

Liberalism believes that the right ordering of society occurs when its processes are made to accord with their natural law–like character. A familiar conception, it finds expression in the theories of the classical economists. A natural, automatic harmony of interests, wants, and relations is expected to prevail wherever society is organized in strict obedience to principles thought to possess the scientific status of the physical laws of nature. Moreover, the stability of these processes will remain as eternal as nature itself. Fascism also embodies the liberal myth of naturalism in its celebration of the "folk," an abstraction that takes on a life independent of the fate of the real individuals who comprise the nation. Regardless of the latters' destiny the folk will survive for it alone is above the "unnatural" vicissitudes of history. Eternal and indestructible, the folk enjoys all the qualities ascribed to nature.

Liberalism's naturalistic interpretation of society is tied intimately to its idea of reason. Central to the natural law of the liberal economy is the notion that progress results from the activity of the individual entrepreneur left completely to his own devices. The public good is furthered by quite ordinary entrepreneurs pursuing their self-interest free from state interference. Reason, Marcuse explains, is realized through private actors, but the rationality of such a "privatization of reason" breaks down the moment the society is plunged into crisis. At that point an embarrassed liberalism can grasp only at justifications for its new developments which clearly appear irrational when measured against its own standard of a privatized rationality. One irrational justification that Marcuse mentions is liberalism's extension of "favors," or "special privileges," to those it heralds as "gifted economic leaders," the unique entrepreneurs who stride forth to conquer new economic frontiers in times of crisis. The gifted economic leader, Marcuse contends, anticipates fascism's charismatic, authoritarian figure.

Private property, liberalistic naturalism, and liberalistic rationalism are in Marcuse's estimation focal points of critical analysis. Around them can be constructed an understanding of the economic and ideological continuity between liberalism and fascism. Underscoring these three elements, Marcuse seeks to shatter the belief that the axioms of liberalism and fascism are contradictory. Fascism, in fact, is "produced" by liberalism as an institutional arrangement securing its highest priorities when the liberal social framework fails to do so. Additional proof for this thesis, Marcuse remarks, is the embryonic presence of the authoritarian state in the monopolistic phase of capitalist development. It is at this point, when the state first acts aggressively on behalf of propertied interests that cannot flourish burdened by the organizational logic of "privatized reason," that the Leviathan is revealed as the secret of liberal capitalism.[6]

If Marcuse concluded his theory of the dynamic relationship between liberalism and fascism at this point, it could be criticized without difficulty and dismissed. Too many factors are omitted from Marcuse's analysis. Among all the criticisms to be leveled, and they are too numerous to entertain, perhaps the one carrying the greatest weight pertains to the significance of the rational elements of liberalism in relation to the value systems of ordinary individuals. This argument can be stated as follows.

Marcuse's claim is that "despite structural variations" among liberal societies their uniform economic and ideological foundations in the long run make them all equally prone to the authoritarian state. If Marcuse's thesis is correct, then authoritarianism matures within the womb of liberalism despite, for example, the establishment of institutions in some liberal societies that make them economically and socially progressive to a greater degree than are liberal orders in which such institutions are absent. Against Marcuse it can be argued that so-called structural variations do not properly encompass ideological and cultural differences among liberal regimes. In those systems where liberal traditions are deeply ingrained and liberal norms are internalized by the society's members, the transition from a liberal to an authoritarian *state* could not occur without contradiction and disruption unless there were a corresponding transition from a liberal to an authoritarian *society*. Where a liberal ethos is firmly rooted in the polity a conflict would occur between popular expectations and authoritarian state tendencies. Liberal institutions would sacrifice legitimacy in the turn to authoritarianism, and faced with popularly held liberal dispositions the state would be sanctioned negatively.

A liberal society, to formulate this criticism sharply, would be forced to contend with the social contradictions that would arise if it engaged in sweeping violations of its own most basic principles, particularly in violations of the sort associated with the total-authoritarian state. Consequently, this problem directly challenges Marcuse's social theory, but he has met this challenge. His analysis does reach beyond a theory of the rise of the authoritarian state to account for the development of the authoritarian society. In this new context Marcuse offers an explanation for the support for fascism forthcoming from individuals socialized into the richest liberal traditions. And once again it is liberalism that is implicated in the rise of fascism for it is the very traditions of liberalism that constitute the underpinnings of the smooth transition from a liberal to an authoritarian society.

Authoritarian Society

Before moving the discussion to these new issues, a few preliminary remarks are in order. In "A Study on Authority," the theoretical investigation now to be considered, Marcuse critically examines the concepts of freedom and authority in the history of "social thought," that is, in religious, philosophical, political, and sociological thought as it evolved in bourgeois society. The family is also a prominent concern in this study. The discussion will be confined to the central parts of Marcuse's investigation, which establish its principal thesis and form the basis of his theory of authoritarian society.[7] In the relevant sections of this study, Marcuse certainly could be viewed as uncovering the ideological constraints that capitalism imposes on social thought and as showing the way in which these constraints are reflected in its concepts. Though such an approach is not incorrect, it limits our understanding of Marcuse by supposing that his primary focus is simply social thought as it is molded by the relations and authoritarian tendencies of capital.

But Marcuse's analysis is not confined to the disclosure of the ideological content of philosophical and theoretical concepts. While this is the ostensible purpose of Marcuse's argument, a crucial underlying assumption animates this study. Marcuse assumes that all the concepts he examines are integral to the ideologies that inform the day-to-day operations of the societies in which the concepts are rooted. He assumes as well, therefore, that the philosophical and theoretical concepts are also common to the belief systems of all individuals within these societies.

When Marcuse's critique of the concepts of freedom and authority in social thought is interpreted as an analysis of the concepts of freedom and authority held by ordinary individuals, the critique is being viewed, and most properly so, as an effort to tie these concepts to the future development of an entire social system rather than just to specific philosophical and theoretical developments. The social system is liberal capitalism and its fate is its historical transformation into authoritarian society.

With these remarks it becomes clear that the following discussion, which is to explore Marcuse's account of the transition from a liberal to a totalitarian society, can proceed only by keeping in sight the two levels on which Marcuse's analysis occurs. Marcuse's investigation will be reviewed on its own terms, that is, as an analysis of particular concepts as they evolve in the social thought situated in the historical context of bourgeois society. His argument then clearly before us, its underlying assumption can be recalled and Marcuse's conceptual analysis tied securely to his explanation of liberalism's authoritarian turn.

Marcuse provides us with a double-edged perspective on the bourgeois conception of freedom as it was born with the Protestant Reformation. Together, the religion and social relations of feudalism bound the individual's spiritual and practical life, the inner and outer spheres of his existence, to repressive institutions. The Reformation broke this total domination of the individual by emancipating the inner sphere. Religious authority could no longer dictate in private, spiritual matters. As Marcuse points out, however, restricting freedom to the private life of the individual permits domination to persist in the realm of practical affairs. The Reformation's concept of freedom is compatible with a social order that functions according to laws beyond the individual's control and that frustrate his efforts to fulfill wants and realize aspirations.

With this Marcuse defines the elements of the bourgeois concept of freedom. The progressive element of the concept rids the individual of a spiritual tyranny, while the failure to take that crucial step into the domain of practice marks the concept's conservative side. True freedom, Marcuse insists, must include two inseparable aspects: freedom of thought must be joined by freedom of action, freedom of the intellect (or spirit) by practical freedom. But Marcuse's argument is not simply that in their preoccupation with the life of the spirit Reformation thinkers justifiably neglected the realm of practical affairs. Rather, the restraints that capitalism imposes on free practice became internal to the Protestant concept of freedom and are reflected in its exclusion of free action. The notion of inner freedom works to blind the individual to external constraints. Marcuse expresses this point by saying that

> the realm of freedom and the realm of unfreedom are not simply contiguous with or superimposed on each other. They are founded together in a specific relation. For freedom — and we must hold fast to this astonishing phrase despite its paradoxical nature — is the condition of unfreedom.[8]

Marcuse explains that Luther first introduced a dualistic conception of individual freedom. Freedom was assigned to the inner person while worldly authority was given charge over all his practical concerns. The sacrifice of the individual's practical interest was of limited spiritual significance for no harm inflicted upon him by worldly authority could compromise his spiritual integrity. Authority as a physical institution, in fact, was looked upon as a product of divine ordination established to protect the faithful. If authorities engaged in corruption it was not a reflection on the institution, which retained its legitimate standing. Because the legitimacy of the institution cannot be compromised by official acts, authority must be obeyed regardless. In practice, at least, the individual is not free to distinguish between obedience to an office and to that office's incumbent.[9]

Obedience to authority is affirmed equally in Calvinism, although Calvin's concept of freedom departs from Luther's in significant respects. Luther's inner spiritual freedom is devalued to an extreme, and the individual's practical activities assume a new importance. The redemption of the individual depends largely on his material success and the vehicle through which success is to be achieved is not chosen freely. On the contrary, the prevailing standards of society are those used to measure success and it is only through conformity to these standards — in the last analysis through absolute obedience to the authority that establishes or represents the standards — that redemption becomes a possibility. Stripped of the Lutheran inner freedom, which allows the individual to make (silent) moral claims against authority's violation of spiritual and temporal law, freedom, which is the condition of material and spiritual success, is reduced to freedom to obey.[10]

With Calvin as well as with Luther, Marcuse has argued, in all matters of practice there is perfect agreement between the freedom of the individual and the aims of authority. At no time is there even a suggestion of possible antagonism between practical freedom and authority. From the outset freedom is defined purely in terms of authority.

Kant improves upon this Reformation scheme by recognizing a fundamental antagonism between freedom and authority. The discipline and obedience necessitated by any social order also infringe upon the prerogatives of freedom. Can this contradiction be eliminated without either restricting freedom or destroying authority and with it social order? Kant's response to this dilemma is to incorporate restraint into freedom as one of its characteristics. Restraint upon free practice becomes voluntary, a free act. In Marcuse's judgment an insight into the structure of bourgeois society is contained in the Kantian notion of a voluntarily imposed restriction upon individual freedom; capitalism must make restraint a condition of freedom. Capitalism, in other words, can tolerate only a substantially compromised freedom, one that could not encroach upon its basic interests. But the insight is canceled when Kant conceives of the *nature* of freedom as including restraint. With this conceptual move the infringement upon freedom ceases to originate within the social order and authority can be obeyed without the implication of coercion. Kant, following Luther and Calvin, in the end elevates authority to the position of final arbiter over practical freedom. Freedom again becomes a private matter. Where the ambitions of freedom would intersect with the public sphere, the former must "freely" defer to authority.[11]

The antagonism between the individual and society, or between freedom and authority, that is recognized but eventually suppressed by Kant reappears with Hegel. Civil society is acknowledged unequivocally to be a coercive order rooted in private property. Propertied interests figure as the source of contradictions responsible for mass poverty, contradictions that perhaps could be managed though not eliminated through civil

society's ventures into imperialism.[12] Bearing no promise of ultimately being resolved, the antagonism between individual freedom and the principles of civil society is sustained. Hegel, however, is not divorced from the cause of freedom. Freedom resides
in the state, which is independent of the interests propelling civil
society and is removed from the pressures and vicissitudes of a
propertied economy. But from Marcuse's perspective, Hegel's
state is an inadequate vehicle for practical freedom because freedom can be realized by the individual only through strict obedience to the state's ethical norms. Marcuse's verdict is that Hegel
mirrors the ideology that saturates the thought of Luther, Calvin, and Kant. Freedom appears again as subservience to authority.[13]

Side by side with the analysis of freedom and authority in Luther, Calvin, and Hegel is Marcuse's description of their theories
of the family.[14] In each case the family emerges as the single
most important factor contributing to the stability and perpetuation (reproduction) of bourgeois society.

The authority that Luther assigns to the temporal sphere is
anchored in the authority of the parents. Educated within the
family to accept rules and commands laid down by the parents,
the individual acquires the proper set of attitudes toward the authority of social institutions.

Calvin adds a psychological dimension to the theory of the formation of authority patterns. The family appears as a unit of
socialization in which particular habits of submission are not
merely learned but also internalized at a deeper psychological
level. Experiences with authority figures within the family, specifically with an authoritarian father, accustom the child to sub-
jection. With Calvin, Marcuse argues, the precise social role and
nature of the family in bourgeois society become transparent.
Through its harsh patriarchal structure the family erects the psychological infrastructure that disposes the individual positively
toward authority and its functions in capitalism.

Hegel's theory of the family resembles Calvin's in its attention
to the psychodynamics of authority relations, although with
Hegel the transmission of authority in the family does not possess
Calvinist harshness. Hegel idealizes the social relations of the
family. As a real community of interests in which no individual

ever thinks to benefit at the expense of the whole, the family generates the selflessness that is a prerequisite for the authentic community sought after by the state. And because individuality is swallowed up benignly by the family, at a higher level of social organization — the state — the dissolution of the individual can be reproduced. The state inherits an individual well taught by the family to subordinate individuality to an authority presiding over the common good.

As Marcuse's analysis moves from concepts of freedom and authority to theories of the family in bourgeois thought, a thesis is beginning to crystallize. Because of the decisive sociological and psychological functions that they attribute to the family, bourgeois thinkers are shown to be at least as concerned with theories of social organization as they are known to be with strictly theological or philosophical defenses of their concepts of freedom and authority. Accordingly, Marcuse's purpose is to expose the social, not philosophical, implications of these concepts. The social implications assume the greater significance when philosophers and religious thinkers, who nevertheless have grounded their concepts in some sort of metaphysics, look to the family as the social institution to *implant* these concepts in individuals as unreflectively held beliefs or attitudes. If individuals were socialized, or in a word "determined," to view authority uncritically, such attitudes toward authority would become the unshakable basis of a relation of domination.

Within liberal society, of course, these attitudes actually may be no more than tendencies toward an authoritarian relation. But Marcuse takes the social theories of the formation of these attitudes to reflect the structural characteristics of bourgeois society. Consequently, to judge from his analysis of freedom, authority, and the family in bourgeois thought, Marcuse certainly wants to claim more than a tendential status for these attitudes as they are nurtured within the social framework of liberalism. The momentum of his argument does seem to be leading to a foreclosure of the possibility that under certain conditions these tendencies could be expressed as any social formation but authoritarianism. This momentum is illustrated further by another measure of the social implications of the authoritarian family examined in "A Study on Authority."

Marcuse's new targets become thinkers wanting to restore the vitality of institutions shaken by revolution and who in so doing assign a special place to the family in society. Focusing on theories of counter-revolution at the times of the French Revolution and the German Restoration, Marcuse primarily considers works by Edmund Burke (*Reflections on the Revolution in France*), Louis Bonald (*Theory of Authority*), Joseph de Maistre (*Considerations on France*), and Friedrich Stahl (*Philosophy of Right*). All defend the interests of the deposed or declining feudal order against the ascendant bourgeoisie. Among the many elements of these somewhat varying theories of counter-revolution dealt with by Marcuse is a basic anthropological assumption that he contends is their essential component. Man is assumed to be immoral and corrupt, with reasoning capacities so defective that the idea of a society founded on the will of rational individuals becomes untenable. In the place of disabled reason is substituted the guidance of an authority based on faith, religion, and the prejudice of tradition. It is here that the family enters as the bulwark of authority. It alone can insure the individual's entry into the ideological mainstream of custom and superstition. The family is drawn into the expansion of state authority at the expense of liberal practices.

Thus, Marcuse's account of the theory of counter-revolution completes his thesis. It is the authoritarian family that marries the authoritarian state to an authoritarian society. The historical detail that counter-revolution and restoration aimed to suppress liberal bourgeois principles becomes theoretically irrelevant. Marcuse's point is precisely that since the theorists of counter-revolution maintain a conception of the family identical to that of bourgeois thinkers, both schools are committed to the authoritarian state psychologically moored in the authoritarian family structure.

Some conclusions can be drawn now that Marcuse's study of freedom, authority, and the family has been reviewed. When it is recalled that the concepts Marcuse analyzes are not simply central elements of certain religious and philosophical systems but are assumed to be common to the belief systems of ordinary individuals, his analyses become much more than expositions of the authoritarian features of bourgeois thought. In effect, they become aspects of Marcuse's own theory of the authoritarian dynamics of bourgeois society. This point deserves emphasis for it places Marcuse's study in a different light. He should not be understood as saying, in other words, that Calvin (for example) believes the family *ought* to manufacture attitudes of obedience toward authority, but rather that the family in bourgeois society in fact produces such authority patterns.

Proceeding with this point in mind, in the context of the work discussed thus far it is evident that Marcuse's theory of the transition from a liberal to an authoritarian state is buttressed by a theory of the total transformation of a liberal to an authoritarian society. Individuals within liberal capitalism are socialized to hold certain beliefs about authority that are supportive of an authoritarian state. When capitalism does suffer the inevitable crisis that gives rise to authoritarian state rule, there is no danger of a contradiction between the policies and practices of the state and the beliefs and values of the people. Never threatened by mass disaffection, the state remains legitimate and strong in its guaranteed reliance on popular sentiments.

Yet, this conclusion is premature for there is an obvious wrinkle in Marcuse's theory. Liberalism may submerge a genuine practical freedom in a powerful disposition to obey and recognize the priorities of authority. But it also has authored an equally strong belief in the *ideal* that practical freedom is realized increasingly in a gradually and steadily improving social system. Coupled to this ideal of practical freedom are beliefs in the possibility of individual happiness and the fulfillment of human potentialities. Armed with and inspired by these ideals, the liberally schooled individual hardly can be expected utterly to capitulate to the authoritarian state, especially because authoritarianism views such promises as false and the excesses of a decadent, bourgeois individualism.

This criticism is anticipated by another of Marcuse's essays, "The Affirmative Character of Culture." Bourgeois society, Marcuse contends, makes a distinction between culture and civilization that functions as a stimulus to material progress. Segregated from the realm of necessity, that sphere of social life in which the individual labors to satisfy basic needs, the cultural sphere articulates values that express the idea of a better, happier life, one free of the travails and anxieties of an unpredictable, insecure existence. Cultural ideals become a driving force behind the willingness of the individual to work hard and sacrifice for a future in which labor and sacrifice will cease to be necessary or at least not as necessary. Culture is critical in as much as it addresses the inadequacies of society and haunts it with reminders of a higher purpose, though at the same time it bestows its blessing by viewing society as instrumental to achieving the visions that are the idealistic stock of all social orders.

It is only theory, however, that understands culture to be, at one and the same moment, both critical and uncritical of society. To the minds of ordinary individuals the ideal, critical character of culture is lost. A pleasurable alternative to the ceaseless toils that are the trademark of civilization, the cultural representation of the ideal is confused with the realization of the ideal in practice. Freedom, happiness, and fulfillment seem to find their perfect expressions in their cultural embodiments. And since cultural experiences, the enjoyment of art, for example, are inner, private experiences, freedom or happiness become internal realities. A strictly internal reality of freedom can exist harmoniously with the most unfree external reality. Culture, Marcuse explains, endorses, or "affirms," the prevailing society. In Marcuse's words, the decisive feature of what he, after Max Horkheimer, refers to as the "affirmative character of culture"

> is the assertion of a universally obligatory, eternally better and more valuable world that must be unconditionally affirmed: a world essentially different from the factual world of the daily struggle for existence, yet realizable for every individual for himself "from within," without any transformation of the state of fact.[15]

First encountered in Marcuse's analysis of Luther, the conception of inner freedom is familiar. When it is taken up within the concept of affirmative culture its meaning and historical significance are elaborated. In his later work, Marcuse will dwell on the unique critical side of affirmative culture.[16] During this early period, too, inner freedom denotes a private space that sets the individual apart from the demands of social organization. Though inner freedom steels the individual to an unfree reality, it also confers upon him a "critical distance" from social constraints. The individual, Marcuse explains, is only "partially mobilized" by social order; inner freedom is still a sanctuary of sorts for freedom of thought and spirit — but only to the smallest extent for the inner freedom nourished by affirmative culture ultimately betrays the individual and is responsible for the complete reversal of freedom into domination.

It is during the Fascist period that the real meaning and historical significance of inner freedom cease to be its role as sanctuary of a critical spirit. As Marcuse understands it at this time, the freedom promoted by affirmative culture is actually a reservoir of dormant energies, ungratified instincts, and unrealized aspirations pent up and pressing for an unsublimated release. When liberalism turns to the authoritarian state to remedy its ills, the luxury of inner freedom, which critically detaches the individual from the social order, can be afforded no longer. In fact, it becomes an asset to fascism rather than a liability, for fascism provides a ready outlet for inner needs. Internalized spiritual cravings are externalized in authoritarian mass culture. Inner freedom, the hallowed liberal retreat for individuality, all along has prepared the individual for "deprivatization," "deinternalization," annihilation. The partial mobilization of the individual in the bourgeois epoch slides gracefully, terribly, into " 'total mobilization,' through which the individual must be subjected in all spheres of his existence to the discipline of the authoritarian state."[17] And the blame for liberalism's turn to authoritarianism is laid squarely upon liberal beliefs.

> That individuals freed [from feudalism] for over four hundred years march with so little trouble in the communal columns of the authoritarian state is due in no small measure to affirmative culture.[18]

> The intensive education to inner freedom that has been in progress since Luther is now, when inner freedom *abolishes itself* by turning into outer unfreedom, bearing its choicest fruit.[19]

No one can study the essays written during this period without being struck by an extraordinary—though some undoubtedly would say outrageous—feature. Marcuse's analyses of the essential properties of liberalism and fascism show them to be congruent without exception. The extensiveness of this agreement, and its startling implications for liberalism, is conveyed by the notion of "total mobilization," which subsequently becomes "one-dimensionality." No thought, indeed, no *form* of thought (art, philosophy, science, ordinary language, etc.), is spared "the reshaping of all human existence in the service of the most pow-

erful economic interests."[20] Although intended as a description
of authoritarianism, this remark is much more a comment on
liberalism's failure to produce individuals, norms, ideals, and institutions that *to even the smallest degree* are able to withstand
assimilation into a totalitarian form of life.

Fascism is the child of liberalism. It is a birth that occurs naturally and in which the entire family of liberal individuals participates. There is not another metaphor better describing the
dynamic (indeed, organic) relationship of liberalism to fascism
as Marcuse understands it. One truer to the actual relationship
would have referred to the rational elements of liberalism that
could abort the Fascist embryo. Individuals educated to liberal
freedoms are not equipped to accept uncritically authoritarian—or any other sort of—rule. In the rational elements of liberalism, in other words, lie the seeds of opposition to the authoritarian state.

These elements did not escape Marcuse's attention. At one
point he declares that "all the tendencies from which the political demands of liberalism derive their theoretical validity (such
as freedom of speech and of the press, publicity, tolerance, parliamentary government) are elements of a true rationalism."[21]
According to Marcuse, however, not because of—as with the
bourgeois concept of authority—but in spite of these elements
the transition to the authoritarian state and the authoritarian society takes place without the least friction. Why are individuals
who are instructed in the elements of liberal reason omitted from
Marcuse's analysis of the transition?

An answer is suggested by Marcuse's assertion in 1934: "Today
the fate of the labor movement . . . is clouded with uncertainty."[22] That Marx's proletariat seemed unable to fulfill its historical mission, though the economic and social conditions for
the revolutionary transformation of capitalism had been present,
meant more to Marcuse than simply labor's uncertain future. As
vehicle of historical development and progress, the proletariat
was the objective ground of Reason and hence the rational foundation for critical theory. While it is not within the power of theory to rehabilitate the ailing revolutionary spirit of the proletariat, it must respond to this development by reworking its rational
foundation. Without such a foundation, the claims against society made by critical theory are weakened. Marcuse responds for-

midably, but the foundation he newly provides proves to be flawed. It contains an implicit set of assumptions that serve to exclude from consideration the politics and rationality of the liberally schooled individual. Later, it shall become clear that it was the fatal blow that fascism dealt to the labor movement that ultimately led to this abandonment of the individual.

There are two equally significant dimensions to what I here choose to call the "abandonment of the individual." This phrase means that the individual is discounted as a *theoretical* factor possibly affecting the transition from liberal to authoritarian society and as a prospective ally in the *practical, political* struggle against the authoritarian state. At this point, my intention simply is to indicate that this abandonment does occur in Marcuse's theory and that it is related intimately to authoritarianism's defeat of the labor movement and to the new foundation Marcuse provides for a critical theory of society. Shortly, this argument will be developed. For now it is merely suggested as a line of criticism. When the discussion turns to a complete explanation of the abandonment, it will become clear that the exclusion of the individual's theoretical and practical significance was not deliberate. As noted, it will be shown to have resulted from a set of underlying assumptions hidden within the analytical framework of critical theory as the latter was conceived in response to fascism. But there is another aspect of Marcuse's theory strangely at odds with this framework, one that therefore deserves first consideration. It is present in Marcuse's analysis of German sociology and carries with it different implications for the rise of the authoritarian state.

Marcuse's studies on freedom, authority, and the family were accompanied by a brief essay critically examining the dominant theoretical approaches to "Authority and the Family in German Sociology until 1933."[23] Marcuse isolates two sociological conceptions of the family that had substantial theoretical purchase within the discipline. Broadly described, the "naturalistic" interpretation of the family regards it as a natural and eternally unchanging structure at the base of society. Because it is prescribed by nature the family and its internal relations are valid and not open to criticism. And not only relations within the family, but also the larger social and economic relations rooted within it, share the quality of naturalness and likewise derive their validity from that quality. While this first school views the family as originating independently of social processes, the "sociologistic" conception denies the family even a relative autonomy from society. Viewed as a unit duplicating on a small scale the structural relations of the entire society, the family is presumed to have arisen from and to be conditioned directly by the social structure.

Marcuse illustrates the faults of these approaches with carefully selected examples. In one seminal work published in the midnineteenth century that was a sociological classic at the time Marcuse is writing, the family appears as the natural ethical foundation of society.[24] Concerned to protect the family from socialist and other tendencies within bourgeois society that could alter its natural structure and functions, its author wages a noble defense. The sanctity of the family and the virtues of liberalism are claimed to go hand in hand. When the family's members are considered, it is the father who plays the major socioeconomic and political role within the society, while women are bound to the family and "naturally" assume no public functions. By offering emotional and spiritual comforts absent from the economic sector, the family serves as a refuge for the embattled male economic subject, thus preparing him for another day's work. Moreover, the patriarchal and economic authority assigned to the father by nature and the equally natural subordination of women are authority patterns transmitted by the family.

As one combination of studies proves, the sociologistic methodology consistently transforms the family into a unit compatible with any social formation.[25] The principle that the individual is capable of thought that can change the shape and direction of social processes is rejected. Not individuals but groups "think" or, to put it differently, being prior to individuals, the structural dynamics of groups determine individual thought and action. The most important group within this environment of social determinants is the family. But though the family molds the individual's thinking, it in turn is formed and reformed by the larger social structure to accord with the latter's imperatives. Marcuse also criticizes a third study for adopting a very similar thesis.[26] This study claims that the family is invaded by society and its functions appropriated. Whatever independence the family may once have had is gradually exchanged for a complete dependence on broader social tendencies.

Since Marcuse criticizes approaches to the study of the family that lie at opposite ends of the methodological spectrum, his own approach in this essay must fall somewhere in between. But although he does not subscribe either to the naturalistic interpretation that the family should entirely determine social processes or to the sociologistic view that it is wholly determined by society, it should not be concluded that Marcuse's approach blends elements of both methods. At least with respect to the family, any sort of naturalism is alien to Marcuse. Marcuse's approach nevertheless can be situated between the two methodological extremes in several important ways. Marcuse understands the family as it appears within capitalism to be a product of a long, precapitalist historical development. Capitalism then imposes its own pressures on the family in order to bring it into conformity with its own dynamics. Quite obviously, these aspects of Marcuse's view correspond somewhat to what he has called the "sociologistic" approach. With Marcuse, however, the family can be bent only partially to the service of capitalism for he strongly contends that "the family has proved itself to be highly resistant to the tendencies described" by those who study the family sociologistically.[27] Historical structures, Marcuse is arguing, are not totally malleable just because they are the results of a long history of social processes. A structure emerging from one historical period to some degree will be unyielding to the pressures of another. Hence, Marcuse's approach clearly is historical but not simplistically reductionistic. And by giving the family a semi-independent status from societal trends, he participates in what might be called the "spirit" of naturalism.

What is the significance of this characteristic ability of the bourgeois family to withstand pressures to conform to the ends of capitalism? According to Marcuse, it is that the family does not simply act as a "psychic agency" within society. It does not, in other words, merely sculpt personalities to fit neatly into the framework of capitalism. It also develops an individual's psychological and rational capacities, which allow him to think critically about the social system in which he lives and works. The individual, like the family, is as much a source of resistance to social processes and political pressures as a source of support.

Now it is readily apparent that this approach to the family is opposed dramatically to that taken by Marcuse in "A Study on

Authority." The investigation examined earlier looks upon the family and its progeny as social atoms moving in unison with the social system. In no uncertain terms, Marcuse judges the individual to be a pillar of the authoritarian state, a lubricant for its growth and development. In retrospect, therefore, it can be seen that Marcuse's approach in "A Study on Authority" seems "sociologistic" — individual development parallels social development, with all individual needs and aims reduced to the needs and aims of society. At this point, an issue of some concern becomes visible. Why is Marcuse's analysis of authority and the family (in "A Study on Authority") informed by an approach that discards the individual as a source of resistance to authoritarian society when his critique of other analytical approaches to the family (in "Authority and the Family in German Sociology") insists implicitly on the existence of such an opposition to authoritarianism?

With this question the discussion finds entry into an analysis of Marcuse's formal conception of critical theory. This entails an exposition and critical examination of its fundamental principles and will secure an answer to our question. But to understand Marcuse's conception of critical theory requires an appreciation of the entire theoretical motivation that lies behind it. Another of his critical essays, "The Concept of Essence," must therefore be considered first. This work remains at the level of a critique of philosophical systems and specifically focuses on the concept of essence.[28] The level at which the analysis proceeds is noteworthy for it reveals Marcuse's purpose in undertaking this effort. Since the theory of authoritarian society excludes the possibility that either collective or individual opposition will be forthcoming, Marcuse's problem now is to discover whether resistance to the authoritarian state has survived within the intellectual division of labor. At least since Plato the Western philosophical tradition has sheltered ideas critical of society. Has the critical disposition of philosophy acquiesced to authoritarianism, or can it aid in rescuing civilization and the socialist vision from barbarism?

Marcuse, in fact, begins by inquiring into the relationship of essence and appearance as it is elaborated by Plato. His starting point is not arbitrary. With Plato, the critical temper of the concept of essence receives one of its finest expressions. For Marcuse, Plato's "essence" derives its critical impetus from the philosopher's investigation into the universal and particular, the One and the Many.

Although all things in the universe are different from one another, through logical procedures they can be classified according to their similarities. For instance, there are various kinds of justice and happiness just as there are types of tables and chairs. What is important, however, is not any particular form of justice appearing to ordinary observation, but the Idea of justice. Contained within the Idea are all possible attributes of the object to which the Idea refers. All possible attributes of an object, its "universal" qualities, that is, justice or happiness in general, are the proper concern of thought and the only basis of true knowledge. Through the Idea knowledge distinguishes between essence and appearance, the universal and the particular, the One and the Many, or between that which is certain and permanent and that which is transient and accidental. Both logic and epistemology are joined in reason's claim to know this difference.

Marcuse argues that the critical dimension of Plato's concept of essence springs from its meaning as "universal." According to the very nature of the universal, no society ever could realize, for instance, all the possible attributes of justice. Societies always could be more just. Consequently, the universal indicts the society for against this measure of true justice the society is inadequate. Furthermore, though essence is established logically and is the basis of knowledge, the universal is not simply an invention of philosophy. On the contrary, the universal is descriptive of the very nature or Being of reality, including social realities. As such, it refers to inexhaustible possibilities for growth and development. Although later in *Reason and Revolution* he grounds the concept of possibility in a logic rather than in an ontology, this ontological character of Plato's universals is of interest to Marcuse. Ontologically, or logically as Marcuse subsequently argues, possibility, or potentiality, remains a given of social life. This is a point that Marcuse will stress constantly in view of the attacks on the validity of universals, and the possibilities they represent, made by logical and epistemological theories after Plato. And there is a final and equally significant aspect of Plato's essence that Marcuse emphasizes: its relation to the world of appearance is not static but dynamic. All universals—justice, happiness, freedom, and so on—are in constant motion toward the realization of their essential possibilities. This is the Plato of the later dialogues. As Marcuse puts it, "The essence as potentiality becomes a force within existence."[29]

At the dawn of the bourgeois era the classical conception of essence undergoes demonstrative changes with Descartes. Marcuse interprets these changes from the standpoint of the historical context of Cartesian philosophy, specifically in terms of socioeconomic constraints that Marcuse already has shown to influence bourgeois thought. Liberated from the oppression of feudal order, the individual acquires an autonomy, a sovereign power to shape his own existence. But the newly emancipated individual is not a subject able to express his freedom practically. Laws governing the economic processes of society are opaque, making it impossible to bring the market under control. Because market relations cannot be mastered, individual intentions and aspirations collide with unanticipated obstacles and produce unexpected consequences. At best, uncertainties accompany the exercise of freedom; at worst, hazards.

Descartes's philosophy reflects the new possibilities and the new constraints of bourgeois society. Deprived of an arena for practical freedom, freedom retreats into a secure world. Freedom becomes freedom of thought. But is it secure? Can thought gain access to certain knowledge or is it, like practice, subject to "blind chance"? Descartes's response, of course, is that the truthfulness of all conceptualization should rest upon a single conception that would serve as the unshakable foundation for all knowledge. Since no person ever doubts the concept of his conscious existence, the *cogito*, or "I think," is the criterion for conceptual certainty. With thought being confident of the certainty of its free exercise, essence, man's universal potentiality, now can reside safely in thought.

Marcuse praises Descartes's concept of essence on two accounts. The certainty associated with thought makes thought rational in an objective sense, while the freedom attached to thought allows for all things to be judged according to the standards reason devises. But Marcuse's praise is balanced equally by two criticisms. Once essence is located in thought it ceases to be a property of existence lying outside thinking processes. What has happened, in other words, is that the ontological character of essence has been lost through the reduction of essence to epistemology. This change in the concept is decisive. It means that the world no longer has a truth (potentialities) of its own behind the way it *appears to*, or is comprehended by, the knowing subject. This first point is crucial. Marcuse means by it that when the distinction between essence and appearance is based upon epistemological rather than ontological assumptions, the critical status of essence becomes fragile. This happens because thinking processes can be influenced by social processes and their ideological supports. Second, the dynamic character of essence is also compromised by Descartes. Restricting essence to freedom of thought means that the inventions of human reason need not be translated into practice. Potentiality remains inert. The critical power of essence is doubly eclipsed.

As the bourgeois era unfolds, the critical dimensions of the concept of essence continue to erode. Kant's philosophy, in Marcuse's estimation, forfeits what critical leverage Descartes had preserved. Essence acquires its new definition in the context of Kant's pure theoretical reason. Marcuse focuses primarily on Kant's concepts of the understanding (such as causality), which give form to the elements of sensual experience, and on the transcendental apperception, that unity of conscious processes that integrates sense experiences and renders them intelligible. Because these attributes of consciousness belong to every individual, they are universal. And as the immutable basis of all experience they guarantee knowledge a foundation in certainty. Universality, permanence, and certainty—all characteristics of pure theoretical reason—constitute essence. But although pure reason makes knowledge possible by *organizing* experience, it provides no standards by which to *evaluate* experience. With Kant, therefore, the critical rationality of Descartes's *cogito* disappears. And following Descartes, the ontological and dynamic qualities of essence are canceled as well. Like Descartes's, Kant's essence is restricted to reason, and the stable forms reason imparts to conscious experience embody no potentiality that is unrealized.

In the decades immediately preceding the rise of the authoritarian state, the critical voice of reason becomes ever more silent. Bourgeois philosophy, like the society of which it is a part, is not in the least antagonistic to authoritarianism. It is the final meaning that is given to the concept of essence which signifies philosophy's tacit consent to domination. Phenomenology and positivism, Marcuse contends, exemplify philosophy's compliance.

Marcuse's analysis shows that Husserl's concept of essence makes no advance over Kant's. He especially takes issue with Husserl's "phenomenological reductions."[30] For two reasons, Husserl's dual reductions fail as reflective vehicles for discovering the essential basis of factual experience. First, the phenomenological "bracketing," which suspends judgments and eliminates biases that otherwise would interfere with reflection on experience, is no more than an indifference to the true social meaning and implications of experience. That all experience is equally significant because reflection is concerned only with its common foundation denies reason the opportunity to discriminate among different forms of experience according to definite standards. For example, it is not within the province of phenomenological reflection to declare experiences within a social system rational or irrational or to identify potentialities for social reorganization and growth beyond those officially recognized. Second, the subject that is found to be the basis of experience is not a particular group, class, or social institution. Phenomenological analysis purges experience of social and historical determinants. Husserl's subject is transcendental — to Marcuse, not a step removed from Kant's pure theoretical reason. As the absolute, certain, essential foundation of all experience, the transcendental subject retains its truth even if the experience is that of authoritarianism. Taking both points together, Marcuse appears to be saying that Husserl permits the irrationality of experience to be neglected and that the presence of the transcendental subject at the basis of that experience allows essence to coexist peacefully with irrationality.

Husserl's phenomenology thus paralyzes the critical power of essence. Essence ceases to represent a truth against which the facts of experience, that is, the way in which the social order appears, can be condemned as false. For all intents and purposes, Husserl has abolished the distinction between essence and appearance. With no truth independent of the world of appearance, the latter assumes the status of truth by default. In this event, phenomenology comes to resemble positivism, which holds that the only valid objects of knowledge are observable facts. Only the facts are real, positivism alleges, and there are no grounds for believing in an essence, a truer world, apart from them. As Marcuse says, using for the first time an expression that will figure prominently in his future work, according to positivism "the world of facts is, so to speak, one-dimensional."[31] And if the given facts are the facts of authoritarianism, positivism and phenomenology collaborate in its affirmation.[32]

The distinction between essence and appearance is no esoteric philosophical conception. It is fundamental. Without it philosophy relinquishes any possibility of thinking critically. Marcuse's analysis of this development is clearly a difficult theoretical study. It is painstaking in its attention to detail, much more so than an exposition can hope to capture. Its detail radiates a certain urgency or perhaps anxiety. It is as though Marcuse is turning over every philosophical stone to recover some critical bearing that remains untouched by the authoritarian dynamics of bourgeois society.

All these qualities of Marcuse's study are indicative of its real purpose. Though it is conducted at the level of a philosophical analysis, Marcuse's critique of philosophy is not designed simply to expose philosophical errors or to stake out an opposing philosophical terrain. Marcuse's great concern is with what the political practice implicit in philosophical discourse shows about the nature of society. Marcuse is waging a battle for ideas that, in the complete absence of other sources of opposition, continue to transcend this society and to call it into question. As an enterprise removed from society in the sense that it makes no contribution to the mechanics of social organization and the productive process, philosophy, by virtue of its "distance," should be less vulnerable to social and political dynamics than is the thought of ordinary individuals. Transcendent ideas should endure within philosophy — that they do not is far more significant than philosophy's affirmation of the status quo. It is revealing of the sheer power of authoritarianism to coordinate the most remote forms of thought with its political ends.

The Theoretical Response to Authoritarianism

Important, then, is not only that philosophy has submitted to authoritarianism by severing its critical lifeline. Its compliance is also an exceptional measure of the extensiveness of the integration of thought into authoritarian society. When critical theory now responds to authoritarian domination, it must respond to total domination. Its conceptual structure must express an opposition that is equally total.

When considering critical theory's response to authoritarianism, it is appropriate to begin with its own concept of essence.[33] For although critical theory is joined by a second fundamental principle, essence is its pivotal concept, the nucleus around which all other articles revolve. Hegel's concept of essence informs that of Marcuse's critical theory, a debt Marcuse willingly acknowledges. Very shortly, the discussion will return to the significance of Hegel's philosophy for Marcuse when there is occasion to consider *Reason and Revolution*. Presently, four aspects of Hegel's concept of essence warrant brief mention.

First, Hegel's essence refers to possibilities or potentialities, in other words, to that which is unrealized. As it appears, for example, society is always false to an extent because its beliefs, relations, and institutions contain possibilities for more rational beliefs, social relations, and institutions.

Next, the realm of possibility denoted by the concept of essence turns essence into a critical concept. Only that is true which has developed its potentialities fully.

Third, Hegel's concept of essence is dynamic and historical. Possibilities are continually in the process of developing, and as they do new possibilities unfold. This dynamic is historical because new possibilities develop through the actions of unique individuals within historical periods, through the norms that constitute cultural epochs, the structural principles of economic and social relations, the practices of the state, and so forth.

Last, though the dynamic process is rooted in the greatest variety of historical factors, it is eventually reduced to an ontological foundation. It is Reason (or Being) that evolves historically. All elements that comprise history — cultures, actors, principles, states — are instruments of Reason, particular possibilities that are expressions of *universal* potentialities. As the expressions of possibilities that are contained a priori in Reason, history is *in fact* the manifestation of a predetermined rational structure. Consequently, not only are the possibilities seized and developed by man not originally authored by him but by the labor of Reason, but also potentiality is limited by Reason in virtue of its being the Absolute (whole or sum of all potentialities).

With the exception of the final characteristic, all are incorporated into Marcuse's concept of essence (though not without modification). For several reasons, Marcuse continues to be hostile to any ontological formulation of essence. Man must be the driving force of the dialectic, not some abstract Reason. And while the possibilities for human and social development are limited within any societal constellation for Marcuse, those actually developed are not determined for man but by him from a range of historical possibilities. Moreover, the possibilities for future historical development must remain open, "indeterminate," and never foreclosed by any self-contained conceptual or societal framework of rationality.

It is Marx's materialism that enables Marcuse to meet these new stipulations for a concept of essence. Man is the author of history, meaning the history of all forms and aspects of social organization. History is the objective, material expression of human potentialities. As man creates history, he also creates himself. Creativity is always self-creation; productivity is self-production. As the fruit of human activity, historical formations (accumulated levels of knowledge and technological development) are the instruments or tools with which man engages in further self-production as well as production. Human potentiality, human essence, therefore, lies as much outside man in his historical creations as it lies within him.

Although man is the author of history, of man's nature, he does not author them freely. Broadly conceived as human historical activity, essence is embodied in every society's perpetually changing relations, in the totality of social processes. As the totality of relations develops, so does man's essence. Historically, however, the totality always has been, as Marcuse describes it, "an inherently multi-dimensional, organized structure."[34] In other words, social, economic, political, and cultural processes have been organized such that one of these levels, the economic, is more fundamental and stamps all relations with a definite character (e.g., feudal or capitalist). The resulting forms of social organization always have disposed over what is to be produced and how production is to occur. In this way, the history of human development has taken place unfreely. In the current historical period it is capital and its production relations that form the basis of and shape all other processes.

Following Marx, Marcuse's view is that the possibilities inherent in the production relations of capitalism are *qualitatively* different from those realized in capitalist and precapitalist social formations. Materialism maintains, of course, that the contradictions of capitalism should lead ultimately to the elimination of private property and to the socialist reorganization of production relations. Socialism, however, is not merely one historical possibility among others. Through the abolition of private property and alienation, socialism restores to the individual the freedom to "assimilate all the wealth of previous development," that is, the freedom to utilize the intellectual and material achievements of history to develop his own potentialities.[35] Socialism is thus the realization of a historical possibility that establishes the preconditions for the realization of all human possibilities. Freely produced, the essence of man then would become truly his essence.

If essence is embodied in the totality of a society's social processes, must not the tendency toward authoritarianism, which is, as we have seen, another possibility within capitalism, be counted as another essential possibility for human development? A second principle of Marcuse's critical theory now becomes pertinent. In its determination of what constitutes man's essence, critical theory is not objective in the sense of being value-free but possesses a normative criterion by which it distinguishes between essential and merely historical, true and false possibilities. Theory's criterion is its "concern for man," its "interest" in his emancipation. It necessarily follows from this commitment that critical theory must incorporate freedom into its concept of essence and that essential possibilities are those that promote freedom. Marcuse argues these points by saying that

> just as the content of the materialist notion is historical and oriented toward practice, the way in which it is arrived at is also determined by historical and practical presuppositions . . . It is determined within the framework set by the historical goals with which materialist theory is linked. Not only do the interests resulting from these goals play a role in establishing what is essential, they enter into the content of the concept of essence.[36]

The "interest of freedom" is "thus preserved in materialist theory."[37] Authoritarianism is not an expression or realization of human essence because it robs man of his self-productive freedom — a freedom that is the essence of all human essence.

In the concept of essence as human potentiality and in the interest of freedom we have the two basic principles of Marcuse's critical theory. Both of these principles, as has been shown, are tied intimately to materialist theory. The conception of potentiality is filled out, so to speak, by an analysis of the possibilities for change and development shaped by the economic structure of society, while the interest of freedom derives from materialism's proof that these potentialities will be realized only through a socialist reorganization of the relations of capital. In "Philosophy and Critical Theory," Marcuse summarizes these principles by explaining that there "are two basic elements linking materialism to correct social theory: concern with human happiness, and the conviction that it can be obtained only through a transformation of the material conditions of existence."[38]

Its specific conceptions of potentiality, freedom, and happiness comprise the truth of critical theory. They appear to theory as the highest good, as the truest aims of social life, because materialism demonstrates that not only the achievements of history but also the social class produced by its most advanced, capitalist, stage converge to bring about their final realization. This last point, now almost commonplace in Marxist theory, is extremely important. Theoretically it means that the truth that critical theory maintains is not true in itself. It is true because it derives from the existence of a class within capitalist society whose *objective* function is to give birth to a new history of human freedom and happiness by radically altering the material conditions of life. This objective revolutionary function of the proletariat gives the truth of critical theory its substance as an empirical, historical truth. In the first and final analysis, the truth of critical theory is a contingent truth.

With the revolutionary agent of historical transformation vanquished by the authoritarian state and society, are critical theory and its truth refuted? To recall the earlier formulation of this problem, how will Marcuse's critical theory respond to the historical situation of total domination? His response is anticipated in this candid recognition of the problem.

What, however, if the development outlined by the theory does not occur? What if the forces that were to bring about the transformation are suppressed and appear to be defeated? Little as theory's

truth is thereby contradicted, it nevertheless appears then in a new
light which illuminates new aspects and elements of its object. The
new situation gives a new import to many demands and indices of
the theory, whose changed function accords it in a more intensive
sense the character of "critical theory" . . . This situation compels
theory anew to a sharper emphasis on its concern with the potentialities of man and with the individual's freedom, happiness, and
rights contained in all of its analyses.[39]

Critical theory is not invalidated by the absence of a class conscious revolutionary agent. It responds to a situation that has
ruptured the bond between theory and practice with, as Marcuse
says, a new stress upon theory. Theory must now underscore conceptual elements that can preserve and protect its truth from the
fate suffered by its practical agency. To do so is an obligation in-
curred by its "interest of freedom," or its "concern for man," in
Marcuse's terms. And, of course, critical theory undertakes to
guard its truth simply because it believes it to be the truth. To
adhere stubbornly to the truth against an authoritarian reality
that threatens it is an authentic act of political opposition.

The precise nature of Marcuse's response to authoritarianism
is now but a short step away. In the excerpted statement Marcuse
has offered several clues. In the present situation, he explains,
theory has a "changed function" and becomes, "in a more intensive sense," a "critical theory" with a new and "sharper emphasis
on potentialities, freedom, and happiness." What this means is
that critical theory becomes emphatically "theory"; that is, it articulates its goals, its truth, without reference or direct appeal to
a practical agent of historical change for that agency is no longer
a conscious revolutionary subject. Critical theory especially retains its theoretical allegiance to political economy because materialism is the basis of its concept of essence and identifies structural tendencies in the social system that can lead to radical
change. Critical theory, Marcuse reaffirms, "is economics itself
insofar as it deals with contents that transcend the realm of established economic conditions."[40]

Also, in the absence of an agent that joins critical theory in an
apprehension of theoretical possibilities as *real* historical possibilities, the transcendent possibilities now sharply emphasized by
critical theory are purely objective but their objective status is
open to question. Claimed to exist independently of any subject's

failure to comprehend them, transcendent possibilities become, as Marcuse says, critical theory's "utopian element."[41] This point can be put differently. Since, in the absence of a revolutionary subject who is aware of objective possibilities for change (conscious of its own objective historical function) these objective possibilities for transformation are attested to by theory only, critical theory is placed in the awkward position of defending possibilities that appear unrealistic or imaginary. Consequently, when critical theory changes its function by becoming strictly theoretical, it must be accompanied by a very important revision in its conceptual framework. An adequate theoretical response to an authoritarian reality that contests its truths as illusory, its essence as fiction, will be to provide this truth with a philosophical foundation that establishes its certainty and rationality!

Marcuse's great work culminating his period of theoretical transition begun in 1933, *Reason and Revolution*, is an interpretation of Hegel offering analyses that converge on the task of providing a foundation for the truth of critical theory. This task, though not the express aim of the study, nevertheless is the indispensable feature without which the study would fail. Written during the era when the National Socialists, and many of their opponents, viewed Hegel as an ideological forefather of the authoritarian state, *Reason and Revolution* is a work explicitly devoted to an elaborate and highly systematic exposition of those tendencies in Hegel's philosophy hostile to fascism. There is also, however, an underlying preoccupation with revealing within Hegel's philosophy a logical and epistemological theory opposed to positivism. But the provision of a foundation for critical theory and the analyses of the antiauthoritarian and antipositivist aspects of Hegel's philosophy are not three separate objectives of *Reason and Revolution*. Rather, they are all accomplished through the development of a single thesis with the foundations argument at its core.

The way in which Marcuse's interpretation of Hegel weaves these three objectives into a single thesis is fascinating. Positivism, as Marcuse also alleges in the earlier essay on the concept of essence, implicitly affirms the authoritarian state. It does so through its claim that knowledge must be confined to observable facts as they are presented in our ordinary experience. Such a principle denies the validity of critical theory's concepts that point beyond the established social and political facts (social orders) to transcendent possibilities. By defending the validity of the conception of transcendent possibility, which is based upon his examination of Hegel's philosophy, Marcuse wages a critique of positivism that simultaneously provides the rational foundation for the truth of critical theory. And at the same time, since Marcuse's foundation is drawn from Hegel's own thought, this foundation frees Hegel from the accusation that his philosophy could certify any established social order as true. The rationality of transcendent possibility, central to Hegel's logic, indicts as irrational and authoritarian all social systems that obstruct the realization of human potentiality.

Marcuse's exposition of Hegel's philosophy is thoroughly comprehensive and exacting in its attention to and affection for Hegel's fine detail. What is salient here, however, is not a review of Marcuse's exposition but its major thesis. In Marcuse's analysis of Hegel's *Early Theological Writings*, the first philosophical writings (the *Difference between Fichte's and Schelling's System of Philosophy, Faith and Knowledge,* the "Relation of Skepticism to Philosophy"), the first political writings ("The German Constitution"), his *System of Morality,* the *Jena* system (particularly the *Jena Logic* and *Philosophy of Mind*), the *Phenomenology of Mind, Science of Logic,* the *Logic, Philosophy of Right,* and the *Philosophy of History,* a single motif appears consistently as Hegel's foremost concern. All the differences among these greatly varied works, though discussed by Marcuse, ultimately are passed over and resolved into the uniform theme of the "universal."[42]

I described the four basic components of Hegel's universal during the discussion of his concept of essence. For Hegel, essence and the universal are in fact one and the same. Only one additional property of the universal should be noted. The universal is true according to the principles of dialectical logic. Thus, Marcuse's insistence on viewing the universal as the central motif of all of Hegel's works implies that their respective arguments are grounded in Hegel's logic, especially the system of the *Science of Logic*. The question of the correctness of this interpretation of Hegel falls outside the scope of this study of Marcuse and is not relevant to it. What is significant is to remember why Marcuse pursues this particular interpretation. The reason, as explained, is that Marcuse seeks a foundation for the truth claimed by critical theory, a task imposed upon him by the historical circumstances confronting critical theory. The main point is that Marcuse seizes upon the logic of the universal as a rational, philosophical foundation for critical theory's concept of possibility. Whether the universal actually is a satisfactory foundation for critical theory is taken up in another chapter.[43] At this time the focus of the discussion is a description of the revised conceptual framework of critical theory when its theoretical weight comes to rest upon Hegel's universal.

Marcuse draws out the implications of the logical properties of universals. A particular fact or set of facts is an expression of a universal but is not its equivalent. The (factual) nature of man within capitalism, for instance, partakes of the universal "mankind," or "man," but according to the logic of universals mankind is more than man appears to be in a capitalist society. Logically, "man" refers not only to men as they have appeared past and present but to all possible men. The same property of possibility belongs to all universals, and everything that has been encountered historically and all that comprises our own world, organic and inorganic, the products of mind or matter, has a universal as well as a particular form.

If thought is to be rational, therefore, it must be guided by the logic of universals. It must refuse to define as true the form that something—be it man, the state, justice, happiness, and so forth—has taken historically or assumes in the present. Reason proclaims truth to be in the continual unfolding of potentiality. And a society is rational and true only to the extent that it contributes to this end.

Rational thought, guided by the universal as the criterion of truth, thus implies a very special kind of thinking. Reason is "negative thinking," as Marcuse calls it. To think negatively, or dialectically, is to conceive of things as they appear as being limited. Such conceptions spring from a recognition of something's potentiality. To think in this manner is to deny, cancel, or "negate" a thing's apparent form. And to think negatively, critically, there must be freedom of thought. Rational faculties must be free from any sort of conditioning by social and political factors that would blind reasoning processes to the existence of possibilities for growth and development.

We need go no further to understand how Marcuse's new interpretation of Hegel, with its singular emphasis on the universal, lays the foundation for the rationality of critical theory's concept of possibility and in the same theoretical sweep lays positivism to rest and vindicates Hegel of all charges of authoritarianism. What must be stressed is that all this is brought to pass only through a defense of the concept of possibility, of the universal. That this foundation for critical theory's truth is the project at the very heart of both Marcuse's critique of positivism and his vindication of Hegel is made clear in this passage from *Reason and Revolution*.

> Positivism, the philosophy of common sense, appeals to the certainty of facts, but, as Hegel shows, in a world where facts do not at all present what reality can and ought to be, positivism amounts to giving up the real potentialities of mankind for a false and alien world. The positivist attack on universal concepts, on the ground they cannot be reduced to observable facts, cancels from the domain of knowledge everything that may not yet be a fact . . . When he emphasizes time and again that the universal is pre-eminent over the particular, he is struggling against limiting truth to the particular "given." The universal is more than the particular. This signifies in the concrete that the potentialities of men and things are not exhausted in the given forms and relations in which they actually appear; it means that men and things are all they have been and actually are, and yet more than all this. Setting the truth in the universal expressed Hegel's conviction that no given particular form, whether in nature or society, embodies the whole truth.[44]

Considered in light of its historical context, *Reason and Revolution* is a remarkable and heroic accomplishment. Appropriating the universal as the new foundation for critical theory, Marcuse responds powerfully to the total domination of authoritarianism with absolute truth, reason, and freedom. By so doing, he introduces a decisive element into critical theory's conceptual framework. With the certainty of truth, reason, and freedom Marcuse forges the sturdiest of theoretical opponents to fascism, an impregnable fortress that safeguards critical theory by turning it into rationalism. In the context of fascism, the rationalistic structure of critical theory becomes its greatest strength. Theory could no longer tie its truth to the proletariat. If it did, the defeat of the working class as revolutionary subject would invalidate the truth of critical theory. Critical theory then had to sever its alliance with the historical agent and, to recall Hegel's portentous comment, "seek refuge from the Present in ideal regions . . . with the view of effecting in its own element, the restoration of its principles from the ruin to which they had been brought."[45]

This is not to argue that when critical theory became rationalism it ceased to be committed to political practice. On the contrary, its insistence on political practice was as tenacious as ever. But critical theory's criteria for political practice express theory's rationalistic structure. Negative thinking, which enjoins political practice to bring the world into harmony with its proposals, abstracts and reproduces the qualities of the proletariat that made it a revolutionary subject. Consider these remarks that set forth the criteria for an authentic political practice.

> The "new" state [of affairs] is the truth of the old, but that truth does not steadily and automatically grow out of the earlier state; it can be set free only by an *autonomous act* on the part of men.[46]

> These become revolutionary conditions, however, only if seized upon and directed by a *conscious activity that has in mind the socialist goal.*[47]

> The revolution requires the maturity of many forces, but the greatest among them is the subjective force, namely, the revolutionary class itself. The realization of freedom and reason *requires the free rationality of those who achieve it.*[48]

"Autonomy," a "conscious activity that has in mind the socialist goal," and a "free rationality": clearly, the subject of political practice must be completely free, rational, and able critically to evaluate the prevailing institutions in view of their tangible intellectual and material riches, as well as to know of their inherent range of possible social and political alternatives. And most important, the revolutionary subject achieves this level of rationality under the yoke of domination. In short, the subject that comes forth to engage in radical politics must meet the standards represented by Marx's proletariat, which are now restored as the rationalism of critical theory. To bring about a rational society, the subject already must be rational in an irrational social order; to achieve a freer existence, the subject must be truly autonomous in a system that distorts the meaning of freedom; to realize the truth, the subject must know what is true in a society that equates the truth with its own practices.

With the conversion of critical theory into rationalism, Marcuse responds deliberately and reflectively to fascism. For as long as the proletariat remains disabled, and the objective possibilities that it still objectively represents remain inert, rationalism will also remain the citadel that preserves and protects the truth of critical theory. Rationalism, as mentioned, is the greatest strength of critical theory.

But it is also the greatest weakness. A rich and complex concept of subjectivity is embedded in the rationalistic dimensions of critical theory. Autonomy, rationality, and a clear, conscious, and certain apprehension of radical goals and of the obstacles to those goals represented by the established order are all characteristic of the subject of political practice. These characteristics constitute critical theory's explicit concept of the subject. But when we now inspect Marcuse's critical theory more closely, it will be discovered that its *implicit* concept of the subject is dramatically different. Critical theory's implicit concept of subjectivity is impoverished.

Because critical theory's criteria for political practice are uncompromisingly rationalistic — now identical to those prescribed by the concept of correct class consciousness, which Marcuse rejects in his early work — any political practice that does not meet these criteria is in no sense authentic political opposition. Marcuse declares the inflexibility of theory's criteria when he says that "theory will preserve the truth even if revolutionary practice deviates from its proper path. Practice follows the truth, not vice versa."[49] When critical theory confronts subjects who express opposition in this manner —

> an individual *feels* discontented as a result of the stresses imposed by the organization of production and the sacrifices exacted through a system of distribution but is not *consciously* socialist;
>
> an individual is partially disaffected from society after witnessing the state's violation of basic liberties and comes to *doubt* the justness and morality of institutional policies but is not *clear* that institutions have ceased to be legitimate;
>
> an individual has an *ambivalent* allegiance to social and political institutions but is not *certain* whether inherent possibilities for structural change would produce a more rational social order —

it concludes that they do not qualify as subjects of correct political practice.

By virtue of its criteria for political practice, therefore, critical theory excludes from consideration the discontented, doubting, disaffected, and ambivalent individual. But the criteria dictated by critical theory's rationalism go much further than rejecting the authenticity of this sort of political practice. The subject whose political practice does not meet theory's criteria for opposition is, according to critical theory, an object of social integration, a source of support for an authoritarian regime.

It appears, then, that the rationalism of Marcuse's critical theory leads him to view the subject as one who can be totally determined, socialized, and manipulated to the point of being made incapable of the least resistance. This view of the subject appears clearly in Marcuse's essay "On Hedonism."

Determined

The labor process, in which the laborer's organs atrophy and are coarsened, guarantees that the sensuousness of the lower strata does not develop beyond the technically necessary minimum.[50]

Socialized

Class situation, especially the situation of the individual in the labor process, is active in them, for this situation has formed the (bodily and spiritual) organs and capacities of men and the horizon of their demands.[51]

Incapable of the least resistance

It appears that individuals raised to be integrated into the antagonistic labor process cannot be judges of their own happiness. They have been prevented from knowing their true interest. Thus, it is possible for them to designate their condition as happy and, without external compulsion, embrace the system that oppresses them.[52]

Since the subject can be so completely assimilated into a repressive social system, implicitly the subject is assumed to possess no faculties that cannot be molded by social structures. In effect, the subject is no more than a blank slate that simply registers the commands impressed upon it by society. *Turned inside out*, critical theory, with its rich and complex rationalistic conception of the subject, can boast only of a skeletal subject who lacks even the capacity to develop a relative autonomy from social conditions.

It is obvious, and in my estimation painfully so, that the concept of subjectivity excluded by Marcuse's rationalistic framework for critical theory is that which inspired and informed his early period. The individual who through labor is able to achieve critical insights that penetrate relations of domination has been abandoned. While there is some continuity between the earlier and the Frankfurt period of Marcuse's work (specifically the hostility to ontology, the retention of Marx's notion of objectification, and the adherence to political economy), the dynamics of lordship and bondage, and the theory of historicity and praxis as it was firmly rooted in Hegel's *Phenomenology of Mind* and Marx's *Manuscripts* have been exchanged for the concept of the universal in Hegel's logic and for purely rationalistic determinants of radical action. Once critical theory's rational foundation and its rationalistic criteria of political practice conceived in response to fascism are in place, it is no longer possible to return to the earlier concept of the ambivalent but reflective and insightful individual. This point must be emphasized. From the standpoint of Marcuse's rationalism, the individual is totally integrated into a system of domination and hence necessarily excluded from further consideration.

But it is not only the subject of "praxis" who is excluded. In retrospect, it now can be understood why Marcuse's analysis of the turn from liberal to authoritarian society excludes the elements of liberalism that would incline the individual to oppose the authoritarian state. Critical theory's rationalistic criteria of political practice would lead it to dismiss liberal practices as political opposition. But much more important, critical theory's implicit concept of the subject would compel it to reinterpret liberal political practices as expressions of the subject's integration (i.e., as limited horizons, false conceptions of true interests, etc.). And it is this implicit conception of the subject that guides Marcuse's analysis of the bourgeois family, in which he argues that the individual can be socialized within the family unit to uncritically accept the authority of the Fascist state.

If Marcuse's critical theory had not been revised along the lines of rationalism, his analysis of liberalism would not have been guided by an impoverished, although implicit, concept of subjectivity. The politics of liberal practices might then have been interpreted in a different light. They might have been viewed as the seeds of opposition to authoritarianism — an uncertain, ambivalent, precarious opposition but opposition nevertheless. It may be, in fact, that in the absence of Marx's revolutionary agent of historical transformation, the "true subject" of radical politics, perhaps similar to the subject of praxis Marcuse attempts to provide a foundation for in his early work, is the individual liberal subject. Critical theory cannot grasp this possibility as long as its conceptual framework sublimates the politics of class struggle into rationalism. For though the liberal subject is not rational according to critical theory, he is not totally integrated either. Like Hegel's subject, the liberal individual gropes toward reason and the universal; unlike Hegel's subject, the liberal individual does not necessarily make progress toward reason without having his beliefs challenged and without being engaged in the discourse and practice of political activity.

All of Marcuse's work after *Reason and Revolution*, with the exception of a single period that will be examined,[53] is guided by the conception of critical theory that evolved out of his experience with fascism. And the impoverished concept of subjectivity, buried deeply beyond the pale of reflection, continues as the hidden subject of Marcuse's critical theory, fused into its conceptual framework — the irrationalism of the rationalistic response to fascism. As of 1941, whenever Marcuse focuses this theoretical framework on the individual's thought and action, he will see a totally mobilized, completely integrated, one-dimensional man; when analyzing social institutions and relations, he will see a one-dimensional society. In a theoretical study the fate of the theorist is not easily distinguished from the fate of his theory. In the ideal region wherein Marcuse's critical theory sought refuge from fascism, it, and perhaps he, became as much victim as the victims left behind.

One of the most impressive qualities of Marcuse's work during this period of transition is the intensive labor expended in mastering an enormous range of philosophical and theoretical ideas. While the preceding review of Marcuse's critical analyses acquaints us with the central influences on his development, a few less pronounced influences that are just beginning to stir beneath the surface of this transitional work deserve mention. One such influence is that of Max Weber. During this period Marcuse occasionally alludes to Weber; at other times his arguments and interpretations are sprinkled with Weberian terms.[54] None of this, however, is indicative of Marcuse's true debt to Weber, which will be discussed further on.[55]

There is also sufficient indication that Marcuse has begun to incorporate the categories of Freud's instinct theory and metapsychology into his critical theory. Though Freud never is referred to explicitly, Marcuse's 1938 essay "On Hedonism" is laced with Freudian language — instincts, repression, sublimation, and so forth. Here Marcuse's purpose is to examine the historical evolution of the conception of happiness beginning with classical hedonism. The aspect of this study tying Marcuse's critical theory to Freud is its concern with the devaluation of pleasure, particularly sensual pleasure, in bourgeois culture. Bourgeois ideology necessarily views sensual pleasure as a debased form of happiness — necessarily, Marcuse argues, because if sensual gratification were permitted by society its productive process would be disrupted.

> The unpurified, unrationalized release of sexual relationships would be the strongest release of enjoyment as such and the total devaluation of labor for its own sake. No human being could tolerate the tension between labor as valuable in itself and the freedom of enjoyment. The dreariness and injustice of work conditions would penetrate explosively the consciousness of individuals and make impossible their peaceful subordination to the social system of the bourgeois world.[56]

The struggle that bourgeois society wages against sensual happiness immediately suggested to Marcuse that human potentiality must possess a sensual dimension. And since labor and the perpetuation and expansion of the productive process depend entirely upon the repression of human sensuality, sensuality must not be merely another potentiality among others but in a strict sense may be the essence of man. Indeed, at one point Marcuse hints that the real possibilities inherent in a freely organized productive apparatus could be exploited fully only if developed under the supervision of what we can infer from this statement would be a "sensual rationality."

> The unfolding of the personality must not be merely spiritual. Industrial society has differentiated and intensified the objective

world in such a manner that only an *extremely differentiated and intensified sensuality* can respond adequately to it.[57]

In fact, this insight anticipates Marcuse's later conception of a "libidinal rationality" as the basis of a "new science."[58]

Of course, Marcuse's new concern with human sensuality follows naturally from the principles of critical theory. It is an extension of his interest of freedom, commitment to human happiness, and a soon to be serious expression of that "sharper emphasis" on the potentialities of man when the historical situation of critical theory warrants such stress. Sensuality becomes the substantive, concrete foundation of critical theory, an essential complement to his preoccupation with theory's philosophical foundation in an abstract universal.[59] Sensuality becomes, in a phrase, Marcuse's "second dimension." But here again we shall see that the rationalistic underpinnings of Marcuse's critical theory infect his interpretation of Freud. When Marcuse's critical theory turns to an analysis of Freud's instinct theory and metapsychology, the hidden subject of theory's rationalistic framework reappears as an image of man ill-equipped to reason, much less to reason critically.

Notes

1. For a history of the Frankfurt Institute and its members during the first years following the Nazi assumption of power see Martin Jay, *The Dialectical Imagination* (Boston: Little, Brown, 1973), pp. 29–40.

2. The ideal region referred to, of course, is the region of theoretical and philosophical thought that no longer enlists any sector of or element in society as a vehicle for the practical realization of its values and objectives. There is a sense, however, in which the ideal region sought for theory is not a strict philosophical and theoretical region. Marcuse also viewed the United States as an ideal environment, and not only for his own work. Feelings of intellectual well-being and physical security are reflected in this passage from *Reason and Revolution*, wherein he pays tribute to his new home. "There is in Hegel a keen insight into the locale of progressive ideas and movements. He attributed to the American rational spirit a decisive role in the struggle for an adequate order of life, and spoke of 'the victory of some future and

intensely vital rationality of the American nation . . .' Knowing far better than his critics the forces that threatened freedom and reason, and recognizing these forces to have been bound up with the social system Europe had acquired, he once looked beyond that continent to this as the only 'land of the future.'" *Reason and Revolution: Hegel and the Rise of Social Theory* (New York: Oxford University Press, 1941), p. xv. Marcuse is alluding to Hegel's analysis of the "New World" in *The Philosophy of History* (New York : Dover, 1956), pp. 86–87. Hegel had argued that "America is therefore the land of the future, where, in the ages that lie before us, the burden of the World's History shall reveal itself . . . It is a land of desire for all those who are weary of the historical lumber-room of old Europe . . . It is for America to abandon the ground on which hitherto the history of the World has developed itself."

3. With his membership in the Frankfurt Institute for Social Research, Marcuse's theoretical perspective acquires the name "critical theory," the theoretical genre of the Frankfurt School. For a discussion of the genesis of critical theory see Jay's *Dialectical Imagination*, pp. 41–85.

4. Although in contemporary social science the terms "authoritarian" and "totalitarian" have different meanings and carry different implications, throughout his work after 1933 Marcuse uses them interchangeably. Totalitarian state, authoritarian state, total-authoritarian state, totalitarian and authoritarian society appear unsystematically. In Marcuse's later work he favors the term "totalitarian." Although he is guilty of the same practice, on one occasion Marcuse expressed his dissatisfaction with the imprecise meanings social scientists attribute to totalitarianism (see chapter four, p. 153). It would be helpful to bear in mind that Marcuse uses authoritarian and totalitarian quite generally to refer to forms of domination that determine thought as well as control action. This does not mean, however, that every authoritarian and totalitarian measure accomplishes both.

5. Herbert Marcuse, "The Struggle against Liberalism in the Totalitarian View of the State," *Negations: Essays in Critical Theory* (Boston: Beacon, 1968), p. 19; originally published as "Der Kampf gegen den Liberalismus in der totalitären Staatsauffassung," *Zeitschrift für Sozialforschung*, 3, 2 (Paris: 1934), pp. 161–195.

6. Ibid., pp. 18–19.

7. Herbert Marcuse, "A Study on Authority," *Studies in Critical Philosophy* (Boston: Beacon, 1973); originally published as "Theoretische Entwürfe über Autorität und Familie: Ideengeschichtlicher Teil," *Studien über Autorität und Familie* (Paris: Félix Alcan, 1936), pp. 136–228. Attention will be confined to the sections on Luther and Calvin, Kant, Hegel, and Counter-revolution and Restoration.

8. Ibid., p. 52.

9. Marcuse considered Luther's *The Freedom of a Christian, The First Lent Sermon at Wittenberg, The Third Lent Sermon at Wittenberg, Sermon on the Ban, Temporal Authority: To What Extent It Should be Obeyed, Admonition to Peace, An Open Letter on the Harsh Book against the Peasants, On War against the Turk, Treatise on Good Works, To the Christian Nobility of the German Nation Concerning the Reform of the Christian Estate,* and *The Large Catechism.* Ibid., pp. 56–78.

10. Marcuse focused on Calvin's *Institutes of the Christian Religion.* Ibid. For an analysis of Calvinism that would contest Marcuse's equation of Calvinism in general with obedience to authority see Michael Walzer, *The Revolution of the Saints: A Study in the Origins of Radical Politics* (New York: Atheneum, 1968).

11. Marcuse concentrated upon Kant's *Political Writings.* See *"A Study on Authority,"* pp. 79–94.

12. Ibid., p. 97. Marcuse is alluding to paragraph 246 of Hegel's *Philosophy of Right*; see the translation by T. M. Knox (New York: Oxford University Press, 1965), p. 151.

13. Marcuse based his discussion of Hegel primarily upon his reading of the *Philosophy of Right.* See "A Study on Authority," pp. 95–110.

14. During this period Marcuse's work on the family takes place within the context of the Frankfurt Institute's first theoretical studies on authority. For a discussion of these studies see Jay's *Dialectical Imagination,* pp. 113–142.

15. Herbert Marcuse, "The Affirmative Character of Culture," *Negations,* p. 95; originally published as "Über den affirmativen Charakter der Kultur," *Zeitschrift für Sozialforschung,* 6, 1 (Paris: 1937), pp. 54–94. The term "affirmative culture" was conceived by Max Horkheimer; see his "Egoismus und Freiheitsbewegung," *Zeitschrift für Sozialforschung,* 5, 2 (Paris: 1936), p. 219. Marcuse acknowledges Horkheimer in the first footnote of "The Affirmative Character of Culture," p. 88.

16. The critical aspects of bourgeois art are especially significant for Marcuse. See chapter eight of this volume.

17. "The Affirmative Character of Culture," p. 124.

18. Ibid., p. 125.

19. Ibid., p. 127 (italics added).

20. Ibid., p. 128.

21. "The Struggle against Liberalism," p. 17.

22. Ibid., p. 42.

23. Herbert Marcuse, "Autorität und Familie in der deutschen Soziologie bis 1933," *Studien über Autorität und Familie,* pp. 737–752.

24. Ibid., pp. 738-741; here Marcuse examines W. H. Riehl's *Die Familie* (1851).

25. Ibid., pp. 742-743; in these pages Marcuse considers L. Gumplowicz's *Die sociologische Staatsidee* (1892) and *Grundriss der Soziologie* (1885).

26. Ibid., pp. 743-744; here Marcuse mentions F. Müller-Lyer's *Die Familie* (1911).

27. Ibid., p. 744.

28. Herbert Marcuse, "The Concept of Essence," *Negations*, pp. 43-87; originally published as "Zum Begriff des Wesens," *Zeitschrift für Sozialforschung*, 5, 1 (Paris: 1936), pp. 1-39.

29. Ibid., p. 46.

30. Marcuse's criticisms are directed at Husserl's *Formal and Transcendental Logic* and *Ideas I, Introduction to Pure Phenomenology and Phenomenological Philosophy*. Ibid., pp. 55-61.

31. Ibid., p. 65.

32. Later, in *One-dimensional Man: Studies in the Ideology of Advanced Industrial Society* (Boston: Beacon, 1964), Marcuse will revise his harsh critical interpretation of Husserl. In that new context the focus is on Husserl's *Crisis of European Sciences and the Transcendental Phenomenology*; see chapter six, pp. 282-283.

33. "The Concept of Essence," pp. 69-87.

34. Ibid., p. 70.

35. *Karl Marx: Early Writings*, edited by T. B. Bottomore (New York: McGraw-Hill, 1964), p. 155.

36. "The Concept of Essence," p. 76.

37. Ibid., p. 77.

38. Herbert Marcuse, "Philosophy and Critical Theory," *Negations*, p. 135; originally published as "Philosophie und kritische Theorie," *Zeitschrift für Sozialforschung*, 6, 3 (Paris: 1937), pp. 625-647.

39. Ibid., p. 142.

40. Ibid., p. 146.

41. Ibid., p. 143.

42. For example, in *Reason and Revolution* Marcuse argues that in the *Early Theological Writings* "Hegel incorporates the basic Aristotelian conception into his philosophy: 'The different modes of being are more or less complete unifications.' Being means unifying, and unifying means movement. Movement, in turn, Aristotle defines in terms of potentiality and actuality. The various types of movement denote various ways of realizing the potentialities inherent in the essence or moving thing. Aristotle evaluates the types of movement so that the highest type is that in which each and every potentiality is fully realized" (p. 41); about the first philosophical writings Marcuse says that for Hegel "speculative thinking compares the apparent or given form of things to the potentialities of those same things, and in so doing distinguishes their essence from their accidental state of existence" (p. 46); the *Jena* system, Marcuse continues, "already reveals the outstanding traits of his philosophy, especially its emphasis on the universal as the true being" (p. 88); in the *Phenomenology of Mind*, Marcuse explains, "setting the truth in the universal expressed Hegel's conviction that no given particular form, whether in nature or society, embodies the whole truth" (pp. 113-114); in the *Philosophy of Right* the "abstract determinations of the *Logic* once again show forth in their historical significance. The veritable being, the *Logic* had said, is the universal, which is in itself and contains the particular in itself" (p. 203); and in the *Philosophy of History* the "true subject of history is the universal, not the individual" (p. 229).

43. See chapter six of this volume.

44. *Reason and Revolution*, pp. 113-114.

45. Hegel, *The Philosophy of History*, p. 69.

46. *Reason and Revolution*, p. 315 (italics added).

47. Ibid., p. 318 (italics added).

48. Ibid., p. 319 (italics added).

49. Ibid., p. 322.

50. Herbert Marcuse, "On Hedonism," *Negations*, p. 185; originally published as "Zur Kritik des Hedonismus," *Zeitschrift für Sozialforschung*, 7, 1-2 (Paris: 1938), pp. 55-89.

51. Ibid., p. 190.

52. Ibid., p. 191 ("determined," "socialized," and "incapable of the least resistance" are my terms).

53. See chapter seven of this volume.

54. Particularly noteworthy is an aspect of Marcuse's interpretation of Marx during this period. When discussing Marx's analysis of the way in which the state functions to stabilize capitalist society, Marcuse argues that "the perpetually conflicting activity, the perpetual struggle between 'opposed particular interests' requires, if the reproduction of the anarchically producing society is to be safeguarded, a universal apparatus which is equipped with all the material and intellectual instruments of coercion: it 'makes practical intervention and control necessary through the illusory *general* interest in the form of the state.' " "A Study on Authority," p. 139. The concept that stands out in this passage is "universal apparatus which is equipped . . ." While it is certainly true that Marx attributed such a function to the state, Marcuse's conception shades Marx's meaning toward Weber's theory of the state as a highly rationalized form of domination. In other words, Mar-

cuse's interpretation views Marx as having developed a theory that anticipates and explains, much more than it actually does, the power of capitalist institutions to reproduce and perpetuate an inherently unstable society. In fact, this is the thrust of Marcuse's entire discussion of Marx herein (pp. 128-143).

55. See chapter four, pp. 179-183.

56. "On Hedonism," p. 187.

57. Ibid., p. 184.

58. See chapter six, pp. 282-286.

59. I am suggesting that viewed in the context of Marcuse's general concern with the foundations issue, the Freudian aspects of "On Hedonism" and these principles should be construed as tendencies toward what eventually becomes Marcuse's anthropological foundation for critical theory. Consequently, the foundations issue, this essay, and the theoretical principles of critical theory together offer an explanation for Marcuse's turn to Freud in addition to that which points to the influence of those members of the Frankfurt Institute who had incorporated psychoanalysis into their work earlier than did Marcuse.

THREE

The Second Dimension

Warum sucht ich den Weg so sehnsuchtsvoll,
Wenn ich ihn nicht den Brüdern zeigen soll.

Goethe, "Zueignung,"
Gedichte

WHEREAS HEGEL'S universal constitutes the philosophical foundation for critical theory, Marcuse's interpretation of Freud's instinct theory and metapsychology is intended to form its anthropological basis. A later chapter will explore the problematic relationship between the two foundations.[1] Essentially, the interpretation of Freud is the human groundwork from which Marcuse derives justification for projecting the possibility for a qualitatively different and rational social order he believes to be inherent in advanced industrial society. As justification for a more rational social system, Freudian theory is at the same time a reasoned defense of Marcuse's critique of late capitalism. Sharing the same foundation, the vision of a future society and the indictment of our present mode of social organization are inseparably bound together through Freud's concepts and categories.

It was not for some time after the publication of Marcuse's comprehensive study of Freud, all later work incorporating Freudian theory in some sense returning to and further developing ideas originating in *Eros and Civilization*, that the implications and perhaps very purpose of that investigation was clarified for Marcuse. In *An Essay on Liberation* the Freudian project at last crystallizes into "a biological foundation for socialism."[2]

89

Prior to all ethical behavior in accordance with specific social standards, prior to all ideological expression, morality is a "disposition" of the organism, perhaps rooted in the erotic drive to counter aggressiveness, to create and preserve "ever greater unities" of life. We would then have, this side of all "values," an instinctual foundation for solidarity among human beings—a solidarity which has been effectively repressed in line with the requirements of class society but which now appears as a precondition for liberation.[3]

By "this side of all 'values' " Marcuse certainly means this side of all conventional value systems only, for he also is claiming that critical standards, or norms, reside *essentially* in human nature. Being this side of all values consequently supposes this morally disposed nature to be presocial in character, standing over and against and in judgment of all social arrangements. Nature becomes the basis of a critical tribunal of reason.

Marcuse arrives at his conception of human nature through a discriminating reading of Freud's instinct theory. And his approach to the metapsychology enables him to generate an impressive set of sociological insights into the complex interrelationships of man and his historical and social universe. Before closely examining this Freudian project, I shall describe its broad outlines. In particular, Marcuse's concept of human nature and its relation to the sociological insights derived from the metapsychology should be made clear. With these bearings the discussion then can turn to the intricate mosaic of ideas comprising Marcuse's "second dimension."

Basic Elements of the Interpretation of Freud

According to Freud, as each person matures and particularly after that level of maturity has been reached coinciding with the final (genital) stage of infantile sexual development, the ego turns completely outward toward the external world and is largely dependent upon it for gratification. So varied are human relations that what is or is not gratifying easily appears to originate within social contexts rather than within the individual. The very notion of gratification as a definite need with universal characteristics is open to question. Prior to the genital stage, however, the child achieves gratification, the pleasurable release of tension responsible for psychological and physical discomfort, through activity directly related to the psychosexual phase of development reached. Stamped with the distinct traits of these phases, such activity not only involves objects, say, people, in the environment. It also takes more direct routes through the autoerotic stimulation of the oral, anal, and phallic zones and the generally eroticized areas of the body. Freud's by now well-known term for these latter forms of obtaining gratification is "polymorphous perversity." Freud's theory of infantile sexuality is decisive for Marcuse. Psychosexual activity during these earliest phases of development, when man is most directly influenced by (his own) nature and gratification is explicitly sexual, proves that the first value rooted in human nature, the first norm characteristic of its moral disposition, is the need for instinctual gratification.

Unless qualified, instinctual gratification is by itself an insufficient basis for critical theory. All social orders provide some sort of instinctual gratification. How can the instinct theory be used critically to distinguish among them? Another and decisive characteristic of the ethical dimension of man's nature limits the sort of gratification that is morally approved. Eros, the life instinct, and Thanatos, the instinct of death and aggression, are Freud's two primary instinctual drives and the central categories of Marcuse's anthropology. *By nature* Eros is the dominant instinct, disposing human nature to a *receptiveness* to human relations and relations with nature. Among other meanings to be considered later, receptivity connotes an erotic or nonaggressive sensibility as the basis for social relations. But a receptive, nonaggressive sensibility would require the emancipation of those senses and sexual drives repressed by a civilization bent on productivity. Productivity, rooted in the aggressive drive, suppresses the nonaggressive, erotic disposition.

Civilization engages human nature by imposing its own values, the most important being the value of productivity. Civilization begins, indeed, is *able* to begin, only at the moment when the need for instinctual gratification is repressed. The needs of social organization are elevated far above those of human nature for the two are irreconcilable. According to the terms dictated by Eros, gratification should be nonaggressive. And according to Freud's "pleasure principle," instinctual gratification must be immediate and complete. Such indulgence, however, would thoroughly undermine civilization, which requires the repressive modification of the instincts in order to accomplish socially productive work. From the standpoint of human nature, that which has truth value is the happiness and freedom bred from the gratification of the instincts through nonaggressive relations governed by the pleasure principle. The hallmark of civilization's morality of productivity, on the other hand, is the denial of freedom, the frustration of happiness, and the suppression of truth — suppression, but not elimination, as we now shall see.

At the point in individual development when instinctual needs and their governing principle must be adapted to the requirements of the environment, specifically to the rules governing reality, the ego becomes a reality-testing ego, equipping the individual with the capacity to negotiate the complex terrain of society. The reality-ego has the task of discovering the "most favorable and least perilous method of obtaining satisfaction."[4] For if the ego, under the hegemony of the pleasure principle, were urged continuously to seek "immediate and unheeding satisfaction of the instincts," this single-minded approach "would often lead to perilous conflicts with the external world and to extinction" of the individual.[5]

Yet there is no simple transformation of the pleasure-seeking ego into an ego structure accommodating social order. Rather, the ego divides into a pleasure-ego and a reality-ego: "With the introduction of the reality principle one mode of thought-activity was split off; it was kept free from reality testing and remained subordinated to the pleasure principle alone. This is the act of phantasy-making."[6] The realm of fantasy preserves the memory of the original aim of the instincts, which is still expressed as the wish for immediate, total, and eroticized gratification. As fantasy, or imagination, the suppressed truth of human nature survives as part of the unconscious. The critical standards of social theory, its foundation, are displaced to the unconscious, which retains the truth of gratification at a repressed layer of existence.

Properly speaking, the two principles of rationality, actually two different modes of reason, two value systems, are divided though not independent of one another. They are as dynamically interrelated as are the id and the ego or the unconscious and the conscious mind. Obeying the pleasure principle, the ego seeks instinctual gratification; obeying the reality principle, it also must insure survival if any gratification is to be obtained. A balance *ought* to occur between the requisites of social organization and the pleasure to accrue to the individual—the greatest pleasure within the limits of maintaining the mutual preservation of self and society. Beyond these limits either pleasure is sacrificed or preservation threatened and social order undermined. Within these limits the rationality of social organization must uncompromisingly serve the ends prescribed by human nature and upheld by critical theory. Marcuse's critical theory of society appears to be teleological by virtue of the relationship between natural order, upon which the theory is based, and social organization.

In Freud's presentations of the relation among social, psychological, and instinctual processes, the emphatic step is never taken to address the issue of the correct balance between social values and natural human values, social order and the moral order embedded in human nature. It is imprecise, however, to claim, as Marcuse does, that to Freud "there was no higher rationality against which the prevailing [civilized] morality could be measured."[7] At the decline of the Weimar Republic Freud invokes the same principle of reason that animates Marcuse's indictment of modern capitalism.

> Men have gained control over the forces of nature to such an extent that with their help they would have no difficulty in exterminating one another to the last man. They know this, and hence comes a large part of their current unrest, their unhappiness and their mood of anxiety. And now it is to be expected that the other of the two "Heavenly Powers," eternal Eros, will make an effort to assert himself in the struggle with his equally immortal adversary. But who can foresee with what success and with what result?[8]

Other examples could be produced showing that Freud was hardly a reluctant critic of Western culture. Frequently he considered the measure of repression exacted by modern civilization to be exaggerated relative to the cost in human happiness and the opportunity to eliminate sacrifice in the face of the accumulated material wealth of a highly productive civilization. Freud knew also that socioeconomic and political institutions impose heavier burdens of repression upon the individual than are necessary.[9] In the final analysis, though, these economic and social factors were given little weight in Freud's explanation for the necessity and justifiability of repression. The orthodox Freudian account of repression leaves little room to entertain an argument for reducing repression by limiting the objective requirements of social organization to the mutual preservation of individual and society. In light of what Freud took to be the antisocial and destructive dangers of biological and psychological drives, repression becomes a fundamental principle of reality, an absolute, indispensable requirement for all social organization: the demands of civilization are always more rational than the rationality of human nature and its needs for gratification.

Marcuse examines Freud's concepts of repression and reality principle critically and from the inside out, so to speak. If there are historical and social processes that contribute to repression, with a change in these processes repression's historical content, its harshness, could change, too. It could be made to vary from one historical period to the next, from one society to another. In order to capture the historical content of the concepts repression and reality principle, they "must be paired with corresponding terms denoting the specific socio-historical component." The corresponding terms thus introduced are

(a) *Surplus-repression*: the restrictions necessitated by social domination. This is distinguished from (basic) *repression*: the "modifications" of the instincts necessary for the perpetuation of the human race in civilization. (b) *Performance principle*: the prevailing historical form of the *reality principle*.[10]

Interpreted through these new terms, Freud's concept of repression is shown to contain within it political as well as social and economic elements. Repression ceases to be simply an unchanging principle of reality. These new elements become visible the moment Marcuse begins his inquiry into the necessity and rationality of repression in the context of the historical development and social organization of the productive apparatus. This inquiry is guided by Marcuse's new terms and clarifies their meaning.

With these new terms Marcuse is extending Marx's conceptual framework. Marx's "socially necessary and surplus labor" become "basic and surplus-repression." Basic repression refers specifically to the degree of the denial of libidinal (nonaggressive) instinctual impulses that is required for labor insuring survival. Or, put differently, basic repression is the repression of the erotic drives required by socially necessary work, work without which survival is inconceivable. Basic, or socially necessary, repression prevails so long as man must labor in the face of natural scarcity. Surplus-repression, on the other hand, refers not to "the brute fact of scarcity" but to "a specific organization of scarcity" brought about through the creation of artificially manufactured needs. With the concept of surplus-repression, it is possible to conceptualize unnecessary repression, or alienation, in biological-instinctual terms. It also allows us to reason that needs fulfilled through surplus-repression, surplus labor not contributing directly to the perpetuation of the human race, are false needs. The greater the production of false needs, the greater is the labor required for production and consumption and the higher the degree of instinctual repression. Capitalism depends on the proliferation and mass acceptance of artificial needs to create patterns of consumption that legitimate the continuing expansion of the productive process and foster the growth of technology.

The concept of surplus-repression also addresses the phenomenon of aggression in modern capitalism. All labor channels aggression at the same time as it represses libidinal instincts. As libidinal impulses are repressed, aggressive energy increases in intensity, and vice versa. The increasing demand for repression brought on by the multiplication of false needs and the expansion of human labor would increase the repression of libido and the release of aggression. Consequently, the labor invested in the development and progress of civilization along the lines of an economic system that raises its overall level of affluence by generating false needs would be threatened internally by the aggressive impulses that surplus-repression releases. Marcuse concludes that "developing under progressive renunciation [of the libidinal drives], civilization tends toward self-destruction." Socialism would eliminate surplus-repression by abolishing false needs, along with the political and administrative apparatus responsible for them; it would expel the surplus aggression with which surplus civilization is burdened.

In a socialist society basic repression would remain. So long as scarcity persists, some labor is socially necessary, hence some degree of repression and alienation must exist, to provide the basic means of subsistence. In a nonrepressive social order the reduction of labor to the minimum required for the satisfaction of basic human needs would sustain the natural predominance of the libidinal over the aggressive instincts. This means that aggression would become socially useful and manageable if society functioned in accordance with the criteria established by the concept of basic repression.

The scientific and technological achievements of modern capitalism create the possibility for eliminating the scarcity of most necessary goods. Once the relations of capital that enforce the organization of scarcity through the promotion of false needs are abolished, the forms of unnecessary labor that fulfill these needs would be abolished, too. And with the abolition of surplus labor would disappear the surplus-repression of the libidinal instincts. Then, as further technological development gradually rendered the remaining forms of socially necessary work obsolete through automation, the corresponding amount of basic repression involved in the human performance of those tasks also would be eliminated. The sum of basic repression would be narrowed to a minimum. In this way, technological progress allows the socially necessary quota of basic repression to be minimized constantly and continuously redefined as surplus-repression.

In a rational society, therefore, the need for repression must correspond to the objective need for socially necessary labor. The progress of science and technology under capitalism, fruit of the repression exacted by capitalist institutions, has forged the means partially to eliminate scarcity and with it instinctually repressive and socially alienating work. The possibilities at hand for qualitatively transforming man's relationship to nature and relations between men are being systematically abused by capitalism. The difference between basic and surplus-repression is an index of both unnecessary alienation and political domination. The difference has become greater and the domination harsher in proportion to the growth of technological possibilities for abolishing repression. This difference indicates that modern capitalism depends upon surplus needs, surplus labor, surplus-repression, and surplus aggression for its very survival.

With the distinction between basic and surplus-repression, Marcuse establishes clearly that repression could vary if measures were taken to reorganize the productive apparatus to unleash its technological potential. Consequently, there is no single principle that makes repression into an absolute burden that must be borne equally by all social orders. Freud's reality principle obscures this theoretical insight. There are only "performance principles," the principles underlying different forms of social organization, that determine the amount of instinctual repression. Surplus-repression is the performance principle of modern capitalism. Basic repression could become the performance principle of socialism. Domination and freedom are based in principles that either violate or obey the norms of human nature.

To this extent and considered at this level of generalized presentation, Marcuse's critical examination of the instinct theory and metapsychology is sound and persuasive. From his biological foundation for socialism rooted in Freud's instinct theory, and through a historical analysis of the metapsychological process of repression, Marcuse generates concepts from which he derives theoretical justification for his assault on capitalism and for his vision of a free society.

Marcuse's work must now be studied closely. Of particular concern is the correctness of Marcuse's interpretation of Freud—the image of man and the new dimension of human potentialities it has produced. As many problems as possibilities, however, emerge from Marcuse's anthropological foundation for critical theory.

Repression and Sublimation

Each of the problems with Marcuse's biological foundation for socialism originate in his usage of Freud's concept of repression. It is appropriate to begin our analysis here. " 'Repression' and 'repressive' are used in the non-technical sense to designate both conscious and unconscious, external and internal processes of restraint, constraint, and suppression."[11] Consider the indexing of the term: "Repression (suppression, oppression)."[12] Caused by the "impact of the reality principle" upon the individual, repression is characterized throughout by sociological and political connotations.

Even a cursory reading of Freud proves Marcuse's rudimentary exposition basically correct. Eventually, though, we shall discover that Marcuse's decision to explicate the concept in this imprecise, nontechnical sense leads to his confusion about the relationship between repression and sublimation and to the complete

loss of the latter concept's critical significance. But a prior serious and fundamental error lies in his application of the concept
of repression, which also will be shown to be related to his misunderstanding of Freud's notion of sublimation.

The predominant form of repression Marcuse identifies is the
"repressive organization of the instincts" under the genital
sphere of sexuality. This results from the impact of the reality
principle as it is transmitted through the Oedipal conflict. Marcuse argues that

> Freud emphasizes the aspect of centralization. It is especially opera-
> tive in the "unification" of the various objects of the partial instincts
> into one libidinal object of the opposite sex, and in the establish-
> ment of genital supremacy. In both cases, the unifying process is re-
> pressive — that is to say, the partial instincts do not develop freely in-
> to a "higher" stage of gratification which preserves their objectives,
> but are cut off and reduced to subservient functions. This process
> achieves the socially necessary desexualization of the body: the li-
> bido becomes concentrated in one part of the body, leaving most of
> the rest free for use as the instrument of labor.[13]

Here Marcuse makes a departure from Freud's theory of infantile sexual development that is crucial to his argument and
upon which its entire critical edifice is built. Freud designated
the nonaggressive (libidinal) and aggressive instinctual predispositions as the two categories of pregenital "component," or "partial," instincts.[14] He explained that "the infantile sexual life, in
spite of the preponderating dominance of erotogenic zones, exhibits components which from the very first involve other people
as sexual objects."[15] An appreciation of the nature of these component instincts in relation to infantile sexual development is required to comprehend fully the flaws in Marcuse's interpretation
of Freud. Freud further described the behavior of the component instincts by saying that they act *independently* of one another
during the early phases of sexual maturity. For the duration of
the pregenital stage the libidinal and aggressive instincts seek
gratification in a radically individualistic manner.[16] According
to Freud this instinctual anarchism prevails because the instincts
are "unalloyed," "unfused," or "disunited."[17] In their search for
pleasure, in their effort to achieve the aim of gratification by re-
lieving tension, the instincts pursue their goals separately
through dominant sexual zones, through polymorphous activity,

and through contact with external objects until the final stage of instinctual development, when the component instincts are fused, or alloyed, by being subordinated to the genital sphere.[18]

What is decisive about this process of fusion and subordination is that it is the natural outcome of a *biological* process of maturation during which an unorganized and unrestrained, in a sense free, distribution of instinctual drives, wherein the instincts had discharged their aims independently, changes to an organized condition in the service of the genital zone. Freud's emphasis on the biological nature of the establishment of genital supremacy is diametrically opposed to Marcuse's sociological explanation. Sociological factors are significant determinants of psychosexual maturation at all stages of infantile development in that they influence personality development, character formation, and dispositions to neurosis, and, of course, the impact of society is dramatized during the Oedipal conflict through Oedipal repression and the creation of the superego. But it is a biological and not, as Marcuse claims, a historical process that determines the organization of the instincts.

This point is not made as a denial of the *ultimate* historical character either of the nature of the instincts or of other biological aspects of infantile sexuality. Phylogenetically all facets of sexuality should be understood as originating in the historical experience of the species. Freud's archaic heritage thesis makes it clear that human nature is the result of centuries of human encounters with social structures all making quite similar demands for the repressive modification of desires and inclinations. Eventually these repressions are assimilated as constitutional factors. Ultimately biology can be reduced to its historical determinants; human nature, in the final analysis to second nature. Once historical experience becomes sedimented as biology, however, we must be prepared to concern ourselves with it as human nature only. Phylogenetically, the subordination of the instincts to the genital sphere and the desexualization of the body may have been enforced by the repressive mechanisms of the performance principle in the interests of domination. Ontogenetically, the establishment of genital supremacy is first and foremost a biological phenomenon such that we must confine our attention to its critical significance as human nature.

Freud did assert that repression occurs during the Oedipal situation, but he used the term in a highly technical sense. When the instincts begin to be localized in the genital zone, polymorphous sexual activity ceases to be an outlet for instinctual aims. Instinctual impulses are directed completely outward and the Oedipal conflict is initiated. The constraints imposed by parental authority prohibiting the Oedipal drive from achieving its aim issue in the repression of the Oedipus complex, the repression of its instinctual designs, and the erection of the superego through the process of identification. When Marcuse incorrectly submits that the "superego is the heir of the Oedipus complex, and the repressive organization of sexuality is chiefly directed against its pregenital and perverse manifestations,"[19] it must be stressed to the contrary that for Freud the repression of the Oedipal drive is necessary *after* the genital organization of the instincts creates the sexual preconditions for the Oedipal conflict. As it is encountered through the Oedipal conflict, the reality (or performance) principle has nothing whatsoever to do with determining instinctual organization. But it influences the selection, in this case through the repression that forms the superego, of the *objects* of instinctual drives for gratification.

Marcuse applies the concept of repression incorrectly by ignoring the biological preconditions necessary to the very occurrence of the Oedipal conflict and Oedipal repression. Since it is axiomatic in Freud's instinct theory that the genital instinctual organization precedes this momentous encounter with the reality principle, Marcuse argues incorrectly that as a consequence of the introduction of the performance principle through the Oedipal confrontation "the autonomous development of the instincts is frozen, and their pattern is fixed at the childhood level."[20]

By identifying the genital organization of the instincts with repression, Marcuse means to imply that the maturation process that Freud believed to be biological and irrevocable is actually social and potentially subject to conscious redirection and control. The obvious implication is that the body does not have to be desexualized. In order to understand why Marcuse is preoccupied with desexualization, the relationship of the body's desexualization to alienated labor must be examined.

It is true, as Marcuse states, that despite sweeping changes in the instinct theory during various periods in its theoretical development, throughout Freud's life work sexuality, the libido, retains the predominant place in the instinctual structure. The view Freud consistently held is that within the mental apparatus the life instincts rule the instincts of aggression. Marcuse mistakenly concludes, however, that "if the primary mental processes are governed by the pleasure principle, then that instinct which, in operating under this principle, sustains life must be *the* life instinct."[21] Following this logic Marcuse exclusively confines the pleasure principle to rule only the life instincts, the instincts of Eros. Cultural activities involving the instinctual drives of Eros and only those activities—although this position is relinquished elsewhere—are pleasurable and gratifying.[22] Seen in this light and returning to Marcuse's equation of desexualization and alienation, since the parts of the body executing labor have been desexualized, or de-eroticized, "work is normally without satisfaction in itself; to Freud it is unpleasurable, painful."[23]

Marcuse errs in regarding only the life instincts as governed by the pleasure principle. In fact, the gratification of the aggressive instincts yields pleasure, too. Because Freud's theory acknowledges the subordination of the aggressive as well as the nonaggressive drives to the pleasure principle, labor based on the repression of Eros would not be totally alienating. Gratification of the aggressive component instincts would occur through work. All labor, therefore, must involve partial gratification and pleasure. Marcuse's conventional Marxist categories of alienated and unalienated labor appear too crude to be insightfully applied to, and the oversimplified dichotomy of unpleasurable and pleasurable work too conventional to be derived from, Freud's instinct theory.

Even allowing for this revision in Marcuse's theory bypasses its central problem and implies concessions where none can be made if Freud is to be understood correctly. The body's desexualization is not a social phenomenon. It is not "socially necessary," as Marcuse contends. Since the organization of the instincts at the genital stage is biological and does not entail a sociological dimension, it is not a form of repression and the desexualization of the body should not be described in sociological terms as alienating. It is not possible to reverse the genital instinctual maturation and it makes little sense to equate this event with a process of alienation supposedly open to social intervention and change.

Marcuse's indictment of the genital stage of instinctual organization also overlooks its most important function. It establishes the biological and psychological preconditions for sublimation, that is, for all intellectual and physical labor. The demand for the resexualization of the body suggests a regression behind the genital organization of the instincts making sublimation impossible. This problem deserves very special attention and a closer inspection of Freudian theory.

Freud's instinct theory associates an interesting and important characteristic with the instinctual drives during the pregenital stage. At this stage, more than at any other in the life of the individual, there is the possibility for nearly total discharge of tension and nearly complete instinctual gratification and pleasure. This possibility arises from the immaturity of infantile sexual development. There is an unorganized division of the instincts into qualitatively distinct and independent libidinal and aggressive component impulses, which derive gratification through the accessibility of external object relations, for instance, with loved ones, and through the polymorphous immediacy of bodily sources corresponding to the pregenital instinctual arrangement.

When we consider explanations for complete gratification during the pregenital stage of infantile sexuality, primary emphasis must be placed not on the object or form of gratification, that is, neither on the child's relations with parents and other figures nor on the polymorphous nature of sexual expression, but rather on the independence and radically individualistic behavior of the instincts. The individual component impulses have a relatively low intensity of instinctual excitation. For that reason nearly complete gratification is possible. Once the component instinctual drives become fused at the genital stage, gratification becomes more difficult to achieve. This absence of complete gratification is the natural consequence of a multiplicity of component impulses, which, once combined into a new instinctual drive but nevertheless retaining the need for discharge as independent aggressive and nonaggressive component instincts, must rely either upon a single or upon many instinctual object relations in order to reach the aim of gratification. Freud explains that "the sexual instinct of adults arises from a combination of a number of impulses of childhood into a unity, an impulsion with a single aim."[24] Elsewhere he makes this point more clearly by saying that "the same object may serve for the satisfaction of several instincts simultaneously."[25] Consequently, only some proportion of the component instincts is gratified in any activity or activities. This is tantamount to saying that the complex instinctual drive structure created through the biological organization of the instincts at the genital stage of sexual development supposes the absence of complete gratification because excitation cannot be eliminated, but at best reduced. This entire discussion must eventually lead, of course, to a consideration of the sorts of social relations that could provide gratification for the instincts after their new stage of biological development has been reached.

Biology clearly appears to be a decisive factor in an explanation for the absence of complete gratification. It is now a small step to realize that biological development is equally prominent in preparing the bases for sublimation (intellectual and physical labor). Whereas the newly complex genital instinctual organization makes gratification difficult, at the same time it compels the development of a sophisticated psychic structure. As of the genital stage the ego is charged with the function of establishing relations in the external world that suitably gratify complex instinctual drives. Hence, the ego is forced to develop its capacities in response to the biological demands thrust upon the individual at the genital stage of instinctual maturity. And the capacities to be developed are those that allow for sublimated modes of gratification, that is, for the labor from which higher sources of pleasure could be derived. But did Freud explicitly make this argument to which his instinct theory leads?

Unsublimated sexual relations are important forms of socially derived gratification. Marcuse interprets Freud as stressing a causal relationship between civilization's constraints on sexual behavior and sublimated activities, as though the restraints make available the instinctual energy to be invested in labor. Freud does say, for example, that "civilization is obeying the laws of economic necessity, since a large amount of psychical energy which it uses for its own purposes has to be withdrawn from sexuality."[26] It would have to follow from this argument that if these restraints were suddenly removed, sublimation would not occur. Freud would hardly be inclined to draw such a conclusion for he did not stop with this rather crude explanation for sublimation.

Freud also considered the possibility that sexual relations are by their very nature limited in the gratification they provide. Perfectly consistent with his instinct theory is the contention that the experience of limited gratification in unsublimated sexual relations is the result of a multiplicity of component instincts that, fused, simultaneously seek gratification through sexual contact. The inadequate gratification of sexual relations would derive not from cultural suppression but from the complexity and intensity of instinctual energy after the genital stage had effected its instinctual reorganization. This would give birth to the natural and necessary tendency of the ego to sublimate its energies in the interest of securing more fulfilling and lasting gratification.

As his work progressed this implication became increasingly clear to Freud. In the second phase of the instinct theory's development Freud remarked that "the possibility must be considered that something in the nature of the sexual instinct itself is unfavorable to the achievement of absolute gratification."[27] He kept to this view in the theory's final stage and suggested that "the sexual life of civilized man is notwithstanding, severely impaired . . . Sometimes one seems to perceive that it is not only the pressure of civilization but something in the nature of the function itself which denies us full satisfaction and urges us along other paths."[28] Such claims are not rare in Freud's writings and moreover express a major thesis of the instinct theory as it developed through its final stage. Freud questioned the degree to which unsublimated social relations can offer gratification and proposed a natural inclination to compensate through sublimation. Sublimation, having the genital organization of the instincts as its precondition, also appears as a developmental stage in a natural process of maturation. It alone holds out the possibility for complete gratification.

Behind this thesis lies an even more fundamental biological consideration that finds expression in the need not simply for labor (sublimation) but rather for particular forms of labor. The complexity of the instinctual structure after the last stage of infantile sexual development explains why it is "the difference in amount between the pleasure of satisfaction which is *demanded* and that which is actually *achieved* that provides the driving factor which will permit of no halting at any position attained."[29] This notion is saturated with the most important implications. It moves far beyond the point at which unsublimated relations are found wanting as sources of gratification. Freud is saying now that some forms of labor are more gratifying than others and that the lack of gratification in labor is the impulse to seek more gratifying forms of sublimation. Freud's presentation of the biological aspects of gratification thus brings us to the horizon of sociological analysis, to a consideration of the historical determinants of labor, to the social and political organization of sublimated forms of gratification. We shall return to these issues later.

In this exposition of Freud, I have drawn out major elements of his instinct theory. They point directly to sublimated activities as potentially the highest source of gratification. Marcuse, however, views sublimation as denial of gratification: "sublimation and domination hang together;"[30] "sublimation involves *desexualization*,"[31] loss of pleasure. Marcuse's reasoning is based upon two errors he has committed.

The first, briefly discussed, is Marcuse's claim that under the impact of the performance principle through the Oedipal conflict, the genital organization of the instincts occurs and transforms the body from an instrument of pleasure into an instrument of toil by spatially reducing its pleasurable areas to the genital zone. Through this event desexualization prepares the *body* for labor, for if it were to remain subject to the rule of the pleasure principle it could not be brought to perform tasks from which instinctual pleasure cannot be derived. Second, this social restriction on sexual behavior makes available instinctual energy for work. Sublimation desexualizes the instinctual *drive*, that is, severely weakens the libidinal component. Libidinal gratification is denied in proportion to the degree of sublimation entailed in the performance of a particular task. Cultures progressing in accordance with an ever expanding set of productive relationships demand continuous sublimation.

Marcuse's initial error originates in a confusion about the historical character of the instinctual makeup. It is true that in Freud's theory the genital phase of organization is the biological product of centuries of historical repression demanding the spatial reduction of the instincts in the service of procreation and sublimation. At the present stage of civilization, however, the genital and pregenital stages and all other universal characteristics of infantile sexuality are firmly rooted in biological processes. By critically grasping the experience of the individual from the standpoint of the experience of the species or, more pre-

cisely, by supposing phylogenesis to be recapitulated ontogenetically in its historical rather than in its biological form, Marcuse
exaggerates the extent to which the instinct theory can be histor-
icized.

To account for the second error is much more difficult. In
fact, there are scattered remarks in Freud's writings, though very
few and apparently made in passing, to the effect that sublimation desexualizes an instinct by weakening (repressing) the erotic
component.[32] But through statements and evidence of the variety I have underscored and, most important, by relating Freud's
particular ideas back to his whole theoretical framework and
then in turn allowing this constantly elaborated and revised
whole to guide further analysis of its parts, the meaning of the
instinct theory unfolds against Marcuse's interpretation. Libidinal and aggressive components remain as strong in their sublimated as in their unsublimated forms. Sublimation emerges as
the means to gratification rather than its denial. If the instinctual drive goes unsatisfied, the blame is to be laid not on sublimation but on the particular form of sublimation (labor) chosen
by, available to, or forced upon the individual. This last point
leads us to a more satisfactory explanation for Marcuse's second
error.

This error can be explained best, perhaps, as the result of
Marcuse's nontechnical use of repression. Freud's technical usage
confined repression to internal, psychological processes of restraint or inhibition. Marcuse expands this term's meaning to include external processes of restraint, constraint, and suppression. In a modern capitalist society *all* labor (sublimation) for *all*
classes is determined by capitalism's performance principle.
Under these circumstances, in light of the broad meaning Marcuse attributes to repression, which includes a sociological as well
as an internal, psychological dimension, all sublimation (labor)
can be interpreted as repression, that is, as domination. Sublimation appears per se as repression; the concepts become interchangeable. It is only when repression and sublimation are restricted to their proper and technical Freudian definitions that
sublimation can be differentiated from repression *and* suppression (oppression, etc.) such that it can be understood to have a
nonrepressive dimension. I have begun to lay the foundations for
these distinctions throughout the foregoing examination.

Marcuse's confusion about the phenomenon of sublimation is highlighted the moment he encounters varieties of sublimated activities not agreeing with his theoretical expectations. An artistic sensibility is gratifying, pleasurable, *and* a sublimation of libidinal impulses. Acknowledging this deviation from his critical evaluation of sublimation, Marcuse awkwardly explains that "artistic work, where it is genuine, seems to grow out of a non-repressive instinctual constellation and to envisage non-repressive aims — so much so that the term *sublimation* seems to require considerable modification if applied to this kind of work."[33] Certainly in great works of art the quality of beauty, which pertains to the erotic and sensuous content of art, may derive from the accomplishment of a highly sublimated aesthetic form. And not only in the great work, but the aesthetic response to such an oeuvre is likewise a sublimation of erotic energy in the pleasurable feelings accompanying the appreciation of art. Yet to characterize aesthetic experience in this way is to demand not a modified concept of sublimation but rather a modified understanding of this concept.

Art instructs us about the actual relationship between sublimation and gratification according to Freud's theory. There is a uniqueness to art that lies not in its sublimated gratification of libido but in its providing for *only* the sublimated gratification of Eros. As such it appears to be the single form of labor based upon the repression of the aggressive instincts. Marcuse, then, is partially correct. Art does grow out of a nonrepressive instinctual constellation through its sublimation of erotic impulses. But it preserves a repressive dimension in that aggressive impulses are not gratified. A completely nonrepressive and unalienated form of activity would be neither art nor labor as we know them but activity sublimating both the libidinal and the aggressive component instincts.

Marcuse has further difficulties with sublimation in his management of aggression. When he speaks of the satisfaction of aggressive impulses, which cuts against his view that only libidinal gratification is pleasurable, he maintains that gratification occurs because "socially useful destructiveness is less sublimated than socially useful libido."[34] In truth, socially useful destructiveness is not sublimated merely to a high degree; in the contemporary period it is perhaps the most highly sublimated of the instinctual drives. Progress through the development of science and technology must mean that the impetus behind the evolution of these sublimated forms of aggression is the need for sublimated satisfaction. This factor should be taken into serious account in any explanation of the course of modern civilization.[35]

In this corrected interpretation of Freud great stress has been placed on two significant elements of the instinct theory. Sublimation emerges as the primary source of gratification. And the genital organization of the instincts establishes the biological preconditions for sublimation. We are now in a position to consider Marcuse's "second dimension" and to discover, as well, that its implications are related to his faulty analysis of both decisive elements of Freud's instinct theory. "Second dimension," it should be noted, is a term I have chosen for two reasons. This phrase seeks to capture Marcuse's dimension of freedom and human potentialities as they are modeled from the theoretical clay provided by Freud. And as a second dimension of one social universe, it is a dimension of freedom presumably just as real as that familiar dimension of repression within which the members of society dwell.

The Second Dimension

Under the rule of its performance principle the scientific and technological achievements of modern capitalism have been so far-reaching that conventional forms of labor have become obsolete. To Marcuse, this means that genital "repression," the historical catastrophe in each life that alters human nature to perform a lifetime of hard labor, is no longer socially necessary and now is to be judged as surplus-repression. A physical regression behind the genital stage of instinctual organization would follow from the abolition of genital repression and the process of desexualization would be reversed.

What is involved in this "resexualization" of the body? Marcuse defines desexualization precisely as the confinement of the entire range of human sexuality, of Eros or the erotic drives, to the genital sphere. Genital sexuality insures reproduction, which explains why genital sexuality is restricted by the norm of heterosexual dominance. And as we saw, after this desexualization of the body, "psychical energy is withdrawn from sexuality." In other words, through labor genital sexuality is subjected to further inhibitions on the pleasure it can provide. Resexualization, therefore, refers to the transformation of sexuality back into Eros, to re-eroticizing the body and the entire personality. Regression behind the genital stage would involve the reactivation of a pregenital polymorphous sexuality. A "libidinal rationality," a rationality of true gratification, would be substituted for a repressive performance principle. A second dimension of human potentiality would be born.[36]

Of no little concern to Freud, however, were the mature sexual counterparts to polymorphous perversity, expressed in such forms of psychosexual pathology as sadistic and masochistic behavior. Metapsychological theory drew out the parallels between the perverse manifestations of infantile sexuality and adult perversions by studying the dynamic relationship between stages of psychosexual development and sexual behavior. Freud's work in this area and its theoretical underpinnings extend beyond the present focus of discussion. A few aspects, however, are salient to a critical perspective on Marcuse's notion of libidinal rationality.

Frequently, in deference to social pressures an individual represses an instinctual aim for which there cannot be found an alternative outlet (displacement) that is both gratifying and socially permissible. In this event, the aim undergoes a regression to an early phase of sexuality. The stimulus for this regression is society's denial of gratification, while its psychological motivation is the unconscious memory of an infantile and particularly intense experience of gratification whose timing and intensity made it a "fixation." The memory also may be of a normal gratification that had been abandoned prematurely as a consequence of a primary or a traumatic repression during childhood. By means of regression the adult gains the satisfaction frustrated by society through a perverse sexuality (or a neurosis), which derives its pathological character from being based upon some form of pregenital sexual expression. The regression causes the instinctual structure to revert to its prior arrangement of independent component impulses. The perversion assumes the sexual characteristics of the component instincts before their genital organization. This is indicated, for example, by Freud's statement that adult sexual aberrations result "from components which have come apart again in the perversions."[37] The perversion's psychological disposition is informed by the infantile psychic memories of the particular pregenital form of gratification. Thus, the *psychosexual* pathology corresponds in its entirety to the nature of polymorphous perversity at some phase of infantile sexual development. Perversion and infantile sexual disposition are inseparable. Freud's theory of regression and perversion suggests that the substitution of a polymorphous libidinal rationality for the performance principle would replace one mode of irrationality with another.

Marcuse, on the other hand, chooses to believe that regression to the infantile phases of sexuality would allow for the free development of polymorphous sexuality and that the instincts would tend toward their own sublimation (a claim to be evaluated shortly). "Self-sublimation," as he calls it, "would also transform the perverted content of these stages."[38] Marcuse's argument proceeds from the mistaken idea that perversion is not rooted in polymorphous perversity but is the outcome of the "explosion" of sexuality "repressed" to the genital sphere and to further sublimated constraints. Abolishing the repressive modification of genital supremacy would subvert the preconditions for perversity. This view is entirely incorrect. Such a primitive explanation for perversion as stemming from dammed up libido might conceivably find some, though very little, support in Freud's earliest papers or in the writings of Wilhelm Reich. It would hardly be sustained by the mature metapsychology. Freud's studies in neurosis proved the relationship between infantile sexuality and perversion (neuroses are the "negative of perversions"). Polymorphous perversity is tied to all subsequent perversion. Constrained sexuality, or frustrated instinctual aims, whether of an unsublimated or a sublimated variety, does not cause perversion but merely triggers the regression that allows for its appearance.

The objective of this part of the critical analysis of Marcuse's second dimension is meant seriously to question his polymorphous libidinal rationality by bringing forward its implications. It is not intended to leave heterosexuality intact as the dominant norm. Marcuse is correct in one respect. The Oedipal conflict is repressive both in the technical Freudian sense and in the nontechnical sense employed by Marcuse not because it affects instinctual organization, because it does not, but rather because it is responsible for the modification of an instinctual disposition that is inherently bisexual to an exclusively heterosexual identification. Heterosexuality as the dominant sexual norm is the consequence of an inhibited sexual development. It is the repression of the Oedipal complex that prepares the ground for this inhibition and its heir, the superego, which insures it. With this exception, Marcuse's inquiry into Freud possesses implications that make his more creative social theory extremely vulnerable. In the final analysis, it will become clear that these theoretical implications efface his theory's critical and heuristic value.

Other and equally serious problems with Marcuse's libidinal rationality arise when he attempts to give this conception a more definite form. He selects the myths of Orpheus and Narcissus to suggest possibilities for freedom in a nonrepressive society. They are meant to create an easily identifiable separation between the established repressive alternatives and future nonrepressive possibilities. These myths are opposed to " 'culture-heroes' who have persisted in the imagination as symbolizing the attitude and the deeds that have determined the fate of mankind," such as "Prometheus . . . the culture-hero of toil, productivity, and progress through repression."[39] Orpheus and Narcissus are "symbols of another reality principle . . . sought at the opposite pole."[40] Prometheus represents the prevailing social order and is the paradigmatic expression of the performance principle, whereas Orpheus and Narcissus represent possible, desirable, and qualitatively different alternatives. As Marcuse says, the "Orphic and Narcissistic experience of the world negates that which sustains the world of the performance principle."[41] But the problem associated with Marcuse's explication of the progressive mythological images is that they possess a meaning other than that he imputed to them, a meaning Marcuse chooses steadfastly to ignore. Their entire realm of implicit possibilities is not presented.

Marcuse's exposition of Orpheus and Narcissus emphasizes their positive qualities: "Theirs is the image of joy and fulfillment; the voice which does not command but sings; the gesture which offers and receives; the deed which is peace and ends the labor of conquest; the liberation from time which unites man with god, man with nature."[42] The images do portray a new harmony between man and nature and among men, relationships that are noncompetitive, nondestructive, peaceful, and eternal. But as such they are distorted, for their undesirable features are disregarded. The myths of Orpheus and Narcissus have always been overshadowed by a morbid, morose, and saturnine character. Orpheus seeks his lost love, Eurydice, in the depths of the underworld and consorting with the rulers of the dead, Pluto and Proserpine, makes a pact that leads to his own demise. Both Orpheus and Narcissus are isolated, unconcerned, and asocial creatures. Narcissus rejects contact out of vanity and self-love and is eventually punished for his indifference. These traits suggest a darker moral nature.

But the distortion of the cultural myths is only the first step. Marcuse then proceeds to reinterpret Freud's instinct theory on the basis of the distortion and he applies this modified psychology of the instincts to social relationships.

Freud's theory requires that the death instinct be understood in terms of a Nirvana principle that governs the "conservative nature of the instincts."[43] This means that the instinctual aim is not merely for gratification but rather for lasting gratification. Under the rule of the Nirvana principle, in other words, the aim is to reproduce the complete absence of excitation characteristic of an inorganic state, or of a deathly state, a state before life. In Marcuse's elaboration of his second dimension, however, Freud's hypothesis is transfigured. Marcuse's mythological prototypes have come to symbolize life and permanency of happiness, their connection with the death instinct and other shadowy connotations having been purged in his one-sided analysis. And since Freud's Nirvana principle expresses the instinctual need for *permanent*, eternal gratification, then to achieve social relations corresponding solely to the positive, eternal characteristics of Orpheus and Narcissus means that the Nirvana principle will begin to rule "not as death but as life."[44] This extraordinary and far-fetched reinterpretation of the Nirvana principle neglects the biological integrity of Freud's theory and its implications (although Marcuse claims to consider biology seriously and criticizes the neo-Freudians for rejecting it). In particular, it entails an unwitting celebration of the death instinct. But through his circuitous manner of analysis this license taken with Freud reveals the true nature of Marcuse's polymorphous rationality. As shall become clear shortly, Marcuse's interpretation of Freud leads to the mental death of the individual.

Marcuse does not end his mythologically based argument here. The cultural myth of Narcissus is extended further into the biological and psychological realms. Where Orpheus and Narcissus were tailored to Marcuse's needs, trimmed of unpalatable mythological details and essentially disfigured to provide for a modification of the Nirvana principle, Narcissus is used again in a comparison with another aspect of Freud's instinct theory, primary narcissism.

Like Orpheus and Narcissus and the Nirvana principle, primary narcissism is understood to contain progressive existential criteria suggesting new forms of social relations between man and nature. According to Marcuse, "narcissism denotes a fundamental relatedness to reality which may generate a comprehensive existential order. In other words, narcissism may contain the germ of a different reality principle." Primary narcissism would mean that "the normal antagonistic relation between ego and external reality" would disappear.[45] The needs of the individual would no longer conflict with the needs of society.

In Freud's theory, however, perhaps what is most important about primary narcissistic behavior is that it is peculiar to the earliest phase of infantile psychosexual development. Here the death instinct, Thanatos, predominates. Libidinal and aggressive component instincts reach their aim of tension reduction to the extent of nearly accomplishing a return to an earlier state of quiescence. If death seems a rather bizarre and uncanny fate of the individual at this stage, it may be more reasonable to suggest that if this pregenital instinctual arrangement were to endure, as it does with Marcuse, there could be no ego development and hence no progress in the interest of mature (unsublimated, aim inhibited, and sublimated) social relations. According to Freud, though, at the mature genital stage of instinctual organization the complete elimination of excitation is not possible and ego development moves forward so that sublimation may occur in order to provide higher forms of gratification.

It is true, of course, that at this earliest phase of infantile sexuality the child's ego has no conception of a division between itself and environment, internal and external worlds, subject and object. There is no antagonism but rather a unity of the ego and its universe. The solipsistic ego essentially is dissolved into the whole of its perceptual and conceptual experience. Certainly, the implication is a world free of conflict, free of the separation between self-interest and general interest, of the distinction between egoism and altruism. There is an absence of differentiation between private and public spheres.

Once again, however, we find a distortion. The freedom that Marcuse infers from his account of primary narcissism could be won only at the expense of an inhibited mental development. Such freedom could be the free expression of an individual not in possession of an ego able either to conceive of or gratify complex spiritual, intellectual, or sexual needs or to cope with the inexorable necessities, challenges, and obstacles of any real world. And as just mentioned, the infantile character of primary narcissism also entails the rule of the Nirvana principle. Freud carefully chose a myth to symbolize the instinctual behavior he described as narcissistic. Over Narcissus and primary narcissism, Thanatos prevails. Needs must be gratified immediately, permanently; there can be no *thought* of postponement. Through Narcissus and narcissism, Marcuse appears to encourage and to participate in the erosion of subjectivity, of thought, of the ego. There is no little irony here. For Marcuse's original purpose in integrating Freud's theory into critical theory was to rescue the subject from the total domination of social order. This goal was to be accomplished by developing an anthropological foundation for a theory whose critical rationality then would be rooted in an element of subjectivity that could retain an autonomy from society. But Freud's instinct theory and metapsychology, which were to provide this foundation, are interpreted in such a way as to lose the singular element of subjectivity, the ego, that must exist if there is to be any critical autonomy.

There is further evidence for Marcuse's theoretical erosion of the subject in his concept of "self-sublimation." It will be recalled that Marcuse identifies the genital organization of the instincts with repression and considers this organization to be the product of social manipulation and coercion. With the exception of art, all mental and physical labor is alienating because it requires the desexualization of the body, the spatial and temporal reduction of the life instincts, of Eros, to the genital sphere. If this alienation is to be overcome and the instincts are to regain their original and natural disposition, social institutions must permit a regression behind the genital stage of instinctual organization. Now this regression supposedly would allow for what Marcuse calls self-sublimation. The self-sublimation of free and unrepressed Eros, of reactivated polymorphous sexuality, would constitute a liberation of all human faculties. For the first time sublimation would be truly gratifying and pleasurable, a "higher gratification." Social relations and relations with nature would come to incorporate the values symbolized by Orpheus and Narcissus.

But Marcuse wants an individual capable of sublimation who is not forced to pass through the developmental stages that make sublimation possible. Infantile sexual development proceeds in strict accordance with a carefully and elaborately defined biological and psychological model of maturation. The logic of Freud's model dictates that its progressive stages are neither repressive nor alienating. Most important, without the completion of all instinctual stages the preconditions for sublimation would not exist. There would not be, on the one hand, the complex instinctual organization making gratification difficult to achieve and, on the other, the complementary development of a psychic apparatus insuring that sublimation can occur so that means of gratification can be devised. By eliminating both of these factors, by reversing the genital organization, as Marcuse does, there would be no self (ego structure), no reasoning faculty to engage in sublimation.

Finally, not only the reasoning capacity of the subject but Reason as such is annihilated through Marcuse's interpretation of Freud. This occurs when Marcuse considers the Nirvana principle directly, without the interpretive mediation of the myth of Narcissus. Here Marcuse is consistent with his previous disregard of the biological realities Freud inferred from the instincts under the rule of the Nirvana principle. Marcuse correctly acknowledges that just as immediate, complete, and permanent gratification is experienced as pleasurable, the relative absence of this state is experienced as painful. The instinctual process originates in an unpleasant state of tension and thereupon determines for itself a path that results in relaxation of tension, for instance, the avoidance of pain (unpleasure, tension) or the production of pleasure.[46] But whereas Freud makes no distinction in *Beyond the Pleasure Principle* between the alleviation of pain (unpleasure, tension) and the elimination of life as an aim of the Nirvana principle, Marcuse contends that "if the instincts' basic objective is not the termination of life but of pain — the absence of tension — then paradoxically, in terms of the instinct, the conflict between life and death is the more reduced, the closer life approximates the state of gratification."[47]

Insisting on such a distinction where none could be drawn out of Freud's theory, Marcuse actually has lost much of the deeper significance of the metapsychology. By claiming that the Nirvana principle refers to the elimination not of life but of tension and pain only, the discovery that led Freud to infer the existence of Thanatos is effaced. And while Marcuse's interpretation can distort the meaning of the Nirvana principle, it cannot alter its reality. Marcuse reduces the conflict between Eros and Thanatos, life and death, only to bring life more securely within the orbit of death. If there is ever a nihilistic strain in Marcuse's philosophy it is at those moments when his inquiry into Freud's theory conceals the latter's real implications. For in addition to its commonplace meaning, because it represents the end of everything symbolized by human life, death also is opposed to all human values, particularly Reason. Correctly understood, however, from the instinct theory it must be appreciated that the submission of the mature ego to a developed instinctual organization and to an "antagonistic reality" is first and foremost an antagonism to death, whatever else it may become thereafter.

This critical examination has uncovered several fundamental errors in Marcuse's interpretation of Freud, and together with these flaws a set of issues and implications was considered forcing the thrust of his argument to be discarded. In the final analysis, Marcuse's interpretation of Freud accomplishes the opposite of its appointed task. His anthropological foundation for critical theory will support neither a reasoning subject nor a critical rationality. The biological foundation, the second dimension in which they are anchored, effectively eliminates both subjectivity and Reason. Now there remains the task of restoring subjectivity and the anthropological basis for the rationality of critical theory. A small contribution can be made by further elaborating the significance of the corrected interpretation of Freud's instinct theory, which has been the ground for the critical evaluation of Marcuse's second dimension. The focus will be on the concept of sublimation. This discussion also will serve as background for considering the final aspect of Marcuse's second dimension — the aesthetic dimension.

Sublimation, Subjectivity, and the Foundation of Critical Theory

It was Freud who first recognized that repression is necessary and fundamental to the preservation and development of both individual and society. While both parties benefit through collaboration, he stressed also that the individual immediately and the society ultimately suffer from the impact of repression. Analysis and therapy perhaps can extricate the individual, but even mental health stands as no barrier to living the eventual fate of social order, which to Freud bore so little promise of redemption. Historicizing the relationship among repression, scarcity, and political domination, Marcuse sheds Freud's darker vision in favor of the possibility of increasingly minimizing repression and the suffering it causes in a way that would insure collective salvation. Although each offers a different perspective on labor's purpose and organization in modern civilization, Freud and Marcuse share an emphasis on labor as the single most decisive factor in an explanation for repression. But they do not share the sense in which work necessarily involves repression!

It is a relatively simple matter to be clear about Freud's notion of repression. The ego inhibits an instinctual impulse, wish, or memory from exercising any influence over its conscious activities. Consciousness may be occupied, for a time, with such material, or it may not, but in either case the ego deflects it away from consciousness into a layer of the unconscious mind. Repression is an internal process of restraint carried out at the behest of society or its internal psychological counterpart, the superego. Ego defense mechanisms protect the individual by adjusting its needs to the conflicting demands of society. But as elementary as it may be to describe the basic characteristics of repression, the discussion is complicated the moment the concept is related meaningfully to labor, for now the concern must be with what precisely is repressed and for what reason. In this regard Freud's theory of aggression is highly instructive.

Although he argued that "man's natural aggressive instinct, the hostility of each against all and of all against each, opposes [the] programme of civilization,"[48] more important, he demonstrated also that the "natural aggressive instinct" is not naturally or inevitably *destructive*. However, Freud did impute a destructive nature to the aggressive component instincts during the pregenital phases. At the oral phase, for example, the component instincts are marked by a primitive and barbaric "cannibilistic" urge, alluding to the biting and chewing activity associated with deriving oral gratification, while the anal instincts are essentially sadistic. At the genital stage of sexual development, however, a significant change in the instinctual structure occurs that binds together the libidinal and aggressive component instincts. This development, in turn, is accompanied by a change of even greater significance. The erotic impulses now *predominate* and "the discharge of the instinct of destruction is habitually brought into the service of Eros . . . The advance from the earlier [pregenital] phase to the definitive genital one would be conditioned by an accession of erotic components."[49] In view of this characteristic of the genital stage of instinctual organization Freud was "driven to conclude that the death instincts are by their nature mute and that the clamour of life proceeds for the most part from Eros."[50]

According to Freud's theory, therefore, the biological progression of the instincts by nature does not permit aggression to enter without design into sublimated social relations (labor) but rather into modes of work wherein the libidinal impulses are dominant. To put it somewhat differently, since the sublimation of instinctual drives is, at the same time, sublimation of an instinctual structure with the erotic impulses harnessing the aggressive impulses, labor by nature is the sublimation of eroticized aggression. By nature labor is nondestructive. It should be noted that this sort of sublimation (labor) has been derived from Freud's theory without once mentioning repression. This insight will receive further attention shortly, but here an indication is given that it is possible and appropriate to speak of nonrepressive sublimation.

Society rests upon labor, however, that exclusively utilizes the aggressive and destructive components of an instinct. Providing basic material needs and other economic necessities requiring the transformation of nature into consumable products means that the raw materials of nature must be destroyed and processed. The erotic instincts preclude destructiveness because they bind and neutralize the destructive tendencies of aggression. Only the elimination of the libidinal instincts through repression will free up the requisite energy that determines that the form of man's relationship to nature and of relations among men will be primarily aggressive and destructive. Repression releases the aggressive-destructive component impulses for sublimation. The societal need for particular types of labor, in other words, has repression as its precondition.

Since the fusion of the erotic and aggressive instincts mitigates the aggressive impulses and the destructive manifestations of aggression, the reemergence of destructive aggression occurs when the libidinal components are eliminated from the instinctual drive, as though a regression to an earlier and pregenital phase of instinctual organization had taken place. According to Freud this is the consequence of repression. Through repression the instinctual drive is "defused" and the destructive impulses, no longer bound and tamed by Eros, are again released. Repression introduces this process of defusion because, as Freud explained, the aggressive components of the instinctual drive must become attached to the superego so that it can act aggressively against the ego to maintain the repression of the erotic impulses. Once repressed, the libidinal impulses can experience any of several fates. They may be displaced as fantasy or expressed as perversion, or they may undergo displacement as symptoms of a neurotic disorder. The outcome depends largely on the individual concerned, his particular history of infantile development, the nature of the regression to an earlier phase of psychosexual experience, and so on. Being repressed and made over to the superego, the aggressive components are "transformed into a sense of guilt."[51] The aggressiveness of conscience reproduces the aggressiveness of society, which had demanded that the repression be undertaken in the interest of production.

A society, such as modern capitalism, developing according to the overriding principle of material growth and progress requires continual repression, and every subsequent demand for a

> renunciation of instinct now becomes a dynamic source of conscience and every fresh renunciation increases the latter's severity

and intolerance . . . The effect of instinctual renunciation on the conscience then is that every piece of aggression whose satisfaction the subject gives up is taken over by the super-ego and increases the latter's aggressiveness (against the ego).[52]

This accumulation of guilt, of aggressiveness against the ego, places the ego in a potentially desperate situation, for "what is now holding sway in the super-ego is, as it were, a pure culture of the death instinct, and in fact it often enough succeeds in driving the ego into death."[53] Elsewhere, Freud again expressed this point by saying that the result of continual repression is "an increase of the sense of guilt, which will perhaps reach heights that the individual finds hard to tolerate."[54]

If the social order is not to succumb to the collective guilt brought on by the repressive demands of productive relations, either this guilt must be deflected or, what is but the same thing in other metapsychological terms, the aggressive components threatening the ego must be displaced. Freud argued that

so long as that [destructive] instinct operates internally, as a death instinct, it remains silent; it only comes to our notice when it is diverted outwards as an instinct of destruction. It seems to be essential for the preservation of the individual that this diversion should occur . . . Holding back aggressiveness is in general unhealthy and leads to illness.[55]

As Freud showed, in the interest of self-preservation and to avoid psychological disorder, the ego turns the aggressive energy responsible for its suffering outward in the direction of the society. But this re-externalization of aggression occurs after a dramatic change has been effected. The postrepression displacement of the aggressive instincts has been de-eroticized. The libidinal instincts are no longer present to neutralize the destructive manifestations of aggression. Nonerotic or destructive aggression then is sublimated in labor. Freud, in fact, inquired as to how he could have "overlooked the ubiquity of non-erotic aggressivity and destructiveness and can have failed to give it its due place in our interpretation of life."[56]

By examining Freud's theory of aggression, forms of aggressivity emerge as the result of a social logic that implicates mental processes in productive processes. Social organization structures a universal network of productive relations and defines the kind of labor to be performed. Individuals cannot avoid the necessity of earning a living and, consequently forced into repressions that place mental health in jeopardy, generate the aggressive energy that finds sublimated means of expression in labor. Repression and sublimation clearly are independent psychological processes. Yet, from the standpoint of mental and social behavior they are related systemically. The socially defined *need* for the sublimation of aggressive and destructive energy in production precedes repression, but actually repression must occur in advance of sublimation in order that noneroticized aggression be made available for work. As a function of repression the cause of the destructive manifestation of aggression originates in society. Though repression can be grasped only as an internal, psychological process, the sublimation of aggression is socially required, making repression socially determined. Thus, one relationship of sublimation to repression is through the social need for aggressive and destructive relationships. Such labor should be termed "repressive sublimation."

Repressive sublimation embraces several crucial aspects of Marx's notion of alienation. A one-sided exaggeration of needs and drives through productive activity excludes a wealth of experience in harmony with the essential constitution of human nature. Within this alienation from human nature must be included an alienation of man from nature as nature would develop if a fuller range of human potentialities could engage it through an appreciation of nature's other than utilitarian value. And just as repressive sublimation determines relations of man to nature, this aspect of alienation has a counterpart in relations among men. Insofar as they require competition, struggle, and other sorts of behavior derivative of the aggressive and destructive impulses, the social relations of production are based upon the repression of erotic impulses. The *essential* disposition of human nature, where aggression is bound to the service of Eros, would eroticize social relations. This is precisely what productive relations do not, indeed cannot, allow, for the problem of alienation is not merely an existential problem caused by scarcity and the necessity of providing for basic needs, as Marcuse has ably demonstrated, but an economic problem in a dualistic sense. The vicissitudes of the instincts, the economics of libidinal and aggressive-destructive energy, depend upon the broader claims of economic "necessity" and its political manipulation.

But is nonrepressive labor, where the instincts harness aggression, feasible and rational? Freud's theory claims nonrepressive sublimation to be a natural disposition following from the biological maturation of infantile sexuality. *Natural* disposition implies both a capacity and a necessity. This point can be understood in this way. The need for nonrepressive sublimation, *for higher forms of gratification*, is the biological stimulus for ego development, that is, for the development of reasoning capacities. These capacities continue to grow with attempts to fulfill this need. And insofar as reasoning processes seek nonrepressive forms of sublimation, they are obedient to a necessity prescribed by nature. Reasoning, as nonrepressive sublimation, then appears as Reason. Yet, although bound by the principles of Reason, reasoning processes are not actually constrained by the values of the natural relation between biology and psychology, instincts and nonrepressive sublimation. The possibilities for all modes of labor remain open. But sublimation that contravenes this relation is both morally and psychologically repressive.

An examination of Freud's theory has produced an all-important distinction between repressive and nonrepressive sublimation. Marcuse's historical terms—basic and surplus-repression and the performance principle—should be retained as well for they also unfold the critical elements in the instinct theory and metapsychology and circumscribe the historical limits of Freud's concepts. The real significance of basic and surplus-repression, however, is captured only when the repression to which they refer is understood as repressive sublimation. The undoing of repressive constraints, whether they are politically or socially necessary, would establish the preconditions for a nonrepressive sublimated mode of existence. And though the difference between repressive and nonrepressive sublimation is qualitative, a correct interpretation of the instinct theory shows that there would be continuity in human activity as labor (sublimation). There is no regression, as in Marcuse's second dimension, to a stage of development inhibiting the formation of the subject's capacities for sublimation, for reasoning. Marcuse's concept of nonrepressive sublimation as self-sublimation, in its association with polymorphous sexuality, cannot maintain a subject with the capacity and disposition for sublimation. By reclaiming the concept of sublimation, a step is taken to reinstate the critical temper of theory. Not only is a decisive element of autonomy restored to the individual, but this element of autonomy is given a natural foundation upon which the objective need for nonrepressive sublimation, nonrepressive, unalienating *labor*, can be defended.

To complete the analysis of Marcuse's second dimension, the restoration of the subject in light of the new conception of nonrepressive sublimation presupposes a revision of a remaining aspect of his theory, the aesthetic dimension. The aesthetic dimension is a further attempt by Marcuse to describe, although this time in strict philosophical terms, the shape that man's relation to nature would assume when governed by a libidinal rationality. As such, the aesthetic dimension is an important expression of Marcuse's second dimension.

The Aesthetic Dimension

The philosophies of Kant and Schiller are attractive to Marcuse by virtue of the function they attribute to an aesthetic sensibility. With Kant the problem is to reconcile the moral autonomy of the individual with an order perceived to operate according to universal empirical laws. The antinomy or essential antagonism of subject and object, man and nature, is overcome through aesthetic perception, a sensuous experience of objects wherein the object, whether "thing or flower, animal or man," comes to assume a form other than that imposed when it is grasped conceptually. In the aesthetic perception no cognitive faculty is instrumental in the mental representation of the object. For if cognition intervened, some definite and limited purpose would be inherent in its conception and attached to the object. Intuition is the mode of apprehension in the aesthetic perception, and imagination is the faculty of a priori intuitions.

The aesthetic perception is receptive, passive, and such mere perception of the object is without regard for any purpose it might otherwise serve. Its appearance without consideration for utility allows an appreciation of its "pure form." The only real purpose of the aesthetic perception is to represent without purpose; its only law, to express lawlessness. Once represented in its pure form by the imagination the object is subjected to reflective judgment — the faculties of the understanding are brought into free play. The harmonious accord of the imagination and the understanding issues in pleasure. Thus, the sensuous and imaginative representation of objects is bound up with pleasure and gratification, and since the basis of pleasure lies not in any sensation of the object but in its form, the perception is universally valid for all sentient beings.[57] Beauty is defined as the universality of form. In its universality, beauty ("purposiveness without purpose," "lawfulness without law," the "pure form" of an object) is symbolic of morality, which is now grounded in universal principles. In this way the aesthetic perception binds together freedom and nature, pleasure and morality.

Kant's treatment of aesthetics does not reflect the history of the concept. Beginning with Alexander Baumgarten in the eighteenth century "sensuousness" and "aesthetic" often are shuffled into a remote sector of the academic division of labor. They appear within a separate discipline as the study of art. Existing on the fringes of society, sensuousness and art are pleasant diversions but not acceptable as part of the real business of the day. Sensuousness is sanctioned only as art and the critical power of aesthetics is neutralized. The nonrepressive aesthetic order and the repressive social order lead a benign coexistence through an institutionalized distance. For Marcuse the importance of Schiller's work lies in his attempt to recapture the critical significance of aesthetics by undoing its sublimated and neutralized expression in art. Schiller somewhat alters the terms of the argument but its spirit is essentially Kantian. Against the repressive order of reason, against the "form impulse," is opposed the order and the "impulse of sensuousness." Freedom resides in the "free play of the imagination," the unfettered "display" of human faculties, of potentiality. The liberation of the senses unleashes a new universal morality by redefining the relations among men and between man and nature as passive, receptive, contemplative. All things unfold according to their own designs as nature — human nature and external nature — is released from the bondage of the performance principle.

No objections can be raised to Marcuse's interpretation of Kant and Schiller in *Eros and Civilization*. His explication is brilliant and through it both philosophers contribute remarkably to the philosophical legitimation of Marcuse's project. The aesthetic dimension of Kant's *Critique of Judgement* and Schiller's *On the Aesthetic Education of Man*, however, is more than the philosophical expression of Marcuse's second dimension; it is also its theoretical critique for it clearly exhibits the weaknesses of Marcuse's position. The aesthetic dimension dictates a relatedness of man to his world essentially *passive by nature*. The point here is not to emphasize some affirmative trait. Without a doubt the aesthetic dimension is a qualitative change in social order. Its break with the past, or with the present, would be so dramatic as to presume the sweeping transformation of culture as it has existed. But although in its legitimation of the second dimension no affirmative character prevails, in the aesthetic dimension a regressive factor is solidly entrenched. Neither the aesthetic nor the second dimension conforms to the disposition of the senses or faculties of human nature according to Freud's theory, where they take on the features of *actively appropriating* the world through labor. Certainly, this appropriation is regulated by Eros, but the libidinal instincts are in association with the aggressive impulses. At worst this may mean that a repressive social order is exchanged for a benevolent form of domination. At the heart of Freud's theory—and this point would be sustained by the concept of nonrepressive sublimation—egoism is always the basis for altruism. Marcuse's second dimension and its philosophical expression in Kant and Schiller are true to the nature of Eros only as it would appear once removed from its natural constitution. Only without the aggressive drive naturally subordinated to Eros, only through the violation of human nature, is the disposition of human nature released to passivity and receptiveness. As it appears in the second dimension and in the aesthetic dimension, Eros is an *alienated* mode of human nature.

In *Counterrevolution and Revolt* Marcuse comes very close to recognizing this problem when he recalls a much neglected interpretation of Marx's *Paris Manuscripts*. Where Marx spoke of the radical emancipation of all human senses in a socialist society, Marcuse realizes that this means that a liberated human sensibility in the broadest sense becomes " 'practical' in the reconstruction of society,"[58] that man's senses "are active, 'practical' in the 'appropriation' of the object world; they express the social exis-

tence of man, his 'objectification' "[59] through *labor*. For this
brief moment Marcuse verges on an insight into the meaning of a
fully reconstituted human nature. The value for Marcuse of his
exposition of Marx would have been the correction of his interpretation of Freud. Before this correction can occur, however,
Marcuse recoils from pursuing the logic of his analysis. Of
Marx's active and practical sensibility Marcuse finally says,
"Marx's notion of a human appropriation of nature retains
something of the *hubris* of domination. 'Appropriation,' no matter how human, remains appropriation of a (living) object by a
subject."[60] Hubris? Perhaps, but Marx was forced to speak without the benefit of Freudian theory. Yet, this concession to Marcuse proceeds too far against Marx and at the same time begs the
question about the Freudian concept of man. Is domination,
even of a benevolent cast, the consequence of an emancipated
human nature? No certain answer can be offered to this all-important question, but no resort to metaphor or symbol must be
allowed to inhibit its sober consideration. As for Marx, however,
I believe he has an informed vision that surely portrays a world
wherein Freud's concept of human nature becomes human nature for man.

> *Communism* is the *positive* abolition of *private property*, of *human
> self-alienation*, and thus the real *appropriation* of *human* nature
> through and for man. It is, therefore, the return of man himself as
> a *social*, i.e., really human being, a complete and conscious return
> which assimilates all the wealth of previous development. Commu-
> nism as a fully developed naturalism is humanism and as a fully de-
> veloped humanism is naturalism. It is the *definitive* resolution of
> the antagonism between man and nature, and between man and
> man. It is the true solution of the conflict between existence and es-
> sence, between objectification and self-affirmation, between free-
> dom and necessity, between individual and species. It is the solution
> of the riddle of history and knows itself to be this solution.[61]

If this proposal means anything at all, it means at least that the
hubris of domination is exchanged for the hubris of having finally conquered the impulse for domination.

Further attempts to develop a critical social theory from Freud's
instinct theory and metapsychology must recognize, as Marcuse
has not, that nonrepressive sublimation, labor, is a central theoretical concept. Sublimation is not necessarily repressive either in

the technical Freudian sense of repression or in the nontechnical sense of repression employed by Marcuse. It is foremost a natural and autonomous human predisposition. In capitalist society, however, the mode of sublimation is largely beyond individual self-determination. It is limited by the relation of the individual to the social division of labor, and the latter is shaped by political restraints and by the objective historical level of cultural and technological development. All these factors converge as determinants of the degree and quality of gratification to be derived from the sublimation of energy in work. We account for the loss of gratification through labor not as a consequence of the nature of sublimation per se but as a result of the repressive inadequacy of the organized division of labor. After focusing on the means to eliminate the socioeconomic, political, and historical forms of repression, we will be left with the categories of labor and pleasure, sublimation and self-realization, and firm grounds to integrate the theoretical priorities and perspectives of Marx and Freud. Sublimation must become a central theoretical concept and foundation of a critical theory of society, for through it we discover in the individual a natural disposition to make history without violence and, beyond that, a history of indeterminate possibility.

Notes

1. See chapter six of this volume.
2. Herbert Marcuse, *An Essay on Liberation* (Boston: Beacon, 1969); the first chapter is entitled "A Biological Foundation for Socialism?"
3. Ibid., p. 10.
4. Sigmund Freud, *An Outline of Psychoanalysis* (1938) (New York: Norton, 1969), p. 5.
5. Ibid., p. 55.
6. Sigmund Freud, "Formulations Regarding the Two Principles in Mental Functioning" (1911), *Collected Papers*, 4 (New York: Basic Books, 1959), p. 17.
7. Herbert Marcuse, *Eros and Civilization: A Philosophical Inquiry into Freud* (Boston: Beacon, 1966), p. 80.
8. Sigmund Freud, *Civilization and Its Discontents* (1931) (New York: Norton, 1962), p. 92.

9. Sigmund Freud, *The Future of an Illusion* (1927) (New York: Doubleday, Anchor Books, 1964), especially chapters 1 and 2.

10. *Eros and Civilization*, p. 35.

11. Ibid., p. 8.

12. Ibid., p. 276.

13. Ibid., p. 48.

14. Although the instinct theory underwent dramatic changes through the various stages of its development, its central concepts are retained fundamentally unaltered throughout Freud's work. When I have relied upon concepts and theories taken from Freud's early work that are occasionally thought to have been discarded in his subsequent formulations, to prove continuity with Freud's mature ideas I shall refer to later writings wherein comparable evidence can be found. Original dates of publication are indicated in parentheses following each title. On Freud's theory of the component instincts see Sigmund Freud, *Three Essays on the Theory of Sexuality* (1905) (New York: Avon, 1971), pp. 58-63, 88-90, 95-98, 104, 107, 111, 137-141, 144; "The Paths to the Formation of Symptoms" (1917), *The Complete Introductory Lectures on Psychoanalysis* (New York: Norton, 1966), pp. 362, 374; *The Ego and the Id* (1923) (New York: Norton, 1962), pp. 31-32, 34, 44; *Civilization and Its Discontents*, p. 86; *An Outline of Psychoanalysis*, pp. 8-12, 43.

15. *Three Essays on the Theory of Sexuality*, p. 88.

16. When describing the behavioral patterns of the instincts Freud explains that "what we see is a great number of component instincts arising from different areas and regions of the body, which strive for satisfaction fairly independently of one another and find that satisfaction in something that we may call 'organic pleasure.' " "Anxiety and Instinctual Life" (1933), *Complete Introductory Lectures on Psychoanalysis*, p. 562.

17. *Three Essays on the Theory of Sexuality*, pp. 95, 107, 138-139; Freud speaks of instinctual fusion, defusion, alloys, blends, combinations, admixtures, and so forth. "The Libido Theory" (1922), *Collected Papers*, 5 (New York: Basic Books, 1959), p. 135; *The Ego and the Id*, pp. 20, 31-32, 44; "The Economic Problem in Masochism" (1924), *Collected Papers*, 2 (New York: Basic Books, 1959), p. 260; *The Problem of Anxiety* (1926) (New York: Norton, 1963), p. 46; "Analysis Terminable and Interminable" (1937), *Collected Papers*, 5, p. 345; *An Outline of Psychoanalysis*, p. 43.

18. This important biological organization of the component instincts first occurs at the third and phallic phase and is finalized at puberty, the genital stage of development. I have referred to the third (phallic) phase of biological organization as the genital stage so that

the psychological differences associated with male and female childhood development commencing with the onset of the phallic phase but not relevant to this discussion can be dispensed with. The overriding concern here is simply with the biological subordination of the component instincts to the genital sphere, which is common to both sexes and which Freud clearly argued is initiated in the third phase. He says, for example, that "in the early phases the different component instincts set about their pursuit of pleasure independently of one another; in the phallic phase there are the beginnings of an organization which subordinates the other urges to the primacy of the genitals and signifies the start of a coordination of the genital urge toward pleasure into the sexual function." *An Outline of Psychoanalysis*, p. 12. And, Freud explains, "the third phase is that known as the phallic one, which is, as it were, a forerunner of the final [genital] form taken by sexual life and already much resembles it" (p. 11). Whenever the issue is the biological subordination of the instincts to the genital sphere it has been a common practice in psychoanalytic literature to refer to the third phase as the genital stage of development.

19. *Eros and Civilization*, p. 55.

20. Ibid., pp. 32-33.

21. Ibid., p. 22.

22. Marcuse acknowledges that the aggressive drives also strive for pleasurable satisfaction. His point is considered later in this chapter and taken up again in chapter five, pp. 243-244, 256.

23. *Eros and Civilization*, p. 81.

24. *Three Essays on the Theory of Sexuality*, p. 136.

25. Sigmund Freud, "Instincts and Their Vicissitudes" (1915), *Collected Papers*, 4, p. 65.

26. *Civilization and Its Discontents*, p. 51.

27. Sigmund Freud, "The Most Prevalent Form of Degradation in Erotic Life" (1912), *Collected Papers*, 4, p. 214.

28. *Civilization and Its Discontents*, p. 52.

29. Sigmund Freud, *Beyond the Pleasure Principle* (1920) (New York: Bantam, 1967), p. 77.

30. Herbert Marcuse, "Eros and Culture," *Cambridge Review*, 1, 3 (Cambridge: 1955), p. 119.

31. *Eros and Civilization*, p. 83.

32. Freud's most famous statement regarding sublimation as desexualization, and the one most often quoted by those who subscribe to Marcuse's position that sublimation is by nature a form of domination, is to be found in *The Ego and the Id*, p. 44. But even this remark does not support Marcuse's contention because in this context Freud is speaking not of sublimation in general but of a particular kind of sub-

limation, "identification," and of particular sorts of identifications, those that define the character of the superego.

33. *Eros and Civilization*, pp. 84-85.

34. Ibid., p. 86.

35. See chapter five, p. 256.

36. In *Eros and Civilization* Marcuse uses a great variety of terms interchangeably to denote what he means by a "rationality of gratification" (p. 228)—"libidinal rationality" (p. 199), "libidinal morality" and "sensuous rationality" (p. 228), and so forth. I propose the term "second dimension" to convey Marcuse's intention.

37. *Three Essays on the Theory of Sexuality*, p. 53.

38. "Eros and Culture," p. 111.

39. *Eros and Civilization*, p. 161.

40. Ibid.

41. Ibid., p. 166.

42. Ibid., p. 162.

43. *Beyond the Pleasure Principle*, pp. 68, 71.

44. *Eros and Civilization*, p. 164.

45. Ibid., pp. 168-169.

46. *Beyond the Pleasure Principle*, p. 21.

47. *Eros and Civilization*, pp. 234-235.

48. *Civilization and Its Discontents*, p. 69.

49. *The Ego and the Id*, pp. 31-32.

50. Ibid., p. 36.

51. *Civilization and Its Discontents*, p. 85.

52. Ibid., pp. 75-76.

53. *The Ego and the Id*, p. 43.

54. *Civilization and Its Discontents*, p. 80.

55. *An Outline of Psychoanalysis*, p. 7.

56. *Civilization and Its Discontents*, p. 67.

57. Immanuel Kant, *Critique of Judgement* (New York: Hafner, 1968), p. 27.

58. Herbert Marcuse, *Counterrevolution and Revolt* (Boston: Beacon, 1972), p. 64.

59. Ibid., p. 68.

60. Ibid., pp. 68-69.

61. *Karl Marx: Early Writings*, edited by T. B. Bottomore (New York: McGraw-Hill, 1964), p. 155.

FOUR

Civilization Without Discontents I: Domination—Political or Technological?

Fairwell, happy fields,
Where joy forever dwells! Hail, horrors! hail,
Infernal world! and thou, profoundest Hell,
Receive thy new possessor, one who brings
A mind not to be changed by place or time.

Milton, *Paradise Lost*

MARCUSE'S ANALYSIS OF the transformation undergone by modern capitalism may seem strangely out of place in an era marked by social decomposition and crises of a universal and unprecedented scope. As "advanced industrial society" is described throughout most of his later work, this new form of modern capitalism could not have been thought to be verging on environmental catastrophe, crippling energy shortages, urban decay, the deterioration of educational institutions at all levels, the dissolution of the family, widespread psychological disorders and retreat into the most private spheres of psychic life, crime and drug abuse of epidemic proportions, renewed possibilities for grave international confrontation over arms agreements and competition for influencing the developing areas of the world, unbridled inflation and unemployment, extensive underemploy-

131

ment and "felt" occupational dissatisfaction, a fiscal crisis of the welfare state threatening the provision of social services to the poor, the disadvantaged, and the aged, as well as to the general public, and, perhaps least to be anticipated in light of Marcuse's portrait, a motivation crisis translating into the individual's unwillingness to support a social system no longer able to guarantee rewards and meet expectations, and a legitimation crisis characterized by political disaffection from the governmental and industrial complex.[1]

In fairness to Marcuse, against this attack on his analytical shortsightedness there could and should be a retort to the effect that Marcuse's critical theory never departs from an orthodox Marxist belief in the persistent and insoluble crisis orientation of capitalism. Two themes, the "final crisis of capitalism" and "socialism or barbarism" (Rosa Luxemburg's historically necessary alternatives to a crisis-prone capitalist economy), endure in writings spanning Marcuse's entire career. They appear consistently whether his focus is on capitalism, as it is in "The Struggle against Liberalism in the Totalitarian View of the State" (1934), *Reason and Revolution* (1941), and *Counterrevolution and Revolt* (1972), or on advanced industrial society, as it is in *One-dimensional Man* (1964).

Despite this standing prognosis of a final crisis, however, with the exception of *Counterrevolution and Revolt* and the work immediately prior and leading up to it,[2] Marcuse continually stressed that in advanced industrial society

1. all material and intellectual sectors of the society are organized to conform to a central ideological dynamic, a repressive rationality of material productivity;

2. all structural contradictions and antagonisms can be managed and contained, perhaps indefinitely;

3. individual hopes, needs, fears, and aspirations are scientifically determined and coordinated with the society as a whole;

4. the great majority of people are comfortable, enjoy and are completely unaware of being manipulated, such that a smooth, efficient, nonterroristic, and democratic unfreedom prevails;

5. absolutely no genuine and effective opposition to the social order is discernible;

6. qualitative change can be prevented for the foreseeable future;

7. critical discussion, where it occurs, is shaped by and limited to the norms of the established social system;

8. tendencies eventually come to dominate that extinguish the vital mental space for the development of individual autonomy and critical capacities;

9. alienation among men, of man from nature, and from his labor has become total; and

10. the entirety of social relations has been hammered into a totally administered, completely integrated, perfectly uniform, pleasant, and hermetically sealed existence to which there is no challenge and from which there is no escape.

All of these claims are elaborated and defended in Marcuse's theory of technological domination and one-dimensional society. From their enormous scope and implications it is obvious that his theory must be as complex as it appears formidable. In this chapter and the next, my goal is to examine Marcuse's theory systematically and critically. In the chapter to follow, the psychological underpinnings of Marcuse's theory will be the focus. The initial half of this chapter will concentrate on the architecture of the theory, drawing out the basic elements of technical reason and tracing the extension of technological rationality into all sectors of society. It is precisely this technological enclosure of the entire society that reduces it to a single dimension. In the critical, second half of this chapter, analysis will unearth from Marcuse's theory its implicit concept of the individual, who is supposedly the helpless victim of the astringent ideological pressures of modern civilization.

I will argue that underlying Marcuse's analysis of a society he determines to be one-dimensional is a conception of human nature that is itself one-dimensional. Marcuse's analysis entails such a minimal set of anthropological characteristics that there can be no surprise when he declares the individual annulled, totally integrated into a repressive set of productive relations. Last, the discussion will critically study many of the sectors of society that Marcuse contends are organized by technological rationality to conform to its ends. The objective of critical analysis is to rediscover a subject, individuals or groups of individuals, influencing or able to influence the structure and outcome of social processes wherever Marcuse has discerned only the influence of technological reason. In other words, the overriding objective of this chapter (and the next) is the same as that of chapters two and three—to reinstate subjectivity, in particular the individual's critical capacity and a degree of individual autonomy, as an active and dynamic force in social life against a theory in which the subject continually vanishes.

Formative Influences on the Theory of Technological Domination

Capitalism, as Marcuse understands it, has evolved into a qualitatively new social formation. "New forms of control" have replaced traditional methods of political and economic administration, which once preserved the frequently awkward stability of earlier stages of economic growth. Domination has been brought to consummate perfection through the rationality of technological processes.

Two major influences, one of a historical and the other of a theoretical nature, have figured prominently in the development of this fundamental but nonetheless radical thesis of Marcuse's critical theory. Historically, National Socialism dramatically proved the effectiveness of a technologically resourceful and calculating economic organization in securing totalitarian rule. Published in the United States during the year of its entry into the Second World War, "Some Social Implications of Modern Technology" is Marcuse's first discussion of technological domination. After a very brief introductory remark explaining what he means by technology and why he considers it significant, a passage follows that is quite instructive about what prompted Marcuse to recognize technology to be a crucial feature of every modern society.

> National Socialism is a striking example of the ways in which a highly rationalized and mechanized economy with the utmost efficiency in production can operate in the interest of totalitarian op-

pression and continued scarcity. The Third Reich is indeed a form of "technocracy": the technical considerations of imperialistic efficiency and rationality supersede the traditional standards of profitability and general welfare. In National Socialist Germany, the reign of terror is sustained not only by brute force which is foreign to technology but also by the ingenious manipulation of the power inherent in technology: the intensification of labor, propaganda, the training of youths and workers, the organization of the governmental, industrial, and party bureaucracy—all of which constitute the daily implements of terror—follow the lines of greatest technological efficiency. This terroristic technocracy cannot be attributed to the exceptional requirements of "war economy"; war economy is rather the normal state of the National Socialist ordering of the social and economic process, and technology is one of the chief stimuli of this ordering.[3]

When Marcuse refers to the Third Reich as a technocracy, he is not suggesting that Fascist Germany be regarded as a society ruled by scientists and engineers. With this initial study of the relationship between politics and technology, technocracy appears as a system *partially* determined by "technics," the technical apparatus of science, industry, the military, government, political organization, education, communication, transportation, and so forth. Politics, it must be stressed, in Marcuse's estimation continues to remain the decisive force in establishing the priorities of totalitarian society. But the sweeping economic, social, and political changes demanded by the totalitarian regime, which prevailed at the unqualified expense of all considerations for the public well-being, required the harnessing of technological to political power. Technical knowledge was an indispensable device to sustain political control.

When taking notice that Marcuse underscores politics as the essential factor in deciding the objectives of National Socialism, the observation must not obscure the principal thesis regarding the deeper nature of the relationship between politics and technology as it is first expressed in the passage on National Socialism. To be precise, technology is Janus-faced. Technics is a social process, a materially conditioning factor in social organization. How great a factor? Despite the obvious authority politics wields, technics is not neutral, but it is also not unambiguously a mode of domination in itself. In 1941 we find Marcuse retaining an implicit distinction between technological domination and the power of domination inherent in technology. This distinction is not the same as that between political ends and technological means. Totalitarian objectives, which include universal manipulation of human thought and action, could not be realized in a framework that did not embrace technology. Offering unique possibilities for domination, technology in the Third Reich appears for the first time to be a form of control in itself.

So while National Socialism's reliance upon technology as an instrument of domination has long been recognized, Marcuse's argument breaks new ground. Once technology and totalitarian politics are understood to be tied together indissolubly, then the totalitarian ends derivative from technology are not ends formally identical to those of National Socialism. National Socialism, in a bizarre sense, is totalitarianism in excess. It employs a "brute [political] force which is foreign to technology,"[4] but up to or beyond the point at which brute force is practiced fascism contains another political and social framework that, although not inclined to terror, possesses an inherent disposition to *universal* domination. This framework is technics itself! In his later work, particularly in four essays exploring the psychological underpinnings of technological domination — "Freedom and Freud's Theory of Instincts" (1957), "Progress and Freud's Theory of Instincts" (1957), "The Obsolescence of the Freudian Concept of Man" (1963), and "Aggressiveness in Advanced Industrial Society" (1967) — and in *One-dimensional Man*, this thesis undergoes a consequential development. In a political setting whose social, economic, and political goals and problems are defined and solved in a *technical* manner, the Janus-like quality of technology is cast off and technology emerges as *the* relation of domination, as the ideological factor that determines all other social factors. Modern capitalism increasingly manages its affairs technically and, depoliticized, becomes advanced industrial society. Capitalism, National Socialism, and, as we shall see, Soviet totalitarianism all hold this technical base in common. Ultimately, Marcuse will argue that this similarity proves to be more important than their differences.

By virtue of the features of technology revealed through the role it assumed in maintaining and extending Fascist domination, National Socialism does appear as a noteworthy influence on the development of Marcuse's analysis of modern industrial societies. Still, though National Socialism could not fail to disclose the secret of its existence, Marcuse requires a theoretical perspective to grasp the real meaning of technics.

Max Weber has certainly made the greatest single contribution to Marcuse's efforts. This claim may seem unusual because Marcuse never acknowledges the Weberian influence; indeed, one of his better known essays, "Industrialization and Capitalism in the Work of Max Weber," is an attack on Weber, thus further concealing his debt. Yet, beginning with "Some Social Implications of Modern Technology," Marcuse's writings on technology closely reproduce Weber's analysis of technical rationality as domination per se. Marcuse focuses, as Weber had predominantly, on the evolution of formal rationality within the social relations of capitalism. At the conclusion of the point by point exposition of Marcuse's theory of technological domination, which will follow shortly, we will be in a position to measure the influence of Weber on Marcuse. At that time the great similarities and few differences between them can be discussed. For now I want only to suggest that without Weber's thorough and groundbreaking examination of the relationship between capitalism and formal rationality, it is very likely that there would have been no "studies of the ideology of advanced industrial society."[5]

After Weber a host of lesser and ideologically disparate influences on Marcuse's view of technological rationality can be charted easily. Their bearing is apparent though, as with Weber, superficially acknowledged. In fact, it is much more accurate to say that such sources as Lewis Mumford (*Technics and Civilization*), Thorstein Veblen (*The Instinct of Workmanship*), Oswald Spengler (*Man and Technics*), Jean-Paul Sartre (*The Critique of Dialectical Reason*), Martin Heidegger (*Holzwege*), and Gaston Bachelard (*L'Activité rationaliste de la physique contemporaine*) should be judged less as influences than as authoritative supports for a thesis springing from Weber.

The same must be said of many of the analyses produced by the members of the Frankfurt Institute for Social Research during the early years of its residency in America. This material is particularly useful in getting an accurate bearing on the origins of Marcuse's views of technological rationality, for it corresponds in time to the publication of "Some Social Implications of Modern Technology."

While there are important differences among them, particularly centering around the issue of the nature of the Fascist state in relation to the economic and political reorganization of capital, Friedrich Pollock ("State Capitalism: Its Possibilities and Limitations"; "Is National Socialism a New World Order?"; and a much earlier 1932 piece, "The Current Plight of Capitalism and the Prospects for a Planned Economic Reorganization"), A. R. L. Gurland ("Technological Trends and Economic Structure under National Socialism"), Franz Neumann (*Behemoth*), and Max Horkheimer ("Authoritarian State") all are concerned to some degree with the advancement of technological rationalization and its potential for domination.[6] A debate that appears to have crystallized from their studies on fascism — over whether Fascist domination means state capitalism at the expense of the interests of private capital (Pollock and Horkheimer), a petit bourgeois antimonopolistic but expanding government sector that benefits from its protectionism of profit and the power of big business (Gurland), or a totalitarian politics that commands and disciplines the growth of a durable monopoly capitalism against existing business concerns (Neumann) — does not seem to have seized Marcuse's attention to the same degree. It is true, as has been pointed out elsewhere, that in *Reason and Revolution* Marcuse's position on this specific issue is closest to that of Neumann. And, I would add, Neumann's view is prefigured somewhat in Marcuse's 1934 essay "The Struggle against Liberalism in the Totalitarian View of the State."[7]

As of 1941, however, the terms of the debate begin to change for Marcuse. No longer is he directly concerned with the possible evolution of fascism out of the structure of capitalism during its crisis periods, as he is in the 1934 article and in passing in *Reason and Revolution*. He becomes preoccupied with the significance of technological development. In this context all the recent studies of the Institute's members become salient regardless of theoretical differences, for taken together they offer an excellent impression of the relative contributions made by capital and the state to the development and application of technics. But qualification must now be added. It is important to note that a comparison of their work with Marcuse's "Some Social Implications of Modern Technology" shows the latter essay to contain a far richer discussion and deeper understanding of technological reason. Following that brief but important passage on the technocratic character of National Socialism, the article concentrates in detailed fashion on the growth and implications of technology within American capitalism. The Institute's work on the Fascist state, therefore, cannot be considered more than a minor influence on the substantive development of Marcuse's theory of technological domination. Moreover, because it is clear that *One-dimensional Man* and the essays dealing with the psychological aspects of technological domination continue to be informed heavily by the first 1941 article on the social implications of technology, Horkheimer's later *Eclipse of Reason* and his collaborative effort with Adorno, *The Dialectic of Enlightenment*, both classics dealing with the history of technical reason, had an impact of similar magnitude on the subsequent elaboration of Marcuse's theory of technological domination.

Before examining Marcuse's arguments about technological rationality and domination, two final influences on his view of technics deserve mention. It is doubtful that Georg Lukács contributed significantly to Marcuse's mature investigations of the technological organization of modern society. In this area Lukács would have proven to be only a poor copy of his teacher, Max Weber. Offering an analytic framework of substantially reduced scope, *History and Class Consciousness* would have severely eclipsed the theoretical conclusions Marcuse drew with the aid of the more fertile Weberian system. Last, Edmund Husserl's *Crisis of the European Sciences* informed Marcuse's critique of science and for that reason merits attention when considering Marcuse's views of the relationship between science and technology and his enigmatic conception of the "new science."[8]

To summarize, National Socialism brought the implications of technology into sharp relief for Marcuse and, as suggested, Weber's analysis of formal rationality provided the theoretical tools enabling Marcuse to grasp the significance of technics. Having attempted to ferret out the probable and ostensible influences on Marcuse's views on technology, we can now proceed critically to explicate the essential elements of technological rationality.[9]

Basic Elements of Technological Rationality

Simply stated, whenever Marcuse speaks of technological rationality he is referring to the modus operandi of the process of material production. He appears to construe production in the
broadest possible sense: all sectors of industrial enterprise—the
whole military-industrial complex, as well as the entire distribu-
tive network of goods and services—are included. In the capitalist countries, manufacture and distribution are co-regulated by
the state and monopolistic concerns, while the task of economic
management falls exclusively to the state within the developed
socialist and communist countries. There is a decisive point that
situates technological rationality within the noncapitalist as well
as the capitalist orbit: the gradual concentration of economic
power, in the sense that the economic mode of production becomes the sector of society determining all other modes of activity, occurs far less as an expression of capital's interest in the
profitable elimination of competition than as a necessary result
of utilizing technological opportunities for the constant development of a productive apparatus that can create more goods more
efficiently.

The dynamics of this process can be described clearly. By its
nature, technology can be exploited most effectively as technological units are progressively bound together into an organic
whole. All parts contributing to technology's operation—individuals, groups, classes, machines, corporations, conglomerates,
and so on—constitute its division of labor. In capitalist, socialist,
and communist countries, the organization of the economy is
propelled by this technological logic of concentration and unification, though under capitalism it is the motive to compete successfully that compels business to adopt the latest technologies.
But in all social systems the uniform result is the reproduction
of technological rationality on an ever wider societal scale. Ever
larger units of production are formed with labor divided according to more elaborately specialized subsystems obedient to fewer
centers of control. Regardless of ideological variations, governmental power follows the pattern laid down by the organization
of production. It expands, centralizes, bureaucratizes, and ra-
tionalizes at a pace set by the exigencies of technologically determined productivity. Thus, the state-capital collaboration char-

acteristic of modern capitalism, the totalitarian state peculiar to contemporary communism, and the democratic state centralism of the developed socialist societies necessarily emerge to insure economic growth *originally* made possible through technological achievements. Given just these few aspects of a technologically ordered process of production considered at a macrolevel of analysis, the technological dynamic that creates Marcuse's one-dimensional society, where all relations are identical to technological relations, begins to crystallize.

This dynamic assumes greater clarity when the elements of technical logic are exposed. At first hearing, "technological reason" seems an odd notion. It is not customary to assign mental powers such as thought and judgment to inanimate objects. Yet, in certain terms that is what is implied by the expression, and it is necessary to keep this point in mind if Marcuse's thesis of technological domination is to be intelligible.

Technological reason means that there are characteristics universal to all technical processes, and these characteristics come to prevail in society to the same extent as does technology. Essential to technics is the discipline and control of production ("regimentation"), the pursual of a narrowly defined means of material and intellectual endeavor ("specialization"), and the absolute uniformity of all regimented and specialized labor ("standardization"). Regimentation, specialization, and standardization together contribute to the precision, calculability, and efficiency of production. Through regimentation all tasks are carried out in accordance with the elaboration of precise and strictly binding rules. Personal qualities, such as reflection and discretion on matters relating to means and ends, and individual initiative are thus removed from the production process. Their removal serves to enhance the predictability of production. Calculability, precision, and predictability increase as the units of labor and production become smaller. Efficient management of productivity follows automatically from this specialization. Standardized techniques establish criteria of performance and define specific types of refined skills and training indifferent to individual distinctions in aptitude, knowledge, and insight. A point to be emphasized, then, is that the concept of individuality embedded in the *logic of technique* limits human capacity to objective measurements to which the agent must unconditionally comply if the rationality of production is to be sustained. Thought and action are transformed into reflex, habit, and reaction.

Technological processes are therefore surrounded by a matter of factness dictating that production be approached with passive attitudes, as though technics contained a will of its own to which all other wills need be subordinated. Nothing that any individual thinks or feels can affect given, determinate operations. Technological rationality proposes, discriminates, judges, excludes, and decides. Its logic establishes a universal language pattern that is to be learned, elaborated through extended application, but cannot be altered.

As technics penetrates or extends to new modes of experience, technical reason becomes ubiquitous and its objectivity completely reshapes the individual subject's activity with which it makes contact. All those engaged in the occupations and professions salient to the productive process share a framework of experience rationalized by technology. Like so many atomic particles, individuals are sorted into a division of labor to perform specialized functions. Thoroughly fragmented, with his mental and physical energies absorbed by a narrow sphere of activity, the individual loses the ability to comprehend the underlying social dimensions of the productive process. In this way the technical control of production is translated into the political control of the laborer.

Rationalization especially affects the working class in a variety of new and significant ways. First, technologically rationalized industry deforms the worker's mental faculties perhaps more than it exhausts his physical strength. In *History and Class Consciousness*, Lukács had argued that there is a greater opportunity for the development of a rebellious attitude in the proletarian than in the bureaucrat for as the worker is not occupied with "mental labor," as is common to bureaucratic tasks, this free mental space leaves him susceptible to a critical perspective.[10] Marcuse's analysis, however, indicates that the technical coordination of mental as well as physical skills, which also entails a debilitating psychological tension, paralyzes the only capacities that could enable the worker to acquire a critical view of a repressive social order. As Marcuse says, "This kind of masterly enslavement is not essentially different from that of the typist, the bank teller, the high pressure salesman or saleswoman, and the television announcer. Standardization and the routine assimilate productive and non-productive jobs."[11] This point is of great significance. Here Marcuse has indicated that the technical rationalization of the productive process subjects *all* individuals at *all* levels of production, including the working-class individual, to the same mechanism of domination. Technological domination becomes as ubiquitous as technological rationalization; as the latter moves toward universality so does the former.

Second, rationalization extends the process of production into a comprehensive technological system that alters the relation of the working class to the means of production. As technical reason integrates production at all levels, the immediate process of production increasingly falls directly under the control of management. Consequently, the working class is less salient to the operation of the productive apparatus and hence less of a politically disabling threat.

Third, rationalization has reduced the overall number of workers in economic sectors. Increasingly reduced in numbers, the working class ceases to be the largest class within society, and its possible subversive impact on production further declines.

Last, modern industrial reform—from profit sharing to the schemes of workers' participation in management and workers' self-management—has encouraged workers to make production problems their problems, with the result that the class distinction between management and labor is erased. Opposing class interests are "technically" dissolved and a new common cause evolves from technological rationalization. A feeling of well-being among workers, and solidarity among workers, management, and capital is fostered, transforming dull proletarian labor into "rewarding activity."

As Marcuse describes them, all the elements of technical logic and the changes in the nature of work introduced by technical reason retard the growth of the individual subject's critical faculties and force the "historical subject," the working class, into precipitous decline.

Other decisive aspects of production and social relations are transformed through rationalization. Control over the goals of the productive process must shift from the owners of the means of production to a location outside the plant, to the universities and private research laboratories. Crucial decisions about what

is to be produced must always be referred to the class of specialists who know objectively what is feasible in terms of the attained
level of scientific knowledge and available resources. Unable to
separate the ends of production from the technical means, the
technician turns questions concerning what is to be produced
and what purposes the production process is to serve into questions limited to *how* production must occur. The transfer of control from political to technical authority precludes opposition to
the ideology of productivity for its own sake. For as their experience with technology has always been shaped by its growth and
development, technicians are singularly inclined to propose and
approve only those projects that follow the rationality of the productive process, from the errand of refining particular techniques to the task of increasing the efficiency and productivity of
the overall process. The technical class is precisely the group
least able to initiate change in the mode of technological organization for it has acquired a historically shaped, or "mediated,"
nature that opposes the arrest of the technological project. Thus,
as technological rationality organizes social relations around
technical logic, technical rather than class status, the ideology of
production rather than the ideology of producers, determines all
goals. Capitalists become bureaucrats, and political domination
becomes administrative rule.

As technological rationalization is advanced, even before the
individual enters the production process his critical faculties are
affected. Already a reality in communist countries and a visible
tendency under capitalism, all levels of education invaded by
technological rationality gravitate toward vocational training.[12]
Because the individual is taught by the educational system to ex-
ecute only the objectively required specialized tasks of production, the growth of individual capacities is inhibited. Sculpted to
carry out simplistic technical operations devoid of personalistic
differences, individual rationality is exchanged for the rationality of technics. Suffering a total loss of personal identity, individuals have been re-formed *essentially* into a crowd and emerge as
faceless members of an association cemented together and swept
along by the movement of an autonomous and self-determining
technological structure.

Originally, technological reason operates not only in accordance with its own laws but equally according to the laws of mass
production. The fate of the individual and class subject, then, is

initially a political fate, determined by technological reason as it unfolds within capitalism. Capital establishes productivity as the goal to which all its efforts and resources must be directed. The material standard of living is improved continually and physical existence is made easier and more comfortable for greater numbers of people. Overproduction, the classic economic crisis of earlier stages of capitalism, is prevented by planned obsolescence, an application of technical knowledge that streamlines and insulates the economic system against such tremors resulting from the internal contradictions of capital. Indeed, planned obsolescence seems to be implied by technological rationality: technical reason obliges production costs to be kept to the barest minimum, which in turn influences the types, quantity, and quality of goods and services to be produced.

Having diminished (real) scarcity, technics also promises a constant reduction in physical and mental labor (basic repression).[13] This is the secret in the perverted elimination of subjectivity by technological rationality. As individual reason is sacrificed to the hegemony of technical logic, subjectivity assumes the purely objective properties of technics. In a strict sense, at this point the individual subject can be apprehended only in the abstract, as an idea no longer having a substantive counterpart. Yet, a progressive feature shows through the technical abolition of subjectivity. The actual dispensability of the individual is proved, for an apparatus that develops the logic and potential of technics to its extreme could become fully automated. As Marcuse puts it, "The elimination of human potentialities from the world of (alienated) labor creates the preconditions for the elimination of labor from the world of human potentialities."[14] This emancipatory dimension of technics, appearing in an alienated form in capitalism, is suppressed by the scientific management of material and cultural needs. Surplus labor is perpetuated by the creation of artificial needs and the individual, harnessed "voluntarily" to a semi-automated apparatus, maintains his status as subject in abstraction.

Two processes occurring simultaneously and interrelated dynamically have been examined. They now emerge as the key to understanding Marcuse's critique of the ideology of advanced industrial society. First, capital develops technological rationality as the universal medium of human labor and human exchange. Technics becomes the historical object (goal) of a particular his-

torical class subject, the bourgeoisie. Second, corresponding to
the evolution of technical reason is the gradual but steady erosion of the individual's subjective capacities. Considering these
processes as one, as the class subject develops technics, the individual subject is developed by technics. Marcuse argues, for example, that "technics hampers individual development only
insofar as [individuals] are tied to a social apparatus which perpetuates scarcity."[15] Eventually, a decisive change takes place.
Technics becomes omnipresent and appears as "reason"; that is,
it acquires the rationality attributed to objectivity and universality by virtue of having become both. The individual subject's
rational capacities have receded proportionately. Technics' rational character is fully a product of its objective universality *and*
the recession of the subject's capacity, not just claim, to reason.
The roles of subject and object have undergone a complete reversal!

With regard to the working-class subject, in response to these
pressures the respective interests of the opposing classes of capitalism have not been merely reconciled. Marcuse's analysis of
technological society does not amount to an *embourgeoisement*
thesis, despite his pronounced emphasis on the scientific management of needs and the political moderation that accompanies
affluence and a rising standard of living. If such were the case,
Marcuse would offer nothing more than a sophisticated "end of
ideology" argument. His analysis, however, runs far deeper.

Technics does not impose a single collective interest that simply cuts across class cleavages as though the latter would re-
emerge at any time the productive apparatus seriously faltered.
Technological rationality materially reconstitutes class society
into a single homogeneous mass. As its defining characteristic,
its technological essence makes it proper to speak of this mass as
a monolithic technical class. The traditional restriction of "technical class" to those with scientific expertise, who now appear as
technics' special managerial class, can no longer be maintained
in light of Marcuse's critical theory. The mass become technical
functionaries in the realm of production. And, equally important, the mass become technical functionaries in the realm of
consumption, too. As mentioned, the goal of productivity for its
own sake immediately translates into the technical manipulation
of needs, which lubricates the wheels of productivity.

As the *fons et origo* of technological reason, productivity had been, without interruption, inextricably bound to technics. With the debilitation of individual subjectivity there is no cognitive lever, no rationality to question the necessity of this relationship. Speculation on the employment of technology without qualifying its every possible use by a concern for its productive output becomes inconceivable. Technological rationality is, at one and the same time, both means and ends. It supersedes the comparatively primitive instrumental rationality that implies a firm distinction between means and ends and that presupposes an individual subject able to contest the norms that technology necessarily administers. In the final analysis, technics qua productivity becomes an end as such.

Here we are taken to Marcuse's conception of politics. Politics is the expression of an autonomous reasoning faculty that is able to distinguish between the rationality of private and public needs, interests, and norms. It is likewise the capacity to evaluate and judge the various claims of these spheres. By eroding this capacity to think critically and reflectively, which is the very essence of subjectivity, "technical rationality cancels politics as a separate and independent function — political problems become technical problems."[16] What comes to pass for politics is, in the technical sense, political *process*, a ritualized series of predetermined operations designed to secure the efficient and periodical exchange of leaders whose function is to pledge to maintain the productive apparatus in peak form. The mass submit to a plebiscitary democracy wherein politics is actually a part of the technical division of labor and is removed from the real political problems that the plebiscitary leadership redefines in technical terms. With universal technical guidelines at this leadership's disposal for managing political problems, "control of the capitalist economy not only requires no special qualification, it is also to a great degree fungible" (interchangeable).[17] That technical, unlike political, leaders are interchangeable in effect dispenses with leaders. The reduction of politics to technics, moreover, recasts politics in a language that the mass, completely dependent on the technical-administrative apparatus, cannot grasp.

Although it is certain that Marcuse's critique of technological rationality is clearly no end of ideology thesis, his argument takes that position several steps further. The *embourgeoisement* theorists identify a minimal set of ideological principles all revolving around affluence. They demonstrate in what manner these principles constitute a unifying set of beliefs that bind modern society together by overriding an array of socioeconomic, geographical, religious, racial, ethnic, and cultural cleavages. The implication of Marcuse's theory, on the other hand, is that a society shaped by a technological mode of production dispenses with organizing principles whose role is to create a working equilibrium between state and society. On two accounts the task of legitimation has grown obsolete—in the wake of the technological unification of society as a mechanical system of interrelated and interdependent parts, which eliminates any problems that would call the legitimacy of the system into question, and with the disappearance of an individual who might require justification for the norms to which the social system is committed. Because the new elements of societal cohesion are purely functional and structural, there is no political and ideological hegemony "from above," no ideological domination by a state acting on behalf of a ruling class. Technological rationality is an ideology of domination that is rooted in a technical base co-extensive with the structure of capitalism's social, economic, and political relations. But technics has substituted technical relations in their place. From the standpoint of political rule, there is no dominant or subaltern political class. The rulers and the ruled are now identical. The interests of the ruling class are newly embodied in technics precisely at that moment when that class's rule is abolished by technics. Technical reason is the real historical expression of a social class that required its self-annihilation fully to realize its inner historical truth. Its annihilation, therefore, is an aspect of that truth.

This discussion brings us to one other point that deserves mention before moving on. Marcuse's theory of technological domination questions the contemporary relevance of the Marxist theory of the state. Against Marx, Marcuse's argument demonstrates that at the more advanced stages of capitalism, the state becomes a simple expression of the technical base. It is no longer charged with the task, as it was during the earlier stages of capitalism, of generating ideological principles or political solutions that would protect the interests of the entire bourgeoisie by unifying a society divided by class interests. This function becomes obsolete because the state comes to share the general fate of subjectivity. Depoliticized, no longer in possession of the capacity to formulate policies other than those narrowly circumscribed by technical reason, the state loses its quasi-independence from the relations of production. This results from the state's assimilation to the universal rationality of technics. The stability of modern capitalism, or rather of advanced industrial society, then would depend upon the effectiveness of technical reason.

The previous discussion has focused on an exposition of the fundamental elements of Marcuse's analysis of technological rationality as it unfolds as a mode of domination within modern capitalism. Technological rationality is a rationality of domination because it eliminates the capacity of all class and individual subjects to form or re-form the goals of society and social relations. Capitalism undergoes a qualitative change precipitated by the quantitative growth of technology. It is transformed into advanced industrial society. At this new stage, domination is a direct function of a technologically rationalized productive apparatus that develops only to reproduce its ability to develop further.

It has been shown that the basic elements of technological domination derive from the technical development of the productive process. And as indicated, these elements are reproduced in all institutions related directly to the management of production, such as the state and research and educational institutions. But the spread of technological rationality does not end with production and those institutions directly related to it. It extends to all cultural and political spheres of society, as well. As these sectors, such as language, the ideologies of political parties, social science, and philosophy, gradually are brought under the influence of technical reason, these forms of thought become technical forms of social discourse. Losing all independence from the rationality of society's basic production relations, cultural and political discourse cease to be critical of the relations and goals of a technologically organized society. All sectors of society begin to conform to the logic of technics. Consequently, the next step in the exposition of Marcuse's theory will be to examine his analysis of the technological organization of the cultural and political spheres of society. This will complete the picture of his theory of one-dimensional society.

As a transition to this important dimension of Marcuse's theory, his analysis of Soviet society merits consideration. There are several reasons for pursuing this course of exposition.

First, published before *One-dimensional Man*, *Soviet Marxism* (1958) builds upon Marcuse's earlier work on technics and clearly and concisely sets forth the complex relations between the basic elements of technological rationality and the cultural spheres of society. It is, therefore, useful as an aid to grasping securely the general theory of technological domination and one-dimensional society. In fact, *Soviet Marxism* is near to an exact theoretical counterpart to Marcuse's subsequent *One-dimensional Man*. In the second work, arguments occasionally are duplicated almost verbatim from the earlier study.[18] Of course, there are theoretical differences, such as Marcuse's concept of "repressive desublimation," which is fully developed in *One-dimensional Man*.[19] (Repressive desublimation forms part of the psychological underpinnings of one-dimensionality and will be discussed in the next chapter.)

Second, the analysis of Soviet domination as technological domination explains the earlier point that according to Marcuse's theory, capitalism, fascism, and Soviet totalitarianism have a common technical base making technological domination their common denominator. In light of what they reveal about the nature of technical reason, as social systems their similarity is ultimately more important than their political and ideological differences.

Last, for both of these reasons Marcuse's *Soviet Marxism* is an important study in itself. It supports the dominant Western view that Soviet domination is not simply political totalitarianism and challenges the Soviet claim that its institutions are neither oppressive nor anything less than a radical break with the principles of capitalism. When in the second half of this chapter the discussion critically examines Marcuse's theory of technological domination, the arguments of *Soviet Marxism* will be critically reviewed as well. For now, the discussion shall focus on presenting its arguments.

Soviet Totalitarianism as Technological Domination

The central thesis of *Soviet Marxism* is that the development of technological rationality, beginning with the rapid industrialization of the Soviet Union in the 1920s and carried out in an international context marked by the antagonistic competition of the communist and capitalist blocs, has determined all past and present and perhaps will determine all future characteristics of Soviet politics and society.

To consolidate the achievements of the revolution and to lay the groundwork for an authentic communist society and a worldwide communist movement, Lenin stressed the importance of bringing the Soviet Union to the same stage of material progress as Western civilization. The policy of rapid industrialization continued through the Stalinist regime. Its purpose was to create the material preconditions for a socialist society and was therefore consistent with Marx's theory of the historical stages that must necessarily be traveled on the road to socialism. During this first phase of socialist construction, individual needs were to be subordinated to the development of heavy industry. In this manner industrialization was to occur. Only after industrialization would there be a means to a social product that could be distributed according to individual needs. The emphasis on heavy industry rather than on a planned consumer economy is explained by the second major reason for the policy of rapid industrialization—the defense of the East from the danger of a capitalist onslaught. Heavy industry was the guarantee of self-preservation. The success of both goals required that the Soviet Union avoid military conflict with the West, which at any time during the U.S.S.R.'s undeveloped stage could only prove devastating to the revolution. This respite, which Lenin declared indispensable to industrialization, could permit the Soviets eventually to attain a level of economic strength competitive with that of capitalism. Once this level had been reached, the Soviet Union could relax its political regimentation of Soviet society. A period of liberalization would follow. Individual rights and freedoms would be restored, and consumer oriented industrial planning would be developed.

Marcuse points out, though, that the introduction of the period of liberalization is not so much an objective of Soviet society while it aspires to socialism as a strategy for subverting capitalism. Here we arrive at the third and equally important basis for the implementation of Lenin's policy of industrialization. The Soviets had consistently and stubbornly rejected the possibility of a permanent consolidation and cooperation among the capitalist powers. Marcuse argues that such an arrangement did emerge as a response to the common enemy of communism. The Soviet Union believed, however, that insuring its national defense by establishing economic parity with the West would safely allow it to alter its internal politics away from political and economic regimentation and in favor of liberalization and the satisfaction of consumer needs. And these changes, in combination with a policy of peaceful coexistence and its moderation of Western communist party politics, would transform communism's aggressive image. With the appearance of a substantially reduced threat of communism, the capitalist countries would become inclined to break their united anticommunist front. The capitalist powers would then revert to their prior and "normal" relations of inter-imperialist competition requiring the construction of a powerful war economy. The permanent war economy, while enriching some capitalists, forces investment in war industries, thus depressing the standard of living and plunging capitalism into an economic crisis. This crisis sharpens class antagonisms and restores the revolutionary potential of the international proletariat, which potential had receded with the conservatism of trade unions managed by a collaborative labor aristocracy. The Soviet policy of industrialization is in this fashion linked to the ultimate victory of world communism.

Marcuse does not proceed to analyze the weaknesses of the theoretical interrelationship of Soviet domestic and foreign policy. At times, however, he notes the faulty calculations of Soviet Marxism—such as the obsolete "orthodox" economic interpretation of capitalism, which blinded the Soviets to the durable and long-range character of the international capitalist consolidation, and the mistaken conviction that capitalism would not be able to maintain a war economy and a high standard of living simultaneously. Instead, Marcuse's examination pursued a different and more insightful direction. His argument succeeds brilliantly in illuminating the extent to which the Soviet policy of industrialization and the policies surrounding it were a reflex of the international constellation of ideological and political pressures. Given the danger presented by capitalism, the Soviets appear to have had no choice but to concentrate all energies on rapid industrialization through the development of heavy industry. Moreover, the pressures do not run in a single direction but are viciously circular. In the face of the Soviet Union's meteoric ascent to a world power, capitalism accelerates its economic development in turn, and this deadlock threatens endlessly to stoke the industrial fires of both sides.

Marcuse accounts for the repressive measures of the Soviet state by emphasizing the priorities forced upon it as a result of being situated within the capitalist environment. At the same time, when evaluating the ideological status of Soviet politics, he rejects as an analytical point of departure the labels "socialism" and "totalitarianism." Socialism is discarded because its conceptual validation requires a consensus on its meaning, difficult if not impossible to achieve. The traditional application of totalitarianism to substantially different social systems renders that term imprecise and ambiguous. In both cases, significant and revealing peculiarities of Soviet society would be excluded from view by such conceptually guided investigations. Instead, Marcuse is concerned with identifying the general features of the construction of Soviet society that have prevailed since its inception. Isolated are industrialization, the collectivization of agriculture, mechanization of labor, postponement of consumer needs until after economic equality with the West has been reached, the development of a work ethic and competitive efficiency, the elimination of elements critical of Soviet state policies, and the strengthening of state, military, party, and managerial institutions in order to accomplish the objective of complete industrialization.

All the characteristics of a highly rationalized socioeconomic and political apparatus are reproduced in the Soviet Union. Nationalization intensifies the centralized regimentation and standardization of production, as it does the coordination of the Soviet people through the coercive organization of the mass media, entertainment, communications, athletics, education, and so on. In the overwhelming interest of promoting industrialization, in effect, of developing and perfecting the technological rationalization of Soviet society, the state is compelled to press all areas of material and cultural life, without exception, into the service of technical reason. As Marcuse describes it,

Autonomy and spontaneity are confined to the level of efficiency and performance within the established pattern. Intellectual effort

becomes the business of engineers, specialists, agents. Privacy and
leisure are handled as relaxation from and preparation for labor in
conformity with the apparatus. Dissent is not only a political crime
but also technical stupidity, sabotage, mistreatment of the ma-
chine. Reason is nothing but the rationality of the whole: the uninterrupted functioning and growth of the apparatus. The experience
of the harmony between the individual and the general interest, between the human and social need, remains a mere promise.[20]

Surveying the dynamic of Soviet politics and progress as Marcuse explains it in relation to the capitalist encirclement, Soviet
totalitarianism cannot be understood as the arbitrary and capri-
cious power of ideologues justifying their oppressive actions
through Marxist propaganda. Soviet Marxism or, more precisely, basic elements of the industrial plan that have become the official communist theory of the Soviet state, along with its political and ideological offspring, emerge directly in response to the
imperatives of furthering technics and indirectly as a result of
the ever present and menacing shadow of capitalism.

Yet, the Soviet state must struggle with contradictions internal
to the rationalization of the productive process regardless of how
efficiently it is carried out.

For example, on the one hand the critical disposition of the
Marxist dialectic can be suppressed as theoretical discourse is
brought into conformity with the objectives of the Soviet industrial plan. Marxist theory is divided into "dialectical" and "historical" materialism. The standard text for this revision of the
dialectic is Stalin's *Dialectical and Historical Materialism*, which
follows the guidelines of Engels's *Dialectics of Nature*. Both
works crudely stress the formal-logical and natural law-like character of the dialectic. "Dialectical materialism" dictates the
values and goals of Soviet society. In this capacity, the dialectic is
transformed from a mode of critical thought into an unchanging
and universal *Weltanschauung* with inflexible rules and regula-
tions. Thus construed, the dialectic can be bent to sanction the
role of the party as historically necessary and as the authoritative
interpreter of the "objective" unfolding of Soviet society. Freedom, rather than the conscious and deliberate cognitive activity
of the subject, as it was for Marx and Hegel, is assimilated to historical necessity and emerges "for" the subject. Systematized, the
Soviet dialectic becomes an inverted caricature of Hegel's dialectic. Unlike Hegel's, Soviet dialectical logic is no extrapolation of

the historical process but rather elucidates history through pre-conceived formal and rigid categories. Substituted for reality, these categories exclude and repress aspects of the historical process standing in contradiction to the official "scientific" view. "Historical materialism" is restricted to a compartment in the ideological division of labor. For Marx, however, historical materialism is the expression of the historical process, and its theoretical integrity is preserved only to the degree that history is understood to contain a higher truth than does any concept or category derived from it. With its Soviet compartmentalization, though, historical materialism becomes "applied dialectical materialism," technically engineering Soviet society to conform with the dialectical vision whose practice and policies it thus justifies.

On the other hand, these ideological acrobatics must ultimately confront the growing contradictions between the relations and forces of production. As the Soviet Union develops technologically, possibilities arise for lessening the regimentation of Soviet society. But they are suppressed through further revisions of the dialectic, which are intended to conceal the fact of progress beyond the established state of Soviet affairs. Contrary to Marx, history need no longer develop through the explosion of material contradictions. The distinction between "antagonistic" and "nonantagonistic" contradictions is introduced, the former insoluble, catastrophic, and endemic to capitalism, the latter a feature of socialist societies and manageable through state intervention. As an ideological weapon, the Soviet distinction justifies postponement of the period of liberalization and concern with the needs of the individual. Where this ideological persuasion is an inadequate means to insure compliance, it is frequently supplemented by outright repressive measures. Eventually, however, the Soviet state is obliged to meet its commitment to introduce changes commensurate with the progress of industrialization. Just as the revisions of the dialectic and political repression were mandated by the original plan of industrialization, this same complex rationale for the draconian measures taken to develop Soviet society technologically commands the Soviet state to pursue the transition to a higher stage of social organization, to a liberal and consumer oriented society.

As Marcuse's analysis of Soviet Marxism develops, its central thesis is without a doubt striking and unique among interpretations of Soviet politics. By virtue of Soviet society's basic commit-

ment to industrialization, its ideological and theoretical machi-
nations can be neither explained completely nor dismissed simply
as propaganda. The revisions of the dialectic are not merely ideological props for an oppressive political system. And they are not
a means of pronouncing the Soviet Union a socialist society so as
to refute claims to the contrary. According to Marcuse's argument the situation is far more complicated. Once institutionalized, the plan of technological development acquires its own
momentum and defines its own objective requirements. The in-
fringements on personal, intellectual, and artistic freedoms, the
domestic and foreign policies of the Soviet Union, the nationalization of the Soviet state, the regimentation and standardization
of work, and the aggregation of power to the party apparatus are
all measures induced by *rationalization* rather than imposed by
political repression.

This argument is extended to the intrabureaucratic politics of
the state. The bureaucracy, although in technical control of the
productive apparatus, must consistently defer its decision-making
power to the social control by the party. Comprised of representatives from the highest levels of the various bureaucratic institutions, the party clearly does not represent homogeneous political
interests. And while one bureaucratic interest occasionally may
prevail over others in certain policy matters, or at other times
there may be an adjustment of all interests to a suitable compromise, the outcome must always "ultimately succumb to the general policy [of technological development] which none of the special interests can change by virtue of its special power."[21] The
bureaucracy taken as a whole, Marcuse concludes, is therefore
representative of Soviet society because the latter's general interest is objectively rooted in the emancipatory promise of the technical base whose development the state, as overseer of the forces
of production, is obliged to carry out lest the very technical foundations from which its power is derived be undermined.

The Soviet Union having reached the stage of heavy industrialization within the decade after the Second World War, the
technical prerequisites of the general industrial plan continue to
override the particular interests within the state and determine
that it must proceed to the second phase of liberalization and
care for individual needs. With the dramatic new technological
possibilities for the creation and distribution of a social product,

the contradictions between the relations of production and the forces of production, between the priorities and power of the state and the progressively unnecessary sacrifices of the individual, can be sustained no longer. The technical basis of Soviet society drives it to the stage of democratization! Technical reason thus has shaped each of the phases of Soviet development — the phase of the oppressive mobilization of Soviet material and intellectual culture and its democratic successor.

Marcuse is quite specific in his characterization of the nature of the Soviet tendency toward freedom. A basic economic trend marking an "increasing use of the growing productivity for consumers' needs" would "generate a corresponding political trend, that is, liberalization of the .repressive totalitarian regime."[22] This would mean a "continuation of 'collective leadership,' decline in the power of the secret police, decentralization, legal reforms, relaxation in censorship, liberalization in cultural life."[23] After completing his examination of national and international developments that lead to this second phase of Soviet socialist construction, Marcuse makes a serious move. He evaluates Soviet progress from the critical perspective of his earlier analysis of technical rationality and offers a prognosis that qualifies the optimism of his discussion of Soviet development.

The new developments of a consumer oriented light industry require a technical and bureaucratic administration equal to that of heavy industrialization. Inevitable is an entrenched bureaucratic class whose power and privilege are reproduced not as a result of any deliberate preservation of self-interest but as a function of this class's technical indispensability to the productive process. At the same time, there is no shift away from a policy of heavy industry, as was originally predicated by the logic of Soviet Marxist theory. The initial theoretical formulation called for an ideological metamorphosis. After reaching the stage of heavy industry, the aggressive Soviet image would be transformed by liberalization and by diverting technology largely into a consumer economy. The normalization of international capitalism would then ensue, paving the way for communism in the West. After Stalin's death, however, this formula was rejected, but no theoretical alternative was devised to push capitalism into its final crisis and remove the threat to the East. In fact, the second phase of Soviet development actually spurred the growth

and productivity of capitalism and contributed to its international stabilization.[24] The result is the indefinitely prolonged
deadlock between the two blocs. And with no visible relief in international stress, heavy industry continues to receive priority
and the democratization of Soviet society becomes a definite by-
product of its development.

With the unequal co-development of heavy and light industry,
technological rationality evolves into a universal practice of Soviet society and begins to reproduce the features of technical reason earlier described as accompanying the rationalization of capitalism. No sooner do the modest democratic gains of the second
phase appear, than they, by establishing the material preconditions for an expanded technical administration, together with
the international pressures to emphasize heavy industry, corrupt
any opportunity for a future transition from socialism to communism. Subjectivity collapses under the weight of technics and
individual reason suffers the same fate under communism as it
had under capitalism. With the entire population and the political and administrative sectors geared to increasing productivity,
all levels of conceptual thought bow to the hegemony of technical reason. In the absence of cognitive levers to reorient Soviet
society from the tendency to one-dimensionality, "administrative
control is secured, and the past is safely transferred into the future."[25] Domination through repressive political practices is exchanged for domination in a technologically liberalized form.

Marcuse's foreboding conclusion is not his final statement on
the future of Soviet society. The second edition of *Soviet Marxism* (1961) is unrevised except for an important preface in which
Marcuse not only emphatically dissociates himself from his original verdict but is suddenly optimistic about the prospects for
breaking the technological convergence of East and West. Marcuse's newly born enthusiasm was inspired by the liberal reforms
and availability of consumer amenities in the short period since
Soviet Marxism was first published, which to others, as well, appeared to inaugurate a new era in Soviet politics.

Marcuse's interpretation of these progressive measures is
unique in an important respect. He views them not merely as the
rewards of de-Stalinization. De-Stalinization was a product of a
more fundamental tendency emerging "through basically different social institutions" from those of Western capitalism, "which

are designed to make for a different development."[26] In other words, although the original text of *Soviet Marxism* remains untouched in 1961, Marcuse's preface alters its central thesis by inverting the relationship between "ideas" and structural (technical) factors. Now Marcuse believes that the Marxist character of Soviet institutions, particularly the commitment to economic development without profit and waste, sets objective limits to technical growth and works against the thrust of technical reason toward domination by reshaping it to correspond to the realization of the emancipatory potential of technological rationality. Marcuse goes so far as to argue that "in eschatological terms, Soviet society contains a qualitatively different society."[27] Marxism, he argues, even in its rudimentary appropriation by Soviet institutions and despite its ideological abuse by Soviet authorities, can very likely override the repressive capabilities of technics.

Marcuse's eschatological characterization of Soviet progress must not be seen as a Hegelian maneuver to draw communism into an evolutionary framework where it would appear as the "unfolding of the idea in history." On the contrary, his intention is to stress the ethical tradition that has legitimated Soviet politics and which for that reason has considerable influence on the course of Soviet history if and only if the international pressures on Soviet communism are relieved. From the Soviet vantage point, achieving economic parity with the West had been an important first step in effecting such a change. It endowed the Soviets with a power that made capitalism seem less formidable and menacing and that allowed for the passage to the second phase. Beyond this, Marcuse consistently underlines the stabilization of deadlocked relations between capitalism and communism. The deadlock continues to postpone the transition from socialism to communism and sustains the danger of technological domination in both realms.

This theme is carried over intact into *One-dimensional Man*. But here, in a very brief analysis of Soviet society,[28] we again discover the tensions between the prospects for domination and those for freedom and social change, which had been the subject of *Soviet Marxism* — the specter of technical reason and the optimism of the new preface. The single difference between the two works is that *One-dimensional Man* adds an expression of concern about the Soviet bureaucracy. Moving away from his earlier position, Marcuse finally concedes that the Soviet bureaucracy may deliberately retard further progress toward a qualitatively different communist society for the purpose of exploiting its technical control of production and also to secure its position in the established hierarchy of social relations. Yet, even this bureaucratic extortion depends on an international situation justifying the perpetuation of the technological administration of Soviet society. Thus, whether technological domination will advance as socioeconomic and political exigency or through the calculations of entrenched bureaucracies, the international deadlock between capitalism and communism appears unfailingly for Marcuse as *the* determining factor. In *One-dimensional Man*, Marcuse offers a summary of his analysis of Soviet society. It should be taken as the statement concluding a significant body of theoretical work.

> The fateful interdependence of the only two "sovereign" social systems in the contemporary world is expressive of the fact that the conflict between progress and politics, between man and his masters has become total. When capitalism meets the challenge of communism, it meets its own capabilities: spectacular development of all productive forces after the subordination of the private interests in profitability which arrest such development. When communism meets the challenge of capitalism, it too meets its own capabilities: spectacular comforts, liberties, and alleviation of the burden of life. Both systems have these capabilities distorted beyond recognition and, in both cases, the reason is in the last analysis the same — the struggle against a form of life which would dissolve the basis for domination.[29]

Ultimately, it seems that the prospects for terminating this continuum of mutual intimidation and spiraling technological domination lie within the Soviet domain — and there only as purely theoretical contingency, as a critical, humanist ethic struggling against its political patron, its ideological opponent, and the hegemony of a Faustian rationality promising in the end to level all vital differences among political systems.

Having drafted an analysis that narrowly forecloses genuine possibilities for change within the Soviet Union, Marcuse then reaches for unlikely candidates to cut the Gordian knot. He speculates that the pretechnological ethos of the Asian civilizations, the antithesis of the values associated with technological rationality, may prove sufficiently sturdy to prevail through industrialization. It then could reassert itself as fertile ground for the exploitation of the emancipatory potential of technology after industrialization has been accomplished.[30] At a later time, Marcuse looks to the student movement of the Vietnam years as a remedial program. However, in light of Marcuse's analysis of the indomitable power of technical rationality, there is no reason to expect, and every reason to doubt, that either area of resistance could admit of the success Marcuse denies to their historical and revolutionary predecessors. Before Marcuse can discover an agency to master technical reason, he first must alter his position on technological rationality as a "new form of control." In less than a decade following *One-dimensional Man* Marcuse will do precisely that, as later we shall see.[31]

The exposition of Marcuse's analysis of Soviet Marxism has moved the discussion an important step beyond that reached earlier with the examination of the elements of technological rationality as they shaped the process of capitalist production. It graphically illustrates the tendency for modes of discourse not at all related in an obvious way to production, such as the Soviet revision of the dialectic, to become coordinated with the rationality of technics. Perhaps the term "centripetal" would be useful for expressing the nature of this tendency. It captures Marcuse's notion of relatively independent thought steadily gravitating toward a technical center of modern society. As the centripetal force of technological rationality increases with the development of technics, the critical and reflective capacity of thinking is exchanged for the logic of technical reason.

To conclude the explication of Marcuse's thesis of technological domination, attention must now be focused on his analysis of these centripetal pressures in capitalist society, on the impact of technical reason on its cultural and political spheres. Here, Marcuse's view of the social sciences, ordinary language, linguistic philosophy, the administration of work, the welfare state, the party systems of the European political left, and aspects of neo-Freudian theory and Marx's philosophy will be considered. (Marcuse's analyses of art and science will be postponed until later discussions; they are significant for additional reasons and should appropriately be treated in other contexts.[32]) At this point, Marcuse's conception of one-dimensional society will have received thorough elucidation, and the discussion can assume a critical stance toward his theory of technological domination and one-dimensionality.

A Mind Not to Be Changed by Place or Time

SOCIAL SCIENCE AS TECHNICAL REASON

Marcuse's analysis of modern social science demonstrates that it incorporates the conservative traits of conventional positivism, which he discussed previously in *Reason and Revolution*.[33] Social science research artificially contracts the empirical world to sets of observations manageable and analytically relevant to an inquiry. An example not chosen by Marcuse, but one that should be considered first because it ties his criticism of the social sciences to his analysis of technical reason more accurately than the illustrations he selects (for reasons to be made clear in the critical section), is the political scientist concerned to explain "democratic stability," with an end, perhaps, to predicting or, more realistically, to generating expectations about the probable future stability of a democratic regime. In this instance, the social scientist must first specify what is meant by democratic stability. As the concept must lend itself eventually to empirical testing, at the outset of the investigation its definition is based on the example of a democratic society judged to be of a stable variety. The surface characteristics of this particular social system are forged into indicators used to evaluate and account for the degree of stability or instability of other political systems. Concepts formed along these lines are referred to as "operational definitions."

By identifying the phenomenon of democratic stability with characteristics of a specific society, the operational definition becomes committed implicitly to the form of social organization that has produced that stable political system. If Western industrial societies furnish the conceptual guidelines for democratic stability, as has been the case frequently,[34] then the operational definition of democratic stability is as much associated with the values of capitalism as with the raw features of industrialization. Evidently, the operational equation of "industrialization and stable democracy" conceals a strong bias in favor of a particular experience of industrialization and of a particular type of stability and democracy. Capitalism, productivity for its own sake, and technological rationality emerge, albeit surreptitiously, as the necessary preconditions for democratic stability. Under the pretense of objective and value-free social science, the methods of modern social science have restricted the meaning of the concept democratic stability to the established social organization of democratic capitalism. Technically, the operational method cannot penetrate beneath the superficial manifestations of democratic stability. Terminating with surface characteristics, without inquiring into the social structures or the ideology of the structures that have given rise to them, the analysis is methodologically purged of any sign of the social and ideological context in which the characteristics are socially constituted. Since its concepts mirror the prevailing social order and present the mirrored image as an evaluative standard, social science reduces thought to the passive exercise of registering and approving the given and inadequate forms of existence. Reason, unable to pass beyond the sophistical boundaries of the fixed society, becomes its ideological handmaiden.

Hence, we can understand why Marcuse has stressed that the methodological a priori of operationalism dictates a political a priori. Stated differently, his claim is that operationalism reproduces the ideology of technical reason in two ways: first, the value of technological rationality is affirmed implicitly by the substantive framework (valuational criteria) of an operational concept; second, and most important, technical reason determines that the social sciences proceed according to a logic of *technique*, according to operations that insure that the correct solution to a problem (e.g., what is democratic stability and which are the stable democratic regimes?) is by definition the technical solution. The second point is especially significant for its explanation of the conservatism of contemporary social science. Marcuse does not contend that social scien*tists* are conservative, by virtue of their class interests, for example, and that they deliberately set out to produce results supporting their political beliefs. If he had done so Marcuse would have contradicted his thesis that domination is rooted in technical reason rather than in politics. Though he would argue that in many cases private inclinations do rule theoretical views, for Marcuse the general rule is that regardless of the ideological orientations of social scientists, their research is driven by operational methods into a position affirming the status quo. In advanced industrial society, reliable knowledge is obtained through science and science is realized only where thought is married to technical reason. Technique, by defining conceptual processes as a logic that substitutes its own propensities for that of the subject (in this case the social theorist), disposes over scientific activity, over its conceptual form. It consistently returns thought to a social reality constituted by technological rationality because the historical factors that gave birth to technics and that could call it into question remain forever beyond the purview of the conceptual operations of technical reason. Technical reason is self-validating and self-perpetuating.

In *One-dimensional Man* Marcuse examines two studies by political scientists whose explicit objectives were to determine whether electoral processes in the United States have been democratic[35] and the extent of political activity among various sectors of the American public.[36] In the first study, Marcuse argues, the criteria for democracy, used as the basis for evaluating elections, are drawn from the electoral processes themselves. Since the evaluations of the elections surveyed cannot pass beyond the criteria of the operational definition of democracy, electoral processes, evaluated on their own terms, necessarily prove to be democratic. In the second study, the operational definition of political activity excludes from consideration the political influence of corporate elites and of the mass media. The first study restricts the meaning of democratic to the familiar, accepted, and established conditions and practices of electoral politics. And the second study's notion of political activity distinguishes only commonplace forms of influence. Broader conceptualizations of democracy would have called into question the democratic character of elections, while a broader conception of political activity would have uncovered types of political influence making commonplace political activity seem far less efficacious than is shown by the second investigation. The *critical* concepts of democratic elections and political influence, Marcuse insists, are rejected because they *cannot* be operationalized. In operational social science, therefore, "the criteria for judging a given state of affairs are those offered by . . . the given state of affairs," such that "the analysis is 'locked' " and "the range of judgment is confined within a context of facts which excludes judging the context in which the facts are made, man-made, and in which their meaning, function, and development are determined."[37] Likewise, the critical, "determining, constitutive facts remain *outside the reach* of the operational concept."[38] By its *very technical nature* operationalism inhibits conceptualization and obstructs criticism.

Do modes of discourse other than empirical social science develop concepts critical of advanced industrial society either by illuminating the technologically organized context shaping human experience or by articulating possibilities for change that would not reproduce the domination of technical reason? With regard to "a whole branch of analytic philosophy," linguistic analysis, whose method has "shut off the concepts of a political, i.e., critical analysis,"[39] Marcuse has clearly answered in the negative. The conservative traits he associates with operational social science are duplicated in linguistic philosophy. To understand this argument, it is first necessary to consider Marcuse's view of ordinary language, the object of analysis of linguistic philosophy.

ORDINARY LANGUAGE AS TECHNICAL REASON

The positivist temperament spawned by the universality of technical reason not only infects specialized, theoretical modes of discourse, such as the social sciences, but also penetrates deeply into our everyday, ordinary language and thought. Critical faculties are eroded as the vehicle of conceptualization and expression, language, becomes entrapped within the fixed meanings promoted by the ideology of technical rationality. The manipulation of commercial and political language through the media reduces ideas to associations that occur and recur with such invariable regularity that word patterns are created that assign inflexible meanings to concepts. The method engendering false associations is again technical. Language is operationalized.

Marcuse refers to this linguistic operationalism as the functionalization of language. The things of which ordinary language speaks are understood only in terms of their behavioral, functional counterparts. Marcuse cites several types of linguistic operationalism. This process occurs where the public is conditioned to accept a single set of conceptual properties in place of reason's office to exercise judgment between alternative concep-

tual meanings. "In the West," Marcuse notes, "the analytic pred-
ication [of freedom] is in such terms as free enterprise, initiative,
elections, individual; in the East in terms of workers and peasants, building communism or socialism, abolition of hostile
classes."[40] Moreover, the ideologically imposed characteristics do
not describe the real state of affairs. The individual is thus burdened with an illusion, but he is comfortably adjusted to it as the
capacity of reason to dispel the illusion is muted. The management of political discourse is also secured as it acquires seductive
and intimate overtones. Elected representatives, public institutions, merchandise—the sum of political and commercial artifacts—"are presented 'especially for you,' " causing individuals
personally to identify their needs, aspirations, and self-interest
with the technologically rationalized general interest. Last, the
"hyphenized abridgement" of language fuses potentially different enterprises in an image that obscures their separate qualities.
The phrase "science-military dinner," which Marcuse takes as an
instance of this sort of manipulation, suggests that science is
bound analytically to military imperatives and finds its most natural function in that specific relation. The nonmilitary, emancipatory potential of science, for example, is suppressed.

In these and in other cases that Marcuse examines, concepts are
identified with the features of organized, repressive, and administered institutionalized practices and procedures of the technical social order. The operational grammar thus enjoins language
to celebrate productivity, affluence, the general social needs and
political objectives that foster ever greater rationalization. Once
learned, standardized popular usages become habitual, spontaneous associations accepted and reproduced without reflection.
Individual reason is powerless to break through the thoughtless
repetition of ideological meanings structured by a technical fa-
cade, to a conceptual universe that would prompt a critical interpretation of social existence.

Moreover, the behavior prodded by the linguistic socialization
validates the distorted conceptual meanings. Functionalized language first suppresses knowledge of the internal contradictions of
advanced industrial society. Then as individual expectations and
technologically molded social relations increasingly harmonize,
not only knowledge of the contradictions but also the contradictions themselves virtually disappear. Welding reason to the pre-

vailing institutions, language becomes the most effective means of drafting the individual to support, preserve, and perpetuate the social order.

LANGUAGE ANALYSIS AS TECHNICAL REASON

As Marcuse would have it, the task of any analysis of ordinary language should be the critical examination of the ideological context within which everyday meanings and usages are formed. It is this project that linguistic philosophy neglects. Marcuse considers the tradition of language analysis that began with Wittgenstein and that includes other notable proponents such as Austin, Ryle, and Hare. Common to their work, as Marcuse understands it, is the principle that philosophical problems arise from the misunderstandings of ordinary language and that the analysis of language's commonplace uses would dissolve such problems. It is the philosophers and not ordinary people who are guilty of muddled thinking, and the precise description and classification of meanings in everyday speech would erase all confusions. At the heart of this principle stands the unexamined assumption that ordinary language is a perfectly suitable means of communication and insight into reality. Although Marcuse proceeds to attack the work of Wittgenstein, Ryle, and Austin exclusively, he intends, unmistakably, for his indictment to apply to the entire movement of linguistic philosophy.

Marcuse's examination of language analysis sifts out the same characteristics he uncovers in his critique of empirical social science and ordinary language. By restricting the meaning of concepts to the domain of everyday speech, linguistic philosophy excludes from view the social relations determining these meanings. Since ordinary language is manipulated by social factors that it cannot express, by refusing to pass behind everyday speech into this ideological context and while, instead, allowing meaning as it appears to common sense to act as the basis for meaning as such, in effect language analysis equates correct meaning with ideology and affirms the dominant social structures. Conceptual discourse critical of the established order and of the society that speaks in its language ipso facto is declared meaningless. Reducing the scope of philosophy to the terms of ordinary language repels criticism and condemns it, at worst, as metaphysics, as unscientific jargon, and, at best, retains it at a safe distance as poetry. One more example of the coordination of thought with the status quo, the operationalism of linguistic analysis leaves the social order intact and contributes to the reproduction of its technical relations.

It should be mentioned that at one point Marcuse does seem to qualify this critique by warning that the ideological character of language analysis should not be prejudged by a demonstration of its conservative features. There is a place, Marcuse appears to be saying, for the general aims of linguistic philosophy: "The treatment of thought in linguistic analysis is its own affair and its own right."[41] Its ban on nonsense, meaninglessness, and metaphysical specters is salient to any philosophy or social theory.[42] By his defense of critical thinking, Marcuse does not want to be misinterpreted as celebrating muddled thinking. Yet, ultimately he retracts all concessions and stresses that language analysis, whatever its aims, can avoid ideological sanctions of the prevailing order only by adopting a sociological perspective. And to insist on an essential distinction between philosophy and sociology is "to make the established division of academic labor into a methodological principle."[43]

Wherever present, operationalism plays a "therapeutic" role. Within the social sciences, ordinary language, and linguistic philosophy, thought is "cured," or relieved of its power to heed the contradictions of advanced industrial society. By the therapeutic adjustment, the symptoms of human decay are repressed, the general illness is safeguarded, and the mind suffers none of the anxiety accompanying knowledge of the need for resistance to a social order whose decadence thought camouflages with the good conscience of scientific procedures authored and authorized by technical reason. Brought into line with the rationality of production, thinking displays positive attitudes as it becomes positivistic.

THE ADMINISTRATION OF WORK AS TECHNICAL REASON

The therapeutic power of operationalism shows forth transparently where technical reason is converted into an explicit method of social control. Such is the case, Marcuse argues, with the techniques of industrial psychology and sociology. Discontents arising from the social organization of work in technological society, whose just remedy demands a fundamental reorganization of social and economic relations, are translated into technical problems that can be addressed and solved with the available resources as they are defined. The technical reformulation of the grievance (e.g., general dissatisfaction with essentially uninteresting and unfulfilling labor is diagnosed as fatigue) turns the universal problem into a personal difficulty. Or the technical reformulation is taken as an acceptable definition of the prosaic character of a certain task, which directs attention away from the technological organization of labor to a particular kind of work, cancels the indictment of the larger social organization of human potential in repressive and alienating labor, and artfully reduces the problem to one manageable within the perimeter of established institutions.

The operational translation of the grievance thus suppresses the real problem. By that act it eliminates criticism of the social order and substitutes a counterfeit problem, implying that all problems are accidental and temporary properties of a not yet perfected productive apparatus. With available resources, the technically defined problem then is resolved in a fashion satisfactory to the grieved parties, thus completing a procedure further rationalizing productivity and developing the rationality of scientific management.

THE WELFARE STATE AS RATIONALIZED ADMINISTRATION

With no form of thought, no mode of discourse appearing to express opposition to technical reason, a coherent and internally consistent ideological universe materializes that provides a frictionless medium through which technological rationalization continues unobstructed. Carried along by its own inertia, automation appears to be inherent in technological progress. There is a natural momentum to push beyond partial automation (the coexistence of automated, semi-automated, and nonautomated labor) and completely to rationalize the productive apparatus. Although automation would unleash the greatest potential for productivity, at the same time it threatens to displace the work force at many levels of technical organization. A twofold contradiction then emerges.

First, the tendency toward the extreme of technological rationalization jeopardizes political stability "at the present stage of advanced capitalism," that is, at the point where class relations have not yet been totally reorganized as technical relations. Creating high levels of unemployment, automation collides with labor, whose hostility to automating the productive process "may weaken the competitive national and international position of capital, cause a long range depression, and consequently reactivate the conflict of class interests."[44] It is only by extending the organizational reach of the welfare state, Marcuse proposes, that this contradiction can be resolved. Through a state-capital partnership negotiating measures that would insure the mutual interests of political stability and economic growth by expansive planning and compensating labor with benefits guaranteeing a prosperous livelihood, rationalization can proceed to its technical limits without opposition.

Second, the result is that the enormous production of goods made possible by automation must be marketed so economic growth can be maintained, and the free time unintentionally made available to individuals by the technical obsolescence of human labor must be repressively utilized. If the free time created by automation were not organized by the social system, individuals released from the technical relations of production might begin to spend their time "unproductively." They could develop interests and capacities contrary to the interests and capacities of a system geared to productivity.

To manage this aspect of the contradiction the social order must resort to "intensified efforts to impose the requirements of the apparatus on the population, to get rid of excess capacity, to create the need for buying the goods that must be profitably sold, and the desire to work for their production and promotion."[45] Planned obsolescence protects markets, the scientific management of needs stimulates demand and creates new patterns of consumption by the manipulation of language and common sense through advertising, and work that is to occupy the free time of the technologically unemployed would be provided by the welfare state, Marcuse argues, through "public works on a grand scale." In partnership with private capital the welfare state nurtures technological growth and successfully harnesses the individual to the technical apparatus—with all its consequences for the deterioration of human reason and subjectivity—while promoting the goal of rationalization. Thus, the dimensions and functions of the welfare state, and the private institutions guiding the production of artificial needs, are required and shaped by technological rationalization and its priorities. Whether the impetus for productivity is ostensibly competition between communism and capitalism or the profit motive, the primary ideology of social organization is technology, not capital. Its relations of domination lay reason to waste and dispense with domination by political coercion. A "new form of control," the new ideology of technical reason swells into a totally administered system of thought and action that is obedient to its desideratum.

POLITICS WITHIN THE LIMITS OF REASON

Even the organized left is not exempt from the jurisdiction of total administration. Without feeling compelled to undertake an analysis of the situation of radical political parties in Western societies, Marcuse offers an impressionistic account of their conservatism. The programs of all parties along the ideological spectrum have become virtually indistinguishable. In the United States, labor has tied its interests to those of corporate power. The German Social Democratic party has long rejected Marxism in exchange for the respectability and rewards of a moderate political stance. The British Labour party supports a mixed economy but is largely indifferent to socialist aims such as nationalization. On the far left, the Italian and French communist parties favor the security of permanent and legal opposition through minimal parliamentary game plans.

Marcuse removes the blame for this widespread conservatism from party leadership and collaborative labor aristocracies.[46] Moderate politics is the strategy necessary to retain a conservative mass, the once politically heterogeneous electoral base assimilated into a homogeneous social order. Preserving its ideological integrity, the left would rescue criticism only to disable the party, while a steady compromise with the status quo saves the party at the expense of articulating a qualitative difference. Adopting the second alternative, the dilemma of the left merely "testifies to the depth and scope of capitalist integration."[47] The left is pulled toward the center by the centripetal pressures of technical reason.

In concluding this exposition of Marcuse's analysis of technological rationality, the few remaining expressions of theoretical and cultural discourse included in his anatomical portrait of advanced industrial society should be considered. Obtaining a composite of his theory presents it at its strongest, lays the groundwork for sound criticism, and conveys the analytical range of Marcuse's work.

NEO-FREUDIAN TECHNOCRATS

Regardless of the criticisms made of Marcuse's interpretation of Freud in the preceding chapter, there is not a doubt that his intention was to develop the critical significance of Freud's discoveries by remaining loyal to the most speculative notions of the instinct theory and metapsychology. Marcuse creatively unearthed their solemn truth, that the fundamental antagonism existing between the nature of man and the manmade "nature" of modern institutions can be resolved in favor of a new dimension of human experience rooted in human nature. Its errors notwithstanding, Marcuse's reading of Freud opened a new dimension for social theory.

As Marcuse views it, contemporary psychoanalytic theory bears no such promise. Examining the neo-Freudian revisionism of Karen Horney, Harry Stack Sullivan, and Erich Fromm, Marcuse emphasizes the ideological conservatism that stems from their understanding of the relationship between psychoanalytic theory and psychotherapy.

Freud consistently stressed the irreducible tension between theory and therapy. The conception of human nature embedded in his metapsychology means that therapy always implies therapeutic adjustment. The terms of membership in a civilized society spell compromise, leaving the individual's needs frustrated to some degree. "Discontent," neurosis, or some other and perhaps more serious psychological disorder is the price exacted by civilization. As psychoanalysis has no power to change the society to accord with the theoretical view of human nature—and, of course, Freud's image of man is not so sanguine as to suggest that such a change would be entirely desirable—therapeutic practices at least resign the individual to personal sacrifice in the interest of a comfortable existence within the limits of social reason. Theory continues to defend the right of the individual, but in principle only, for the imperatives of social order are *irrecon-*

cilably opposed to those of psychic order. Mental health becomes an unattainable ideal.

Marcuse's criticism of the Freudian antinomy (psychic order versus social order), revealing the sociological elements of the theory, the historical limits of the established reality principle, and the possibilities for a higher, libidinal rationality, is turned into purely academic exegesis by the neo-Freudian dismissal of much of the metapsychology as metaphysics and by its interpretation of other aspects of the theory to end its breach with therapy. Lacking a materialist framework that would provide a grasp of the historical content of Freud's metapsychology, the neo-Freudians reject the instinct theory as a species of biological determinism. By this move the depth dimension of Freudian psychology, the id, libido, pleasure principle, the formative significance of the stages of psychosexual development, is excluded, and theoretical attention is focused exclusively on the ego. Having lost the substance that gives it an integrity apart from and against the norms of social order, the personality is redefined as an entity that grows in response to social pressures instrumental to its fullest development.

The neo-Freudians do differentiate between positive and negative features of society affecting the personality, but with a theoretical view that maintains that society has shaped the decisive aspects of human nature, the undesirable features are distinguished from the desirable in terms of the prevailing institutional values. The measure of psychological health then becomes the ability of the individual to transform social pressures into personal strength and psychic growth. Once

> health, maturity, and achievement are taken as they are defined by the given society . . . this "operational" identification of mental health with "adjustive success" and progress eliminates all the reservations with which Freud hedged the therapeutic objective of adjustment to an inhuman society and thus commits psychoanalysis to this society far more than Freud ever did.[48]

With all standards of excellence and psychological stability being originally social standards, it follows that the individual must be held responsible for his conflicts with social order. And since the society is no longer implicated in the cause of individual misfortunes, the individual's struggle against society cannot be seen as political but rather as a moral contest wherein individual needs and rights become mere self-interest opposed to the general welfare. Not only illness but all forms of personal and political rebellion, too, are interpreted theoretically as violations of universal ethical codes rather than of the particular values of a particular society.

Beyond the rejection of the biological and sexual aspects of Freudian theory, neo-Freudian psychology eliminates all other conceptions "that are unverified and unverifiable in accordance with accepted scientific standards."[49] For instance, Freud's death instinct (Thanatos), and with it Marcuse's elucidation of its implications for comprehending the dynamics of aggression in advanced industrial society,[50] is methodologically omitted from serious consideration by the revisionists. Such "wild" hypotheses are shut out, together with the insights they produce, which question a psychological theory having no doubts about the objective of therapeutically adjusting the individual to modern society. In the final analysis, the scientistic purge of the metapsychology by the neo-Freudians brings theory into conformity with the requirements of therapy. Theory is revised to complement the designs of therapy or, more precisely, of *technique* — a procedure whereby the individual is made functional to society, whereby individual functions become identical to social functions. Theory and therapy, theoretical, practical, and individual reason are united by the logic of technics. Technical reason not only effaces the psyche through its organization of the cultural and material process of production but invades even the disciplines that treat those who would resist such coordination.

MARX AS TECHNOCRATIC HUMANIST

Marcuse is also careful to examine aspects of his own theoretical moorings for signs of technical reason. At the conclusion of the last chapter, I pointed out that Marcuse distinguishes his concept of human emancipation from that of Marx. He argues that Marx's notion of unalienated labor preserves the characteristics of the active, practical appropriation of nature. As such, Marx's theory is closely allied with an ideology of domination, specifically with repression (for Marcuse, "sublimation"). If Marcuse had pressed this criticism within the context of his analysis of technical reason, perhaps he would have claimed that Marx's conception of unalienated labor is inadequately sensitive to the dangers of an anthropology that bases the prospects for human development on the unfettered use of technology. The impact of Marxism on contemporary social theory could very well encourage progressive theorists to incorporate the Marxist anthropology and thus to seal the technological fate of the individual while opposing capitalism on his behalf.

In fact, Marcuse does offer a similar indictment of Marx. Though Marx discovered the material laws of historical development, his thesis in the *Poverty of Philosophy* and the *German Ideology* that the hand mill gave birth to feudalism and the steam mill rise to capitalism, fails to grasp that the technological mode of production responsible for capitalism, and which was to be developed further under socialism to create the material preconditions for communism, was also responsible for advanced industrial society. Hence Marx did not (or could not) perceive the most serious form of domination latent in capitalism, which could prevent all further *human* progress. Given his emphasis on the emancipatory significance of technology under socialism and communism, Marx did not take notice of the technological domination that would come to prevail in those societies, of which Soviet Marxism may be judged one version.

Other facets of Marx's anthropology conform to the ideology of advanced industrial society. In the *Economic and Philosophic Manuscripts*, the *German Ideology*, and *Capital*, Marx spoke of the individual who once freed from socially necessary labor could develop his capacities to their fullest extent. Free time would be invested in developing human potential through a great variety of activities. Marcuse suggests that Marx's all-round individual can be assimilated into the repressive fabric of modern civilization. Today, free time is actually manipulated leisure time, wherein diversity of activity, in avocations, hobbies, and so on, is managed by the culture industry. Likewise, within the productive process such advances as polytechnical education give the semblance of all-round development. The standardization of tasks makes individuals as interchangeable as any part of the productive apparatus. Consequently, Marx's image of protean man "pertains to a stage when the intellectual culture was still divorced from the material culture."[51] In other words, it conforms to a historical period when the representatives of higher culture could not imagine their creative privileges universalized in a perverted form by technical reason.

THE TECHNICAL MANIPULATION OF DEATH AS THE TECHNICAL MANIPULATION OF LIFE

There is no aspect of life so private that it does not fall within the domain of technological rationality, as Marcuse's concern with the "ideology of death" proves. The ideological interpretation of death, exaggerating its terror, emphasizing its horror as the end of all things, intensifies the anxiety over the reality of death and transforms life into a means for deriving all the gratification one can from existence. But as existence is socially organized existence, gratification turns out to be the repressive satisfactions offered by modern society. The culturally manipulated view of death thus serves to make the impoverished material and spiritual offerings of advanced industrial society appear pleasurable and rewarding. As Marcuse puts it, "The power over death is also the power over life."[52]

One-dimensional Society

By recalling the earlier discussion of Marcuse's evaluation of the role played by technology in National Socialism, we acquire a clear insight into Marcuse's conception of one-dimensional society. The politics of brute force was the decisive tool of Fascist totalitarianism, and technology was an indispensable though partial factor insuring its "success." Common to fascism and advanced industrial societies, including the Soviet Union, is a technical base. From the standpoint of comprehending the nature of technological rationality, the crucial difference among these social systems lies in the weight technics assumes in each. With fascism, politics unleashed the powers of domination inherent in technology. Before technology could become the predominant factor in totalitarian rule, however, fascism was defeated and the evolution of Fascist totalitarianism concluded with politics as its primary force. In advanced industrial societies the reverse is true. As Marcuse declares,

> In this society, technics is not one particular factor or dimension among others, but is the *a priori* of all reality and realization. The

relation between the technology and the politics of advanced industrial society *is not that of an external force brought to bear upon a
purely technical ensemble.* [The technical ensemble is] not only the
medium in which the social controls are exercised in and over the
individuals but also an apparatus of social controls in its own
right.[53]

Technological rationality determines that the "era tends to be
totalitarian even where it has not produced totalitarian states."[54]

Clearly, for Marcuse the essence of totalitarianism is technical
reason. Embodying this rationality in their productive base, fascism, modern capitalism, and Soviet Marxism tend toward the
elimination of all vital political differences such that the distinguishing characteristic among these systems ultimately is time —
the duration permitted for technological development. Once
technological rationality progresses to the point of becoming the
ubiquitous basis of production, as it never did under National
Socialism, all social relations become the organized domination
relations of technical reason. The implication is that having had
the historical opportunity, fascism would have evolved into a
qualitatively different form of domination. Or, turning this point
around, one-dimensional society is fascism minus brute force.

Grasped in all its manifestations within the material and cultural process of production, the relationship between politics
and technology as it emerges from Marcuse's analysis leads to a
precise understanding of what is meant by one-dimensionality.
Marcuse's conception of subjectivity views the individual as the
potential architect of his own history. The potential freely to dispose of his own fate, rationally to judge the society, and autono-
mously to order it according to the standards of reason remain
the ideal prerogative of the individual. It is this capacity for reason, the critical faculty, the "power of negative thinking," the essence of subjectivity, that is eroded by technological rationality.
All potentiality is now projected by technics. Technical rationality is the single dimension of human experience.

Society is totally mobilized; every sector of society and every field of
human activity is involved. Intellectual and material culture, public and private life, mind and soul, thought and language — all these
are adjusted to fit in with the needs of the apparatus.[55]

The Theory of One-dimensional Society as a
One-dimensional Theory, or the Limits to Domination

THE APPROACH OF CRITICAL ANALYSIS

On the surface, there appears to be no obvious passage of entry through which to initiate criticism of Marcuse's theory of technological domination and one-dimensional society. By Marcuse's account each and every aspect of advanced industrial society shares identical features, and all verify his thesis and extend its reach. Those with special interests in any of the areas Marcuse attacks could take issue with a particular analysis, offer an opposing view, and be satisfied that the rebuttal defended that sphere of society from implication in one-dimensional practices. Such a focused critical approach, however, either would leave standing the remainder of Marcuse's theoretical edifice or, reproduced point counterpoint, would chip away at the entire structure, thus proving that the greater part or perhaps the totality of the social order has not fallen prey to the hegemony of technological rationality.

Beginning in this manner, however, criticism would have little value insofar as the underlying suppositions of Marcuse's central thesis would remain uncontested. If his argument that technological rationality is a new and virulent form of domination passes unchallenged, refutations of the order "linguistic philosophy, or social science, or ordinary language, and so forth, does not confine its conceptual possibilities to the limits of technical reason, uncritically embrace a technologically rationalized society, and contribute to the reproduction and perpetuation of its institutions" can be disarmed as they are turned into qualified disclaimers — "has not *yet* become rationalized and coordinated with a repressive social organization of social relations, though given time the logic of technics will compel it to do so." Marcuse's thesis allows for this sort of theory saving caveat because of its emphasis on the historical tendency *toward* one-dimensional society. Consequently, criticism is paralyzed and discussion is reduced to speculations on the future, unless the central thesis is somehow questioned.

Restating this problem, a challenge to Marcuse should avoid moving within the framework of his analysis. There should be no debate about "Domination — Political or Technological?" Posing the issue "is technical reason closing or has it closed the material, cultural, and political universe of discourse?" is prima facie acceptance that technological domination is a correct notion, even though proof may have been offered that it is not immediately, or is only potentially, a menace. A critique that does not leave Marcuse's thesis intact must test the conviction that technological rationality can be a mode of domination, as Marcuse describes it, under *any* circumstances.

With this objective in mind, the critical approach adopted in the remainder of this chapter will be to pursue answers to variations of a single question: what is the nature of an individual who can be so completely dominated by technical reason? This question is designed to draw out the concept of the subject implicit in Marcuse's theory of technological domination and one-dimensional society. If, in fact, the concept of the individual implicit in his theory appears untenable, then there would be grounds for suggesting that a different concept of subjectivity may define firm limits on the extent to which technical reason could become a rationality of domination, as Marcuse understands it, under any circumstances.

The first concern of this critical analysis is the nature of the individual engaged at all levels of technically organized processes of production. Later, the results of this analysis will be developed into a critique of Marcuse's view of the relationship between technological rationality and the cultural and political spheres of society. It is highly appropriate to begin the analysis by considering Marcuse's relation to Weber, as will become clear shortly.

WEBER FOR AND AGAINST MARCUSE

Marcuse's relationship to Weber is not ambiguous in the least. As can be appreciated readily from the foregoing exposition of Marcuse's analysis of advanced industrial society, although there is an incidental difference in the specific empirical targets of their analyses, on the whole Weber's theoretical model of the development of formal rationality is duplicated in a striking manner by Marcuse. Drawing out the parallel, it clearly extends to a common emphasis on the progress of technical reason within the historical context of industrialization, to a concern with the impact of mechanization, routinization, the calculability of rules and results, standardization, depersonalization, and a highly specialized division of labor. Both theorists are concerned, as well, with the rationalization of education, bureaucratic structures and the superiority of technical elites, the centralization and rationalization of authority and planning, plebiscitary democracy, obedience to authority and depoliticization, factors obscuring class and power relations, the penetration of technical reason into the cultural spheres of society, cumulative technological rationalization and the universality of instrumental norms in the public and private sectors, the comprehensive "disenchantment of the world," and the disappearance of all elements that cannot be rationalized (which for Marcuse translates, for example, into a consideration of the implications of operationalism, specifically, the positivist debunking of metaphysics and the general elimination of transcendent concepts). Last, Marcuse and Weber are similarly interested in the servitude accompanying the rise of welfare institutions, the uniformity of life under modern capitalism, and the unification of politics, economics, and culture into an administered apparatus upon which the entire society depends and that produces a streamlined social organization ideally marked by the absence of tension and conflict. In the broadest sense, it is quite evident that the major features of Marcuse's analysis first appear in Weber's work. It is not stretching the truth to say that the theoretical foundations of Marcuse's technological domination thesis were laid by Weber, nor is it an exaggeration to claim that without Weber Marcuse's work in this area cannot be imagined.

Equally significant, and decisive to a critique of Marcuse, is his departure from Weber. In the social formation Marcuse has labeled advanced industrial society there is no distinction between formal and substantive rationality. In other words, "formal," technical rationality is ideological, a rationality of domination. Weber had argued, however, that although once developed formally rationalized institutions appear virtually indestructible, in principle they remain the administrative *means* for those in political control of the technical apparatus. Weber left as an open question, of course, the issue of whether technological and bureaucratic rationalization at some future time would prevail over substantive political directives; he had insisted that within any particular social structure the weight that formal rationality acquires cannot necessarily be regulated despite the objectives and the power of the society's political masters. Hence, Weber's position regarding the *ultimate* relationship between formal and substantive reason, technology and politics in modern society, does seem ambivalent and, in fact, as often as not the ambivalence appears resolved in the direction of means elevated to the status of ends—which is to say that the ambivalence is not resolved at all.

At times, Marcuse also states that the technical apparatus is controlled by men and that at bottom domination is the consequence of political manipulation. For Marcuse, though, after the early stages of capitalist development the distinction between technological and political domination cannot be solidly established. At the advanced stage of capitalism, the political determination of ends *begins* to decline and technical rationality *begins* to predominate. To this point, Marcuse could yet be judged quite plausibly to have followed Weber's lead in the examination of the means-ends relation because he appears to sustain Weber's ambivalence. The crucial step undertaken by Marcuse is his analysis of the erosion of subjectivity. With this thesis Marcuse moves far beyond Weber's treatment of the possible dominance of formal rationality and the possible elimination of substantive reason, to the substitution of technical for human reason through the gradual but sweeping eclipse of the individual's critical, "substantive" *faculties*. Weber's nearest approximation to such a radical thesis as the reduction of thinking to a single dimension comes in such references as "the settled orientation of man" for keeping to the formal rationality of administration.[56] For Weber, technical reason is habituating, but politics, values, and their subjective basis are not dissolved. Rather, they continue to exist beside the apparatus and often in conflict with it.

Further differences between the two theorists are illuminated by Marcuse's own critical essay on Weber. In "Industrialization and Capitalism in the Work of Max Weber," Marcuse argues that Weber's conception of formal rationality is too closely aligned with the rationality of capitalism. Particular historical practices of capitalism—specifically, free enterprise, continual profit opportunities for capital in order to allow for the general satisfaction of the public's material needs, the separation of the means of production from the worker, and the selling of labor power for wages—become necessary to the development of formal reason and are idealized and elevated to the status of reason as such by Weber. Evaluated according to the (operational) criteria of formal reason, the irrationality of capitalism emerges as the very embodiment of universal rationality, as being truly rational. And, since Weber is unaware that his concept of formal rationality is tied to substantive capitalist rationality, through Weber's theory, formal, technical reason must then appear as a form of domination. Recapturing the historicity of Weber's formal rationality, Marcuse severs the equation of formal and capitalist rationality, to which Weber is blinded, and the emancipatory potential of technics is brought to the surface. Freed from the organization of social relations in the interest of profit and productivity, formal reason can be seen to have established the material preconditions for human emancipation—the elimination of scarcity and the reduction of work to the barest minimum relative to basic repression. Once formal reason is purified of its ideological content, the irrationality of modern capitalism stands out distinctly.[57]

While Marcuse's criticism of Weber is basically accurate, it does tend to be one-sided. Weber is not so sanguine about formal rationality that its highest expression in modern capitalism would leave it free of blame. He is extremely critical of the dangers to democracy and personal freedom constituted by formal reason and aware of the threats to human happiness presented by the routinization of an oppressive, religiously inspired work ethic. Moreover, although Weber's definition of formal reason incorporates many of the essential characteristics of capitalist rationality, it contains an insight that may very well explain the origin of Marcuse's theory of technological reason. Marcuse's argument that historically the rationality of capitalism becomes embodied in technical reason, that is, modern capitalism is transformed into a qualitatively new social formation, advanced industrial society, is prefigured by Weber's concern with the future of freedom, democracy, and happiness in a fully rationalized society. Although Weber reproduces many of the features of capitalism in his concept of formal reason, his concept and criticisms of formal reason unwittingly recognize it as the advanced historical form of capitalism. Weber's formal rationality thus anticipates and may have suggested to Marcuse the notion of advanced industrial society. Consequently, Weber's error, as Marcuse has described it — the confusion of formal and capitalist rationality — may have been the germ of Marcuse's theory.

Nevertheless, however suggestive Weber's concept and criticisms of formal reason may be of Marcuse's theory of advanced industrial society, a firm dividing line between the two must be drawn. Weber and Marcuse part company on the final status of the subject in a totally rationalized society. This crucial difference cannot be explained in terms of their analyses of the universal organization of social relations by technical reason because their frameworks parallel each other so closely. Marcuse's divergence from Weber lies not in Marcuse's structural examination of technics but in the anthropological assumptions that underlie and inform his theoretical analysis and its conclusions regarding the fate of subjectivity. This all-important difference between Weber and Marcuse brings us to the decisive question: what is the nature of an individual who so utterly collapses under the pressures of technical reason that he can be transformed into "one-dimensional man"?

ONE-DIMENSIONAL ASSUMPTIONS

Consider these assertions.

> With all its rationality, the Welfare State is a state of unfreedom because its total administration is systematic restriction of . . . the intelligence (*conscious and unconscious*) *capable of comprehending* and realizing the possibilities of self-determination.[58]

> The coordination of the individual with his society *reaches into those layers of the mind where the very concepts are elaborated* which are designed to comprehend the established reality.[59]

> But this radical acceptance [by linguistic analysis] of the empirical [ordinary language] violates the empirical, for in it speaks the mutilated, "abstract" individual who experiences (*and expresses*) *only that which is given to him* (*given in a literal sense*), who has only the facts and not the factors, whose behavior is one-dimensional and manipulated. By virtue of the factual repression, the experienced world is the result of a restricted experience, and the *positivist cleaning of the mind brings the mind in line* with the restricted experience.[60]

Quite evident in these passages, and in many others that could be cited, is the image of the inner world of the mind assuming the shape of the outer social world. Yet, what is extraordinary is that nowhere in Marcuse's analysis of the impact of technical reason on mental processes is there an analysis of the mental processes themselves. We are furnished with a finished portrait of subjectivity after formal rationality has completed its work, but there is no examination of the actual individual to determine whether he corresponds to the theoretical *concept* of one-dimensional man. Immediately it will be objected that Marcuse in fact has examined the psychological basis of one-dimensional thought and has studied the internal dynamics of the mind as much as the dynamics of technics in relation to it. This project will be considered in due course. Despite that project the objection is invalid, however, for his discussions of the psychological basis of one-dimensional thought, including the notion of repressive desublimation, either focus on the earliest stages of psychological development or are restricted to biological-instinctual forms of domination, which Marcuse fails properly to relate to mental functioning. In the event that this objection is pressed further, the argument of the following chapter shows that Marcuse's theory of the psychological underpinnings of one-dimensionality is incorrect. It is, in fact, a theory that views all mental capacities as developing and taking shape in direct response to and conformity with social pressures and social requirements.

Marcuse's theoretical omission is of great consequence. Without a view of the empirical subject after he has been reduced to the one-dimensional state, it must be assumed that prior to that condition the nature of the mind was such that its aggregate dispositions held the possibility for total assimilation to technological rationality. If this assumption were not implicit in Marcuse's conception of one-dimensional man, if there *were* essential features, or "dimensions," of human reason distinguishing it from technical reason, then regardless of the universal scope of technics and the strain under which it placed the mind, mental processes could never be exhausted by technical processes. The essential differences would have introduced an antagonism between the logic of the mind and the logic of technics. In Marcuse's account of this important relationship, no such tension is apparent. Indeed, what is emphasized without equivocation is the correspondence, conformity, coordination, and harmony of the objective spheres of structural intercourse and the subjective spheres of human discourse.

Where, then, does this conception of the mind's nature under-lying the theory of one-dimensional man originate? The implicit anthropology of mental processes disposed to total objectifica-tion through technical rationality bears a strong resemblance to the concept of reason embedded in technics. When we consider the evidence Marcuse offers for the dramatic redefinition of thought, we are consistently referred to a description of the logic of technical reason. The mind is inferred not from its own phe-nomenology but rather from elements that lie outside the mind. Mental processes are derivative. Marcuse seems to have extrapo-lated his notion of subjectivity from the constitution of struc-tures. Mental features not peculiar to technological rationality also do not pertain to the manipulated individual. Having no prior knowledge of Marcuse's extensive work on Freud, or for that matter on Hegel, a reader of Marcuse's analysis of techno-logical rationalization could conclude appropriately that his crit-icisms of modern society notwithstanding, he has produced a theory whose psychological presuppositions not only allow for but are verified by the individual's comfortable and functional relationship to the behavior required by technical reason. This interpretation would be intelligible and plausible for in his criti-cal analysis Marcuse never probes the inner world of the subject within advanced industrial society but inherently conceives of this world as it is projected from one-dimensional behavior and the technical, structural logic of one-dimensional society.

Behaviorism, then, and a variety of the most radical sort, is not a methodology alien to Marcuse's critical theory. The empir-ical subject's attitudes, dispositions, capacities, personality, and character are inferred from the social behavior of the individual. Certainly, Marcuse has another conception of human nature that cannot be reduced to its behavioral counterpart. But this concept belongs to the rationalistic framework of critical theory, carefully removed from any empirical referent in the established social universe and preserved in the abstract as a free, autono-mous, and rational subject. And in view of Marcuse's critique of neo-Freudian psychology, his behaviorism is truly ironic. The revisionists discarded those aspects of Freud's theory that ques-tioned the therapeutic aim of adjusting behavior to prevailing norms. Marcuse, in a similar fashion, develops a theory of one-dimensional man whose implicit theoretical assumptions about the nature of the psyche anticipates the one-dimensional behavior that the neo-Freudians sanction. At a later point it will be asked whether Marcuse's slide into behaviorism is related to his interpretation of Freud, specifically to that part of the interpretation that establishes the psychological underpinnings of the one-dimensionality thesis.

Intimately related to Marcuse's behaviorist tendencies are quite visible signs of what could be properly called "epiphenomenal reductionism," or, to use an older, similar, and somewhat more familiar term, "materialist determinism." These phrases, however awkward, adequately express the idea that one-dimensional thought occurs as a direct result of or reaction to a one-dimensional technical apparatus. A one-way causal relationship holds between the mind and the rationalized organization of production. And since Marcuse fails to consider any mental events that accompany the impact of structural factors upon the mind, mental behavior appears to be nothing but material behavior. It is an epiphenomenon, a mere shadow of material processes. Marcuse turns the mind into a dependent variable, a black box passively processing information. The mind is identified with the functions it performs, which in turn are identical to technical functions.

Marcuse's determinism situates his critical theory near to the orthodox Marxist framework of historical materialism. Although Marx clearly was not the crude economic determinist of the orthodox Marxist school many of his interpreters have claimed him to be, there are quasi-determinist features to Marx's theoretical work. While it is unnecessary to take up the debate about Marx's so-called determinism as it might be associated with many facets of his social theory, in the context of the present discussion brief attention to two of its aspects will aid in clarifying the nature of Marcuse's much stricter technological determinism.

MARX AGAINST MARCUSE

In the *German Ideology*, the text that perhaps goes the furthest in establishing the nature of Marx's determinism, history is described as a history of generations one after another confronting predetermined sets of objective material conditions. These objective factors place a limitation upon the orientation of man's intellectual and physical energies in that human faculties and capacities must be brought to bear and concentrated upon the material means of production. The subject of historical development, be it individual, class, or society, is structurally limited, not *strictly* determined by material conditions. Within the realm of necessity and beyond it a realm of choice is open, containing a variety of possible human projects circumscribed by material conditions, yet sufficiently broad to allow for a degree of autonomy and discretion and, most important, for politics. The possibility of choice and political contest would be meaningless unless Marx had supposed a subject, sketched philosophically and anthropologically in the *Paris Manuscripts*, able to dispose over historical opportunities. Subjectivity is always bound by the material limits to historical change, but at the same time the subject's capacities are greater than the material possibilities already realized in the forces and relations of production.

Marx's conception of a semi-autonomous subject appears in a different form in the relation of "base and superstructure." Whether the focus is on the state, science, religion, art, or philosophy the superstructure always maintains a semi-independent relationship to the material basis of production. Ideology can no more be reduced to material factors than the latter can fully account for the origin and substance of ideology. The semi-autonomous status Marx grants to the subject in fact prompts Marcuse to argue that Marx's materialism has a concept of a "reduced" material basis of society because it "undervalues" the impact of science and technology in forming and determining "man's being and consciousness."[61] For Marcuse, in other words, ideology no longer receives emphasis, as it did with Marx, as a repressive means of organization and socialization. Rather, "by virtue of the way it has organized its technological base, contemporary industrial society tends to be totalitarian."[62] The reciprocal relationship of base and superstructure as conceived by Marx is altered by Marcuse decisively in favor of an all-pervasive and all-determining material basis encroaching upon, manipulating, and coordinating ideology until there ceases to be any difference between base and superstructure, ideology and reality, subject and object. By underlining the greatly expanded role of technological rationality in modern civilization, Marcuse corrects Marx's "error," inflates the influence of technical structures on the subject, and bestows upon subjectivity the characteristics of technical reason. Marcuse's theory emerges as a caricature of the determinism falsely imputed to Marx. Weber's theory of the development and implications of formal rationality has thus led Marcuse to a revision of Marxism. Important to recall, however, lest it be inferred that I am suggesting that Weber's and Marcuse's theories of rationalization share similar anthropological assumptions, Weber's view of man in technological society preserves a complexity that Marcuse's has implicitly denied. Weber maintains a distinction between "internal states and external demands."[63] Ideas, attitudes, and dispositions cannot be equated with those implied by the performance of required behavior. Needless to say at this point, Marcuse's theoretical categories are not those of human thought and action but categories—structures—standing outside of and determining both.

In fairness to Marcuse, there is an element of truth to his critique of Marx: Marx did underestimate the forces of social integration and cohesion deriving from science and technology. Yet it is important to remember that for Marx the subject of historical development beyond capitalism was the proletariat. If the thrust of Marcuse's critique is the obsolescence of the revolutionary proletarian class subject, Marcuse's indictment of Marx is valid. That, however, is not Marcuse's point. Marcuse's critique breaks down when he suggests that Marx was wrong in undervaluing the impact of technics on *"man's being and consciousness."* Against Marcuse, however, the depth and complexity of Marx's anthropology would have enabled him to place technical reason in its proper theoretical perspective. In other words, for Marx *man* includes all forms of subjectivity, not merely the proletariat, and *being* and *consciousness* refer to man's entire nature, his cognitive, emotional, and biological constitution. If Marx had feared or even foreseen the possibility of the integration of the proletariat, as is sometimes indicated in his writings, would he have interpreted that development as the erosion of *all* aspects of subjectivity associated with man and, therefore, with the working class? Marx's notion of the subject, of which the revolutionary working class, with its revolutionary capacities, is but one concrete historical expression, would have prevented such a conclusion. Revolutionary capacities of the subject would have been assimilated, perhaps, but not all human critical capacities. Now a similar question must be put to Marcuse: in view of the behaviorist and determinist implications brought to light by revealing the underlying anthropological assumptions of the theory of one-dimensional man, what would correctly evaluating the effect of science and technology on man, as the universal human subject, mean for Marcuse?

A complete agreement between social being, the composite traits of the individual's private and public existence, and social (technical) consciousness would have to occur, a perfect psychic-social fit. The relationship between the individual and the social role he occupies would entail an absence of tension and conflict. At no level of conscious or unconscious existence would there be expressions of discontent, frustration, hostility, and apathy in response to the submissive, passive, dependent, and powerless station to which the individual would have become accommodated. Nor would there be the least perception of such enslavement. No longer applicable to individual psychology would be the Freudian dynamic that a necessary concession to an ungratifying or otherwise repugnant social demand, in effect, to the reality or performance principle, would cause emotional distress or a neurotic symptom of some sort. Furthermore, as the society became progressively rationalized, as production units became less complex to increase their manageability, there could be no expectation of an intensifying contradiction between individual needs and abilities and structural requirements. As different and as complex as individuals are, they would be standardized by rationalizing their technical roles. The question of the limits of human tolerance to rationalization would never arise.

Marcuse's behaviorism, determinism, and, by allusion, "role theory"[64] clearly neglect highly significant areas of resistance to a rationalized social organization of production. Only a notion of subjectivity richer than that implicit in Marcuse's theory of one-dimensional man would heed signs of discontent, which, no matter how primitive, constitute a source of opposition. A critical theory whose underlying assumptions suppress recognition of these signs also suppresses a basis for politics and forecloses the possibility of the intervention of political movements or organizations in social life. It is guilty of a fundamental hostility to politics. No doubt that at the bottom of Marcuse's implicit anthropology is the mistaken tendency to evaluate the modern subject in terms of Marx's revolutionary subject and from the standpoint of the rationalistic structure of Marcuse's critical theory.[65] Consequently, a grave injustice is done to the far less politicized but no less alienated figure of modern man. With presuppositions excluding any but a positivist conception of subjectivity, that is, an image of the individual merely reflecting the a priori concept of subject rooted in technological rationality, Marcuse's critical theory is depoliticized in advance of further analysis. It thus contributes to the very process of integration and to forms of political mobilization it abhors. If critical theory is to move beyond a one-dimensional society, it must first move beyond a theory laden with one-dimensional assumptions. Once it does, the categories of critical theory will no longer be anchored in the laws of history but rather in the laws of human nature.

Reinstating subjectivity against its suppression in Marcuse's critical theory restores a basis for politics and at the same time qualifies considerably the possible impact of technics upon the individual. Discovering the limits to technological domination as it affects the individual within the process of production forces the next question: are there also firm limits to its influence on a subject engaged in activities removed from those sectors of society directly related to production processes? Now the concern is to determine whether Marcuse is correct in arguing that the critical distance between the cultural and political spheres of advanced industrial society and technical reason can be attenuated completely or, contrary to Marcuse, whether a degree of subjectivity and a critical dimension remain and will continue to remain intact. This final part of the critical examination will focus only on those spheres of society for which Marcuse's analysis appears to make the strongest case for his theory. Social science, ordinary language, linguistic analysis, the administration of work, and political parties are the pertinent areas to be considered. The discussion will conclude with a critical look at *Soviet Marxism*.

OPERATIONALISM IN SOCIAL SCIENCE

When the evidence is considered, there is not the slightest indication that Marcuse has correctly grasped operationalism as it has been used methodologically in the social sciences. This is the mildest criticism that can be made of his indictment of empirical social science. For if he does correctly understand operationalism in a manner not revealed by his work, then it must be concluded that by offering critical expositions distorting social science research, Marcuse has deliberately misrepresented operational analysis to make it appear the crudest sort of ideological thought. These serious accusations are confirmed by reexamining the studies Marcuse selects as illustrations of the rationalized coordination of the social sciences with the technical basis of production.

Marcuse, we recall, argues that operationalism is committed to a technical conceptual framework that necessarily evaluates societal relations in terms of criteria extracted from societal practices. Analysis becomes "locked" within the given ideological universe of established institutions. By means of operational methods social science can do nothing but affirm a repressive social order. Marcuse's argument is based upon his examination of two empirical investigations by political scientists who inquired into the democratic character of elections and the extent of political activity and influence among different sectors of the American public.

In discussing a study by Morris Janowitz and Dwaine Marvick, "Competitive Pressure and Democratic Consent," Marcuse claims incorrectly that "a set of three criteria is offered" to judge the degree to which the 1952 presidential election produced a process of consent or manipulation. He cites the authors' criteria, which define what they refer to as the "competitive theory of democracy," as follows.

(1) A democratic election requires competition between opposing candidates which pervades the entire constituency. The electorate derives power from its ability to choose between at least two competitively oriented candidates, either of whom is believed to have a reasonable chance to win.

(2) A democratic election requires both [!] parties to engage in a balance of efforts to maintain established voting blocs, to recruit independent voters, and to gain converts from the opposition parties.

(3) A democratic election requires both [!] parties to be engaged vigorously in an effort to win the current election; but, win or lose, both parties must also be seeking to enhance their chances of success in the next and subsequent elections.[66]

After quoting Janowitz and Marvick's criteria, which he explicitly states were used to assess the effects of electoral competition, Marcuse remarks that since "these definitions describe pretty accurately the factual state of affairs in the American elections of 1952, which is the subject of the analysis,"[67] then the actual electoral practices constitute the basis for evaluating the elections, "the investigation becomes circular and self-validating," and the electoral "process is democratic prior to the results of the investigation."[68] Criteria other than those employed by the authors to judge the election, Marcuse argues, and which would have contributed a genuinely critical perspective and proven the election to be far less democratic than the authors concluded, could have been furnished by some other definition of democracy. Such a concept was at Janowitz and Marvick's disposal, but they rejected this classical "mandate" theory of democracy, which postulates that "the process of representation derives from a clear-cut set of directives which the electorate imposes on its representatives," because "it assumed a level of articulated opinion and ideology on the campaign issues not likely to be found in the United States."[69] Marcuse notes this explanation for rejecting the mandate theory but contends that the "precise" reason for the authors' rejection lay in the concept's "non-operational" status.[70] Concepts belonging to a critical theory, Marcuse is saying, "remain outside the reach of the operational concept."[71]

Several important objections to Marcuse's treatment of the Janowitz and Marvick article must be raised. First, the authors provided not three criteria but *five*.

    I. The Quality of an Election Depends on the Degree to which Competition Produces High Levels of Citizen Participation among All Social Groupings.[72]

   II. The Quality of an Election Depends on the Extent to which Citizen Participation Is Based on Predispositions of High Political Self-Confidence as well as the Traditionally Emphasized Self-Interest in the Outcome of Elections.[73]

  III. The Quality of an Election Depends on the Extent to which Competition stimulates Effective Political Deliberation on the Issues and Candidates and Creates a Meaningful Basis on which Citizens Can Make Their Voting Decisions.[74]

  IV. The Quality of an Election Depends on the Extent to which Limitations Operate Precluding Either Side from Monopolizing or Even Exercising Pervasive Influence by means of the Mass Media.[75]

V. The Quality of an Election Depends on the Extent to which the Influence Exercised by Interpersonal Pressures Operates Substantially Independent of the Influence exercised by the Mass Media.[76]

Second, obviously none of their operational criteria bears any resemblance to those that Marcuse lists. Those Marcuse identifies as evaluative criteria were never used by the authors to determine the election's democratic stature. The authors did not argue that those three conditions, which certainly *do* factually describe the election, were met, ergo democracy! Their objective was to consider whether, *in spite* of these conditions, the election was undemocratic, because competitive party activities—which these three conditions served only to outline—may have generated pressures that ultimately involved manipulation of the public and inhibited a process of consent!

Third, as the article makes clear, of the five criteria devised for the investigation the "fifth criterion, involving the patterns of interaction between the impact of the mass media and interpersonal pressures, isolated a political process with important manipulative potentials and some observed manipulative consequences."[77] Taken together, through their operational criteria the authors

point to a series of weaknesses in the American election process; they delineate conditions under which such weaknesses would become exacerbated. Moreover, these weaknesses are clearly profound enough to warrant the conclusion that constructive measures are required to prevent the growth of that type of competition which can only result in increased and dangerous manipulation. There is little ground for believing that these defects are likely to correct themselves merely in the "course of events."[78]

Clearly, the analysis hardly can be said to be uncritical of American elections. Yet, when the study concludes that "in planning for and assessing future elections, it would be a grave error to deny that these manipulative pressures were present,"[79] Marcuse dismisses this warning as "a hardly illuminating statement beyond which the operational analysis cannot go."[80]

Marcuse's sarcasm leads to a fourth and final objection. In the first place, even if Marcuse is correct in arguing that a critical examination cannot be properly accomplished through operational methods, his sarcastic response to the authors' conclusion is unwarranted. Showing, as did Janowitz and Marvick, that manipulation was a profound factor in the 1952 election, particularly as it was related to the mass media, a topic in which Marcuse is supposedly interested, is a significant finding. It is highly unlikely, however, that Marcuse could have recognized or disputed the significance of their findings so long as he neglected the authors' real operational criteria, especially the fifth criterion, and, most important, was mistakenly convinced that operationalism excludes critical perspectives a priori.

As it stands, Marcuse's comprehension of operationalism is as poor as his reading of the essay. He contends that through an operational analysis the authors "cannot raise the decisive question whether the consent [which the investigation claimed was far in excess of manipulation] itself was not the work of manipulation."[81] Only the so-called nonoperational mandate theory, or by implication nonoperational concepts in general, Marcuse suggests, could have posed the crucial issue whether the electorate that some view as free and autonomous is actually indoctrinated. While it is true that the competitive theory of democracy is less critical than the mandate theory, Marcuse's argument is nevertheless false in an important respect. In principle *any* concept can be operationalized, including theoretical terms such as classical definitions of democracy, for example, the mandate theory. To understand this rather basic point, operationalism must be conceived broadly, as it has been in social science, to denote not merely physical operations but mental, particularly verbal, operations, too. Marcuse unduly restricts operationalism to purely physical operations. Janowitz and Marvick did not reject the mandate theory of democracy because it cannot be defined operationally. On the contrary, levels of articulateness, consent *as* manipulation, and so forth, can be operationalized quite easily. Their choice between the competitive and mandate theories was not a choice between an operational and a nonoperational concept but rather a choice between *alternative operational definitions*. The reasons for Janowitz and Marvick's selection of the less critical concept must be sought elsewhere than in a universally objective requirement to provide scientific analyses that end by imposing a strictly technical exclusion of authentically critical notions.

Further evidence for Marcuse's confusion about operationalism appears in his examination of "Political Activity of American Citizens," by Julian Woodward and Elmo Roper. Marcuse argues that the operational criteria that the authors used to measure political activity—"(1) voting at the polls; (2) supporting possible pressure groups . . . (3) personally communicating directly with legislators (4) participating in political party activity . . . (5) engaging in habitual dissemination of political opinions through word-of-mouth communication"[82]—cannot identify the influence of business on government and that of the mass media in the formation of public opinion. Regarding this particular article, this criticism is, of course, true. It is one that would also come as no surprise to the authors of the study because they made the same point.

> It has not been maintained that the "top tenth" [of those sampled] are actually the most influential group of people in determining the course of political events.[83]

> And it is of course also possible that the kinds of activity covered in the Index [of political activity] are not good measures of political *influence* at all and that some other approach . . . might be more fruitful.[84]

> No doubt most political scientists would make some additions to or subtractions from the list [of operational criteria] . . . There may be many different tests for political activity.[85]

Woodward and Roper were careful to point out that there are forms of political activity and types of political influence that this study did not consider but that may be as significant, if not more so, than the focus of their analysis. The activity of elites and the influence of the mass media, which other social scientists have studied extensively and with which Marcuse is concerned, could be included among possible inquiries. Most important, the authors recognized that an investigation producing results more critical than theirs does not "remain outside the reach of the operational concept" but lies within the method's conceptual domain. This is the point Marcuse consistently misunderstands.

It is still true that Woodward and Roper, like Janowitz and Marvick, opted for operational definitions that contributed findings less critical of elections, political influence, and political activity than other concepts and criteria would have yielded. A decisive question must now be posed: if domination, in this case the exclusion of critical concepts, is not asserted through the hegemony of technical rationality, in other words, if the technique of operationalism does not in itself explain how criticism is repelled or reduced to the terms of the prevailing ideology, what other than Marcuse's fetishized view of social science methodology can offer an explanation?

In *One-dimensional Man*, Marcuse refers to Percy Bridgeman's *Logic of Modern Physics* (1928) for the authoritative statement on the meaning of operationalism.[86] Bridgeman had stressed the use of physical operations in that text. Marcuse also acknowledges Bridgeman's subsequent revision of operationalism to include "pencil and paper" (types of mental) operations.[87] However, Marcuse seems to assume that Bridgeman's continued preference for physical over mental operations determined that the former would become the dominant trend in social science, as though modern social science based its methodological orientation upon Bridgeman's original 1928 *Logic*.

Consequently, it appears as though Marcuse either is unfamiliar with or is deliberately ignoring the significant debates about operationalism among social scientists and philosophers lasting for nearly three decades after the publication of Bridgeman's influential book.[88] Though these debates cannot be discussed in any detail, what they immediately disclose is that social scientists and philosophers feuded over the general implications of operational analysis for the social sciences, over the relative merits of physical versus mental operations, the relationship between social theory and operational methods, and the possibility and desirability of ever agreeing on the definition of any single operational concept. At the very least, these debates indicate that physical operationalism was not the dominant tendency in social science. And, most important, where mental operations were to be employed widely in social science research, the key issue remained the validity of any particular operational concept. Validity could never be guaranteed through objective, technical operations except where physical operations were concerned. Physical operations, however, allowed for the formulation of only the most elementary social science concepts, those that would be of little use to social science (e.g., to the studies conducted by Janowitz and associates). Theoretically significant concepts were to be constructed through mental operations, and their validity depended upon prior agreement on criteria of validity by the members of the social science community. To put it differently, personal, professional, and political values and beliefs were tied to the formulation of operational concepts and to evaluations of their scientific validity. As is well known, the relationship between the norms and commitments of the scientific community to scientific truth emerged controversially in the wake of Thomas Kuhn's *Structure of Scientific Revolutions*, but this issue was as central to the earlier debates about operationalism.[89]

From this analysis of Marcuse's views of operationalism and social science an important conclusion can be drawn. When it is recognized that operationalism as it is broadly conceived in the social sciences does not exclude concepts of a critical nature by virtue of a methodological a priori, then technical reason cannot be held directly responsible for the conservatism of modern social science. The affirmative character of any particular (mental) operational definition must be referred back to the values and beliefs of the individual social scientist, and eventually if the concept is generally acknowledged as valid, its validity must be explained by reference to the values and beliefs of the social science community that agreed on its scientific status. Yet, even a passing familiarity with social science literature would pay testimony to the fact that most terms of significance, such as those Marcuse underscores, do not enjoy such credibility. Definitions are contested, data are disputed, and alternative concepts and criteria are proposed. If the time does arrive when contest subsides, critical terms are abolished, and a single paradigm emerges as dominant, as has happened occasionally throughout the history of social science, it will occur as an act of consensus by whatever forces constitute or influence the social science community.

In short, it is not technical reason, not a methodological a priori, but subjective reason, in the last analysis politics, that animates social science and accounts for its coordination with the technological organization of social relations. Both the existence of a subject and its political, ideological expressions are missed by ignoring decisive differences between technical rationality and the rationality that informs social science methodologies. Once more Marcuse seems to have made an assumption, albeit explicitly in the case of social science, that blinds his theory to factors that limit the domination by technical rationality. The assumption is that social science continues to attempt to replicate the model of natural science,[90] or, more exactly, that operationalism in social science is identical to physical operationalism in the hard sciences. By making such an assumption, Marcuse joins the diminishing ranks of those few social scientists, throwbacks to an age of an obsolete and untenable positivism that collapsed under its own weight, who represent the most negligible tendency in social science today.

ORDINARY LANGUAGE

At one point Marcuse does seem to have supposed a concept of subjectivity allowing a margin of individuality to survive the onslaught of technical reason. On the perimeters of ordinary language there are expressions of discontent, small pockets of resistance opening it to criticism. Against the one-dimensional, functionalized speech of everyday life "the popular language strikes with spiteful and defiant humor . . . Slang and colloquial speech have rarely been so creative."[91] Here subjectivity possesses the capacity to reassert itself by designing a specialized vocabulary of new and extended meanings that fall outside the restrictions of conventional usage.

Besides these extralinguistic elements, whose critical spirit derives from a cynical or idiosyncratic temperament, Marcuse also suggests that there exists a critical dimension *within* ordinary discourse. Marcuse refers to the work of Karl Kraus, whose analyses of the uses of the basic components of language, such as grammar, vocabulary, and syntax, disclosed the real social and political context of values and beliefs that lies behind and is concealed by the surface meanings of the spoken and written language. The critical elements revealed through Kraus's analyses were originally hidden, but not completely. Marcuse suggests that these deeper, critical layers of meaning enter "with various degrees of awareness and explicitness, into the individual communication."[92] The depth layers, or what Marcuse refers to as the "multi-dimensional universe" of meaning, are critical, "antagonistic," yet "interrelated," "merged," and "overlap[ping]" with the ideologically distorted surface communication. Marcuse chooses Kraus's work for an important reason. It is Marcuse's example of the sort of linguistic analysis after which contemporary language analysis ought to be modeled. The implication is that it is just as possible today to "make the established language itself speak what it conceals or excludes, for what is to be revealed and denounced is [still] operative *within* the universe of ordinary discourse and action."[93] In other words, our universe of discourse is at least as open as that during the period before and after the First World War, when Kraus wrote.

Marcuse's consideration of these critical features of language incorporates a threefold set of implicit themes: (1) it suggests that the deeper layers of meaning, the extralinguistic terms and the meaning buried within the structure of ordinary discourse, reveal the ideological aspects of officially established meanings; (2) it affirms that linguistic analysis cannot hope to clarify meanings by enlisting as its final interpretive standards those ideologically distorted meanings of ordinary language; (3) it implies that the universe of ordinary discourse is not totally closed to negative elements and that critical and affirmative elements are not two entirely different worlds of meaning. Rather, they cohabit the same speech acts in the sense that criticism to some degree is manifested within ("interrelated," "merged," and "overlap-[ping]" with) the positive, uncritical language of common affairs. This last theme certainly emerges from Marcuse's second example (of Kraus) relating depth to surface meanings. It likewise emerges from his first illustration if slang is taken to be an addition to ordinary language and colloquial speech is taken to be a revision or extension of established meanings. Both forms of unconventional discourse, then, are integral to rather than removed from ordinary language.

All three points stand together inseparably and are extremely significant, particularly the third. They are indicative of a view of ordinary language to which Marcuse, if I am correct in discerning their presence within his discussion of meaning and language, nearly subscribes. This view, in some form held in common by interpretive, hermeneutic, and intersubjective modes of inquiry, maintains that linguistic meaning is formed within a network of social relations, is shared by all individual participants, and that meaning can be grasped by regarding its various layers not as independent of one another but as internally related; that is, one set of meanings cannot be explicated without reference to another set. Meanings are internally related and can be so comprehended because they all originate in the general practices of a social context that involve its participants or, to put it differently, because they are constituted intersubjectively.

Since from the standpoint of the concept of intersubjectivity all meaning springs from the thought and action of the (individual and collective) subject, even ideological meaning engineered by institutions within the social system must share at least partially the linguistic meaning of intersubjective terms. This sharing of intersubjective meanings, which derive from the practical social basis of language, which in turn establishes the internal relation of meaning, makes it possible for ordinary individuals critically to grasp the ideological distortion of surface meanings by reference to other and internally related deeper layers of meaning. Hence, in terms of the concept of intersubjectivity, in principle as well as in practice the authors of speech acts permeated with ideological content should be able to comprehend the deeper meaning, which clarifies the real meaning of the ideologically distorted expression, because these layers of meaning are internally related. The significance of intersubjectivity is clear. Even a subject totally submerged within ideology is potentially able to move beyond it to become a critical subject.

Just as this view of language, the conception of intersubjectively constituted meanings, with its implications for critical subjectivity, begins to crystallize in Marcuse's discussion of the multidimensionality of ordinary language, his analysis ends prematurely. Although his discussion touches upon the many decisive aspects of ordinary discourse, specifically the concern with layers of meaning and their internal relations (that a knowledge of the deeper meanings is required for a correct exposition of ideological meanings), and though he insists all along that the social context of meaning receive attention, he fails to push the notion of social context to a concept of an intersubjectively constituted context of meaning. For Marcuse, social context appears to mean social structures or political institutions that create ideological meanings completely independent of the language and meaning constituted by the activity of the society's members. The pragmatic ideological meanings, pragmatic in the sense of being functional to the social system and to the individual who must live and work in it, are learned but apparently bear no resemblance to the linguistic meanings formed by the participants in the social process. It is as though the individual comes to know two entirely different languages, one constituted intersubjectively and the other structurally determined, neither of which can be understood in the least in the other's terms. Only such a structural theory of the formation of the "prevailing universe of discourse" could explain how ideological meanings are closed to critical perspectives.

Marcuse's view of ordinary language is thus ambiguous. On the one hand, he maintains that discourse is relatively open. Slang, colloquial speech, and the deeper, "concealed" meanings which Kraus addressed, all to a greater or lesser extent enter consciousness and introduce a critical edge to subjectivity by calling into question the internally related meanings of ideological discourse. On the other hand, Marcuse argues that critical access to ideological meaning is blocked; the universe of discourse is closed.

This ambiguity can be rendered intelligible in the following way. Because he failed to develop his view of ordinary language to include a concept of intersubjectively constituted meanings, for Marcuse meaning beyond ideologically distorted language cannot be accessible to the members of society from whose social practices meaning originates. But since he develops his argument to the level of a concept of internally related meanings, the universe of discourse does remain open, yet if not for the individual then for whom? — for the theorist or analyst! Thus, underlying what initially appears to be an ambiguous view of ordinary language is a rather consistent and ultimately objectionable theory of the relationship among subjectivity, language, meaning, and ideology. Since Marcuse has a conception of internal relations but lacks a concept of intersubjectivity, it is no paradox that the ideas within what the individual thinks and says are critical though the individual is not. On the contrary, according to Marcuse ordinary consciousness is imprisoned within the "straightjacket of common usage," within a "totally manipulated and indoctrinated universe" characterized by a "purged and impoverished language." Establishing the true meaning of whatever is thought or spoken — in effect, establishing the connection between a repressive social order and the ideological meanings it manufactures to conceal the relations of domination — "is not the job of ordinary thought in ordinary speech."[94] The authoritarian implications of this statement by Marcuse, and of the theory of meaning that lies behind it, are all too transparent. The tragedy, and an irony for a theorist whose critical framework should have included a more adequate concept of (inter-)subjectivity, is that these implications could have been avoided.

A critical subject about to be born through an analysis stressing the multidimensionality of ordinary language is thus aborted just as it stirs beneath the surface of an argument having a foreshortened conception of subjectivity. It is not as though intersubjectivity were a concept with which Marcuse could not have been familiar. It is central to the phenomenological tradition, for example, in the philosophy of Hegel, Heidegger, and Husserl, three figures crucial to Marcuse's theoretical development, and more recently it is present in analytic philosophy in such texts as Peter Winch's *Idea of a Social Science* (1958), though Marcuse's antipathy to analytic thought would blind him to the significance of the latter contribution. As we saw in chapter two, the plight of critical theory in the historical context of fascism compelled an interpretation of Hegel that emphasizes the logical structure of the dialectic and the "universal." Such an interpretation led Marcuse elsewhere than to the concept of intersubjectivity and the critical subject associated with it. And as we saw in chapter one, in his early work Marcuse rejects Heidegger, a rejection no doubt obscuring as well the important intersubjectivist dimensions of Heidegger's philosophy. With regard to Husserl no such excuse can be provided. For in *One-dimensional Man*, Marcuse's critique of science relies heavily on Husserl's *Crisis of the European Sciences*. In this work by Husserl intersubjectivity figures prominently. Furthermore, there was another and immediate opportunity at Marcuse's disposal for developing a view of critical subjectivity very similar to that implied by the concept of intersubjectively constituted meanings. This source is particularly relevant to the present argument.

In *One-dimensional Man* there is a brief but important discussion of the Platonic dialectic that occurs within a broader context exploring the differences between pretechnological and technological rationality, dialectical and formal logic, critical and one-dimensional thought.[95] Marcuse recognizes and draws out the significance of a decisive aspect of Plato's dialectic.

The experience of a divided world finds its logic in the Platonic dialectic. Here, the terms "Being," "Non-being," "Movement," "the One and the Many," "Identity," and "Contradiction" are methodically kept open, ambiguous, not fully defined. They have an open horizon, an entire universe of meaning which is *gradually structured in the process of communication itself, but which is never closed.* The propositions are submitted, developed, and tested in a *dialogue,* in which the *partner is led to question the normally unquestioned universe of experience and speech, and to enter a new dimension of discourse* — otherwise he is *free* and the discourse is addressed to his freedom. *He is supposed to go beyond that which is given to him* — *as the speaker, in his proposition, goes beyond the initial setting of the terms.* These terms have many meanings because the conditions to which they refer have many sides, implications, and effects which cannot be insulated and stabilized.[96]

This passage is striking for many reasons. First, in his reference to "meaning which is gradually structured in the process of communication itself, but which is never closed," Marcuse describes a Platonic conception that has as its implicit presupposition a notion closely approximating that of intersubjectively constituted meanings. Meaning can be structured, that is, reconstructed through dialogue (communication), because it is assumed that meanings are formed and shared by the participants in the larger social process even before they enter into a critical dialogue. While Plato does not suppose so precise a concept of intersubjectivity, its characteristics are very nearly embodied in his theory of knowledge as "recollection," that that which has been learned in the context of social life and then forgotten under the constraint of public opinion can be recalled through discourse.[97] The significance of recollection is comparable to that of intersubjectivity. Both locate the critical elements of meaning within the cognitive experience of the subject and as such are accessible to the individual. Although the philosopher appears to have the authoritative edge in guiding the evolution of the dialogue, in principle he does not formally teach the participants. Rather, the individual's acquired meanings are learned through speech because they were already contained within the rich and varied network of socially constituted meanings. The potentially critical disposition of the subject and the nonauthoritarian role of the theorist in relationship to the individual are two points central to Plato's dialectic and should have occurred to Marcuse in light of his familiarity with the doctrine of recollection and his exposition of the structure of the dialogue ("the *partner is led to question* . . . ").[98]

Second, Marcuse makes it clear that the purpose Plato attributed to dialogue is to engage participants in a critical examination of their commonplace beliefs and, through a private or public discussion that poses questions and possible answers, to eliminate the distortions of opinion and to arrive at a truer understanding of the object of inquiry (virtue, justice, the good, etc.). For Plato, in other words, although discourse is constrained and structured by the social system, these constraints can be shattered through dialogue. By revealing what has been hidden from conscious awareness and reflection, by disclosing what the participants in discussion already know at a deeper level of conscious and unconscious existence, by making explicit what is implicit in the fabric of socially constituted meaning, Platonic discourse is at the same time a highly *politicized* discourse. Marcuse senses this aspect of the Platonic dialectic when he says that the partner is not only led to question ideological meanings but by so doing "enters a new dimension of discourse." Yet, when it comes to developing his own view of the relationship between thought and meaning, Marcuse's insights into Plato's dialectic are neglected. For Marcuse has neither a concept of politicized discourse nor a concept of a critical subject disposed to politics.

Marcuse's theory, therefore, could have benefited from the opportunity to seize the critical dimensions inherent in Plato's dialectic. In fact, the opportunity actually had been present in an early essay perhaps more emphatically than in *One-dimensional Man*. Discussing the bearing of the Platonic dialectic of the later dialogues (*Theaetetus, Sophist, Philebus*) on Hegel's dialectic, Marcuse says of the former that "the truth of being is discovered and preserved in human speech (*Logos, legein*). Human speech is essentially talking with another about something; *only in discussion (Durchsprechen)* with another can [speech, the dialectic] fulfill its discovery and preservation function."[99] The language is more abstract than that of *One-dimensional Man*, but the thesis is clear. Knowledge of the true nature of existence, including "socially organized existence," is "preserved" (deeply embedded) in everyday meaning and can be "discovered and preserved" (consciously grasped) only through practical human discourse.

Marcuse takes a further step and contends that philosophical inquiry is able to be dialectical, that is, critical, only when it is grounded in the concrete activity of speech (*Konkretion für das menschliche Miteinander-reden*).[100] Following Plato, Marcuse indissolubly joins language, meaning, speech, and critical subjectivity. Here it is not, as it is with Marcuse's own view of the relationship between ordinary language and the individual in *One-dimensional Man*, the philosopher (theorist, analyst) claiming truth by abstracting in an authoritarian manner the critical elements of discourse. Rather, it is the individual philosophizing through discourse. Plato certainly did not restrict philosophizing to the philosopher — only the slave (excepting the slave of the *Meno*) was limited in this capacity. But the slave, unlike the ordinary individual, could not become a critical subject because *he lacked the faculty of reason*. If Marcuse consistently views the universe of meaning as relatively open but in his later work maintains that the individual is limited in his awareness to the surface meanings of ideologically distorted language, then Marcuse's subject, like Plato's slave, is incapable of reason. Marcuse's individual would not have the capacity for critical insight, much less a critical perspective on society. This analogy thus produces conclusions consistent with the earlier argument that Marcuse's theory of one-dimensional society contains assumptions about the nature of the individual that dispose him to complete domination by technological rationality.

In fact, Marcuse may even believe meaning to be open to a degree greater than is indicated by his discussion of extralinguistic terms and the multidimensional universe of meaning within ordinary language. At one point he remarks of the one-dimensional, functionalized language that "people don't believe it, or don't care, and yet act accordingly."[101] Here it seems that the subject is not so credulous as to be caught within the web of ideological discourse. The subject preserves a critical detachment. From the perspective of the individual, established meanings are pragmatic but false. It would seem reasonable to conclude, though Marcuse draws no such conclusion, that the interpretation the individual has of his social behavior and of the operation of the social system derives its meaning not from the prevailing and institutionalized modes of discourse but from some other and perhaps critical standpoint. Consequently, an open universe of meaning is *potentially* an open universe of dialogue and involves *potential* contests between the ideologically dominant meanings and layers of meaning that challenge established norms. It involves, as well, a *potentially* critical and politicized subject. As long as Marcuse maintains, to any extent, the openness of meaning, as he does clearly in several ways, he is obliged to return the problem of meaning to the subject, for whom it must be most meaningful, if criticism is to mean anything more than critical *theory*.

LINGUISTIC ANALYSIS

Now turning our attention to linguistic analysis, we discover that that "whole branch of analytic philosophy," which Marcuse regards as an essentially conservative discipline, preserves a definite critical edge in its orientation to ordinary language. For instance, in his essay "When Is Ordinary Language Reformed?" (1961), Manley Thompson argues that ordinary language incorporates erroneous beliefs even after false but well-established beliefs have been proven wrong because language will lag behind alterations in belief systems.[102] People continue to speak in ways that express mistaken beliefs although they have come to hold others. Ordinary language is "pretheoretical" and is to be accepted as valid only until inquiry suggests reasons to change beliefs. Thompson's points are significant. They underline the inadequacy of ordinary language, indicate that beliefs can contradict the prevailing universe of meaning, and that one of the tasks of philosophical inquiry is to question beliefs expressed in ordinary discourse. Implicitly, he inserts a distance between what the individual believes to be meaningful and the impoverished established meanings of spoken and written language. At the same time, emphasizing the pretheoretical status of ordinary language dissociates theoretical language from the given ideological terms and clearly rejects the latter as the final criteria of truth and falsehood.

Similar views are expressed elsewhere and differently by a wide range of analytic philosophers. To note other examples, in his article "Moore and Ordinary Language" (1942), Norman Malcolm argues that the use of ordinary language frequently entails a view of the world that is *linguistically* correct but empirically false.[103] Alluding to the time when the common view was that the world is flat, he declares that "it is perfectly possible for *everyone* to say what is wrong."[104] On this claim, Marcuse and language philosophy are in agreement; indeed, Marcuse maintains an identical position. The entire one-dimensional society speaks in the language of established meanings, meanings that are linguistically correct, appropriate in terms of the criterion of ordinary meaning, but otherwise profoundly wrong. And concluding an argument that ordinary language does not have the philosophical significance many philosophers attribute to it, Roderick Chisholm writes in "Philosophers and Ordinary Language" (1951) that there is "sufficient reason for believing [the statement that] 'any philosophical statement which violates ordinary language is false' " is itself false.[105] Moreover, in "Philosophical Discoveries" (1960), R. M. Hare praises the Socratic method of arriving at knowledge through dialectical (!) analysis.[106] The dialectic reveals the incorrect use of words and moves toward a truthful understanding of concepts. Provisionally, he concurs with the metaphysicians (!) that philosophy must contain statements that conform neither to the actual use of words (ordinary discourse) nor to philosophers' decisions about how words ought to be used. In other words, philosophy must contain statements that refer to possible levels of empirical existence other than those expressed by the simple facts, or "mere data," of immediate experience.[107]

Virtually endless are the instances of philosophers' locating, or rather relocating, the boundaries of meaning far beyond the universe of ordinary discourse. One final illustration is Stuart Hampshire's "Interpretation of Language: Words and Concepts" (1957).[108] Here it is argued that the task undertaken by linguistic philosophers to distinguish among and to describe the various usages of language should properly and primarily include a historical dimension. Since the meaning of concepts changes gradually from one historical period to the next, it is quite misleading of linguistic analysts to speak generally about language as though an entire range of discourse could be founded on the restricted study of a few terms. Insisting on the historical character of concepts, Hampshire also questions the disposition of philosophers to judge as meaningless those concepts whose conditions of application no longer exist. Indeed, concepts having no corresponding reality can be understood and used meaningfully and correctly in ordinary speech even if that to which they refer is historically remote. With its all-important emphasis on history, Hampshire's argument retains an antipositivistic region of experience against which the prevailing social system may be evaluated. That is, it opposes the efforts of some linguistic analysts to close the meaning of concepts around established and simplistic functional definitions. Opening conceptual discourse to the rich and varied historically evolved meanings is simultaneously an opening to a critical perspective. Recalling what decisive philosophical concepts have meant in the past is to question implicitly how and why they have acquired their newly formed meanings within the present social order.

All published before *One-dimensional Man*, the examples I have selected portray linguistic philosophy in a radically different light from that of Marcuse's characterization. Obviously, Marcuse's view of ordinary language philosophy is exaggerated; more than adequate evidence was available to him demonstrating that, at the least, linguistic analysis does not subscribe to the principle that ordinary language offers sound criteria for differentiating between truth and falsehood. Furthermore, the critique I have provided is deliberately modest though it is sufficient to establish Marcuse's error. An elaborate investigation of language analysis would reveal many additional critical elements.[109] And while linguistic philosophy does not engage in the sort of sociological analysis Marcuse demands of it, its refusal to equate meaning per se with ordinary meaning raises questions about meaning that can be examined sociologically. To make this point more strongly, linguistic philosophy does not exclude critical sociology but implies sociological theory as the completion of its own enterprise.

THE ADMINISTRATION OF WORK

As an example of the therapeutic operationalism of industrial psychology and sociology, Marcuse chose the study of labor relations of the Western Electric factory in Hawthorne, Illinois, conducted by Elton Mayo. Though this is an old and classic study (late 1920s), in Marcuse's opinion the "substance and function [of its methods] have remained the same" in the considerably refined operational techniques of scientific management developed since that time.[110] Certainly, there is a sense in which Marcuse is correct. Research continues, at what must be described as a furious pace, to seek newer and more sophisticated technical procedures for therapeutically adjusting the needs of the worker to the goals of organized production. Surveying the voluminous writings of organizational theorists since Taylor and Mayo (research produced through the collaboration of private industry, private consulting firms, the academic establishment, and frequently governmental agencies),[111] it is easy to be impressed by the extent to which scientific management has reached ever higher levels of technological perfection. Technical reason certainly appears to be servicing the goals of rationalization and productivity. But this supposed tendency toward more efficient domination through the application of technical reason to problems in labor relations can be evaluated from another, and I believe more insightful, perspective.

At one point in the development of industrial management schemes, and it is difficult to ascertain when the "breakthrough" occurred because the literature is massive, it was discovered that the worker is not simply an infinitely pliable entity who can be reshaped to mesh with the productive process any time he expresses some sort of dissatisfaction or recalcitrance. In 1960, for example, we find *The Human Side of Enterprise*, a text by Douglas McGregor that reconceptualized the worker in terms of Abraham Maslow's "hierarchy of human needs."[112] At least from the period marked by its publication, industrial psychology acknowledged that the employee's needs are substantially more complex than was assumed by the management models of either Taylor or Mayo. To begin with, in the long range the veteran techniques had never been successful. Now, in the fully modernized world they were clearly obsolete. Newer techniques — "job rotation," "job enlargement," "participative management," "work teams," "human relations training," "sensitivity training," "job enrichment," "encounter groups," and even the philosophies of the East (Taoism, Buddhism), just to name a few — were developed and underwent variation in organizational theories that multiplied at an exponential rate to take into account not only the complexities of the worker's rational abilities but his emotional needs, as well. Employees were suffering from one or more maladies caused by rationalization—frustration, feelings that their work was meaningless, psychological failure, reduced output, errors, postponement of difficult decisions, daydreaming, impatience, aggression against and conflict with subordinates and superiors, and so forth.[113] As rationalization progresses, so does the scope and intensity of these ills. And workers in the plant and on the assembly line were not the only group targeted for research; rationalization also affected white-collar employees positioned all along the organizational hierarchy. "Personality and Organization (P and O)" theory, for example, stressed techniques fostering "growth needs" and "self-actualization."

Marcuse would interpret these developments, whose "substance and function have remained the same" as the methods of the classical studies, as so many examples charting the progress of domination through technical rationalization. An alternative interpretation, however, is suggested by the very proliferation of these technical theories and practices. Adjustive, therapeutic methods of labor management continually and rapidly evolve not because of the administrative success of technical procedures but because of their *failure*.[114] "Irrational" human factors increasingly appear in response to rationalization as it moves forward. What is therefore indicated by the almost frenetic rush and dispersal of theoretical energies invested to reshape the "human side of enterprise" is a fundamental contradiction between human nature and the nature of work in a technological society that scientific management cannot eliminate. Human nature apparently reaches a threshold of socialization beyond which the technical administration of work can no longer bend human nature to an alien logic. What this suggests is that the increasing rationalization of production results not in more extensive domination but in increasing *resistance* to domination. Technological domination may therefore reach its limits long before total rationalization has been consummated, and at the highest stages of rationalization this process may be sowing the seeds for its reversal.

The contradiction between human nature and the nature of work in a rationalized society cannot be identified through Marcuse's theory. On the contrary, for Marcuse the operational techniques applied to adjust the worker's needs to the imperatives of productivity completely reshape the subject to accord perfectly with the ongoing process of rationalization. According to Marcuse, when forming operational definitions the researcher merely follows "the worker's own translations" of his general grievances.[115] In other words, the worker has no conception of his own needs apart from those most suitable to the technician and the organization (and society) on whose behalf the technician works. Yet, the opposite seems to be the case. Old techniques are disposed of, new techniques proposed, each attempting, without compromising the ends of production, to meet the needs of the worker, which always seem to *defy* the inventiveness of technical reason. With needs and dispositions more complex than can be translated into operationally defined behavior, the individual subject is in permanent opposition. Technological rationality is frustrated by the rationality of subjectivity.

This remains true even where the anthropological model of the subject that informs the development of new techniques and operational translations is only as complex as Maslow's hierarchy of needs. The irony is that Maslow's model itself is an operational conception of man in that it severely underestimates the complexity of human nature, but even *its* anthropological characteristics (human needs, capacities, etc.) cannot be operationally translated and adjusted technically to the most advanced technological mode of production. If Maslow's concept of human nature, or more exactly the human needs to which it refers, cannot be technically translated into the operational terms of functional behavior without leaving a significant residue of discontented, frustrated, and alienated subjectivity, then an *adequate* anthropological account of human nature, as is represented by Freud's metapsychology, would reveal the actual depth dimensions of subjectivity that surface in resistance to all technical translations. Scientific management, however, can never embrace a Freudian psychology because it establishes firmly the absolute limits to technical reason — that human needs and the needs of a technologically advanced society whose substantive rationality is capitalist are ultimately incompatible. If Marcuse's theory of technological domination and one-dimensionality had taken Freud's metapsychology as its analytic point of departure, as we would have expected, instead of a minimal set of anthropological assumptions that are intrinsically behaviorist, or if he had even assumed a concept of human nature derived from Maslow's or a comparable theoretical view, he would have begun to identify the limits to domination and to define the subjective basis for critical theory and political practice.

POLITICS

Just as a study of the travails of the management sciences of labor relations implies an anthropology far more complex than is assumed either by organizational theorists or by Marcuse, a consideration of the tendencies of electoral and party politics in advanced industrial societies will shed further light on the actual nature of subjectivity. Marcuse's explanation for the conservatism of political parties on the left is superficial in an important sense. This is not necessarily to say that the increasing moderation of left party politics is not ultimately a response to a progressively conservative electoral base, but rather that merely asserting this as a brute fact of rationalization belies analyses of the real conditions influencing electoral conservatism. These analyses reveal a highly politicized process where Marcuse believes politics simply to have receded in the face of technological advancement. Higher standards of living, reflected in the income, wealth, and status of the newly affluent worker, and a mass culture industry engineering false needs, in Marcuse's estimation are sufficient to account for the movement away from radical ideologies. Mass support for the system is rooted in its ability to deliver ever greater quantities of material goods and services.

"Mainstream" or "bourgeois" social science, however, has done an excellent job in demonstrating that the matter cannot be explained in such elementary terms. The studies to which I allude either were designed explicitly to test the validity of the end of ideology thesis or bear directly upon it. Quite generally, the end of ideology argument is that material deprivation precipitates extremist ideological views and radical, if not revolutionary, political practice; whereas ameliorated economic conditions mitigate conflict by altering its basis and gradually but inevitably lead to a consensus on the legitimacy of the social system in which all major classes come to participate democratically.[116] As we have seen, Marcuse's analysis of advanced industrial society is substantially more complex than this argument, which is certainly crude in comparison. Nonetheless, to a limited extent, specifically and only with regard to electoral conservatism, Marcuse does focus on material rewards as the factor most influential in determining the possible erosion of class based party loyalties. This erosion occurs if parties fail to moderate their ideological and programmatic elements in favor of a consensual politics, that is, in favor of the established economic order and of the political institutions under which it flourishes. Against Marcuse, however, numerous studies have shown that political attitudes are not strictly a function of material conditions but are shaped by a wide range of factors other than, although frequently associated with, economic development. Three examples of these studies will be adequate to demonstrate their important implications.

In *The Affluent Worker: Political Attitudes and Behavior*, J. H. Goldthorpe, D. Lockwood, F. Bechofer, and J. Platt rejected the view that a large segment of the British working class supported the Tories as a result of improved socioeconomic conditions.[117] They conceded that the period after the Second World War, especially during the 1950s, was characterized by a marked increase in the number of families receiving a middle-class income. These same years saw undisputed dominance of the Conservative party. At the same time, there were indications that in the most progressive economic areas the Labour party lost electoral support. Was affluence per se responsible for the decline in the Labour vote, or was some other factor or set of factors at work?

The workers studied were in many ways what could be referred to as the "well-to-do lower strata," meaning that they were middle class in terms of income and material advantages despite a working-class occupation and education. The authors' findings invalidated the thesis that as things get better materially, and even are perceived to have improved, these differences have an effect on party allegiances. Their findings specifically indicated that, although clearly affluent by comparison with lower middle-class white-collar and other blue-collar workers, the sample as a whole was strong and stable in its allegiance to Labour. This was the most significant aspect of the study and it falsifies the thesis that improved economic conditions completely break down class based parties. Instead, it was shown that the social structure in which the worker lives and works influences, or "mediates," political convictions. Everything the worker is exposed to in his environment at work and at leisure reinforces convictions and isolates the worker from social pressures that could alter them. The central factor at issue is the worker's environment, that is, sociopsychological factors.

This last point is supported in *Political Change in Britain*, by David Butler and Donald Stokes.[118] Noting that the impact of class affiliation on electoral behavior differs from region to region in Britain and has done so for decades, the authors suggested that variations among regions may be explained through a ratio of regional class composition in relation to a degree of persuasiveness in the formation of political attitudes, opinions, and party allegiances. From their complex empirical investigation it seems that the higher the ratio of class composition in a particular region, the greater the expectancy that the electoral support for the party of the dominant class in that region will exceed the simple ratio of class composition. Electoral support, in other words, does not merely reflect class composition but exceeds it by a figure related to the magnitude of the ratio. If the ratio of working to middle class in region X is three to one and in region Y two to one, electoral support for the dominant class based party in both cases is greater than the ratio of classes, and just how much greater is a function of the size of the ratio. The magnitude of the ratio is a measure of the intensity with which the concentration of a given class acts as a persuasive force that attracts electoral support for its party from other classes in the region. Once again, the factors directly affecting party allegiance are primarily sociopsychological.

Both of these studies bear an interesting theoretical resemblance to Richard Hamilton's *Affluence and the French Worker in the Fourth Republic*.[119] Hamilton's express aim was to examine the validity of the end of ideology thesis. As a test case he took Fourth Republic France during a period (1950s) in which a relatively high rate of economic growth was experienced. During the same period the vote for the French Communist party remained stable. Hamilton demonstrated that socioeconomically improved conditions had little effect in pulling French workers away from radical commitments and convictions. Rising standards of living made no significant difference in the basic pattern of workers' lives. Under the influence of factory and neighborhood communists and party workers, material improvement, in short affluence, was interpreted largely within a left-wing frame of reference. The key variables that account for the persistence of working-class support for the French Communist party are sociopsychological and organizational, that is, underlying group pressures and a highly structured interpretive frame of reference influencing political attitudes and behavior. Hamilton pointed out, in fact, that with certain forms of social organization economic development is accompanied by an increase in radicalism and not by the usually anticipated conservatism. An instance from Hamilton's study concerns the worker who migrates from a rural to an urban sector to take advantage of economic opportunities. He becomes exposed to a communist milieu, a veritable subculture, extending from the factory to the neighborhood. He comes to live in an insular workers' world, psychologically removed from the impact of moderating cross-pressures as the latter are critically interpreted through radical norms and standards.

Each of these studies carries an important set of implications, and the full significance of these implications is brought out most clearly in Hamilton's project. In each case considered, sociopsychological factors played a decisive role in shaping political opinions and electoral behavior. The specific content of such influences would change, of course, with changes in socioeconomic conditions. As Hamilton indicated, for example, changes in income can be accompanied by changes in employment, working conditions and experience, residence, organizational affiliation, informal communications channels, reference groups, and other standards of comparison. The worker's environment is the paramount factor in influencing political attitudes, although they could be swayed in a variety of directions by an altered surrounding. Of very great significance, therefore, is the shape of this influence, the texture of the environment, which can be designed organizationally. Consequently, Hamilton's study takes the importance of environmental factors a step further by underscoring the place of party structure—its organizational network, strategies, and tactics—which, if present, possibly can counter the conservative influence of affluence.

In a double sense these studies, particularly Hamilton's, offer a perspective critical of Marcuse's explanation of the centripetal movement of left political parties. First, communist and socialist parties are not simply coerced by the progress of technological society to tailor their programs to a pace keeping with the supposed conservative dispositions of their class bases; rather, they must do so insofar as competing environmental pressures prove more effective than organizational influences in shaping opinion. Hence, such a necessity arises only where party organizational structure is weak. Second, where party organizational networks are extensive and disciplined at all levels, as they have been in Italy during the past decade, the abandonment of radical ideologies thus must lie with the party leadership. Such party leadership would then resemble the classical model of social democratic reformism and gradualism.

The problems with Marcuse's thesis are obvious. It ignores the highly politicized nature of the formation of attitudes influencing electoral behavior, emphasizing instead purely technical-economic factors. Stressed are affluence, an ideology of material progress, and the impact of the mass culture industry on the determination of needs and beliefs favoring the perpetuation of the status quo; neglected are the political-psychological dimensions of this process, which outline the prospects for the intervention of political organizations. In the final analysis, which refocuses attention on the motivation of the party rather than on the *embourgeoisement* of the working class, Marcuse's account of left party electoral reformism serves as an apology for social democratic labor bureaucrats who have imposed a course of social integration upon Marcuse's working-class subject.

SOVIET MARXISM

Soviet Marxism is one other context in which technological rationalization acquires an apologetic cast. As we learned earlier, according to Marcuse all facets of Soviet leadership were constrained and justified by the commitment to industrialize the Soviet Union as quickly as possible. Rapid industrialization was justified in turn by a vision of socialism that viewed a highly developed technical base as its essential precondition, by the necessity to construct an adequate system of military defenses to ward off threats from the West, and by the theory that a liberal second phase of Soviet socialism resulting from technological progress would transform the image of an aggressive communism, break the international consolidation of capitalist powers, and plunge them into normalized relations issuing in a final capitalist crisis. This overriding objective of the rationalization of Soviet society shaped its domestic and foreign policies, aggregated power to a centralized party apparatus, placed the bureaucracy in a position to become an independent power base, promoted the comprehensive regimentation of work and education, and fostered the curtailment of political, cultural, and personal freedoms. Once fully industrialized on a parity with the West, Marcuse argued, the rationale for these measures would have become obsolete and the Soviet leadership would be obliged by the logic of its technical plan to introduce political decentralization, reduce the power of the secret police, initiate a liberal phase ending all censorship and the repression of freedoms, and continue the collective leadership. This new stage would occur despite the continued emphasis on the development of heavy industry. For liberalization was contingent only upon industrialization and, as Marcuse recognized, the achieved level of technical progress after the Second World War could bear the weight of the simultaneous development of heavy and light (consumer oriented) industry.

Marcuse's predictions or, more precisely, his projections of what must necessarily occur given the logic of technical rationality as he believed it was to unfold within the Soviet Union have proven to be false. While the political power of the secret police has declined, its administrative power has increased considerably. What this means is that high ranking political and administrative officials in the party and bureaucracy are no longer subjected to arbitrary and brutal purges, as they had been under Stalin, but the ordinary citizen, intellectual, artist, and so forth, have become the unhappy victims of threats, exile, unemployment, and a variety of other less and more subtle forms of administrative harassment. Decentralization of decisionmaking certainly has not taken place. For a brief period beginning in 1962 Khrushchev attempted a partial decentralization and division of industrial and agricultural functions, but this move was made for administrative reasons and ended abruptly with his ouster in 1964. Collective leadership has continued though in itself is hardly evidence of a progressive and democratic form of government, particularly as the basic domestic policies of the Soviet

Union have not changed in the past twenty years. Most important, it cannot be claimed that Soviet society has become less repressive. The state management of cultural life and the suppression of individual freedoms have risen steadily.

Needless to say, "liberal" or "liberalized" are not terms descriptive of contemporary Soviet society, as Marcuse thought that they would be. A single change has been the attention to consumer needs, such that "welfare-state totalitarianism" or "welfare-state authoritarianism" far more accurately describe this repressive social system that abides a limited consumer ethic.[120] The absence of liberalization in Soviet politics questions fundamentally the validity of Marcuse's thesis that Soviet development was and is constrained within the parameters of a technological project. Clearly, the failure of the liberal phase to materialize after industrialization was accomplished is proof that in the contemporary period politics operates independently of the restraints imposed by an ideology of rationalization and technical progress. Suppression by political means, in other words, continues beyond the point at which, according to Marcuse, it could be justified by technical considerations.

Only in the contemporary period? Since political domination can be judged now to have escaped what initially appeared to be technical constraints, it is necessary to inquire retrospectively whether the plan of technological rationalization ever could explain and justify the forceful coordination of Soviet society with that goal. The answer must be that it cannot, for although it is possible to conceive of the justification for the regimentation of those sectors of Soviet society directly related to the rationalization of material productivity, no theory of socialist development could defend the legitimacy of the suppression of cultural and individual freedom that characterized the first phase of socialist construction. One that would attempt to do so, such as Marcuse's thesis of the technical determinants of Soviet politics, would constitute an apology for an oppressive state apparatus. Yet, supposing that Marcuse's theory of a technical justification for total suppression could be defended, the more basic question is whether technical factors did actually constrain Soviet politics during the first phase. To this question it must be responded that if the achieved stage of industrialization obviously has not altered Soviet political practices, which indicates that politics is now independent of technical pressures, there is every reason to assume that politics has always been independent of technical logistics.

On these grounds two final points can be made. In light of the truly repressive *political* nature of Soviet institutions, it is rather doubtful that, as Marcuse contended, they are progressive in a way that would allow Soviet society to harness a fully rationalized technological base to realize a Marxist humanism. Second, since political domination is required despite the benefits of material progress and, most important, despite what is becoming a comprehensively rationalized technological society, it seems as though technical reason has not succeeded in introducing a qualitatively new form of domination that renders repressive political measures indispensable. This last and crucial point reveals the true relationship between political and technological domination, which in its Soviet form is actually an exaggerated expression of the relation as it prevails within advanced industrial societies of the West.

SUMMATION

The criticisms offered of Marcuse's theory of technological domination each captures in a different way the defectiveness of Marcuse's theory, and each in its own way is meant to contribute to reinstating subjectivity. Where a subject can be discovered actively participating in the formation of the rationality of social order, or where a subject appears in opposition to a fully constituted technical rationality, there also survives a basis for a critical theory with a critical political practice. Reversing the sequence of analysis, a few summary remarks are in order.

The analysis tried to show that Marcuse is incorrect about the relationship between politics and technology in the Soviet Union. Recent developments there have proven that domination is political rather than technological, and the evidence for this view also questions whether tendencies toward technological domination in fact ever existed. Furthermore, the very clear and precise function of Soviet politics discloses the secret of the actual relationship between politics and technics in the advanced industrial societies generally and indicates that an evaluation of the role of politics from the standpoint of an apparently universal technical logic veils the hegemony of politics together with its irrationality.

My examination of electoral and party conservatism argued that technological rationality is a poor explanation for both and that in light of the significance of sociopsychological and organizational factors in the formation of political attitudes, the political reformism of left-wing parties is more likely the cause rather than the effect of a moderate electoral base.

The inability of technical rationality to transform the individual into an expression of its own logic stands out clearly in an examination of the difficulties scientific management encounters in a progressively rationalized social order. It seems that more rather than fewer characteristics of subjectivity appear in the course of rationalization, suggesting a tendency toward a threshold beyond which rationalization cannot at the same time mean the socialization of the individual to complement technical norms, procedures, and objectives. The subject gradually reappears, so to speak, behind the back of rationalization.

Even a modest appraisal of linguistic analysis proves that it does not simplistically equate conceptual meaning with the meaning assigned to concepts within the prevailing universe of discourse. The manner in which such a distinction appears within language philosophy implicitly raises questions that can be investigated properly through sociological analysis. If it is then claimed that by not explicitly incorporating a sociological framework linguistic analysis thus assumes such a benign critical stance toward the established universe of meaning that it becomes affirmative, it must be countered that by virtue of their specialized (aesthetic, philosophical, sociological) "forms," or "modes," of presentation, each mode of discourse offers a unique critical perspective that must be preserved.

An examination of Marcuse's view of ordinary language demonstrated that his position is ambiguous — that the universe of ordinary discourse is both open and closed and that the ambiguity is resolved as the critical dimensions of language are open to the theorist but closed to the ordinary individual. Moreover, if Marcuse had had a notion of subject and of context from which he could have developed a conception of an intersubjectively constituted context of meaning, then the deeper and critical layers of meaning embedded in language would have been accessible to the individual. Opportunities had been available to Marcuse to develop such a theoretical conception, specifically from his readings of Hegel, Heidegger, Husserl, and even Plato. His interpretations of their thought prevented him, however, from stressing the significance of the quasi-autonomous spheres of subjectivity for which in different ways their writings establish grounds.

At least as far as operationalism is concerned, within the social sciences there is no identification of reason with technique. While technical (operational) criteria guide the researcher's conceptual and empirical investigations, these are not criteria whose validity already has been established independently of the disposition of the social scientist or social science community. Operational methods for determining conceptual criteria are neither chosen by nor imposed upon social science by virtue of the aura of an objective and universalistic model of science. It is the nature of positivist scientific rationality to suppress values and substitute (an equally substantive) technical logic. But what has occurred within social science around the operationalism debate is the emergence of a definite *self-consciousness* about the explicit relationship between technical norms and criteria and the interests of social science research. Through operationalism, technique expresses rather than suppresses values in every instance and apparently and deliberately so (as evidenced by the examples discussed earlier). Consequently, the rationality or irrationality of social science through operationalism lies not with technical reason but with the subjective rationality self-consciously underlying the logic of this research conducted by individuals or groups within the social science community.

Finally, laying bare the behaviorist and determinist assumptions implicit in the theory of technological domination establishes one-dimensionality as an untenable thesis. Although proposing an analysis intended to discern the extent to which technological rationality has come to supplant and to prevail over all other forms of reason that would otherwise continue to animate the thought and action of the subject, Marcuse, in his investigation, presupposed a minimal anthropology determining in advance that modern society and, most important, the individual within it are one-dimensional. As it has been conceptualized by Marcuse, the validity of technological domination depends upon the validity of a behaviorist and determinist anthropology. Any anthropology or philosophical anthropology that posits a quasi-autonomous or quasi-transcendental subject would sustain, at the very least, a theory of two-dimensional man and society, though it could very well be compatible with a notion of one-dimensional *behavior*. Thus, both the theory of one-dimensional man and the tendency *toward* one-dimensionality are plausible only if Marcuse's limited anthropology is accepted. In that event, technical reason would be victorious by default.

We have now to ask whether Marcuse's slide into an uncritical anthropology is related to his interpretation of Freud and to the rationalistic conceptual framework critical theory adopted in response to fascism. This question leads directly to a consideration of the psychological underpinnings of one-dimensionality.

Notes

1. Marcuse will eventually revise his theory of advanced industrial society to take account of many such crises. See chapter seven of this volume.

2. See chapter seven.

3. Herbert Marcuse, "Some Social Implications of Modern Technology," *Studies in Philosophy and Social Science* [*Zeitschrift für Sozialforschung*], 9, 3 (New York: 1941), p. 414.

4. Ibid.

5. Herbert Marcuse, *One-dimensional Man: Studies in the Ideology of Advanced Industrial Society* (Boston: Beacon, 1964).

6. For an extended analysis offering a somewhat different interpretation of these works see Martin Jay, *The Dialectical Imagination* (Boston: Little, Brown, 1973), pp. 152–167.

7. Jay points to the similarity of Neumann's view and Marcuse's position in *Reason and Revolution*. Ibid., p. 155.

8. See chapter six, pp. 282–286.

9. The discussion of the basic elements of technological rationality is based upon, in addition to the works cited, a consideration of Marcuse's "Some Social Implications of Modern Technology." Perhaps more than any other work, this essay presents the fundamental aspects of technological reason as Marcuse understands them.

10. Georg Lukács, *History and Class Consciousness* (Cambridge: MIT Press, 1971), p. 172.

11. *One-dimensional Man*, p. 25.

12. "Some Social Implications of Modern Technology," p. 427.

13. See chapter 3, pp. 94–97.

14. Herbert Marcuse, *Eros and Civilization: A Philosophical Inquiry into Freud* (Boston: Beacon, 1955), p. 105.

15. "Some Social Implications of Modern Technology," p. 436.

16. Herbert Marcuse, "Language and Technological Society," *Dissent*, 8, 1 (New York: 1961), p. 74.

17. Herbert Marcuse, "Industrialization and Capitalism in the Work of Max Weber," *Negations: Essays in Critical Theory* (Boston: Beacon, 1968), p. 221; originally published as "Industrialisierung und Kapitalismus im Werk Max Webers," *Kultur und Gesellschaft*, 2 (Frankfurt: Suhrkamp, 1965), pp. 107-129.

18. Compare, for example, Marcuse's analysis of the manipulation of ordinary language in *One-dimensional Man*, pp. 90-92, with his examination of the same practice in *Soviet Marxism: A Critical Analysis* (New York: Random House, Vintage Books, 1961), pp. 70-72; all citations from *Soviet Marxism* are drawn from this edition, which is distinguished by a preface added three years after the work was first published (New York: Columbia University Press, 1958).

19. *One-dimensional Man*, pp. 56-83.

20. *Soviet Marxism*, p. 69.

21. Ibid., p. 100.

22. Ibid., p. 158.

23. Ibid., p. 159.

24. For example, Marcuse explains that "the two social systems are locked in a global struggle in which the renunciation of socialist violence is found to strengthen the realm of capitalist exploitation." "Socialist Humanism?" in *Socialist Humanism*, edited by Erich Fromm (New York: Doubleday, 1965), p. 108.

25. *Soviet Marxism*, p. 168.

26. Ibid., p. xii.

27. Ibid., p. xiv.

28. *One-dimensional Man*, pp. 39-45, 52-55.

29. Ibid., p. 55.

30. *Soviet Marxism*, pp. xv-xvi.

31. See chapter seven of this volume.

32. On science see chapter six, pp. 282-283; on art see chapter eight.

33. See chapter two, pp. 73-76.

34. The classic study in this area is Seymour Martin Lipset, "Some Social Requisites of Democracy," *American Political Science Review*, 53, 1 (Washington, D.C.: 1959), pp. 69-105.

35. By Morris Janowitz and Dwaine Marvick, "Competitive Pressure and Democratic Consent," in *Political Behavior*, edited by H. Eulau, S. J. Eldersveld, and Morris Janowitz (New York: Free Press, 1956), pp. 275-286; see *One-dimensional Man*, pp. 113-118.

36. By Julian L. Woodward and Elmo Roper, "Political Activity of

American Citizens," in *Political Behavior*, pp. 133-137; see *One-dimensional Man*, pp. 118-120.

37. *One-dimensional Man*, pp. 115-116.

38. Ibid., p. 119 (italics added).

39. Ibid., p. 181.

40. Ibid., p. 88.

41. Ibid., pp. 170-171. But elsewhere Marcuse suggests that by exercising this right, that is, by restricting itself to the "clarification of particular thoughts and speech acts which are unclear," analytic philosophy is guilty of an "arrogant modesty" (*überheblicher Bescheidenheit*). "Zur Stellung des Denkens heute," in *Zeugnisse: Theodor W. Adorno zum 60. Geburtstag*, under the sponsorship of the Institut für Sozialforschung, edited by Max Horkheimer (Frankfurt: Europäische, 1963), p. 47.

42. Marcuse argues that "exact thinking, the liberation from metaphysical spectres and meaningless notions may well be considered ends in themselves." *One-dimensional Man*, p. 170.

43. Ibid., p. 195.

44. Ibid., p. 37.

45. Ibid., p. 35.

46. Herbert Marcuse, "The Obsolescence of Marxism?" in *Marx and the Western World*, edited by Nikolaus Lobkowicz (Notre Dame: University of Notre Dame Press, 1967), p. 411.

47. *One-dimensional Man*, p. 21.

48. *Eros and Civilization*, pp. 256-257.

49. Herbert Marcuse, "Theory and Therapy in Freud," *Nation*, 185 (New York: 1957), p. 200.

50. Marcuse's analyses of aggression in advanced industrial society are considered in chapter three, pp. 95-96, 107-108, and in chapter five, pp. 243-244, 256.

51. "Socialist Humanism?" p. 112.

52. Herbert Marcuse, "The Ideology of Death," in *The Meaning of Death*, edited by Herman Feifel (New York: McGraw-Hill, 1959), p. 76.

53. Herbert Marcuse, "The Problem of Social Change in the Technological Society," in *Le Développement social*, edited by Raymond Aron and Bert F. Hoselitz (Paris: Mouton, 1965), pp. 148-150; volume printed for limited distribution; address presented to a UNESCO symposium on social development, May 1961.

54. *Eros and Civilization*, p. xxvii.

55. Herbert Marcuse, "Socialism in the Developed Countries," *International Socialist Journal*, 2, 8 (Rome: 1965), p. 144; originally published as "Perspektiven des Sozialismus in der entwickelten Industriegesellschaft," *Praxis*, 1, 2-3 (Zagreb: 1965), pp. 260-270.

56. *From Max Weber*, edited by H. H. Gerth and C. Wright Mills (New York: Oxford University Press, 1972), p. 229.

57. Marcuse does not contradict himself by arguing that technological rationality is both a form of domination in itself and the means for establishing the preconditions for freedom. Technological rationality is purified of its ideological content, or rather its rationality of domination is neutralized or contained, once the society ceases to develop along the lines of technical reason, technological progress is *arrested*, and social relations are organized according to a new principle of reason that does not compel the individual to engage in labor for the sake of productivity. Technology becomes rational to the extent that it permits freedom *from* work, *from* scarcity, and *from* further technological production. To do this technological progress must be advanced — and then suspended. See chapter six, pp. 282–286.

58. *One-dimensional Man*, p. 49 (italics added).

59. Ibid., p. 104 (italics added).

60. Ibid., p. 182 (italics added).

61. Herbert Marcuse, "The Concept of Negation in the Dialectic," *Telos*, 8 (St. Louis: 1971), p. 131: originally published as "Zum Begriff der Negation in der Dialektik," *Filosoficky casopis*, 15, 3 (Prague: 1967), pp. 375–379.

62. *One-dimensional Man*, p. 3.

63. *From Max Weber*, p. 62.

64. Stanley Aronowitz was correct when he called attention to the similarity between Marcuse's theory and Parsonian "role theory." See *False Promises* (New York: McGraw-Hill, 1974), pp. 57–58.

65. For an analysis of the rationalistic structure of Marcuse's critical theory see chapter two.

66. *One-dimensional Man*, p. 115; Marcuse is quoting from Janowitz and Marvick, "Competitive Pressure and Democratic Consent," p. 276; the exclamation marks are Marcuse's. I have consulted the original article in all cases.

67. *One-dimensional Man*, p. 115.

68. Ibid., p. 116.

69. "Competitive Pressure and Democratic Consent," p. 275.

70. *One-dimensional Man*, p. 116.

71. Ibid., p. 119.

72. "Competitive Pressure and Democratic Consent," p. 276.

73. Ibid., p. 278.

74. Ibid., p. 280.

75. Ibid., p. 282.

76. Ibid.

77. Ibid.

78. Ibid., p. 276.

79. Ibid., p. 285.

80. *One-dimensional Man*, p. 116.

81. Ibid., p. 116 (brackets added).

82. Ibid., p. 119; Marcuse is quoting from Woodward and Roper, "Political Activity of American Citizens," p. 133.

83. "Political Activity of American Citizens," p. 137.

84. Ibid.

85. Ibid., p. 133.

86. *One-dimensional Man*, p. 13.

87. Ibid., p. 12, n. 5.

88. A partial listing in chronological order follows. S. S. Stevens, "The Operational Definition of Psychological Concepts," *Psychological Review*, 42, 6 (Washington, D.C.: 1935), pp. 517–527; A. C. Benjamin, "The Operational Theory of Meaning," *Philosophical Review*, 46, 6 (Ithaca: 1937), pp. 644–649; P. W. Bridgeman, "Operational Analysis," *Philosophy of Science*, 5, 2 (East Lansing: 1938), pp. 114–131; R. H. Walters and L. A. Pennington, "Operationism in Psychology," *Psychological Review*, 45, 5 (Washington, D.C.: 1938), pp. 414–423; Hornell Hart, "Operationism Analyzed Operationally," *Philosophy of Science*, 7, 3 (East Lansing: 1940), pp. 288–313; George A. Lundberg, "Operational Definitions in the Social Sciences," *American Journal of Sociology*, 47, 5 (Chicago: 1941–1942), pp. 727–743; Frank E. Hartung, "Operationalism: Idealism or Realism?" *Philosophy of Science*, 9, 4 (East Lansing: 1942), pp. 350–355; Stuart C. Dodd, "Operational Definitions Operationally Defined," *American Journal of Sociology*, 48, 3 (Chicago: 1943), pp. 482–489; Frank E. Hartung, "Operationism as a Cultural Survival," *Philosophy of Science*, 11, 4 (East Lansing: 1941), pp. 227–232; H. Israel and B. Goldstein, "Operationism in Psychology," *Psychological Review*, 51, 3 (Washington, D.C.: 1944), pp. 177–188; "Symposium on Operationism," *Psychological Review*, 52, 5 (Washington, D.C.: 1945), pp. 241–294; P. W. Bridgeman, "The Operational Aspect of Meaning," *Synthese*, 8, 3 (6–7) (Dordrecht: 1950–1951), pp. 251–259; "The Present State of Operationalism," *Scientific Monthly*, 79, 4 (Washington, D.C.: 1954), pp. 209–231.

89. For example, Gideon Sjoberg, "Operationalism and Social Research," in *Symposium on Sociological Theory*, edited by Llewellyn Gross (New York: Harper, 1959), pp. 603–627.

90. "In the academic tradition," Marcuse argues, "these dichotomies [e.g., manual versus intellectual work, labor versus leisure, necessity versus freedom, operational versus nonoperational thought] once found their parallel in the distinction between the natural sciences on the one hand, and all others on the other, the social sciences, humanities, etc. This distinction between the sciences has now become entirely obsolete." "Remarks on a Redefinition of Culture," *Daedalus*, 94, 1 (Cambridge: 1965), p. 192.

91. *One-dimensional Man*, p. 86.

92. Ibid., p. 197.

93. Ibid., p. 195.

94. Ibid., p. 180.

95. See chapter six, pp. 276-277, for Marcuse's examination of Plato's dialectical logic.

96. *One-dimensional Man*, p. 131 (italics added).

97. For another view that is quite suggestive of the one I present here see Alvin W. Gouldner, *Enter Plato*, part 2 (New York: Harper & Row, Torchbooks, 1971), especially pp. 96-112.

98. Marcuse refers to the doctrine of recollection in *Counterrevolution and Revolt* (Boston: Beacon, 1972), pp. 69-70.

99. "On the Problem of the Dialectic," *Telos*, 27 (St. Louis: 1976), p. 33; originally published as "Zum Problem der Dialektik" (part 2), *Die Gesellschaft*, 8 (part 2), 12 (Berlin: 1931), pp. 541-557.

100. Ibid. Elsewhere, in fact, Marcuse insists that in *every* act of speech the individual has knowledge of the universal, of an essence or potentiality, and that without such knowledge communication would be inconceivable. He argues that "all communicative speech (*mitteilende Reden*), which can be true or false, understands the particular as the universal (because only as such is it communicable and understandable)." "Zur Geschichte der Dialektik," *Sowjetsystem und Demokratische Gesellschaft*, 1 (Freiburg: 1966), p. 1194.

101. *One-dimensional Man*, p. 103.

102. Manley Thompson, "When Is Ordinary Language Reformed?" in *The Linguistic Turn*, edited by Richard Rorty (Chicago: University of Chicago Press, 1970), especially pp. 203-204.

103. Norman Malcolm, "Moore and Ordinary Language," in *The Linguistic Turn*, pp. 111-124.

104. Ibid., p. 117.

105. Roderick Chisholm, "Philosophers and Ordinary Language," in *The Linguistic Turn*, p. 182.

106. R. M. Hare, "Philosophical Discoveries," in *The Linguistic Turn*, especially pp. 208, 216-217.

107. Ibid., p. 217.

108. Stuart Hampshire, "The Interpretation of Language: Words and Concepts," in *The Linguistic Turn*, pp. 261-268.

109. Critical theory has not continued to neglect the critical dimensions of ordinary language and linguistic philosophy. In this area the writings of Jürgen Habermas are perhaps the best known, but investi-

gations by contemporary social theorists into all aspects of language are far more extensive.

110. *One-dimensional Man*, p. 108.

111. For example, see *Work in America*, Report of a Special Task Force to the Secretary of Health, Education, and Welfare (Cambridge: MIT Press, 1972), and its bibliography, pp. 219–253.

112. Douglas McGregor, *The Human Side of Enterprise* (New York: McGraw-Hill, 1960). The work by A. H. Maslow was *Motivation and Personality* (New York: Harper, 1954). The influence of Maslow's theory on McGregor's book is well known though Maslow is not explicitly acknowledged in the text.

113. See Chris Argyris, "Personality vs. Organization," *Organizational Dynamics*, 3, 2 (New York: AMACOM, 1974).

114. Harry Braverman makes this point precisely when he argues the "schools and theories [of industrial psychology] have succeeded one another in a dazzling proliferation of approaches and theories, a proliferation which is more than anything else testimony to their failure." *Labor and Monopoly Capital* (New York: Monthly Review Press, 1974), p. 143.

115. *One-dimensional Man*, p. 111.

116. The literature on or relating to the end of ideology is enormous. A basic introduction is provided by *The End of Ideology Debate*, edited by Chaim Waxman (Princeton: Princeton University Press, 1967), a collection of essays by Aron, Shils, Feuer, Lipset, Bell, Mills, Mannheim, and others.

117. John H. Goldthorpe and others, *The Affluent Worker: Political Attitudes and Behavior* (New York: Cambridge University Press, 1968).

118. David E. Butler and Donald Stokes, *Political Change in Britain* (New York: Macmillan, 1974).

119. Richard Hamilton, *Affluence and the French Worker in the Fourth Republic* (Princeton: Princeton University Press, 1967).

120. See Merle Fainsod's entry on "Communism" in the *International Encyclopaedia of the Social Sciences*, 3 (New York: Macmillan and Free Press, 1968), pp. 102–111, and George W. Breslauer, "On the Adaptability of Soviet Welfare State Authoritarianism," in *Soviet Society and the Communist Party*, edited by Karl Ryavec (Amherst: University of Massachusetts Press, 1978), pp. 3–25.

FIVE

Civilization Without Discontents II: The Regime Within and the Regime Without

> Whoever ventures on the enterprise of setting up a people must be ready, shall we say, to change human nature, to transform each individual, who by himself is entirely complete and solitary, into a part of a much greater whole, from which the same individual will then receive, in a sense, his life and his being. The founder of nations must weaken the structure of man in order to fortify it, to replace the physical and independent existence we have all received from nature with a moral and communal existence. In a word each man must be stripped of his powers, and given powers which are external to him, and which he cannot use without the help of others. The nearer men's natural powers are to extinction or annihilation, and the stronger and more lasting their acquired powers, the stronger and more perfect is the social institution.
>
> Rousseau, *The Social Contract*

NO SOCIAL THEORY ever dispenses with a theory of human nature. Attempts have been made to do so, much as there have been efforts to develop presuppositionless philosophies. When not an explicit theoretical objective an anthropology is at least implicit

229

in a social theory, and when brought to the surface it helps render theory intelligible, though not necessarily plausible, for that account. Such is the case, I have argued, with Marcuse's theory of one-dimensional man. One-dimensionality both requires and implies a theory of subjectivity that makes sense of the hermetically sealed universe of technological domination.

This portrait is complicated somewhat when we consider now that Marcuse's analysis of the impact of technological rationality on the individual not only contains a set of implicit anthropological assumptions but is (supposedly) carried out in full possession of an explicit anthropological framework, that of Freud's metapsychology. An interesting and important question can be posed here: why not begin the discussion of the anthropological dimensions of Marcuse's theory with his explicit interpretation of Freud's categories, which has led him to the conception of one-dimensional man? Is there not perhaps an unnecessary duplication of effort in first inferring Marcuse's anthropological categories from his theory of one-dimensionality and then turning to his explicit interpretation of Freud in order to follow how the theory is formulated? Put simply, would it not have been more appropriate to begin where Marcuse began rather than with his conclusions?

In fact, Freud's metapsychology only *appears* to guide Marcuse's investigation of the subject in advanced industrial society. The earlier analysis that internally reconstructed the anthropology informing Marcuse's theory identified his *actual* analytical point of departure by demonstrating that his anthropological categories are merely social categories by another name. Characteristics of subjectivity originate not in the subject but in the structure of the social system. They derive from institutional practices, social behavior of the narrowest variety, that is, socially useful and required behavior, from technical reason generally. In this way the individual is reduced conceptually to social, the subject to object-ive, factors. Subjectivity emerges *essentially* constituted by reified social processes. *From the beginning*, the individual is no subject at all. No dynamic relationship holds between the subject and the external world. Rather, Marcuse's subject is a social atom through and through, a pure object of theoretical *and for that reason practical* manipulation.

At this time the particulars of this argument must be thrashed out. Its validity rests largely upon a demonstration that Freud's metapsychology prescribes a view of the subject that Marcuse would have omitted from consideration if his anthropological theory were in fact structurally conceived. This will follow the exposition of Marcuse's thesis on the psychological underpinnings of technological domination, clearly one of the most fascinating aspects of his work.

The Psychological Underpinnings of One-dimensionality

In advanced industrial society ideological norms are not "internalized," as they are in traditional forms of domination. They do not become anchored within the individual's unconscious. To understand Marcuse's critical theory this point must be appreciated in its fullest significance.

The dynamics of internalization presuppose an individual equipped constitutionally with certain psychological faculties, capacities, and dispositions. Alongside an ego that seeks personal identity at the same time as gratification of needs, a superego functions as a repository for ideological beliefs generated by the social system and acquired through a process of institutional socialization (e.g., through the family). These institutions do not simply impose themselves and penetrate the deepest recesses of the mind. The ego is engaged willfully in all phases of the formation of its superego, actively constituting this inner censor, perhaps over a lifetime, by internalizing norms through "identifications" with significant persons in the environment. Obvious examples are early identifications with figures within the family. While the internalized ideological beliefs hold sway over and to a great extent regulate individual thought and action, as reason the ego can question their legitimacy, doubt their certainty, obey, disobey, and re-form the superego, locus of social rationality.

Although an ideology, technical reason, however, is acquired by means of no such process of internalization and identification. Nor does the ego ever submit it to critical evaluation. Acquisition and reconstitution of beliefs supposes an active subject playing a decisive role in socialization. Technical reason cannot be *acquired*: it involves the dissolution of ego and superego. The essential elements of subjectivity, the psychic apparatus itself, are eroded by the technical apparatus.

According to Marcuse, the development of capitalism up to and including the advanced industrial stage presupposes both the existence and the annulment of the individual. Subjectivity is either an asset or a liability to capitalist growth and stability depending upon the objective requirements of the achieved level of economic organization. During the early laissez-faire period of capitalism, the economy flourished through the activities of freely competitive individual entrepreneurs—freely in the sense that the capitalist succeeded or failed in his ventures as a consequence of his individual initiative, aggressiveness, skill at managing human and material resources, and so on. Capitalism's success as a productive economic system rested upon its "social production" of individuals able to compete effectively and aggressively. Economic productivity alone was insufficient to guarantee the reproduction (perpetuation) of laissez-faire capitalism. Equally central to the reproduction of the system were social institutions, the family in particular, which "manufactured" individuals with the psychological and cognitive equipment that enabled them to assume their dominant economic roles.

The well-known internal contradictions of this period of capitalism forced both the transition to a monopolistic market economy increasingly regulated by public institutions and a gradual transformation of the social institutions of production. The radical individualism characterizing the laissez-faire economic subject was incompatible with an economy reorganized into ever larger monopolistic concerns. Concentrating power in the technical and political administration of large-scale industry, monopoly capital dispensed not only with free enterprise and the independent entrepreneur but also with the driving force of the free enterprise system, the individual suited to be the dominant economic subject. Monopoly capital meant the elimination of the would-be bourgeois entrepreneur *and* his absorption into a universally rationalized division of labor. As the new rule of economic life, absolute subordination to a technical apparatus of production rendered the individual—who once had set goals, devised means, applied and tolerated the pressures of free and unorganized competition—obsolete.

Subordination of such an oppressive nature could not be imposed upon the individual without introducing antagonisms between economic imperatives and human needs, provoking resistance undermining the rationalization of the productive process. Scientific management can mitigate, if not, as Marcuse contends, resolve, this conflict. Even if it is true, as I have argued, that scientific management secures but precarious and temporary resolutions that continually break down and must eventually fail as the limits to the rationalization of human nature are reached, Marcuse (perhaps) can dismiss this criticism as ultimately irrelevant. Scientific management attempts to resocialize the individual to accept technical translations of employee discontents into solutions that trim the critical edge from the original grievances. Marcuse can now say for an important reason, that this practical application of technical reason, regardless of how effective it may or may not be, belongs to the earlier stages of technological development. That is, the system attains a qualitatively new level of stability when socialization comes to be completed *prior* to the individual's entry into the productive process. A new "psychic-social fit" occurs, which would make scientific management dispensable. Primarily responsible for the creation of the now obsolete economic subject, the bourgeois family underwent an internal restructuring. Marcuse historically situates this structural alteration of the family between the two world wars.[1] Linking, as he does, the emergence of a new phase of economic organization with a new phase of social organization, Marcuse must conclude that theoretically the bourgeois family and the subject it produced became historically obsolete with the first stirrings of monopoly capital. In other words, the traditional family structure was in contradiction to economic tendencies in most capitalist countries beginning approximately in the mid-nineteenth century.

When we look closely at the socialization process as Marcuse understands it, these developments acquire deeper meaning. During entrepreneurial capitalism the bourgeois family is the primary agent of socialization. By virtue of his role within society as the dominant economic subject, the father's economic power establishes him also as the family's pivotal figure through whom are passed on the norms of social order. Patriarchal supremacy is founded primarily on economic authority. Having no independent means of support, the female is absolutely dependent, subordinate; she is a minor factor in the socialization of the child. Free enterprise and patriarchal family enterprise are complementary. Laissez-faire capitalism requires patriarchalism to produce the "fathers" who as the reigning economic and familial subjects reproduce the society in its prevailing form.

Socialization during this stage of economic development is not confined to the formation of the superego. As the father imposes his authority upon the child, the child constantly resists the father's demands to compromise his needs and desires. Although the superego is implanted as the internal counterpart to external authority, the child's rebellious confrontations with the father serve to develop a strong ego structure. This development is decisive for its ambiguity. While the tenacious ego is later instrumental to a successful performance in the economic sector, it also equips the subject to do battle with a society determined to bend individual needs to satisfy its requirements. With regard to behavior the social order may and usually does prevail, for internalized norms work unconsciously to obstruct the conscious formation of rebellious motives, inhibit the expression of those consciously entertained, and consciously and unconsciously censor with guilt and anxiety those acted out. But the ego is also a sanctuary of inner freedom. Having matured to the point of being a durable entity aware of itself possessing an identity apart from external constraints and their internal psychological counterpart (the superego), the ego at the very least retains a *capacity* for rebellion. And because of its obligatory sensitivity to repressed and unconscious needs, and as the embodiment of needs that are properly ego needs, the ego is disposed to engage in sublimated and unsublimated behavior contrary to ways of life that deny its integrity. As capacity and disposition for opposition, this ego, which has grown strong through persistent combat with paternal authority, becomes a faculty of reason. In the struggle between the individual and society, "the conscious ego plays a leading role." The decision as to which needs are to be satisfied, those of the individual or those of the society, "is really *its* decision." The ego is, "at least in the normal case of the mature individual, the responsible master of the psychic processes."[2]

Hence, the family is not merely the arena for the individual's socialization; the socialization process itself sets into motion a complex series of mediations such that the ego cannot develop for an-other (the society) without simultaneously developing a self against the other. Entrepreneurial capitalism is caught in a contradiction. It cannot reproduce itself without also creating faculties that stand over and against and that critically oppose it. In its most servile and purely instrumental function the family, *structured patriarchally*, is likewise a private sphere in that it generates and protects reason from a total encroachment by the public sphere. The family both resists and supports structures of domination.

With the sweeping organizational transformation marking the shift from laissez-faire to monopoly capitalism, the father is deprived of his status as the dominant economic subject. Incorporated into a rationalized economic system demanding absolute subordination, the father is no longer buttressed by his economic power. This dissolution of the father's authority is extended to his role in the family. Once they are exchanged for submission to hierarchical command, for resignation to a fate dictated by the administrative apparatus, and for obedience to universally applicable and impersonal rules, individualism, aggressiveness, and competitiveness cease to structure the father's relation to the child. Released from the discipline of patriarchal rule,[3] the child's new freedom is acquired at the expense of a retarded psychic development. Without the antagonistic relation to the father, the child's ego fails to mature. Forever remaining a weak entity, the ego can neither evolve into a rational faculty nor develop its capacity for independent thought and an autonomous disposition. What began with the assimilation of the entrepreneur into a higher stage of capitalist organization leads to the obsolescence of the bourgeois father and to the shattering of the traditional family as a sphere of privacy and a refuge for critical reason. The internal changes in the family and in the psychic structure prepare the conditions for the invasion of the mind by the public sphere.

This decay of the traditional family oriented mode of socialization reverses the process of individuation. Extrafamilial agents of socialization, such as the mass media, step in to replace the patriarchal family structure. Socialization becomes a public affair. Exposed to cultural and political instructions articulating quite similar values, aspirations, hopes and fears, children are socialized collectively. And "the more the models and examples are taken from outside it, the more unified and uninterrupted becomes the 'socialization' of the young generation in the interest of public power, as a part of public power."[4] But the true impact of the public sphere on the minds of the new generations cannot be appreciated by recognizing only the sociological factors involved. The extent to which the child is vulnerable to suggestion and manipulation can be grasped completely only by considering the interrelationship between the structural decay of the family and the decay of the individual psyche. Here the weak and defenseless ego becomes the focus of attention.

If infantile psychosexual development occurs normally, the superego will result from the successful repression of the Oedipus complex. In light of the changes in the internal structure of the family and their dramatic effect on the ego, it would be plausible to conclude that since the father has come to play such a negligible role in one crucial aspect of the child's psychological maturity, his diminished significance would pertain also to the disappearance of the Oedipal conflict and to the eclipse of the superego. Such a conclusion may seem justifiable, too, because Marcuse unfortunately does not give due consideration to what must necessarily appear to be the fate of the Oedipus complex within the modern family. Nevertheless, this conclusion would be incorrect. Marcuse does note that in the modern family "the father continues to enforce the primary diversion of sexuality from the mother."[5] This point deserves mention because those believing that Marcuse has erred by excluding the father from the contemporary socialization process must take note of his thesis that the continuation of the Oedipal conflict is evidence supporting the continued role of the father in socialization. Marcuse allows for the Oedipus complex but still insists that socialization and psychological development have altered in the manner he describes. But Marcuse has not contradicted himself, as will now become clear.

Although the father retains a presence that sustains the Oedipal conflict and enjoins the repression of Oedipal wishes, to which the superego is heir, this superego can never have practical bearing on the individual's mental life. Transfixed at an immature stage of psychic development, the ego lacks volition, the conscious power to will, exercise discretion, conceptualize needs and goals and the means to their satisfaction and achievement. All cognitive functions are impaired, particularly the capacity for reflective thought. In brief, the ego lacks *identity* and a self-consciousness of an identity in relation to the surrounding social universe. At the same time, the superego is frail because subsequent to its formation it is not reinforced by the father, who now is socially marginal. Given the enfeebled state of the ego it need not be censored or restrained by the superego, while the frailness of the superego excludes it from possibly providing the identity of which the ego is in desperate need. This "regression" of the ego, as Marcuse calls it, shows forth "above all in the weakening of the 'critical' mental faculties: consciousness and conscience."[6]

Ego identity is essential to mental life. Without identity, understood in terms of those characteristics associated with it above, the individual is hopelessly crippled and unequipped for survival. This is the predicament in which the individual is caught by virtue of the nature of socialization within the modern family. At this point, Marcuse adopts certain aspects of Freud's group psychology theory salient to his analysis of the individual in advanced industrial society.

To survive, the undeveloped ego must compensate for the deformity that has occurred. In the absence of identity, the ego reaches out beyond the boundaries of the psychic apparatus and identifies with an agent, a political leader for instance, possessing those qualities of identity for which the individual is in want. This agency is internalized and becomes part of the psychic structure. Such identifications are not arbitrary. Those established emulate prior attachments with authority figures, usually the father, and were described by Freud as "ego-ideals." "Ideal" refers simply to the ideals or values that first had been represented by the father and had been internalized as the superego with the repression of the Oedipus complex. Ego-ideals, to be precise, are idealized versions of the internalized father, who, as superego, provides the unconscious model for all identifications (transferences, projections) undertaken by the ego in its effort to constitute its identity. The ego-ideal, therefore, is *not* the superego but a substitute for it, although it serves the same function as the superego, with this difference: unlike the superego, which *pressures* the ego to think and act in socially desirable ways, the ego-ideal *rules* the ego for, at the very moment that it takes the place of the superego, it also *becomes* the ego; that is, it now constitutes the ego's identity. In a real sense, the internalized ego-ideal is the fusion of the ego and superego (functions). And this newly formed ego, its thought and action, is "identical" to the thought and action of the agent upon which it was originally based.

Marcuse does not adopt these elements of the group psychology model without introducing revisions that he claims are implied in Freud's theory. Freudian categories, Marcuse argues, are fundamentally historical (social, economic, political), meaning that they take shape within one set of historical conditions and contain within them the possibilities for their revision or dissolution should these conditions change in specific ways.[7] By considering these revisions this argument can be understood, along with the broader conclusions of Marcuse's analysis.

First, Freud applied his group psychology model to particular sorts of groups, those whose members are bound together by the attraction of an unusually strong leadership. The egos of the group's members have fallen into the plight described above, though for reasons very different from those offered by Marcuse and which need not concern us here. However, all other elements of the group psychology model already noted pertain. Freud's groups, such as the church and the army, which he used to illustrate the dynamics of the group mind, are cases in social as well as individual pathology. Societies, on the other hand, are comprised of individuals who largely retain the moral, psychological, and intellectual independence that the mob, the mass, or the group unconsciously has resigned and reembodied in the (father-)leader. Freud is correct, Marcuse's theory holds, because societal institutions, most notably the family, give rise to individuals with psychic structures enabling them to distinguish themselves to a significant degree, and critically, from the norms facilitating social order. Individuality requires the traditional family; the concept of individual presupposes a definite historical logic, that is, material conditions that produce such a family unit. Conversely, according to Marcuse the Freudian concept of individual, of ego, implies its historical limits—internal changes in the society and family that breed structural changes in the psyche make the group psychology model applicable to the entire society. The society becomes one of permanent mass psychology. Furthermore, Marcuse maintains, the extension of the group psychology model to the entire society carries with it more than a revision of the group psychology theory. Meaning as it does the collapse of the individual, the dissolution of the *ego* — a central category in psychoanalysis — the Freudian concept of man, if not psychoanalytic theory in general, is rendered obsolescent.

Second, by recalling an earlier point the psychoanalytic model can be seen to be obsolete in another way. Normally, through the repression of the Oedipus complex the superego is established and influences the ego to a greater or lesser extent depending upon the strength of the ego's identity. Social reason becomes domination through "introjection." With the institutional changes leading to the deformity and enfeeblement of the ego structure, this phenomenon of introjected domination is now surpassed. The superego is formed but has become obsolete because there is no longer a strong ego to reprimand. And as noted, this superego has become frail because it ceases to be reinforced by the father for he now holds a weakened position in society and in the family.

Third, the superego is not the only form of introjected domination that is surpassed. We arrive now at the most controversial aspect of Marcuse's theory of the psychological underpinnings of one-dimensionality. A further revision, Marcuse argues, is that ego identifications are no longer formed according to the psychodynamics of Freud's group psychology. Marcuse departs from Freud in this respect: identifications are not internalized or introjected as part of the individual's psychic apparatus. Instead, identifications are "immediate." They occur as imitations. Introjection gives way to "mimesis." What has altered to force this revision of the group psychology model and what exactly does the alteration mean?

The answer to the first question can be put succinctly. Advanced industrial society does not function by virtue of the power and authority of leaders. There are no agents who are also representatives of the unconscious father image. The meaning of this development is truly significant. As we have seen, Marcuse stresses certain economic developments that have transformed the father into a social and psychological factor of negligible importance within the family. At the same time, the longer range tendencies of these developments is toward the comprehensive rationalization of society and, it will be recalled, a system organized completely according to the logic of technical reason dispenses with leaders.[8] Considering these developments together and from a psychoanalytic perspective, Marcuse has not argued merely that technical rationality eliminates the traditional role of the father in the family and of the leader in society. Capitalist social structures, which are *essentially patriarchal structures*, are being eliminated. Now, in the group psychology model the leader (as symbolic father) or the ego-ideal (as substitute superego) determines for the individual all his thought and action, including the designation of circumstances under which it is or is not permissible to think and act aggressively. The technical elimination of the father-leader thus creates the supreme danger. Where individuals are deprived not only of sturdy ego structures and superegos but also of ego-ideals that can determine the manner in which aggression is to be harnessed (through repression, sublimation, etc.), we are

> faced with a reality which was envisaged only at the margin of psychoanalysis—the *vaterlose Gesellschaft* (society without fathers). In such a society, a tremendous release of destructive energy would occur: freed from the instinctual bonds with the father as authority and conscience, aggressiveness would be rampant and lead to the collapse of the group.[9]

Rationalization leads, inevitably, to barbarism.

Drawing out this far-reaching implication from Freud's group psychology—the fatherless society and the inherent danger of barbarism produced by rationalization—is the decisive step taken by Marcuse in formulating the distinction between introjection and mimesis, which is his final revision of psychoanalytic theory and the one most salient to the theory of technological domination. Modern civilization has not yet reached the stage of the society without fathers, although Marcuse views this as the dominant tendency of technological rationalization. For the present, advanced industrial society has replaced the father-leader with an agency fulfilling a similar psychological function, though with an important difference. This new agent is not embodied in a person; the ego-ideal is no father image. Rather, it is an abstraction, an idea and ideal whose power and authority derive from its association with *all* of the "various competing power elites, leaders, and chiefs" of society but with *none* of them in particular. Through its diffuse association with societal institutions and personages within them who simply administrate their organizational logic, technical reason constitutes this abstraction, whose universality establishes it as the ego-ideal.[10]

A major point of Marcuse's thesis of the fatherless society is now brought forward into this new context. In the group psychology model, introjections (identifications actually internalized as part of the psychic apparatus) take place only where ego-ideals are also father images. Barbarism would result where there were no father images to be introjected for without such an ego structure there can be no inhibiting of aggressive energy. Marcuse appears to argue that since the ego-ideal of advanced industrial society is no father image, identifications are considerably weakened. They are sufficently strong to provide an ego identity—and one that can check the threat of a barbaric release of aggression—though the identifications are too weak to be internalized. Consequently, identifications become mere reflections of the diffuse and universal ego-ideal embodied in the society as a whole. In effect, as the ego-ideal the logic of technical rationality determines the thought and action of the individual just as it determines the behavior of institutions and of those who manage them. Weak and defenseless, and in dire need of identity, the ego "submits quickly to required modes of thought and behavior."[11] As far as domination is concerned, is there really a significant difference between introjection and mimesis? In principle, advanced industrial society is still a society without fathers, and the moment the rationality of technics and the engines of production falter, there will be no ego-ideal to intervene and provide that collective identity which could stave off civilization's descent into barbarism.

It can be seen readily that Marcuse's analysis of the psychological underpinnings of technological domination is likewise the basis for his theory of one-dimensional man. There is no longer any sense in which it is possible to speak of a subject. All individ-

ual aims originate within the society. Domination is so deeply entrenched within the psyche that human nature can be said to
have been supplanted by a second, social nature. Two statements by Marcuse adequately summarize this shift from a quasi-
autonomous individual to complete social heteronomy.

> In the contemporary period, psychological categories become polit-
> ical categories to the degree to which the private, individual psyche
> becomes the more or less willing receptacle of socially desirable and
> socially necessary aspirations, feelings, drives, and satisfactions.[12]

> It is as though the free space which the individual has at his disposal
> for his psychic processes has been greatly narrowed down; it is no
> longer possible for something like an individual psyche with its own
> demands and decisions to develop; the space is occupied by public,
> social forces.[13]

At this point in the exposition of Marcuse's theory, there can
be no doubt that there is a singular characteristic establishing
definite boundaries between modern capitalism and advanced
industrial society. The erosion of the critical faculties, the virtual
annihilation of subjectivity, distinguishes advanced industrial society *qualitatively* from its predecessor.

Thus far, the discussion pertains only to Marcuse's analysis of
the effects of rationalization on the members of the younger generations. For it is the newer generations who directly experience
the structural changes in the family, the loss of the father, and
who suffer the psychological deformities endemic to advanced
industrial society. As a result of their childhood socialization, individuals will enter the productive process as preformed and fully
credentialed one-dimensional men.

But children are not the only candidates for one-dimensional
society. Historically situating it in the interwar period, the rationalization of the family and psychic structures, according to
Marcuse, has emerged late in modern civilization. Several generations belonging to contemporary society therefore have escaped
this particular development. Nevertheless, the rationalization of
culture and production has occurred in other ways that as efficiently and effectively integrated the older generations into the
technical apparatus. Technical reason not only claims the critical faculties directly by undermining their development through
the rationalization of the family but likewise impairs the func-

tioning of the fully matured faculties by reaching into the individual's biological structure. Deeply rooted instinctual ties between the individual and society are established.

Advanced industrial society enslaves the individual biologically by providing the instrumental means, labor, for the gratification of the aggressive impulses. Basic to the rationality of advanced industrial society is that constant material growth is a necessary condition of its preservation. This is the substantive dimension of technical reason. Artificial needs must be promoted to insure the expansion of the system. A social order that thrives on the creation of artificial needs is able to furnish in enormous surplus the labor to be fueled by human aggression. Rooted in the instinctual structure the social order derives its support by satisfying the aggressive impulses through the process of production, while the individual sustains the process by consuming and also by contributing the aggressive energy requisite for productivity. The result is a symbiotic tie based on a dynamic relationship between biological and social needs.

Moreover, there is an additional complexity to this dynamic suggesting another way in which an impetus for rationalization originates in its instinctual moorings. As the process of production reaches its highest levels of rationalization, the degree of gratification labor offers begins to decline. The technological apparatus becomes a less adequate means for the gratification of unsublimated aggression than its earlier and less rationalized counterparts. "Technological aggression" does not allow for the satisfaction of the aggressive drives in their primitive ("primary") form. Production sustains instinctual tension and frustration. Marcuse argues that the net effect is the ever greater demand for a productive and cultural apparatus that can gratify the aggressive instincts. This leads, in turn, to further rationalization and to the reproduction of the entire cycle and, along with it, of the established social order. Marcuse speaks of a "vicious circle of progress"[14] and of a pattern of "repetition and escalation."[15] His analysis is an ingenious application of Freud's theory of "repetition compulsion."[16]

The term "escalation" further indicates that the pattern is not simply one of repetition, that it resembles less a circle than a spiral in this sense. Rationalization does engender the demand for greater rationalization by progressively reducing the gratification that can be acquired through labor. Because rationalization only partially gratifies the aggressive impulses it has released, an outlet for the ungratified aggressivity must be found. A target for this aggression is presented as the "enemy" of the established order. It seems, then, that according to Marcuse progressive rationalization spurs a dynamic that begins by partially gratifying aggressive drives and ends by repeating this process of rationalization and channeling impulses denied gratification in the direction of threats to the social system. The enemy is protean — communism, capitalism, intellectuals, Jews, foreigners, and so on. Providing the gratification denied through rationalized labor, the enemy serves further to consolidate the society around its goal of rationalization, while the progress of technical reason steadily expands the aggression, which is then directed against its target. Aggression escalates and with it — if the enemy targeted is capitalism or communism — the danger of international confrontation. Regardless of a communist or a capitalist government's official stance towards the enemy, the cumulative effect of rationalization is to release aggression, which finds its expression among the public as the demand "for more militant, more uncompromising, more risky policies, sometimes blatantly irrational and endangering the very existence of civilization."[17] These psychological dynamics of technological domination lend depth and a new dimension to Marcuse's thesis on the nature of the deadlock in relations between capitalism and communism first submitted in *Soviet Marxism*. As we saw, technical reason reinforces this deadlock and forecloses any possibility of breaking out of it.[18] Now having considered the psychological underpinnings of rationalization, it becomes clear that the aggression released by rationalization intensifies the opposition and threatens to end it with catastrophe.

Marcuse's essays on the psychological underpinnings of technical reason call into question, by his own admission, the aptness of the term "domination" as a description of the state of affairs prevalent in advanced industrial society. To the extent that rationalization is anchored in the biological structure, there is a sense in which the social system is not opposed to the individual's needs. Indeed, we have just seen that according to Marcuse advanced industrial society derives support from its satisfaction of these needs. How, then, is criticism of the society to be restored?

Gratification appears as domination where the needs satisfied are not natural human needs but are first and foremost socially determined needs. Here we return briefly to a point discussed in an earlier chapter. The examination of Marcuse's second dimension stressed the importance of his claim that a fundamental aspect of repression is the centralization of the instincts to the genital sphere. This so-called social organization of the instincts desexualizes the body, thus turning it into an instrument of labor while also restricting gratification to genital sexuality and its sublimated expressions. In other words, biological needs are not natural but are preshaped by the social system. What is gratified is not human nature but "second nature." Consequently, since second nature already comprises a primary layer of domination, the social satisfaction of such an artificial nature cannot be said to be anything less than a secondary form of domination. The second nature hypothesis saves the critical dimension of social theory.[19]

Aggressive impulses are not the only side of the individual's second nature affected by the dynamics of rationalization. "Repressive desublimation," one of Marcuse's most original contributions to a critical theory of society, focuses on the libidinal underpinnings of technological domination. The desexualization of the body through the repressive centralization of the instincts in genital sexuality, the confinement of sexuality to heterosexual relations and to the monogamous family, and the further restrictions placed upon sexuality through the demands for its sublimation in socially productive labor all contribute to the social organization of production. Most important within this context, the confinement of the libidinal impulses to the genital sphere, reinforced by the other restrictions, not only negatively affects the quality of pleasurable gratification (by transforming Eros into sexuality) but also intensifies the instinctual need for gratification. Sublimation, Marcuse contends, further frustrates the satisfaction of this need. But as the society proceeds toward advanced levels of rationalization, such a comprehensive repressive transformation of the instincts is no longer warranted by the technical apparatus. According to Marcuse, a fully rationalized productive enterprise can dispense with several types of conventional repressive constraints on libido. In the society at large there occurs a liberalization of sexual morality, and at all levels of the production hierarchy this relaxation of sexual taboos is reflected in the dress, language, and everyday relations among workers. Sublimation, the channeling of instinctual energy into cognitive activity, becomes extraneous. Marcuse submits that "the Pleasure Principle absorbs the Reality Principle . . . This notion implies that there are repressive modes of desublimation."[20]

The consequences of repressive desublimation must be drawn out. Repressive desublimation refers to the immediate gratification of intensely felt instinctual drives within a framework of domination organized according to the logic of technical reason. Technics regulates productive relations independently of the subject. No longer required to sublimate, that is, to manage the technical apparatus through intellectual labor, the subject becomes obsolete. Social relations can then be governed by the pleasure principle, biologically wedding the individual to an apparatus of domination. Rationalization develops libidinal roots just as it had developed moorings in the aggressive impulses. With the social need for sublimation obsolete and immediate gratification at hand, there is little need for a strong ego able to discharge the complex tasks of production and to search for means of gratification within or outside the confines of social order. The ego structure declines precipitously and the fate of the critical faculties in the modern family is replicated.

Beyond the debilitation of the ego, repressive desublimation affects the psychic apparatus in another crucial respect. With the immediate gratification of biological needs at the "organism's" disposal, that is, without a relatively independent ego engaged in seeking gratification, there ceases to be any conflict between the individual and society. The absence of conflict would mean that there are no norms necessary to regulate conduct or, expressed differently, there would be no need for a superego to inhibit the activities of the individual. The superego is overcome. Without the possibility for guilt and anxiety, the ego would be contented. This, Marcuse argues, is precisely what has happened in advanced industrial society. Consciousness is blissful, "happy." Furthermore, this "happy consciousness," as Marcuse calls it, being a psychic entity without the encumbrance of conscience, censors the behavior of society as little as it censors the behavior of the individual. The major institutions of society can act with impunity, without fearing that disagreement, judgment, or constraint would be forthcoming from the individual. The "loss of conscience due to the satisfactory liberties granted by an unfree society," Marcuse explains, "makes for a *happy consciousness* which facilitates acceptance of the misdeeds of this society."[21]

With the subversion of ego and superego, the once mature critical faculties are dissipated. Marcuse does qualify this thesis somewhat. Apparently, the ego is preserved to a small degree, for it continues to experience vague feelings of discontent. Biological needs, it seems, can never be gratified completely. Yet, without a sufficiently strong ego structure to raise these feelings to the level of conscious thought and reflection, they remain obscure, intangible, but disquieting. And these confused, uncomprehended dissatisfactions can be easily mobilized by the political system. The inclination of the repressively desublimated happy consciousness is fascistic.

Marcuse's theory of the psychological underpinnings of technological domination thus is inclusive of the effects of rationalization on all generations belonging to advanced industrial society. No individual escapes the repressive transformation of the psychic structure, and no part of the psychic apparatus remains unscathed. The id, ego, and superego of each subject is either preshaped or reshaped to conform to the mold of one-dimensionality. The society has been reduced to mass society and one where the masses are not, and can never be, in opposition. The steady and irreversible tendency of this state of affairs is toward a final barbarism. Having fully explored Marcuse's thesis we can now examine it critically.

Toward a Reconstruction of the Subject

A serious effort has been made to capture the impassioned and complex nature of Marcuse's arguments, all the more so because the psychological underpinnings thesis is the basis for his conception of one-dimensional man. Whatever approach critics may adopt in confronting Marcuse's thesis, it cannot be denied that his work, particularly on the family, contains fundamental insights that are significant. Rationalization undoubtedly has altered the family and continues to do so in dramatic ways. The sort of individual produced will be different, perhaps substantially different, from the offspring of the traditional family struc-

ture. Against this development as Marcuse understands it, however, a subject can be reclaimed with confidence. I intend to
leave outstanding the issue of the effect of rationalization on the
factors to be brought forward to account for this subjectivity.
What is certain, though, is that Marcuse neglects to recognize
these factors and his theory is flawed to that extent. Should these
factors be given weight, as I believe they must, the fate of the individual must be reevaluated in their terms and according to the
impact of rationality upon them.

Despite Marcuse's pretensions to a grasp of the effects of rationalization on the family and the individual from a psychoanalytic perspective, very little of his analysis bears a resemblance to Freudian theory. Of the greatest consequence to
Freud's theory of ego development are two factors—the notion of
the bodily ego and the central role played by the mother in childhood socialization. The former includes both constitutional
(sometimes called maturational) and experiential elements; the
latter refers primarily to experiential ones, although the child's
relation to the mother also incorporates a constitutional element
deserving of mention. After considering these two factors and
drawing out their critical implications for Marcuse's analysis of
the family, the discussion will turn to a critical examination of
Marcuse's claim that technological domination is secured as it
becomes firmly entrenched within the instinctual structure of
man. The conclusion of the discussion will return us to the arguments made at the outset of this section.

That the human mind is nothing more than a blank slate
upon which society inscribes its many codes is a belief alien to
Freud's metapsychology. On the contrary, the psyche is comprised
of a wealth of capacities that Freud conceded he had but begun
to describe. The newly born infant is best characterized, according to Freud, as an undifferentiated ego-id, a bundle of instinctual needs and drives with no mental activity owning a sense of
being either distinct from these needs or divisible from the envi-
rons. Mind, so to speak, is intertwined completely with the body.
In a very short time, however, the ego functions—specifically,
the sensory and perceptual apparatus, memory, and motor controls—develop within a basic context of experience (described
below) and with them the first awareness of a self distinct from
the inner world of impulse and the surroundings. An illustration

will demonstrate how this process of individuation is intimately related to biological and physiological maturation.

Infantile needs are gratified through autoeroticism and through parents or parent substitutes. Frustration occurs whenever particular needs are not met immediately, or some not at all, and is a brute fact of the child's existence. Frustration forces the perception of the ways in which needs are and are not gratified, thus teaching the infant about its dependence on sources of gratification outside itself. Concepts of "self" and "not-self" are formed quickly — "concepts," because the experiences of frustration, dependency, and gratification are stored in the memory and influence future behavior aimed at satisfying needs. The sensory and perceptual apparatus provides the information to be preserved by memory, while the development of motor controls enables the infant to undertake behavior necessary to the mastery of its environment. At the same time, the child's reliance on the parents and the displeasure prolonged until needs are gratified forcefully develop the child's capacities for mastering its own needs and extinguishing frustration. "Primary repression" — a capacity for willfully denying impulses and wishes that in a context of dependency provoke the child's earliest and inescapable experiences with frustration — contributes to differentiating the ego from its corporeal needs and contributes to self-mastery. No sooner, in other words, do we begin to elaborate the basic ego functions than we recognize a process through which the formation of the ego is also the ego forming a concept of ego (self), of boundaries within an internal psychic world between ego and id, and between the internal and external worlds. Repeated over and over again, these experiences (perceptions) of a need, frustration, dependency, gratification, retention of information, mastery, and so forth, further differentiate the ego, crystallize its boundaries, and develop its identity.

What Freud leads us to understand, then, is the manner in which constitutional factors, in the broad sense of capacities and needs, combine with experience (also partially constitutional as in the *perception* of needs), for instance, the continual frustration of ever more complex needs, to shape the ego as a durable and independent entity. Eventually, through the interrelationships of constitutional and experiential factors, the ego's mastery of its inner and outer worlds and its concept of self are enhanced

by the development of its other capacities, such as the mechanisms of defense and fantasy. Basically, the successful management of needs requires a strong ego. Memories, defense mechanisms, fantasy, and thought in general are all cognitive vehicles
of the ego for managing needs and stimulating its further development. For example, as one alternative to repression, fantasy
offers temporary gratification and thus aids the ego in mastering
the id, avoiding frustration and a possible confrontation with the
environment. But the inadequacy of illusory gratification ultimately must compel either the repression of the need or the discovery of a means for real gratification. Hence, fantasy both reinforces the ego's powers of self-mastery and places the ego in a
situation where it must learn to be independent of another of its
functions, that is, to discriminate between fantasy and reality.
The ego appears always to be developing beyond the sum of its
parts *and* simultaneously to be developing beyond the sum of its
developing parts.

Before moving on an important point must be noted. It would
be a mistake to argue that a particular form of social organization creates what has been described here as the fundamental
ground of experience for the development of the ego; no social
system could reduce the level of frustration below that required
for the maturation of the ego's capacities. If Marcuse had considered the aforementioned aspects of Freud's theory of ego development, I believe he also would have agreed with this last
statement for the following reason. Marcuse frequently has been
misunderstood as saying that all repression can be eliminated at
some time in the future. Against those critics who wrongly accuse
him of such a utopianism, Marcuse has replied by arguing that
some level of basic repression always must remain, though he has
not made it clear why this is so or exactly what he takes this basic
repression to be. It is precisely the primary repression that develops the ego, I would argue, that constitutes what Marcuse
calls basic repression. As both a constitutional and an experiential factor, basic, or primary, repression cannot be eliminated.

A second way of expressing the relationship between constitutional factors and ego development is to approach the notion of
bodily ego from another angle. Freud claimed that there is a
parallel development between instinctual organization, the passage through the oral, anal, and genital phases, and ego functions. The mechanism of identification, for instance, reproduces

at a higher level of psychological organization the primitive characteristics associated with the oral phase. Properly stressing Freud's meaning, we see that the ego cannot fail to develop the capacity for identification by virtue of the intimate developmental relationship between this ego function and biological maturation. The same general relationship holds true for all ego capacities.

Because of its position in Marcuse's theory of domination, the mechanism of identification requires closer inspection. Noting the parallel development of identification and the oral phase correctly locates the emergence of this capacity very early in the infant's life. In fact, it develops well before the first year is completed. Through the capacity for identification, the newly developing ego at first forms identifications that are immediate. In other words, they are "unmeditated," that is, unreflective, automatic imitations of significant figures in the infant's environment. Immediate identifications do not, as Marcuse argues, result from the absence of certain structural elements, notably the father, which causes the ego to remain enfeebled and in pathological need of a readily available identity. To the contrary, immediate identifications are normal; they are responsible for developing the embryonic ego. For the most part, these early identifications enrich the ego considerably by giving it form and direction.

In light of those aspects of Freud's theory of ego development already surveyed and with this newly acquired understanding of Freud's conception of identification, at this point a decisive move can be made against and away from Marcuse's theory of the psychological bases of domination.

Contrary to Marcuse's interpretation, nowhere in Freud's extensive writings does he equate ego development with cognitive development. As it appears in Freud's work the relationship between ego and cognitive development can be most accurately described in these terms: the facets of ego development and of the early identifications thus described are necessary, though not sufficient, psychological preconditions for the development of the intellect. The capacities of the ego and, as I have referred to it, its "embryonic" character (earliest identifications) are first brought into play and then the cognitive faculties begin to mature. Cognitive faculties, however, certainly cannot be reduced to the prior formation of ego functions. So although Freud did not furnish a complete theory of cognitive development, his the-

ory of those factors contributing to the development of the ego is
rich in possibilities for a general theory of the intellect. (The significance of this distinction between ego and cognitive development is established on page 254.)

Two important and related questions can be posed now: with
which parties are identifications most likely to be formed and
why? Contrary to Marcuse's analysis of the family and his interpretation of Freud, the infant's mother is the principal figure in
its maturation and ego development. Freud stressed that the two
"objects" most heavily cathected by the infant are its body (autoeroticism) and its mother, for with these objects lie the most accessible, suitable, and natural relations through which libidinal
needs can be gratified. Since highly cathected relations are a
prerequisite for identifications to occur, the mother becomes the
leading candidate for identification.

But the nature of the psychological relations between mother
and child beyond the gratification of needs must be emphasized.
Love, affection, interest, attention, and other such attitudes offer the greatest contribution to the development of a strong ego.
Relations defined by these sorts of qualities breed vital character
traits in the child — to name but a few, trust, confidence, and security, all of which nurture an active, exploratory, and inquisitive
spirit. The relationship among these qualities of identification,
the salience of the mother, and ego development flatly contradict Marcuse's argument that the emergence of a strong ego depends upon *combat*, particularly with the father.

In fact, taking Freud's theory several steps further, object relations characterized by aggression or hostility on the part of an
authority figure are normally *rejected* by the child and are unlikely to serve as the basis for identifications. And in addition to
identifications formed on the basis of affective ties, they are frequently established as the result of the *loss* of an object. The implications of these last two points are significant. According to
the first point, the traditional family's dominant father, as described by Marcuse, would destroy the possibility of the child's
identifying with the father, thus minimizing his impact on the
development of the ego structure. While in terms of the second
point, the increasingly diminished role of the father in the modern family could very well encourage the child to identify strong-

ly with him in order to compensate for his absence (loss). The former implication further underscores the part played by the mother in ego development, and the latter reintroduces the father into the family (actually into the child's psychic structure) in spite of, or rather because of, changes in social structures compromising his presence within the family unit.

One final comment must be made, this time regarding Marcuse's understanding of the formation of the superego. Marcuse definitely has exaggerated the impact of the father in resolving the child's Oedipal complex. Though Freud can be read most consistently as underlining the father as predominant in forcing the repression of Oedipal wishes, Freud qualified this view by arguing that the actual identification establishing the superego is with the "parents."[22] Hence, the mother is as much implicated in the unconscious influences of the superego as is the father. From this hypothesis it can then be doubted whether the superego engendered within the traditional family actually provided the patriarchal support for capitalism, as Marcuse believes. But this issue is controversial and if pursued would take the discussion far afield of its primary critical focus. In any event, it is not the chief point I intend. Regardless of whether Freud meant ultimately to place the responsibility for superego formation squarely upon the father or equally upon the parents, he claimed that however severe the child's parents (or father) in repressing Oedipal and future wishes, the child's superego *rarely corresponds to the severity of the authority.* The norms, beliefs, and aspirations expressed by the superego may be more or less harsh than those represented by the parents. The implications of Freud's claim are extremely important. On the one hand, it offers very little basis for Marcuse's belief that the superego is simply the internal counterpart to external authority. Consequently, the superego cannot be thought to contribute unambiguously to the reproduction of social relations. On the other hand, since the sternness of the individual's values may well exceed those after which the superego has been modeled, the superego may not become frail as a result of being in the presence of a father whose position in the society and family has been weakened. Thus, the individual may continue to maintain critical standards when confronted with a public sphere whose authority is irrational or whose authority breaks down under the strain of internal contradictions.

By way of summary, in opposition to Marcuse's thesis on the psychological underpinnings of technological domination, I have enlisted Freud's metapsychology to establish four central and theoretically interrelated claims.

First, the metapsychology provides a theory of ego development that portrays the ego as rather more durable and stable than Marcuse contends. Freud's theory depicts an ego structure sufficiently resilient to defeat an attempt to extend the group psychology model to contemporary society as a whole. The ego develops according to a biological and constitutional logic that prevents the distinction between the private and public spheres from being eclipsed through rationalization.

Second, the overall strength of this ego structure meets the preconditions for cognitive development, meaning that despite the social or ideological fate of the cognitive faculties, the presence of a constitutionally intact ego structure insures the potential for a less conditioned cognitive (re-)development. Likewise, the irreducibility of cognitive to ego development means that cognitive development can continue even where structural factors affect the developing ego beyond its constitutional determination. On both accounts the presence of cognitive faculties potentially resistant to and relatively independent of ideological manipulation is indicated. Rationalization cannot erode them though it clearly may hold the critical faculties in bondage.

Third, a coherent Freudian perspective on the structure of the traditional family emphasizes the crucial role played by the mother in the development of the child's ego, character, and cognitive capacities. At the very least, this means that structural alterations in the modern family brought about by rationalization eventually must affect the mother (or mother substitute) if ego, character, and cognitive development are to be influenced in a dramatic way. However, the developmental significance of the mother also questions Marcuse's entire analysis of the traditional family and its father imposed structural reproduction of individuals equipped with a psychic apparatus instrumental to the evolution of capitalism.

Last, a corrected view of the relationship between the severity of the child's superego and the norms articulated by the parents suggests that whether the beliefs internalized as part of the superego are represented by one or both parents (the traditional family) or by the mass media or other agencies within the public and private spheres (peer groups, educational and governmental institutions) that invade the modern family and appropriate its role in childhood socialization, the individual's personal value system can be more rigorous and critical than those of other sectors of society.

To conclude the critical analysis of Marcuse's theory, I now want to examine his proposition that rationalized domination becomes secured as it is anchored in the individual's biological structure.

My initial objection begins by recalling a principal argument of chapter three. The stages of psychosexual development follow a natural biological process of maturation completed with the genital organization of the instincts. This centralization of the instincts is not a sociologically determined phenomenon. It conforms to a constitutional order rather than to the logic of social order. Human nature, rather than second nature, is developed in this process. Of paramount importance here is that the genital organization of the instincts establishes the preconditions for sublimation. Unsublimated relations provide inadequate sources of gratification, forcing the individual into sublimated modes of activity in order to derive more complete and fulfilling gratification. In other words, the individual is compelled by nature to graduate from more immediately biological (unsublimated) activities to cognitively mediated practices. Freud's theory of instinctual organization is at once a theory of mental activity, of a purposeful intellect, though neither theory exhausts the other.

This argument penetrates to the heart of Marcuse's thesis by revealing its cardinal error. The immediate gratification provided by repressively desublimated modes of activity is insufficient gratification. An apparatus deriving support from its indulgence of unsublimated aggressive and libidinal impulses would be faced with mounting discontents and quickly would discover allegiance falling away. Repressive desublimation thus introduces a contradiction into the tendencies toward rationalization. If, as Marcuse argues, by spurring a liberalization of sexual morality rationalization desublimates the libidinal drives, it does so only by causing unhappiness. The response would be the demand for highly sublimated activities, thus challenging the organized creation and division of labor.

Curiously, Marcuse's analysis of aggressivity actually describes this contradiction, but his theory of sublimation as repression prevents him from recognizing it. The earlier discussed pattern of repetition and escalation, Marcuse explains, leads to further rationalization but only partially gratifies the instincts. But why would there be a repeated and escalated demand for forms of sublimation that result in insufficient gratification? Of course, there would not. The need for gratification is the driving force behind all instinctual demands. Because rationalization issues in partial gratification, the demand to escalate it is also a demand to escalate gratification. Otherwise, the dynamic of repetition and escalation is unintelligible. Only partial gratification occurs through rationalization because its logic excludes forms of labor that would be truly gratifying. Consequently, Marcuse's aggressivity thesis inadvertently shows that rationalization would not oppose gratification where sublimation would be enhanced. Rationalization must therefore oppose gratification where it systematically desublimates the instinct, as it does with the repressive desublimation of libidinal impulses. Hence, Marcuse is correct in arguing that the rationalization of aggression derives further support for rationalization but wrong in thinking that this support would be forthcoming if the primary aggressive impulse were denied gratification. He is correct, too, in believing that technical reason promotes the repressive desublimation of libido but incorrect in regarding desublimation as a means for securing domination by fostering harmony between individual and social needs.

From this first line of argument a related objection to Marcuse's concept of repressive desublimation immediately surfaces. There can be no doubt that Marcuse's interpretation of the metapsychology views it as a crude "economic" model. Instincts press for immediate discharge. Sublimation, or cognitive activity in the widest sense, is forced upon the subject, denies gratification, and is a perpetual obstacle to it. Any slack in the social demand for sublimation, any opportunity for unsublimated relations, would be seized upon hungrily by the individual. Freud's concept of sublimation belies this economic formula of the automatic redistribution of instinctual energy in the direction of instant gratification. Pleasure is taken from the psychical representative(s) of an instinct; for instance, from an idea. Thought mediates pleasurable feelings and experiences such that a relationship holds between the thinking (sublimation) constituting an activity and the pleasure derived from it. Contrary to Marcuse's economic interpretation, according to Freud's theory the mental apparatus is a selective, discriminating entity whose conception of pleasure cannot be reduced to a species of biological determinism.

Several other objections could be raised against the notion of repressive desublimation. Only one other will be mentioned. Earlier I noted that Marcuse speaks of gratification weakening the ego structure and ushering in a happy consciousness. In point of fact, Freud argues that gratification strengthens the ego, for example, by freeing it from the strenuous labor of maintaining a repression. Conversely, the absence of gratification strengthens the id impulses, as though a need denied then ever more intensely pressures the ego until an adequate means of gratification is found. According to this reasoning, by gratifying needs repressive desublimation would invigorate the ego and impel it to seek higher forms of gratification.

Against Marcuse's analysis of the fate of the individual in the modern family and in advanced industrial society generally, my criticisms have attempted to reconstruct dimensions of subjectivity. Subjectivity fades more from the pressures of Marcuse's theory than from the pressures of technological rationality. Whether attention is focused on the many factors and facets of ego development, the formation of the superego, or the functioning of the mature psychic apparatus, in each and every instance subjectivity and its critical capacities can be reclaimed. But such progress on behalf of the subject can be made only if a rich, complex theory of subjectivity is embraced.

Rationalism, Determinism, and the Preinterpretation of Freud

By way of this conclusion we are returned promptly to the claims made at the outset of this chapter and to those of the last. I believe my argument clarifies the real logic of Marcuse's investigation. After examining Marcuse's writings on the psychological underpinnings of one-dimensionality, it would appear to the reader that Marcuse arrived at his understanding of the impact of technological rationality on subjectivity by launching the analysis through the categories of the metapsychology, when actually he had first grasped the metapsychology through the categories of technical reason. Marcuse's work on the psychological underpinnings of one-dimensionality does not, therefore, entail an interpretation of Freud but a *preinterpretation* rooted in an approach that analyzes subjectivity from the standpoint of technical rationality. This becomes quite evident when comparing the conclusion that Marcuse draws from his explicit interpretation of Freud's metapsychology—namely, that mental processes deteriorate completely to the point of becoming identical to one-dimensional technical processes—with the behaviorist anthropology shown in the preceding chapter to be implicit in the theory of one-dimensional man. Freud's metapsychology has been turned into a behaviorist psychology, a consequence whose impulse springs from a prior allegiance to a rationalistic conceptual framework for critical theory that necessarily, though implicitly, views the individual as being completely integrated into the network of productive relations. Because he had adopted a theoretical framework that views the individual as totally assimilated into society, Marcuse is naturally disposed to comprehend social life exclusively in terms of historical conditions, material factors, in the final analysis, structural elements *constituting* and *determining* the subject. Metapsychological categories are then automatically interpreted, that is, preinterpreted, from a hidden though solidly entrenched perspective of an individual determined by technical-structural factors. The result: Marcuse's (pre-)interpretation of Freud can produce no other effect than to erase all limits on the extent to which the individual can be socialized.

These last points must be stressed. It is the preinterpretive aspect—and just this aspect—of Marcuse's theory that establishes technical reason as unique in the history of domination relations. For technical reason can be claimed to have such a devastating impact on psychic processes only if theory is initially disposed either to neglect the critical dimensions of the metapsychological categories it believes to be pertinent to its analysis of the individual in technological society or to disregard those crucial developmental factors in the psychic life of the individual to which I have drawn attention. Furthermore, Marcuse's neglect of that other important factor, the mother's part in childhood development, is also dictated by his disposition to a determinist perspective. Such a perspective would be expressed immediately in an easy causal inference from the father as dominant economic subject to the father as dominant subject within the family. So the impetus for Marcuse's neglect of all these factors stems from his commitment to a rationalistic framework for critical theory, which translates into a disposition to judge the complexity of the subject on the basis of the structure of the social system. And if the latter is understood as organized according to the logic of technics, subjectivity becomes a mere extension of technical reason. Because Marcuse is predisposed to a one-dimensional view of the subject, theoretically the subject is exhausted by the prevailing social rationality; practically, domination of the individual appears total.

Whether or not it is finally agreed that Marcuse has foreclosed the issue of subjectivity by virtue of a set of one-dimensional theoretical presuppositions, one thing is certain. Marcuse believes that for all "practical" purposes subjectivity has vanished. Without subjectivity, there is no sense in which it is possible to speak of human reason. There is no reason other than the universal objective rationality of technics. Technological rationality appears as the ground for Reason itself. If there is to be a critical theory of technological society, it must stand upon a ground other than that which supports the society it seeks to indict. Theory must discover an opposing but equally objective foundation for rational criticism. What, then, is the nature and status of a "critical" theory of society in a one-dimensional universe? It is to this problem, as Marcuse confronts it, that the discussion now turns.

Notes

1. Herbert Marcuse, "The Obsolescence of the Freudian Concept of Man," *Five Lectures* (Boston: Beacon, 1970), p. 46, originally presented as an address entitled "The Obsolescence of Psychoanalysis," at the annual meeting of the American Political Science Association, 1963, but first published as "Das Veralten der Psychoanalyse," *Kultur und Gesellschaft*, 2 (Frankfurt: Suhrkamp, 1965), pp. 85–106.

2. Herbert Marcuse, "Freedom and Freud's Theory of Instincts," *Five Lectures*, p. 14; originally published as "Trieblehre und Freiheit," *Freud in der Gegenwart: Ein Vortragszyklus der Universitäten Frankfurt und Heidelberg zum hundersten Geburtstag, Frankfurter Beiträge zur Soziologie*, 6 (Frankfurt: 1957), pp. 401–424.

3. Herbert Marcuse, "Progress and Freud's Theory of Instincts,"

Five Lectures, p. 37; originally published as "Die Idee des Fortschritts im Lichte der Psychoanalyse," *Freud in der Gegenwart: Ein Vortrags-zyklus der Universitäten Frankfurt und Heidelberg zum hundersten Geburtstag, Frankfurter Beiträge zur Soziologie*, 6 (Frankfurt: 1957), pp. 425-441.

4. "Freedom and Freud's Theory of Instincts," p. 15.

5. "The Obsolescence of the Freudian Concept of Man," p. 47.

6. Ibid., p. 50.

7. See "Freedom and Freud's Theory of Instincts," p. 1, and "The Obsolescence of the Freudian Concept of Man," pp. 44-45. Also, see the discussion of basic and surplus-repression in chapter three, pp. 94-97.

8. See chapter four, p. 147.

9. "The Obsolescence of the Freudian Concept of Man," p. 53.

10. Ibid., p. 54.

11. Ibid., p. 51.

12. Herbert Marcuse, *Eros and Civilization* (New York: Random House, Vintage Books, 1962), p. viii; this statement appears in the Preface to this edition only (the 1962 Vintage Preface was omitted from the later, Beacon Press editions of *Eros and Civilization*).

13. "Freedom and Freud's Theory of Instincts," p. 14.

14. "Progress and Freud's Theory of Instincts," p. 36.

15. Herbert Marcuse, "Aggressiveness in Advanced Industrial Society," *Negations: Essays in Critical Theory* (Boston: Beacon, 1968), p. 264; originally published as "Aggressivität in der gegenwartigen Industriegesellschaft," *Die Neue Rundschau*, 78, 1 (Frankfurt: 1967), pp. 7-21.

16. On the concept of repetition-compulsion see Freud's *Beyond the Pleasure Principle* (1920) (New York: Bantam, 1967), pp. 40, 42, 44-46, 61, 65-66, 78-79, 103.

17. "The Obsolescence of the Freudian Concept of Man," p. 59.

18. See chapter four, pp. 150-162.

19. I have indicated my disagreements with Marcuse's conception of second nature in chapter three, pp. 99, 105-106.

20. Herbert Marcuse, *One-dimensional Man: Studies in the Ideology of Advanced Industrial Society* (Boston: Beacon, 1964), p. 72.

21. Ibid., p. 76.

22. For example, see *The Ego and the Id* (1923) (New York: Norton, 1962), p. 21.

SIX

Civilization Without Discontents III: The Foundations of Critical Theory and the New Science

> If God held all truth concealed in his right hand, and in his left hand the persistent striving for the truth, and while warning me against eternal error, should say: "Choose!" I should humbly bow before his left hand, and say: "Father, give thy gift; the pure truth is for thee alone."
>
> Lessing, *Werke*

EARLY IN *One-dimensional Man* Marcuse poses two questions from which a critical theory of society today must depart. Is the stabilization of advanced industrial society temporary, he first inquires, in that it does not affect the roots of the conflicts Marx found in the capitalist mode of production, or does it signify a "transformation in the antagonistic structure itself"? If the second alternative is true, Marcuse then asks, "How does it change the relationship between capitalism and socialism which made the latter appear the historical negation of the former?"[1] After comprehensively examining Marcuse's analysis of technological domination, it is clear that he believes the evidence attests to the second alternative. The structure of capitalism has been transformed essentially, with no foreseeable possibilities for the emergence of an opposition able to propel the society to a higher, more rational level of social organization. Traditional categories, such as class, individual, family, and private, no longer denote spheres of conflict within society, as we have seen. Under these circumstances what, then, according to Marcuse, is the relationship between capitalism and socialism? Stated precisely, if there is no opposition to the rationality of the prevailing society, how can the ideals of socialism be claimed to be more rational than the capitalist practices they oppose?

Marcuse's problem can be appreciated clearly when the traditional bases of theoretical criticism are briefly recalled and it is understood why critical theory now considers them to be obsolete.

First, for Marx, of course, no such problem existed. The laws of capitalist development determined that a historical agent must objectively bear the irrepressible single alternative to the established order. Reason's material expression was the proletariat, which represented the culmination of an evolutionary process leading to a superior stage of social organization. Historical laws conferred objectivity and universality upon socialist criteria of rationality.

In the wake of the dissolution of the proletariat as the historical agent of progress, however, socialism ceases to be the theoretical as well as the practical successor to capitalism. Individuals who comprise the working class experience the same fate as all other individuals in advanced industrial society. This fate is the erosion of subjective capacities and the total assimilation into the network of productive relations. Being so totally integrated into the social fabric, the proletariat not only ceases to be the conscious subject of historical change but, most important, is no longer the *objective* basis for historical development. This is the real meaning of the "transformation in the antagonistic structure itself" brought about through technical reason. Critical theory is thus left without an objective foundation for criticism.

Certainly, capital and wage labor remain the basic categories of advanced industrial society, as Marcuse emphasizes.[2] On this issue there is no qualitative distinction to be made between capitalism and a completely rationalized society. Like the individual, the basic laws of capitalism have been assimilated by technical reason. So although the proletariat is no longer the subjective and objective vehicle of historical change and hence not the objective basis for the indictment of modern society, "class" is no less efficacious as a conceptual tool for analyzing the many inequalities of capitalism obscured but preserved through rationalization.[3] Technical reason, however, has proven its resourcefulness in gradually rectifying these inequalities; hence, no critical ground is to be acquired here. And since the laws of political economy still pertain to the advanced stage of technical development, the crucial difference between capitalism and technological society lies in the course the "higher" stage of society must eventually run. With advanced industrial society integrating all potential opposition, its inevitable collapse must result in barbarism. This is another implication of the practical obsolescence of the socialist alternative. But although advanced industrial society must collapse violently, and perhaps with it what remains of civilization after it has been hollowed by rationalization, apparently the peril of barbarism is insufficient to establish the objective irrationality of the prevailing order. Theory's critical substance is violated where it is no longer rooted in or can no longer appeal to a class subject. When subjectivity receded, the Marxist conception of historical development went bankrupt and with it critical theory's claim to truth.

Second, Marx's theory of history is not the only foundation for reason that terminates in one-dimensional society. "Internal criticism," which takes the social system to task for failing to meet commitments extolled by its own ideology, while also demonstrating its institutional inabilities ever to do so, also becomes ineffectual. In 1941 Marcuse was able to declare that

> critical rationality derives from the principles of autonomy which individualistic society itself had declared to be its self-evident truths. Measuring these principles against the form in which individualistic society has actualized them, critical rationality accuses social injustice in the name of individualistic society's own ideology.[4]

In advanced industrial society, however, reason must search elsewhere for a critical edge. The individual has become so thoroughly identified with the aims of the society that social needs, values, and aspirations appear to *originate* with the individual. Alienation has become total.[5] Reproducing society spontaneously from within, the subject appears autonomous. Freedom,

Marcuse laments, becomes an impossible concept.[6] The society seems to conform most to its ideological principle of individualism at the very moment when the individual has ceased to exist. The contradiction between subjectivity and the denial of subjectivity is flattened out.

Internal criticism is vitiated in a second way. It is not that the dialectic inherent in the relations of capital has been paralyzed; rather, technical reason has neutralized its manifest contradictions. The society celebrates the profitability of weapons systems, argues that waste contributes to progress, that war will insure peace. Unquestionable and unquestioned necessities, no matter what the cost, and the negative consequences of such development are merely an integral part of the technical balance sheet, the acknowledged and agreed upon price to be paid for a high standard of "living." Even the terms of critical theory are assimilated to their opposites. The meaning and intent of socialism is sacrificed where socialist parties work for the defense and growth of the established way of life.[7] Marcuse first noted this practice as characteristic of fascism, where the principles of political economy served as "ideological instruments for the attack on 'Jewish capitalism,'" concealing the actual relationship among capital, material and spiritual impoverishment, crisis, and totalitarianism.[8] The unification of opposites — destruction for profit, waste for progress, war for peace, socialism for capitalism, the critique of capital as the defense of fascism — obliterates the distinction between the rational and the irrational.[9]

Deprived of all foundations, of its historical grounding in a logic of class relations, of its appeal to an individual subject, of an indictment of the social system on its own terms, and confronted with the reconciliation of rationality and irrationality, critical theory must then ask, Marcuse declares,

> In what counter-tongue can Reason be articulated?[10]

With this question we arrive at one of the most interesting and significant aspects of Marcuse's work. It is a question that has been foisted upon critical theory by the development of technical rationality, just as once before it had been imposed on critical theory by the emergence of the authoritarian state and society. But Marcuse's theoretical response to the dilemma posed by technical reason differs dramatically from his response to fascism. On this occasion, Marcuse's reply to total domination clarifies the true nature of reason and subjectivity and their proper relationship to the conception of a foundation for critical theory.

The Philosophical Foundation

On what new philosophical basis is advanced industrial society to be reproached? Regarding this matter Marcuse's position applies not merely to contemporary industrial civilization but to all social orders past, present, and future. The new basis contains judgments, made unabashedly and without cunning, resting squarely on a personal but reasoned commitment to specific norms or values. For the moment I elect to defer the issue of whether Marcuse successfully defends the objectivity of these judgments and whether he believes they even require defense.

Marcuse's argument is that "the established rationality becomes irrational when, in the course of its *internal* development, the potentialities of the system have outgrown its institutions."[11] From this "initial premise," as I will call it, an approach to evaluating the present stage of modern civilization is defined. Advanced industrial society is to be evaluated "in light of its used and unused or abused capabilities for improving the human condition."[12] Two value judgments support this argument.

First, "human life is worth living, or rather can be and ought to be made worth living," and, second, "in a given society specific possibilities exist for the amelioration of human life and specific ways and means of realizing these possibilities."[13] The second normative judgment is also a straightforward empirical proposition and tests could be constructed to prove or disprove its factual validity. In advanced industrial society it is certainly beyond dispute. By its normative side Marcuse is implying that such possibilities ought to be exploited and that the available means ought to be applied to exploit them.

The first judgment can be misinterpreted and requires some clarification. If it is necessary to declare that life is, can be, or ought to be made worth living, on the one hand Marcuse could be understood as implying that under present circumstances life is not worthwhile though it would be under changed social conditions. As it is stated imperatively, however, Marcuse's meaning is that life *as such* is worth living. On the other hand, if this is so it could be argued that standing without qualification the judgment hardly brings critical pressure to bear on modern society. Could it be that "life is worth living" means the same as all forms of life, including that form which prevails, are, can be, or ought to be made *equally* worth living? Certainly Marcuse means to deny this, for he is loath to agree that the established form of modern society can be made rational. By his first judgment Marcuse clearly intends to say that life must be made as worthwhile as intellectual and material resources permit. And this is precisely what advanced industrial society cannot do because by its very nature technical reason both creates and suppresses potentialities.

It is important to be clear about what Marcuse has offered thus far. His initial premise defines the standard of rationality in terms of a social system's use of, misuse of, or failure to use intellectual and material resources in obedience to the values implicit in this premise. This fundamental critical standard and the standards (value judgments) presupposed are contestable and open to the charge that their objectivity must be defended. Marcuse, it must be stressed, recognizes this problem emphatically. He says, for instance, that it is "perfectly logical" to reject the claim that life is, can be, or ought to be made worth living. Furthermore, since he means by this first value judgment that life must be made as worthwhile as resources allow, his argument is complicated by the additional task of establishing criteria that objectively distinguish between the rationality of *improved* forms of social organization. A critical theory of society therefore has two essential and inseparable components for Marcuse. Criticism begins "negatively" by acknowledging the "possibility" of alternatives to the prevailing institutions and proceeds to the consideration of the "positive" or "content" of the alternatives. Once again, though, by his own admission the objectivity of both these dimensions is in need of demonstration.[14] Lacking certainty all critical judgments and evaluations may be no more than relativistic. May be! Does the absence of objectivity, certainty, perhaps foretell not relativism but an attempt to reconstitute the terms of critical discourse by reconceptualizing the very notions of foundation, objectivity, and certainty? This point will be returned to shortly.

Marcuse endorses a philosophical foundation for the negative function of critical theory that combines linguistic, logical, and ontological characteristics. (Further on it will be seen that Marcuse disavows the ontological dimensions of critical theory.) Recommended is a "classical philosophy of grammar," according to which the subject of a sentence (proposition) is a "universal" and its predicates descriptive of the forms and conditions in which the subject appears.[15] The subject is expressed through its predicates but is never identical to them. Justice is a particular moral and legal treatment of persons, but it is also more than, and not to be equated with, a particular moral and legal practice. Essentially (ontologically), the properties of an object never can be conceptualized fully. Logically, this essentially inexhaustible "excess of meaning" implies a wealth of potentialities above and beyond those already realized in a society. Language provides a vehicle through which ontological and logical characteristics become known, though in itself it is no foundation for criticism. Through language, however, an objective ground for Marcuse's standard of rationality is disclosed. The ontological and logical basis for "potentiality" is at the same time an objective basis for "unused capabilities."

Marcuse's concern with universals was earlier encountered in the discussion of *Reason and Revolution*.[16] As can be seen, nothing about the critical significance of universals has been added in this new context, where he alludes briefly to their relationship to language. With little exception this remains true in a closing chapter of *One-dimensional Man*, where the status of universals is raised again and for a last time.[17] Here the most important point made is that "universals are primary elements of experience."[18] Through ordinary experience, for example, the individual necessarily learns contrasts. That everyday familiarity with societies offering varying qualities of freedom and opportunity, with persons more or less compassionate, and even trivial encounters with objects of varying shades of a particular color or with climates of varying temperature, teaches that the concept (of freedom and opportunity, compassion, blueness, heat and cold) cannot be reduced to a particular quality or sum of qualities. Experience teaches the distinction between the particular and the universal, actuality and potentiality, the achieved and the promise of greater fulfillment. Experience, and that which is experienced, is grasped implicitly as limited. Negativity, so to speak, is lived.

It is this ontological, logical, and experiential status of universals that constitutes an objective basis for the negative function of critical theory. In what sense, though, can the universal be said to offer standards for critique, a foundation for critical theory? Even granting the validity of such a foundation, through this route very little progress can be charted on behalf of objective criteria of *rationality*. Merely upholding an objective basis for potential modes of existence, possible forms of social organization, leaves us with the initial problem. Is not the prevailing social order one possibility among the inexhaustible range of possibilities represented by the universal? Should it not then be granted the same validity enjoyed by all logical possibilities? The true significance of negative reasoning must now be put into focus. Its logic forces a consideration of alternative possibilities, but failing to defend the rationality of any one against all others, the established society must be included among them as a prospective candidate. At the least, however, negative thinking compels reflection, discrimination, the quest for knowledge of what may be judged the limitations of both the given and other possible social systems. A decisive question is thus pressed to the surface. According to Marcuse, are there to be further grounds for distinguishing the rationality of potential forms of social organization? Put differently, what is the foundation for the positive content of critical theory?

Marcuse has been followed to the point where he must now differentiate between rational and irrational possibilities for social organization. His first move is to limit the range of possibility he must consider by identifying factors that act as constraints on the parameters of critical thought.

To this end Marcuse draws attention to two sets of inescapable historical constraints. The first affects theory specifically and directly. Without a concrete historical foundation, that is, in the absence of a class subject in principle bearing the promise of becoming theory's practical realization, critical theory necessarily becomes abstract. For Marcuse, in other words, theory must resort to such critical devices as value judgments and universals. This abstractness does not mean, however, that critical theory can then proceed from a vantage point external to and unaffected by society, as though within its abstract domain lies *all* possibility. Theory is also broadly constrained by general material conditions. The abstractness resulting from the dissociation of theory and practice does not free thought from this embeddedness in history. But while theory's abstractness is not a transcendental standpoint, the other extreme, too, is false. Ideas and values are not determined by historical conditions. Objectivity need not collapse in virtue of material constraints. Rather, thought has great latitude within these constraints and is bound only by a "common framework" of social existence in which all individuals share the "same natural conditions, the same regime of production, the same mode of exploiting the social wealth, the same heritage of the past, the same range of possibilities."[19]

Within this range of general material factors, which both create and limit the possibilities for historical development, specific choices are made. Here we arrive at the second type of historical constraint. Marcuse borrows Sartre's concept of "project" to distinguish what he means by choice. Among the array of historical possibilities one is "seized" or settled upon through conflict among competing individuals, groups, and classes; in light of this possibility the society's dominant cultural, social, economic, and political institutions are designed. The decision is determinate in that it leads to the restructuring of the general historical factors (described above), which then gives birth to, or "projects," subsequent possibilities, that is, definite tendencies toward particular historical possibilities, while excluding others.

Marcuse's first step has not altered the terms of his problem in the least but has defined it more clearly. We are advised that the potentialities to be speculated upon are generally limited by the achieved level of historical development and, further, by a societal project that has shaped institutions and social relations that define tendencies limiting (constraining — not determining) future possibilities. Theory is not autonomous, but neither is the societal universe heteronomous regarding theoretical discourse. Objectivity is yet possible but continues to stand in need of demonstration. Furthermore, objectivity must be demonstrated in view of the alternatives that may or may not become available and in light of their tendencies (or consequences) after a new "project" has been undertaken.

In comparison with the terms Marcuse finally selects to express the aim of critical theory, "objectivity" is a rather benign characterization. Marcuse is seeking nothing less than "criteria for objective historical *truth*," although he claims that this truth "can be best formulated as the criteria of its rationality."[20] Marcuse obviously intends a distinction between criteria of truth and criteria of rationality, or at bottom between truth and rationality. Still, he offers no explanation for why one is the better formulation of the other. I will offer an explanation for his distinction momentarily and then relate this distinction to what I believe to be the logic underlying Marcuse's entire discussion of the foundation for critical theory. First, what are Marcuse's criteria of rationality?

(1) The transcendent project must be in accordance with the real possibilities open at the attained level of the material and intellectual culture.

(2) The transcendent project, in order to falsify the established totality, must demonstrate its own *higher* rationality in the threefold sense that

   (a) it offers the prospect of preserving and improving the productive achievements of civilization;

   (b) it defines the established totality in its very structure, basic tendencies, and relations;

   (c) its realization offers a greater chance for the pacification of existence, within the framework of institutions which offer a greater chance for the free development of human needs and faculties.[21]

Marcuse's criteria specifically address the rationality of possible "transcendent" projects, those that presuppose the abolition of the established society. Temporarily leaving aside the question of whether these standards do in fact distinguish the rationality of a transcendent project from that of the established social order, I want to pose a series of problems with Marcuse's criteria of rationality. Each problem is a counterpart to a criterion listed above.

(1') Even if it were possible to make an empirical assessment of intellectual and material resources at the established society's disposal upon which everyone would agree, and if it were possible also to elicit agreement that the established institutions do not merely inhibit but systematically obstruct the realization of new possibilities, what is and what is not a "real [i.e., technical] possibility" is an issue subject to dispute and likely to produce extremely divergent views. We would have to ask next whether the range of possible disagreements is narrowed by the criteria demonstrating the "higher" rationality of one project as opposed to another.

(2a ') What meaning is to be attached to "improve"? Are the improvements to be qualitative or quantitative? Similarly, what many consider a "productive achievement" of civilization, others, Marcuse particularly, would not, and vice versa.

(2b ') What sort of methodological approaches and epistemological claims are to inform efforts to define social structure, tendencies, relations? Are not further criteria required to enable the social sciences to avoid becoming entangled again in traditional debates?

(2c ') Finally, is not the question of the "free development of human needs and faculties" tied inseparably to the conception of what they are? Both agreement and disagreement over the existence and nature of most needs and faculties would considerably influence possible agreement on whether they can or ought to be developed, much less developed freely.

These few problems certainly do not exhaust the inadequacies of Marcuse's criteria, but they are sufficient to certify his failure to provide grounds that objectively discriminate between rational and irrational projects. So long as the essential terms of Marcuse's propositions are contestable, none of the criteria can be applied objectively to any potential form of social organization to determine whether it is "rationally transcendent." As they are stated, the criteria are too vague not only to adjudicate but even to entertain disputes. For if the meaning of the concepts constituting each criterion remains indefinite, it is impossible to judge whether the criterion is being met! But ultimate proof of the inadequacy of Marcuse's criteria lies in their inability to exclude the limiting case, the prevailing society. With no certainty about the nature of human needs, for example, it can be claimed with a plausibility at least equal to that of the disclaimer that needs and faculties are being developed and freely. This is not necessarily to say that it is possible to define human needs objectively, but such an obligation is implicit in Marcuse's criterion (2c).

If Marcuse's argument is interpreted as an attempt to *reconstitute* the foundations of critical theory, then an indictment of the

sort I have offered is sound and justified and must not be abandoned so long as it is agreed that the interpretation need not
proceed further. Now, however, I want to suggest an alternative
view that may deepen the interpretation of Marcuse's argument
and that turns the indictment into a defense. I believe that this
second view is correct, but it becomes apparent only after Marcuse's criteria have been evaluated and the charges—as obvious
as they are necessary—leveled. The accusations centering on the
general inadequacy of Marcuse's criteria are well founded; however, once made, they appear facile. Surely Marcuse anticipated
such a critique and for that reason a definite intellectual strategy
must reside behind his highly vulnerable "best formulation." If
this hypothesis has a remote possibility of being true, Marcuse's
strategy should be permitted to surface.

What could be the real point of Marcuse's discussion of standards for critical theory? Is it to pose the question of foundation
and to work toward a definition that sharply distinguishes the
rationality of competing projects, in which case he clearly has
failed? Or is it to pose the question and deliberately to provide an
answer that in virtue of its shortcomings implies that this question, which appears today as one of the overriding obstacles to a
critical theory of society, has in the past been both posed and answered incorrectly?

"The criteria for objective historical truth can best be formulated as the criteria of its rationality." The key to unlocking the
meaning of Marcuse's proposition is to be found in the relationship between truth and rationality that it expresses, *together*
with the inadequacies of Marcuse's criteria as outlined. Marcuse
is preoccupied with neither criteria of truth nor criteria of rationality but rather with the *criteria of the rationality of truth*.
What the rationality of truth is, is to be revealed by his criteria
though in an uncommon way. Since Marcuse's criteria do not
serve as criteria in the usual sense, that is, as standards of judgment, could it be that he intends to convey a different sense of
"criteria"? In other words, whereas the "formal" status of criteria
of rationality allows them to discriminate, evaluate, and judge
objectively, that is, to be applied independently of the disposition of any subject, to establish criteria of the rationality of truth
would be to disavow formalization. A sure method of avoiding
formalized criteria would be to leave open all their essential

terms and not to foreclose the meaning of any concept used to articulate a value, evaluate a practice, and so forth. In this event, the rationality of truth would emerge as reason or, more precisely, as reasoning and the purpose of the criteria to do nothing more — or less — than to engage us in a consideration of the criteria themselves and of their component concepts. The failure of the criteria to legislate judgment becomes the mark of their success. Marcuse's criteria would prove that the rationality of truth is reason because the criteria of its rationality compel us to *reason* about the rationality of its criteria! Hence, the basis of critical theory is no foundation, objectivity, or certainty in the traditional sense. To seek a universal, unchanging standard that merely is to be applied is to contribute to the very thing critical theory opposes — the eclipse of reason, the elimination of subjectivity. The best formulation of the philosophical foundation of truth reformulates its goals. The objective (objectivity) of truth becomes reasoning, the persistent striving for truth. Reason is its own foundation. As Marcuse says, "The concept of truth cannot be divorced from the *value* of Reason."²²

Upon examination Marcuse's new inquiry into the foundations for critical theory has made an impressive turn. Reason now approaches as nearly to an absolute freedom as can be imagined, its constraints limited only to those general material factors earlier described. Paradoxically, this new freedom has arisen at the moment in history that is least free. How can this paradox of absolute freedom and absolute domination be explained? Technological rationality has eliminated the reasoning agent, the individual subject. At the same time, this rationality of domination has destroyed the logic of historical development. There are no contradictions internal to advanced industrial society, as there were within capitalism, that would be expressed inexorably through a revolutionary class, vehicle of qualitative change. This logic of "determinate negation," wherein the socialist successor to capitalism was defined by the dynamics of the latter's property relations, was the subversion of the established order but *also* the subversion of reason as Marcuse now conceives it. It predetermined the historical subject and limited socialist consciousness to particular values and aims. History was objective *Reason*, but with limited *reasoning*. With the obsolescence of this evolutionary model history becomes contingency, an open system, its telos

sheer potentiality. One-dimensional society is thus the benefac-
tor of reason as freedom, but since the individual as well as the
class subject has been eliminated, it is a reason and freedom for
theory only. In and for theory, history is the realm of freedom
and determinate choice, the ground for the play of reason. In
practice, however, no such subject remains for Marcuse who can
rationally exercise this freedom.

With this conception of the status of critical theory, Marcuse
has taken an important step forward. Technical rationality has
abolished the traditional foundation for theory, a development
threatening the viability of criticism. Marcuse's insight is that
from these ashes a phoenix has arisen. What first appeared to
end theory's claims to objective rationality actually has emancipated theory from the yoke that prevented its appreciation and
celebration of the real nature of reason. Theory's release from
the Marxist conception of history allows it to represent the values
of reason, subjectivity, and freedom without dictating what reason, freedom, and subjectivity ought to be. Critical theory also
escapes its theological past as it was shaped by Hegel as well as
Marx. Marcuse argues that "in the Hegelian dialectic negation
takes on a false character: notwithstanding all the negation and
destruction, it is always being-in-itself which ultimately develops
and rises to a higher historical level by negation."[23] No longer, it
is implied, is theory to be expected to follow or discover a path
leading toward the realization of some a priori, ontological essence, some pregiven substance unfolding historically through
agents reduced to instrumentalities.

Behind Marcuse's notions of history as an open system, the
emancipation of theory and reason, and reason as its own foundation, lies optimism. If history is truly contingency, as Marcuse
comes to believe, then the one-dimensional society is as tentative
as any potential historical project. Emerging from Marcuse's
writings is a perspective on history that forbids the exclusion of
none of the possibilities created by the progress and oppression of
technical rationality. The abstract theoretical subject is free to
liberate the fruits of generations of toil and renunciation as it so
chooses. That history has brought the individual to the stage at
which his freedom is limited virtually by only the achieved level
of intellectual and material resources is indicated fully by Marcuse's declaration that man is now (theoretically, though not

practically) in a position to "ask again what is good and what is evil."[24] Not only theory's past claims to reason but all historical conceptions of rationality can be transcended. With this emphasis upon negation (determinate choice) as the modus vivendi of the reasoning subject, such a radicalizing of the dialectic voids any claim to a positive content for critical theory. Consequently, Marcuse's entire discussion of the standards for critical theory belies his lament that today "the critical theory of society possesses no concepts which could bridge the gap between the present and its future."[25] In a moment of transition from the theoretical to the practical subject, and such a moment is predicated by the notion of history as contingency, individual subjects will devise such concepts themselves. Any concepts critical theory would prescribe in advance of that moment compromise reason, freedom, and subjectivity as they are understood by Marcuse according to the terms of his new foundation.

To this point, however, Marcuse's theory remains wedded to the thesis that technological domination is absolute and the severing of theory and practice irrevocable. (In the following chapter we will see that this perspective, too, changes.) Indeed, it is apparent that the new claims he makes about the nature and status of history, theory, reason, freedom, and subjectivity grow out of this thesis. But Marcuse's argument need not depend upon the extreme version of technological domination. As I have contended throughout, since Marcuse's implicit conception of the subject is inadequate, predisposing his analysis to a theory of one-dimensionality, a richer, more complex notion of individual subjectivity would form the basis of a revitalized practice. During the course of the last three chapters especially, I have argued that a subject continues to prevail actively in and against the process of rationalization and theoretically in Freud's metapsychology. In fact, these dimensions of subjectivity are quite compatible with Marcuse's new and highly significant views on history, theory, reason, and so on.

This point will be returned to shortly. First it is necessary briefly to consider a final aspect of Marcuse's position on the status of critical theory. The claims he has made for the emancipation of theory and reason from Marx's conception of history presuppose a subject able to think reflectively. The question can thus be asked of Marcuse what the necessary social preconditions are for the development of such a subject. I believe Marcuse provides an answer to this query. His response, though, will be modest, for an elaborate description of the preconditions for a critical subject would preclude the subject's right to determine these conditions freely. And this is exactly what must be avoided according to Marcuse's foundations argument. What has occurred is that the foundations discussion, which placed individual reason at the basis of theory, leads to a consideration of the social preconditions of individual reason. Put another way, the question concerning the philosophical foundation of critical theory has been turned into the question regarding the foundation of individual subjectivity.

In this context two interesting arguments should be examined. There is no obvious relationship between them and both take up the question only indirectly. Nevertheless, a relation can be discerned between them, and taken together the arguments contribute insight into Marcuse's preconditions for reason and subjectivity.

Marcuse's first argument, exceptionally abstract, is expressed through a creative reading of the central categories of Platonic logic. Beginning with Plato's concept of reason, Marcuse stresses the significance of reason for ordinary experience. Reason is dialectical, its task being to scrutinize experience in order to discover those of its aspects that are true manifestations of Being. Since Being is a universal, by differentiating between truth and falsehood, reality and appearance, reason is seeking to fulfill Being's real potential. As its dialectical opposite, non-Being is an actual as well as a logical property of Being. Logically it is the negation of Being, and in ordinary experience this negation is expressed actually as that which threatens to arrest or annihilate (Being's) potentiality. Reason's struggle for truth therefore translates into a struggle to realize human potentiality and a struggle *against* that which threatens stasis or destruction of that potentiality. Inseparable from the nature of Reason, the struggle for truth saturates human existence for as long as man can reason. Marcuse refers to this struggle as "the essentially human project," which "commits and engages human existence."[26]

Why is this *struggle* for truth the *essence* of reason? Does this conception of reason speak as well to the nature of reality? In fact, it does. It is a conception that "reflects the experience of a world antagonistic in itself—a world afflicted with want and negativity, constantly threatened with destruction."[27] Marcuse is here offering his view of the human condition—the limits to viability, the impossibility of completely eliminating scarcity, the "natural" individuality of mankind setting people apart in virtue of their uniqueness, and so forth.[28]

However, while reality is essentially antagonistic, forming an ontological ground of human reason, Marcuse does not mean to glorify struggle as such. Reason's purpose is to reduce the struggle to a minimum, to conduct the quest for truth in an environment utilizing the achievements of civilization to mitigate toil, misery, aggressiveness. Reason's struggle for truth goes hand in hand with the necessity of creating and improving the conditions for reason. As its precondition this necessity becomes a definite standard of reason for unless it is met there can be no pursuit of truth. Any social order opposing Marcuse's "essentially human project," denying the individual the right to reason, is irrational and must be brought into harmony with the standard of reason. Truth can become reality only when the project becomes the universal project for mankind, that is, when all have equal access to the intellectual and material resources making reason a possibility.

Waged at a high level of abstraction, Marcuse's argument is revealing of his own project. His aim seems to be to provide a logical defense for the social and universal preconditions of individual reason, for the minimal requirements of subjectivity. Beyond this, no other claims for reason or on behalf of the subject are intended by Marcuse. This initial argument, then, attempts logically to redeem the preconditions for reason in reason itself; that is, reason must posit certain definite objectives as rationally necessary if reason is to become its own objective.

Next, it is possible to infer, as I have, what specific preconditions Marcuse has in mind. Such inference proves unnecessary. The idea of equal access for all to the intellectual and material resources making reason possible appears in his second argument, the essay "Repressive Tolerance."

If there is any work of Marcuse's that has made him notorious it is surely "Repressive Tolerance." Marcuse argues that the "pure tolerance" of liberal societies unwittingly fosters intolerance and repression. Although in principle equal toleration of all views is advocated, in societies characterized by institutions of inequality those interests having disproportionate power and resources have a disproportionate influence over policy and the shaping of all material and cultural spheres of life. Where the "background limitations" of wealth and power to tolerance prevail, tolerance is turned into its opposite. Conservative voices dominate to the exclusion of the radical opposition. Needs, hopes, aspirations, fears, beliefs, and values are molded and in a single direction.

To this extent Marcuse has said nothing startling, and he falls in line with many moderate critics of liberal capitalism. What is so explosive is the conclusion he draws from the logic of his analysis. Marcuse proposes to end the repressive practices sanctioned by pure tolerance by substituting a "liberating" or "discriminating" tolerance, meaning "intolerance against movements from the Right, and toleration of movements from the Left. As to the scope of this tolerance and intolerance: it would extend to the stage of action as well as of discussion and propaganda, of deed as well as of word."[29] Accomplishing the practical intent of tolerance demands intolerance, a proposal for which Marcuse has been criticized and attacked.

On the issue of the implications of liberating tolerance there is very little to be gained either by launching a new defense of Marcuse's position or by taking the side of his critics. Regardless of the strengths and weaknesses of either side, the real controversy lies elsewhere, as I will argue. Marcuse even supplies reason to doubt his own commitment to liberating tolerance. This point deserves first consideration for it places Marcuse's radical proposal in a new perspective.

Marcuse confesses that his argument for liberating tolerance contains a *petitio principii*. The conclusion assumed but not proved is that the radical objective of discriminating tolerance is practicable. But this conclusion is false because it presupposes a mass actually perceiving the necessity for and willing to support a leadership that would exercise liberating tolerance and, of course, Marcuse's critique of pure tolerance, as well as the entire theory of one-dimensionality, is an argument against the existence of such a mass. Consequently, Marcuse's extreme measure has no purchase, by his own admission, because it is unrealistic.[30] Qualifying his argument to such a degree, what, then, is his real purpose?

"Repressive Tolerance" was meant to draw attention, in a dramatic way, to the absence of the preconditions for reason and to recreate "in the society at large, the mental space for denial and reflection."[31] The alternative to the "semi-democratic process" of liberal tolerance "is *not* a dictatorship or elite" charged with the responsibility of exercising tolerance in a discriminating manner, "no matter how intellectual and intelligent, but the struggle for a real democracy."[32] Real democracy does not flourish when reason is subjected to indoctrinating and manipulating rule. The background limitations of tolerance must be abolished so that institutions can promote that equality of education and distribution of material resources that adequately prepares the individual to discuss and evaluate competing values, ideas, practices, and policies and to exercise rational choice. Marcuse submits that "The subject whose 'improvement' depends on [this] progressive historical practice is each man as man, and this universality is reflected in that of the discussion, *which a priori does not exclude any group or individual*."[33] But in a society marked by a pure tolerance compromised by background limitations, how can such a progressive historical practice succeed if not through the installation of an intellectual elite? The answer, according to Marcuse, is through the militant activity of radical minorities "who are willing to break this tyranny and to work for the emergence of a free and sovereign majority."[34]

This last statement raises the controversial issue. Are militant minorities to work on *behalf* of majority rights or *with* the majority to secure its rights? There is no evidence in Marcuse's writings (up to *Counterrevolution and Revolt*) suggesting an allegiance to the second strategy. Politicizing the majority, or even a portion of it, presupposes the existence of subjectivity, of individuals in possession of faculties enabling them to reason at least when they are called upon to do so. And this presupposition follows from a theory of subjectivity that can detect areas of resistance to, and capacities not eroded by, technical rationality and ideological manipulation. Lacking such a theory Marcuse is forced to turn to militant struggle.

With this the discussion is returned to the earlier point concerning both the basis for a revitalized practice and its relationship to the conception of reason emerging from Marcuse's new analysis of the foundations of critical theory. This point can now be reformulated as a question: what sort of individual subject is

inclined to political practice? To this most significant of questions Marcuse has given two different and conflicting answers.
Each of these answers must be made perfectly clear.

First, in this chapter it was discovered that Marcuse has offered a new foundation for critical theory. The terms of this new
foundation provide a theory of emancipated reason, that is, reason as the persistent striving for truth, which presupposes an individual capable of reflective thinking — but reflection in a highly qualified sense. Since a decisive characteristic of Marcuse's
emancipated reason is the open and contestable property of all
conceptual thought and discourse, the most important quality of
reflection becomes *uncertainty*. Accordingly, the reasoning of
the reflective individual presupposed by this new concept of reason would have about it a precariousness, a groping, an insecur-
ity of belief and perhaps a skeptical design, a reluctance or at
least a cautious inclination to act, an uncertainty expressive both
of cognitive and psychological needs for discussion, deliberation,
and of a receptiveness to being challenged and persuaded if possible. Embedded in Marcuse's new foundation for critical theory,
therefore, is what I choose to call the "true subject of politics."

Second, Marcuse has two other and intimately related conceptions of subjectivity. Earlier he was committed to a rationalistic
framework for critical theory. The explicit conception of the
subject entailed here is of one possessing a *certainty* of knowledge
and belief, an autonomous critical rationality. Now, with "Repressive Tolerance," this critical subject has been embodied in
the radical minorities who act aggressively on behalf of the assimilated majority. And who is this assimilated majority? It is the
one-dimensional subject implicitly contained within Marcuse's
rationalistic structure for critical theory.

To which of Marcuse's three subjects are we to subscribe?
Thus far, even Marcuse has not satisfactorily answered this question for himself; in subsequent work he will take a definite position, as the next chapter will show. Marcuse's implicit conception
of the subject is impoverished, one-dimensional. And the rationalistic theory responsible for this one-dimensional subject is explicitly committed to a radical subject fully matured and loaded
down with an arsenal of critical faculties hurling it toward the
barricades. But between these two extremes lies Marcuse's new
foundation for critical theory — a theory of emancipated reason

that presupposes a subject both more and less capable than those entailed by the extremes. This is the true subject of politics! But as it underlies Marcuse's new conception of reason it remains abstract. With *Counterrevolution and Revolt* it will be given a definite shape. Whether this is the subject to which critical theory ought to subscribe cannot now be answered. What is first required is a rich and complex theory of subjectivity that can determine whether such a subject really exists. Although my critical examination of Marcuse's work does not constitute this theory, it has tried to demonstrate that certain dimensions of subjectivity prevail in and against the process of rationalization but are neglected by Marcuse. This subject, in fact, is remarkably similar to that presupposed by the terms of Marcuse's new foundation for critical theory and its concept of emancipated reason and is a parallel to the reflective, radically disposed subject of Marcuse's early work (see chapter one).

Thus, an adequate concept of the subject arises as the overriding objective for a critical theory of society, but it is an objective that cannot be met either by taking refuge in rationalism, in critical "theory," or only by developing a richer and more complex theory of subjectivity. To grasp the true nature of subjectivity is to grasp the subject in practice, as well. Marcuse has expressed this point succinctly.

> In the interplay of theory and practice, true and false solutions become distinguishable — never with the evidence of necessity, never as the positive, only with the certainty of a reasoned and reasonable chance, and with the persuasive force of the negative.[35]

To complete the analysis of Marcuse's argument regarding the foundations of critical theory, a final problem needs to be considered. The problem originates in an appreciation of Marcuse's broader and more ambitious theoretical objective: to lay foundations for critical theory that extend beyond the philosophical basis we have just examined. Briefly, the problem can be described in this way: what is the relationship of Marcuse's philosophical foundation to his interpretation of Freud's instinct theory and metapsychology, to the anthropological basis of critical theory Marcuse summarized by the phrase "a biological foundation for socialism" and which I have referred to as his "second dimension"? Are the philosophical and anthropological dimensions of

Marcuse's critical theory complementary? It is appropriate to explore this issue within the context of Marcuse's criticism of scientific reason, as will become evident, for it is only by reference to this critique that we can obtain a clear and adequate grasp of the quite special claim he makes for *anthropos*.

The Anthropological Foundation and the New Science

What is the essence of scientific reason? Specifically, is the rationality of science also a logic, a body of inherent principles that determine a necessary, in the sense of unavoidable and unchangeable, relation to its object of inquiry? Repeating an argument from Husserl's *Crisis of European Sciences and Transcendental Phenomenology*, Marcuse answers in the affirmative.[36] The object of science — nature — is comprehended through a language denying it any meaning except that which can be expressed quantitatively. The "mathematization of nature," in Husserl's words, is a symbolic conceptualization transforming all of nature's qualities into quantifiable attributes — physical laws, universal relations. Two problems then arise. The abstractness of science's conceptual structure conceals its inherent relation to nature and also prevents science from being translated directly into a means servicing nonrepressive social aims and practices.[37]

Science's necessary relation to nature is already expressed in the symbolic representation of nature, the reduction of quality (e.g., beauty) into quantity through nature's mathematization. The scientific transformation of quality into quantity is in essence a domination of nature. In Marcuse's words, "Pure science has an inherently instrumental character prior to all specific application."[38] But this intrinsic relation assumes a far less benign form in the only practical mode of expression, or application, available to science — technology. "Science and society," Marcuse explains, "theoretical and practical reason, meet in the medium of *technology*."[39] A societal project committed to the development of science *necessarily* universalizes scientific reason and therefore the technological rationality and technological domination of nature and human nature inherent in it.

Technological domination, in all its manifestations considered thus far, is the "hidden subject" and "inherent limit of the established science and scientific method." With this argument Marcuse reaches a crucial juncture. If society is to become truly free, its rationality must be other than the rationality of science. Or, what is but the same thing, the established science must be exchanged for a "new science," a qualitatively new idea of theoretical and practical reason. Such a departure, Marcuse declares, would be so radical as to be "catastrophic" for the prevailing society, the complete abolition of existing order, the end of our present way of knowing and conceptualizing.

What precisely does Marcuse mean by a new science? In *One-dimensional Man*, where the idea first appears in contradistinction to the established scientific reason, there is little in the way of a precise elaboration. Nor is there further elaboration in any subsequent work that explicitly argues for a definite conception of a new science. Yet, in *One-dimensional Man* Marcuse attributes particular characteristics to, and offers hints about, the new science; elsewhere he provides a description of (another) radical notion of reason. From such evidence it is easy to say what other and major aspect of his thought fills out this conception.

First, the new science entails the arrest of technological development, for only that measure can neutralize technical reason and reverse the process of technological domination. "Arrest" is a decisive term. Marcuse is not a modern Luddite. The break with technics signifies a departure from its "rationality," while the fully developed technical base, the apparatus of production, is "reconstructed," that is, utilized with a view to different ends.

Second, labor is reduced to a bare minimum, to the level at which the vital needs of all members of society can be satisfied with the least amount of toil and aggressivity.

Third, the arrest of technological development and the furthest possible reduction of labor are intended physically to separate the individual from the productive process, to render obsolete the need for his participation. The release from labor would be accomplished through the automation of productive labor and its centralized organization and control.

Fourth, Marcuse's radical idea of reason is based upon new concepts of time and progress. Progress will no longer be evaluated quantitatively with productivity for its own sake as the highest value. Rather than ceaseless labor, discontent, and the denial of gratification for the benefit of future material goods, progress will mean peace, contentment, and the happiness of gratified human needs. Linear time will cease to be meaningful.

Happiness would have permanence and would no longer be experienced as a series of momentary pleasures fleeting in the present, distant and uncertain in the future.

These characteristics of the new science add up to significantly more than the preconditions for a rational society. They would be expressive of a new reality principle, which could, as Marcuse requires, bind the growth of science in the modern world as religion had in the Middle Ages.[40] Marcuse alludes to this new reality principle in *One-dimensional Man* when he suggests that it "pertains to the metaphysics of liberation — to the reconciliation of Logos and Eros. This idea envisages the coming-to-rest of the repressive productivity of Reason, the end of domination in gratification."[41]

With this suggestion Marcuse promptly returns us to his interpretation of Freud, to Eros as Reason (Logos), to the notion of libidinal rationality, the logic of gratification. The return is hinted at in the fourth characteristic noted above because the new concepts of progress and time were first developed in *Eros and Civilization*.[42] There the philosophies of Aristotle (the *nous theos*), Hegel (the Absolute Spirit), and Nietzsche (the myth of eternal return) express, albeit in different ways, the highest idea of reason, that of attained and sustained fulfillment, when all potential has become actualized, where individual needs and capacities are no longer alienated to an imposed rationality of either sacrifice or domination, necessity or the social organization of necessity. Elsewhere Marcuse recalls the cyclical theories of history, those of Thucydides, Machiavelli, Vico, Toynbee, and Spengler, each symbolizing the concept of freedom as gratification, fulfillment, and rest.[43]

The metaphors of philosophers and historians are approximations of Marcuse's new idea of reason. What must be stressed is not merely that technological development could be arrested and bound securely by the substitution of a new principle of reason for the productive rationality of technics, but that this principle must be of a particular kind with a definite content. It cannot be other than the reflection of a subject capable of a radically different disposition to and experience of nature and human relations — a disposition that is passive, an experience that is receptive. Passivity and receptivity are qualities antithetical to those that animate the active and appropriating subject of technical reason. Technical rationality would cease to rule where and only where those former qualities prevailed. Marcuse's new science is his second dimension. The erotic, passive, receptive sensibility of the libidinal rationality is also the biological need for gratification, fulfillment, rest, peace, beauty, and solitude. It is, in a phrase, the "biological foundation for socialism."

Nothing more in the way of a critical analysis of Marcuse's second dimension and its many fallacies need be pursued. It is appropriate, however, to recall a major point of the argument developed in chapter three for the purpose of acquiring a perspective on the relationship of Marcuse's new science to his philosophical foundation for critical theory.

If it is correct to argue, as I have done, that Marcuse's new science is synonymous with his second dimension, then it is also correct to claim that the relation of the new science to Marcuse's philosophical foundation is actually a question about the relationship between two different sorts of foundations, the second being anthropological. It is evident, though, that the foundations do not complement one another. In fact, they accomplish two entirely different and contradictory objectives.

Marcuse's philosophical foundation for critical theory restores, in the fullest sense, the subject as reason, subjectivity as reasoning. By this is meant that what the individual aspires to become, the forms of social organization he devises, and the values and standards he adopts to guide his every thought and action are open, contestable, and liable to change through critical reflection. At the limit, what should be provided for the subject, and what Marcuse does provide, are the theoretical preconditions for rational discourse.

But this philosophical foundation is undermined in two ways by Marcuse's anthropological basis for critical theory. First, the latter foundation is a positive content for theory legislating all dimensions of subjectivity—its cognitive, psychological, and biological constitution; ethics; relatedness to man and nature; and so forth. The anthropological conception determines the subject and the subject's mode of being in advance and in a manner precluding the issues and problems with which a free subject would contend. Second, and paradoxically, this conception of the subject is inadequate and actually contributes to the eclipse of subjectivity. Here I refer to the thesis of the third chapter, where it was argued that Marcuse's interpretation of Freud supposes a regression behind those stages of psychosexual development establishing the biological preconditions for reason (sublimation). Consequently, the second dimension is intended as a comprehensive anthropological foundation for critical theory, but it is one that ultimately fails because it achieves both too much and too little. An anthropological basis for critical theory should do neither more nor less than establish the existence of the subject, of an individual possessing the capacity and the will to reason.

Notes

1. Herbert Marcuse, *One-dimensional Man: Studies in the Ideology of Advanced Industrial Society* (Boston: Beacon, 1964), p. 21.

2. Ibid., pp. xii–xiii; see also Marcuse's "Socialism in the Developed Countries," *International Socialist Journal*, 2, 8 (Rome: 1965), p. 140; originally published as "Perspektiven des Sozialismus in der entwickelten Industriegesellschaft," *Praxis*, 1, 2-3 (Zagreb: 1965), pp. 260-270.

3. Marcuse argues that in "the advanced industrial countries there *is* a class society; all the fine talk about a levelling out of the classes or a property-owning democracy is no more than pure ideology." "Socialism in the Developed Countries," p. 140.

4. Herbert Marcuse, "Some Social Implications of Modern Technology," *Studies in Philosophy and Social Science*, 9, 3 (New York: 1941), p. 423.

5. *One-dimensional Man*, p. 11; also see Herbert Marcuse, "The Individual in the 'Great Society' " (part 2), *Alternatives*, 1, 2 (San Diego: 1966), p. 29.

6. Herbert Marcuse, "Freedom and Freud's Theory of Instincts," *Five Lectures* (Boston: Beacon, 1970), p. 12; originally published as "Trieblehre und Freiheit," *Freud in der Gegenwart: Ein Vortragszyklus der Universitäten Frankfurt und Heidelberg zum hundersten Geburtstag, Frankfurter Beiträge zur Soziologie*, 6 (Frankfurt: 1957), pp. 401-424.

7. *One-dimensional Man*, p. 89.

8. "Some Social Implications of Modern Technology," p. 424.

9. Other examples of the "unification of opposites" can be found in *One-dimensional Man*, pp. 226-227, and in Herbert Marcuse, "Epilogue to the New German Edition of Marx's *18th Brumaire of Louis Napolean*," *Radical America*, 3, 4 (Cambridge: 1969), p. 59; originally published as the Epilogue to Karl Marx, *Der 18. Brumaire des Louis Bonaparte* (Frankfurt: Insel, 1965), pp. 143-150.

10. "Epilogue to the New German Edition of Marx's *18th Brumaire of Louis Napolean*," p. 59.

11. *One-dimensional Man*, p. 221.

12. Ibid., p. x.

13. Ibid., pp. x–xi.

14. Ibid., pp. x, 217, 219.

15. Ibid., pp. 95–96.

16. See chapter two, pp. 68–69, 74–76.

17. *One-dimensional Man*, pp. 203–224.

18. Ibid., p. 211.

19. Ibid., p. 218.

20. Ibid., p. 220 (italics added).

21. Ibid.

22. Ibid (italics added).

23. Herbert Marcuse, "The Concept of Negation in the Dialectic," *Telos*, 8 (St. Louis: 1971), p. 130; originally published as "Zum Begriff der Negation in der Dialektik," *Filosoficky casopis*, 15, 3 (Prague: 1967), pp. 375–379.

24. Herbert Marcuse, "Eros and Culture," *Cambridge Review*, 1, 3 (Cambridge: 1955), p. 109.

25. *One-dimensional Man*, p. 257.

26. Ibid., p. 125.

27. Ibid.

28. Even in a truly rational or "utopian" society, Marcuse explains, there would not be "perennial happiness. The 'natural' individuality of man is also the source of his natural sorrow. If the human relations are nothing but human, if they are freed from all foreign standards, they will be permeated with the sadness of their singular content. They are transitory and irreplaceable, and their transitory character will be accentuated when concern for the human being is no longer mingled with fear for his material existence and overshadowed by the threat of poverty, hunger, and social ostracism." "Some Social Implications of Modern Technology," pp. 438–439.

29. Herbert Marcuse, "Repressive Tolerance," *A Critique of Pure Tolerance* (Boston: Beacon, 1965), p. 109.

30. Ibid., p. 123.

31. Ibid., p. 112.

32. Ibid., p. 122.

33. Ibid., p. 88 (italics added).

34. Ibid., p. 123.

35. Ibid., p. 87.

36. *One-dimensional Man*, pp. 162–166.

37. Hannah Arendt makes a similar point about the inherent conceptual limits of scientific language. "Wherever the relevance of

speech is at stake, matters become political by definition, for speech is what makes man a political being. If we would follow the advice, so frequently urged upon us, to adjust our cultural attitudes to the present status of scientific achievement, we would in all earnest adopt a way of life in which speech is no longer meaningful. For the sciences today have been forced to adopt a 'language' of mathematical symbols which, though it was originally meant only as an abbreviation for spoken statements, now contains statements that in no way can be translated back into speech. The reason why it may be wise to distrust the political judgement of scientists *qua* scientists is not primarily their lack of 'character'—that they did not refuse to develop atomic weapons—or their naïveté—that they did not understand that once these weapons were developed they would be the last to be consulted about their use—but precisely the fact that they move in a world where speech has lost its power." *The Human Condition* (New York: Doubleday, Anchor Books, 1959), p. 4.

38. Herbert Marcuse, "On Science and Phenomenology," in *Boston Studies in the Philosophy of Science*, 2, edited by Robert Cohen and Marx W. Wartofsky (New York: Humanities, 1965), p. 286.

39. Herbert Marcuse, "The Problem of Social Change in the Technological Society," in *Le Développement social*, edited by Raymond Aron and Bert F. Hoselitz (Paris: Mouton, 1965), p. 147; volume printed for limited distribution; address presented to a UNESCO symposium on social development, May 1961.

40.   Herbert Marcuse, "The Responsibility of Science," in *The Responsibility of Power: Historical Essays in Honor of Hajo Holborn*, edited by L. Krieger and F. Stern (New York: Doubleday, 1967), pp. 439-440.

41. *One-dimensional Man*, p. 167.

42. Herbert Marcuse, *Eros and Civilization: A Philosophical Inquiry into Freud* (Boston: Beacon, 1955), pp. 106-126.

43. Herbert Marcuse, "Karl Popper and the Problem of Historical Laws," *Studies in Critical Philosophy* (Boston: Beacon, 1973), p. 199; originally published as "Notes on the Problem of Historical Laws," *Partisan Review*, 26, 1 (New Brunswick: 1959), pp. 117-129.

SEVEN

Revolutionary Subject, Revolutionary Class

> Often, the outward and visible material signs and
> symbols of happiness and success only show them-
> selves when the process of decline has already set in.
> The outer manifestations take time—like the light of
> that star up there, which may in reality be already
> quenched, when it looks to us to be shining its
> brightest.
>
> Thomas Mann, *Buddenbrooks*

CRITICAL THEORY, in at least one sense, conscientiously attempts
to resist falling into the miasma of ideology. Many varieties of
contemporary Marxism have held fast to the unqualified belief
in the proletariat as revolutionary agent of historical transformation, although this belief certainly has not been expressed in similar ways or for similar reasons. Marcuse and the other members
of the Frankfurt School recognized that the historical development of capitalism both produced and abolished the proletariat
as vehicle of qualitative change. Since Marx critical theory has
been a theory of the transition to socialism and of those factors
that explain why the transition has not occurred and perhaps
never will occur.[1] In the present stage of capitalism the failure of
socialism appears to critical theory to be as inevitable as did its
success during capitalism's earlier stages.

With this sober conclusion pressed by history upon critical theory, it would be a simple matter for theory to take flight from

reality and seek refuge in the fantasy of a proletarian mythology. Such flight would be perfectly understandable in view of the depth of emotional involvement of the critical theorists in their work, evidenced by the frequently depressive tone of their writings and by remarks of this sort offered by Marcuse — "I literally couldn't stand it any longer if nothing would change. Even I am suffocating."[2] Pathos can be a measure of the temptation to fall into ideological solutions to the plight of modern socialism and of the theoretical objectivity that is exercised to resist the temptation.

Reflecting on critical theory's prognosis of the once promising but now dismal prospects for radical social change, Marcuse charges that such theoretical objectivity is not without fault.

> If the same theory can equally well deal with the development A as well as non-A, prosperity as well as crisis, revolution as well as the absence of revolution, or the radicalization of the working class as well as its integration into the existing system, then although this may indicate the validity of the theory, it also indicates its indifference.[3]

"Indifference" casts a new light on a theory that otherwise is approved for its objective analysis and portrayal of historical tendencies. It strongly suggests that regardless of the evaluation of tendencies, and especially where the evaluation stresses that the dominant tendency is toward the preservation of the status quo, theory ought to adopt a strategy of identifying sources of resistance to the prevailing institutions and practices, even if those sources of "negativity" identified cannot be accorded the stature of revolutionary agents. Critical theory, in other words, must overcome its indifference, which does not mean sacrificing its objectivity, and become political in a practical sense. It must strive toward politics though social reality is invested only with the forces of a primitive, chaotic, unorganized opposition.

Marcuse's Moral Turn

By way of introduction I choose this issue of critical theory's fealty to objectivity and its imposed burden of indifference weighing upon the theorist because I believe it will explain why Marcuse's well-known but imperfectly understood and (only for that reason) "notorious" association with the New Left, which begins roughly in the middle 1960s, marks a break with the theory of one-dimensionality. This break may have appeared obvious and in no need of explanation, for during approximately the next decade we find Marcuse writing extensively and enthusiastically about the composition of the New Left, its prospects for initiating change, and the nature of change it represents. Yet, a study of these works does not support the obvious interpretation that Marcuse viewed the New Left, and other oppositional strata with which he was concerned, as a new historical agent of social transformation. The New Left and its rebellious company did not prove to him that the domination of technical reason was not as effective as he once firmly believed. Assuming the contrary would introduce a contradiction into Marcuse's work during this period because such a view would be inconsistent with the theory of one-dimensionality—a theory that was retained in the bulk of Marcuse's writing on the New Left. Falling far short of a modern counterpart to Marx's proletariat, the New Left could not have prompted Marcuse to break with past theoretical claims.

A break did occur, however, and it is heralded by Marcuse's self-proclaimed alliance with the New Left. "I believe," Marcuse exclaimed in 1968, "that the New Left today is the only hope *we* have."[4] In what sense, then, does Marcuse's intense interest in the New Left signal a departure from the one-dimensionality thesis?

While the New Left came to occupy a definite place in Marcuse's theory as a practical force for sweeping change, though a place revised considerably over the years, at first its most prominent theoretical function was *symbolic*. Restoring a humanitarian dimension to radical politics, the New Left's criticism of advanced industrial society was moral in kind. The New Left had begun to "relearn what we," Marcuse lamented, "forgot during the Fascist period . . . that humanitarian and moral arguments are not merely deceitful ideology."[5] Only moral discourse could succeed where traditional indictments of capitalism, those emphasizing material inequalities and deprivations, had been made obsolete by technical progress. Specifically, in Marcuse's estimation, what sort of case on behalf of humanity was made by the New Left? This question will be considered in greater depth when the discussion turns to Marcuse's "new sensibility." For now, it can be said simply that the New Left gave expression to new conceptions of human need, happiness, and freedom, to goals transcending the established form of life. Moral criticism of this nature could be persuasive, though moral outrage was not: "Genocide, war crimes, crimes against humanity are not effective arguments against a government which protects property, trade, and commerce at home while it perpetuates its destructive policy abroad."[6]

Theoretically, the New Left's attack was a sign that the quantitative progress of technological rationality was inadequate as a social cement to bind together the institutions of advanced industrial society. The system's inexhaustible technical resources, organized to "deliver the goods," were not appreciated by some groups within the society as equivalent to the highest public good. Soon Marcuse realized that "very different from the revolution at previous stages of history, this opposition is directed against the totality of a well-functioning, prosperous society."[7] Overwhelming material achievements may be capable of eroding the traditional bases of contradiction but generate new antagonisms in their place. "Revolution aus Ekel!" Revolution out of disgust at the "general inhumanity, dehumanization, waste and excess of the so-called consumer society."[8] Later, in *Counterrevolution and Revolt*, Marcuse will argue a refined version of this thesis. Affluence does not merely create opposition out of disgust but delegitimizes the society by emptying its most salient normative structures of content.

Resisting the temptations of prosperity, insisting on an experience of the world no longer mediated by "things," giving expression to humanitarian values and objectives, in short, symbolizing the aspirations of those who should one day found a nonrepressive social order, the New Left created problems for the theory of technological domination. At a point in its evolution, by virtue of its own technical and material accomplishments one-dimensional society becomes not more but less impervious to internal contradictions. At the same time, however, for reasons to be made clear shortly, the New Left could neither fulfill the role assigned to the historical agent of social transformation nor perhaps even constitute a genuine threat to stability. Yet, the New Left must be, and in fact is, incorporated by Marcuse into his theory. On what grounds?

The theoretical development that occurred was not at first a complete break with the one-dimensionality thesis. That would not come about until 1972, with *Counterrevolution and Revolt*. Of a rather more subtle nature, the change in Marcuse's thinking can be described best as a *theoretical revision* and a *moral break*. In its capacity as moral agency the New Left became a theoretical and moral inspiration for Marcuse or, more emphatically, it became actually as much of a moral force within his work as he believed the New Left to be a moral force within society. Viewing the New Left as an unorganized, frequently anti-theoretical and anti-intellectual but morally armed opposition, Marcuse is first moved by its moral character to take it into account. But why should moral discourse have had this impact upon his thought? Marcuse's opening to the left is an accommodation, a theoretical revision, but foremost a moral response to moral pressures that educated him to the immorality or, to recall the earlier term, indifference of critical theory. Theory now must be committed to discovering oppositional tendencies regardless of how limp or ill-defined they appear according to the traditional (rationalistic) framework of critical theory. The New Left represented one such tendency. Acting in good faith is the ultimate meaning of Marcuse's assertion that "we," the intellectuals, the theorists, "must finally relearn what we forgot during the Fascist period . . . that humanitarian and moral arguments are not merely deceitful ideology."

What cannot be overestimated is the broader, long-range significance for Marcuse's theory of the humanitarian dimension symbolized by the New Left. Ostensibly, the New Left was a historical development that compelled Marcuse to reflect upon his theoretical claims. Incorporating it into his theory was an initial theoretical revision that refocused his analysis on social processes that would become increasingly unstable. Attuned to these processes, Marcuse then followed with additional revisions. Consequently, prompted by his moral turn, the first theoretical revision, of which more now will be said, is also the first and decisive stage giving occasion to a gradual transition to a richer conception of subjectivity in a radicalized critical theory. As we saw, the new conception of subjectivity was present already, but only implicitly, in Marcuse's philosophical foundation for critical theory.[9]

Before this transition is completed, continuity is preserved in Marcuse's critical theory. The revision allowing for the accommodation of oppositional tendencies occurs within a single framework. The one-dimensionality thesis remains fundamentally unchanged. Revolution depends upon the emergence of a mass base, but suffering from the paralysis induced by technological domination there is little likelihood of the mass's becoming politicized. A "perfect barbarism where freedom and automatism coincide" is yet the dominant tendency of advanced industrial society.[10] The task of liberation can go forward only where the radical opposition recognizes that "society has invaded even the deepest roots of individual existence, even the unconscious of man."[11] But liberation *can* go forward. Although Marcuse continues to remind us that "under total capitalist administration and introjection, the social determination of consciousness is all but complete and immediate," now, in the era of New Left politics, he contends also that

> under these circumstances, radical change in consciousness is the beginning, the first step in changing social existence: *emergence of the new Subject*. Historically, it is again the period of enlightenment prior to material change — a period of education, but education which turns into praxis: demonstration, confrontation, rebellion.[12]

An exceptional remark! Side by side with a strong affirmation of the one-dimensionality argument lies an equally forceful expression of belief in the possibility for freeing the individual from an internalized enslavement that is (no longer?) thought to be fathomless. Marcuse has taken a serious step toward a new project, the reunification of theory and practice. In this spirit he proposes that "the idea of revolution is never a 'mystification.'"[13] His support for the New Left becomes unqualified, tempered only by the advice that the movement must avoid both defeatism and illusions of success.[14] In fact, Marcuse can now claim what his theory previously denied — that his concern is to project not merely the objective technical potentialities for liberation but the subjective possibilities for revolution as well.[15]

To this point, I have proposed that the New Left conveyed a very special and, perhaps in a deeper sense, even personal significance for Marcuse. Investigating the moral as well as the theoretical aspects of Marcuse's critical theory made possible certain important clarifications. The nature of his theoretical response to the New Left could be explained in such a way as to account for the extension of the one-dimensionality thesis into this stage of his work, while also entertaining the suggestion that he may be taking strides toward closing the distance between theory and practice. Given this perspective, an abrupt development that certainly would have appeared to embody a contradiction is proven to have an underlying coherence with previous theoretical work. With this argument the path is now cleared for an analysis of Marcuse's critical theory as it further developed in the historical context of New Left politics. The remainder of the chapter is arranged as follows.

Once Marcuse had incorporated subjective factors as progressive tendencies into his theoretical framework, he was obliged to introduce certain other theoretical revisions. Marcuse's greatest challenge lay in the redefinition of the concept of revolution. Faced squarely, the theoretical implications of New Left politics required modifications in that concept amounting to a nearly complete reformulation of the traditional Marxist theory of revolution. Inquiring first into Marcuse's theoretical revisions, I provide an overview of the amended economic basis and social composition of revolution and of revolutionary strategies and their justifications. In this context, it will be shown that all conceptual revisions and proposed strategies are consistent with the theory of one-dimensionality. This point would be less significant theoretically than as a historical detail if it were not for two interesting and important questions that it raises. First, since Marcuse conceived revolutionary strategies from the standpoint of the one-dimensionality thesis, could the New Left's real strategic prospects for influencing a political practice beyond its own (organizational) frontiers be obscured by Marcuse's theory? Second, *if* the New Left had adopted Marcuse's proposed strategies, what would have been the result? The second question directly concerns the relationship of theory and practice in Marcuse's critical theory and addresses the issue of whether his theoretical revisions contributed to healing the separation between theory and practice. Both questions quite obviously offer the opportunity for arriving at a better understanding of the political as well as the theoretical implications of Marcuse's critical theory during this time. These questions will be answered in the course of discussion.

Next, a series of related issues will be explored. Marcuse's "new sensibility" will be examined, lending depth to the prior consideration of the humanitarian dimension represented by the New

Left. A fascinating parallel between Marcuse's anthropological foundation for critical theory, the new sensibility, and the New Left will be observed. At the same time, the new sensibility will be shown to be the theoretical development that compelled Marcuse to make a complete break with the one-dimensionality thesis. As such, it is the theoretical bridge to *Counterrevolution and Revolt*.

Finally, the discussion will turn to *Counterrevolution and Revolt*. I have singled out this work because it does appear to realize, or comes very near to realizing, the promise of a reunified theory and practice intimated in Marcuse's writings during the previous New Left years. A new concept of subjectivity is supposed, and revisions of prior revisions occur. A complete break with the theory of one-dimensionality has been made at last.

Redefining Revolution

FACTORS IN THE SOCIAL COMPOSITION OF REVOLUTION

After retrieving the concept of revolution from a premature grave, Marcuse submits it to a reevaluation in the context of political developments associated with the New Left. One such development already has been noted. In the advanced industrial societies, economic prosperity rather than economic crisis becomes a material basis for generating opposition. Crisis is no longer a *necessary* condition for social transformation, an important revision of the orthodox Marxist formula for revolution. As we have seen, of course, even if prosperity were not to figure in the conceptual renewal of revolution, crisis would still have to be rejected as part of Marcuse's conceptual apparatus. The psychological underpinnings of domination weigh heavily against the possibility that in the midst of crisis a socialist consciousness would be bred.[16]

Prosperity does not only spur opposition. Along with the deeply entrenched psychological roots of domination, affluence continues to secure the yoke of domination on the vast majority of the population, including the working class. Together with crisis, then, class is jettisoned by Marcuse as an element of the conception of revolution in advanced industrial society. This is to be expected where the central aspects of the one-dimensionality thesis are retained.

For Marx, the revolution was to be a majority affair. Marcuse also subjects this aspect of the concept to revision. This does not mean, however, that the revolutionary minority is as it was in "Repressive Tolerance."[17] Marcuse's theory of revolution has moved beyond that argument. The New Left must forge alliances, among which is to be included an alliance with the working class. (This point does not contradict the revision that eliminated class from the concept of revolution, which shall become clear.) Even an alliance with the working class, however, would not make the revolution a revolution of the majority. Technical factors, such as the rationalization of the productive process, have reduced considerably the size of the proletariat to the extent to which it is no longer the class of the majority.[18]

From Marcuse's analysis of the situation of the working class in advanced industrial society, another important revision follows. Since the revolution is not to be waged (primarily) through the large-scale, mass action of the proletariat, the dictatorship organizing the transitional stage from capitalism to communism would not be a revolutionary dictatorship of the proletariat. It necessarily would be a joint dictatorship of New Left forces and the working class.

Greatly extended, the new social basis for revolution is as different from its class based predecessor as the new material basis, prosperity, is from economic crisis. Cutting across class and racial lines, the social composition of the New Left includes civil rights groups, intellectuals, students, and other youth groups such as hippies. Marcuse argues that "corresponding to reality," that is, to the empirical character of the opposition in advanced industrial society, this circumstance nevertheless "is a real nightmare for 'old Marxists.' "[19] Marcuse's assessment is that this new social basis is neo-Marxist rather than Marxist. It is difficult to grasp why he attaches the neo-Marxist label to these groups collectively though, as he does when he praises the New Left for its distrust of old leftist parties and their ideology.[20] Somehow Marcuse has overlooked the fact that these groups were highly politicized around a plethora of Marxist and neo-Marxist ideologies that distinguished often hostile factions within the New Left.

Marcuse extends the social basis for revolution far beyond the New Left. He is optimistic about the chances for the emergence of socialism in the Third World because its masses seem not to be "integrated into the value system of the old [presumably colo-

nial] societies."[21] Marcuse's conception of revolution, though, is
not intended to project separate tendencies for revolution in the
Third World and in the advanced industrial societies. Rather,
Marcuse's concept includes a "global" perspective that attempts
to demonstrate the objective possibility and necessity for an alliance of revolutionary forces in the West and in the Third World.
What are the dynamics of this global perspective and what is the
nature of the alliance?

"In today's situation," Marcuse argues, "there is no longer
anything 'outside capitalism.' "[22] "The opposition is concentrated
among the outsiders *within* the established order."[23] Here Marcuse begins to speak less of advanced industrial society than of
capitalism or, more exactly, of a world capitalist system. Capitalism's systemic character means that a change in one area
causes changes in other areas. Third World struggles against imperialism, specifically the colonial and neocolonial penetration
upon which the economic and political strength of capitalism depends, could undermine capitalist stability. While Marcuse does
not say explicitly that these struggles would produce an economic crisis, as much can be inferred from his assertion that capitalism "can survive only if its expansion is not blocked."[24] Does
Marcuse mean to reintroduce crisis into his conception of revolution? He does, though not according to the traditional Marxist
format. Crisis is not instrumental to the emergence of *subjective
factors* for revolution but would complement, in a decisive way,
the tendencies toward change within the capitalist societies once
they had begun to be developed consciously by oppositional
forces. The crisis induced by Third World liberation movements
must be "synchronized" with the standard antagonisms burden-
ing the advanced stages of capitalism, such as those produced by
the rationalization of the productive process (e.g., unemployment and a declining margin of profit associated with increasing
automation) and by the efforts to retain neocolonial holdings
(e.g., war costs draining subsidies from the welfare state). At the
same time, the morale and discipline required for work under
capitalism weaken as artificial needs are satisfied—a satisfaction
breeds indolence and lethargy syndrome. Strategically located
socioeconomic groups (the working class, professional and technical classes) affected by these contradictions would be organized
and mobilized by the New Left to paralyze the central economic

structures. Alone, however, the New Left in alliance with these groups could not succeed for the capitalist system is too powerful. At this point, an economic crisis manufactured through revolution in the Third World would deliver the crippling blow. Hence, the success of revolution depends on an international alliance of Third World forces and forces within the advanced capitalist countries. Neither the New Left nor the Third World, Marcuse advises, can succeed independently of the other.[25]

In explaining Marcuse's conception of the global dynamics of revolution I have alluded to a crucial factor that now can be brought to the fore, namely, the socioeconomic groups with which the New Left must enter into alliance under conditions of economic stress. The issue can be clarified by posing a question that uncovers another aspect of Marcuse's concept of revolution. According to Marcuse's view of advanced industrial society, what must be the principal strategic target of a revolutionary struggle? "For the totalitarian control of society," by which Marcuse means to include the nonviolent totalitarianism peculiar to advanced industrial society, "it is not necessary to control directly *all* or 'nearly all' relations because control of the *key* positions and institutions assures control of the whole."[26] It follows that seizing the "key positions and institutions" would break totalitarian domination.

"Objectively" this makes the proletariat decisive to the revolution because it still forms much of the social basis of the immediate process of production. Consequently, the alliance forged by the New Left for the purpose of crippling the productive apparatus would be with the working class—but not with this class alone. In a technically rationalized social system, wherein the institutions are functionally interdependent, the key institutions would include, as well as the major industrial concerns, the communications, educational, and research establishments. Theoretically, the practice of the New Left also would entail an alliance with the professional and technical classes, who along with the proletariat comprise the entire social basis of production.

Marcuse's redefinition of the material basis and social composition of revolution clearly revolutionizes the concept but also makes significant, albeit qualified, concessions to the traditional Marxist conception. His economic analysis ultimately includes a political economy of prosperity *and* crisis, even though the role

Marcuse assigns to the latter does not agree with Marx's crisis theory. And although class is rejected in favor of a heterogeneous social composition, the proletariat's strategic relation to the production process is not ignored. Here Marcuse's essential difference with Marx is his disqualification of the proletariat as the subjective factor in *initiating* revolutionary struggle.

Once Marcuse grasps the scope of the material and social factors of revolution within a single concept, he moves to a consideration of what ought to be the practical relations between them. To this end, Marcuse discusses both the strategies that should be adopted by the New Left for building alliances among its respective groups, between it and the working, professional, and technical classes, and the obstacles to the success of these strategies within these constituencies and the prevailing society.

ORGANIZATION AND STRATEGY

Like the revisions of the concept of revolution, from which they were born, Marcuse's strategies for revolutionary change are consistent with the theory of one-dimensionality. Sharing the general fate of the mass, the working and technical classes are assimilated into the social fabric of society but are potentially at variance with the system by virtue of the effect of the contradictions of advanced capitalism. Technically, their position in the productive process makes them crucial to its operation. In other words, subjectively these classes are nonrevolutionary; objectively the revolution's success or failure depends upon their conduct. The New Left is consciously opposed to the established order, but independent of the working and technical classes it could have little direct impact on its stability. Subjectively the New Left is revolutionary; objectively it is not. Under these circumstances critical theory is without practice, without a revolutionary agency. A strategy must be devised to unite subjective and objective factors, to ally the New Left with the social classes of production, which together would reconstitute a revolutionary agent. Comprehending the need for revolution, the productive classes would become disposed consciously, "subjectively," to social transformation. Acting to bring to these classes the consciousness of this need and of their objective function in the revolution, the New Left, too, would become an objective element in the revolutionary process. In this identity of subjective and objective factors would be the reunification of theory and practice.

The task of reunification must be the work of the New Left by virtue of its conscious opposition to the prevailing social order. As this movement evolved throughout the 1960s, its political practice was not suited to accomplish that end. Time and again Marcuse urged the New Left toward a theoretical understanding of society. Without a knowledge of the conditions, limitations, and capabilities of change, he argued, there can be only private rather than revolutionary practice, which at best delivers advantages to particular groups while preserving the status quo. At bottom, Marcuse understood, the New Left had far less of a hostility to theory than to organization. The former, in fact, was a reflection of the latter. Without a cohesive organizational life there could be no coherent view of advanced industrial society. Theory would be limited to the solipsistic perspectives of individual groups.

Organization, however, seemed to conflict with the philosophy of the New Left's student contingent. Hierarchy, authority, and oligarchy were too intimately associated with the system the students opposed. And student radicals did not view these features to be unique to the establishment but rather to be common to the repressive ideological practices of Marxist-Leninist parties. Sympathetic to their fear of reproducing the authoritarianism of the eastern European left and the oligarchies of the left in western European democratic societies, Marcuse praised the spontaneous anarchism of student groups. Although he suggested that the New Left develop "a new, very flexible kind of organization, one that does not impose rigorous principles, one that allows for movement and initiative . . . without the 'bosses' of the old parties or political groups,"[27] Marcuse failed to be more thoughtful about the problem of joining spontaneity with the imperative of organization.

His very concept of revolution prevented Marcuse from doing that. Alone, the students perhaps could raise a flexible organizational structure. But as Marcuse had made clear, organization must extend beyond the New Left to encompass the entire social basis of production. Dividing the subjective and objective factors for revolution neatly among completely separate constituencies, for Marcuse the productive classes had to be the *object* of the New Left's revolutionary politics and organizational aim before they could become the *subject* of a revolutionary struggle. This division and the politics it prescribes imposes a much stricter organizational function and structure upon the New Left—and one certainly irreconcilable with its anarchistic nature. Charged with the function of "radically enlightening" the nonrevolutionary classes, with respect to these classes as they are characterized by Marcuse, the New Left would have to adopt a traditional organizational framework and traditional pedagogical techniques because only such a framework and techniques are designed to cope with a traditional pedagogical problem—the instruction of those who do not know by those who do! Only if the classes forming the social basis of production were thought to be inclined similarly to a spontaneous activism could there be a relaxed organizational structure. This would mean, however, that the productive classes as well as the New Left necessarily would be seen as subjectively disposed to change from the outset. Such a view, and with it a sounder theory of organization, is not to be found until *Counterrevolution and Revolt*.

Is it mistaken to argue that Marcuse's concept of revolution mandates an organizational strategy that reproduces the oligarchical tendencies of traditional organizations? Any doubts are removed by statements such as this.

> The basic idea is: how can slaves who do not even know they are slaves free themselves? How can they liberate themselves by their own power, by their own faculties? How can they spontaneously accomplish liberation? They must be taught and must be led to be free, and this the more so the more the society in which they live uses all available means in order to shape and preform their consciousness and to make it immune against possible alternatives. This idea of an educational, preparatory dictatorship has today become an integral element of revolution and of the justification of the revolutionary oppression.[28]

Elsewhere Marcuse's language occasionally softens. Paired with "dictatorship," for example, we read "counteradministration."[29] In such instances, of course, not only the language but also the meaning softens. It may certainly be true, as he claims, that a counteradministration "would be very different from the Marxian dictatorship of the proletariat" and would eliminate, as apparently a Marxist dictatorship would not, he implies, "the horrors spread by the established administration."[30] Nevertheless, Marcuse's counteradministration is still very far removed from the flexible organizational structure that in *Counterrevolution and Revolt* is to blossom from the spontaneous, improvised practices of the New Left. It seems that Marcuse's ambitious organizational strategies are compromised wherever the one-dimensionality thesis reasserts its earlier (and uglier) influence.

In fact, the influence of the theory of one-dimensionality on Marcuse's strategic analysis is equally prominent in cases to which the theory seems least to apply. Besides those groups composing the New Left, there are two others Marcuse believes to have withstood integration into advanced industrial society and which should become targets for the New Left's educational work. An alliance with the poor can be formed because their needs are not met by the established institutions. Of the black population in particular, Marcuse has said that it "appears as the 'most natural' force of rebellion."[31] At the same time, blacks are not central to the productive process, making their objective function in the system and in the revolution negligible. Women are candidates for organization, Marcuse contends, because "in general [they] are more accessible to humane arguments than men are. This is because women are not yet completely harnessed into the productive process."[32] But other than implying that these groups are significant for their popular support of rebellion or, as in the case of women, for their electoral support of leftist aspirants for political office, Marcuse assigns to them no active or creative political role. Once again, this appears to be an omission encouraged by a theory that attributes subjectivity, the capacity to evaluate the society critically, to a select group of individuals who, for some unexplained reason, have escaped the pressures of technological domination.[33]

Organization clearly is a decisive strategic aim for Marcuse, though not one free of impediments. Before the New Left can begin to organize beyond its own constituencies, the antibureaucratic tendencies of its student contingent must be suppressed in favor of the more traditional organizational rationality denoted by counteradministration and educational dictatorship. The complete integration of the productive classes into society is an obstacle to democratic organization at one extreme and at the other to any form of organization that would incorporate these groups. Blacks and women are to be included in the organization but play a subordinate role apparently because they are not centrally related to the process of production. On all these accounts and in all matters, in other words, the New Left assumes the vanguard.

But the integration of the classes forming the social basis of production can be disputed for those reasons I advanced earlier. These classes may not be the critical subjects required by the concept of historical agency, but neither are their critical faculties so numb as to justify turning them into the objects of an educational dictatorship. And allowing Marcuse's economic analysis of blacks and women, though even here there is much room to doubt their place in the productive process as Marcuse understands it, their negligible role in production hardly can justify their subordination to an organizational leadership. Blacks and women, too, for Marcuse are far less the subjects than the objects of political practice.

Once the true subjective dispositions of these groups are taken into account, the theory of organization can be revised. No longer presupposing the need for a revolutionary subject over and against a potentially revolutionary object, it would be possible to dispense with an organizational logic that grows out of the absolute distinction between critical and uncritical, revolutionary and nonrevolutionary subjects, between those who know of the need for change and those who do not and are opposed to it. This point answers the two questions raised earlier about the New Left's strategic prospects for influence if its organizational structure, function, and strategies were shaped by Marcuse's theory of one-dimensionality. Bringing this point to bear directly on these questions, it can be argued that conceptions of subjectivity and revolution and strategies for change that affirm and enforce these distinctions obscure the real prospects for influencing a political practice beyond the organizational frontiers of a minority such as the New Left. This is so for three reasons. First, taking the form of an educational dictatorship, the political practice of the left would be rejected for its alien, coercive, and manipulative appearance. Second, if the groups at which the counter-administration is directed are really as integrated as the theory assumes, then *no* radical enlightenment could pry loose the psychological staples binding them to society. Last and most important, if these groups are not bound fast to the system but by experiencing discontents and uncertainties are somewhat disaffected and have suspended an unquestioned allegiance to the social order, then only a democratic framework emphasizing discussion, interpretation, and debate would be acceptable and appropriate.

The theory of technological domination weighs heavily upon Marcuse. His proposal for organization is locked up as tightly within his theoretical framework as his one-dimensional men are within his totally administered society. When he finally does liberate his strategies from the one-dimensionality thesis he will have recognized that human nature is not so malleable as his theory of domination supposes. At that point Marcuse will have arrived at a different conception of subjectivity.

That point, however, has not yet been reached. The theory of one-dimensionality not only disposes Marcuse's general proposal for organization toward an organizational function and structure consistent with it, but also dictates particular methods through which an organization is to attract support and achieve revolutionary aims. Most prominent among the methods that Marcuse believes have strategic significance is the "demonstration." Within this context arises the controversial issue of the relationship between violence and the critical opposition.

In his interpretation of Freud, Marcuse stressed the theoretical significance of Eros. Committed to an anthropology that celebrates nonaggressiveness, Marcuse should be constrained to adopt the principle of nonviolent struggle. It would be inconsistent first to indict the established social order on the anthropological ground that it represses the nonaggressive side of human nature and then to affirm that very repression as a justifiable revolutionary means to achieving a free society.

This anthropological constraint is wed to a second rational constraint of a Marxist persuasion that is accepted by Marcuse: the ends of a revolution are shaped during the revolution itself. If this were not to be the case, then the goals of the new society would be other than those born out of struggle and freely chosen by the participants. With Marcuse, as will be seen when his "new sensibility" is discussed, this rule must be true in form as well as in content. If an objective of the order is nonaggressiveness, it is not enough to espouse this ideal during struggle. The revolution must embody this value in its very practice. On one occasion Marcuse stated this position with particular forcefulness.

Our goals, our values, our own and new morality, our OWN morality, must be visible already in our actions. The new human beings who we want to help to create — we must already strive to be these human beings right here and now.[34]

Anticipating a particular political practice on the basis of uncovering certain rational constraints embedded in Marcuse's theory leads to a decisive question: is Marcuse obedient to these constraints or does he violate the discipline of his own theory?

At first there is no disappointment. Without the least equivocation Marcuse approves only nonviolent demonstrations. "Passive resistance" is an appropriate characterization of the approach he supports, though such resistance must be of a peculiar variety. Qualities belonging to a different, erotic sensibility also must be present. Describing a Berkeley demonstration that was on the verge of erupting into a violent confrontation, Marcuse applauds a dramatic turn of events. "After two or three scary minutes," Marcuse recalls, "the thousands of marchers sat down in the street, guitars and harmonicas appeared, people began 'necking' and 'petting,' and so the demonstration ended." Marcuse refers to this as a "new dimension of protest, which consists in the unity of moral-sexual and political rebellion."[35]

In this example, as in several others scattered throughout Marcuse's work at this time, both constraints implicit in Marcuse's theory are heeded. The strategy of demonstration is consistent with the principle of nonviolence, and as a primitive expression of Marcuse's libidinal rationality radical protest entails the nonaggressive ends of a nonrepressive society. By itself, however, demonstrations cannot alter the prevailing institutions even if conducted on the broadest scale. Their purpose, Marcuse argues, is educational.[36] Demonstrations interrupt normal, everyday affairs and create a public space in which issues and events are given new interpretations and explanations. Attracting a critical mass, demonstrations provide the basis for organization, from which more systematic educational work can proceed. Demonstrations are preparatory.

It appears, though, that this preparatory stage is destined to terminate prematurely and unsuccessfully. While Marcuse advises that all opposition must strive to preserve peace by discovering forms of democratic struggle that neither are violent nor provoke the violence of established institutions, ultimately "it is

meaningless to speak of the legality of resistance."[37] At the point
at which organizational practices constitute a direct challenge to
the fundamental values of the prevailing society, ipso facto the
state can be expected to react violently. Demonstration inevitably turns into confrontation; nonviolent opposition necessarily
passes over to violence. If, however, violence is avoided at *all*
costs, this would mean not only working peacefully within democratic channels but also agreeing to the nonfundamental, status
quo oriented changes that formal democratic institutions permit.[38] "The alternative," Marcuse regrets, "is not democratic
evolution versus radical action, but rationalization of the status-
quo versus change."[39]

Marcuse concludes that the opposition is caught in a series of
contradictions. It must support democracy, for without the protection that democratic institutions afford the left could not even
begin to organize. Once the left is organized, however, a commitment to actions calculated to maintain democratic institutions by not forcing them to respond with violent suppression of
the left's civil liberties requires the left to compromise revolutionary aspirations. Since this compromise is unthinkable, for
the left the contradiction admits only of violent resolution. But
violence leads to a second contradiction. To accomplish its aims
the left must forge alliances; yet violence dissuades and forecloses
the possibility of attracting mass support.

> The conclusion? The radical opposition inevitably faces defeat of its
> direct extraparliamentary action, of uncivil disobedience, and
> there are situations in which it must take the risk of such defeat — if,
> in doing so, it can consolidate its strength and expose the destruc-
> tive character of civil obedience to a reactionary regime.[40]

Increasingly isolated from groups crucial to the success of its
organizational aims by virtue of being compelled, by the logic of
the system it opposes, to adopt self-defeating strategies, the left
remains confined to a minority even though its strength may be
consolidated and the system's underlying hostility even to democratic opposition may be exposed. But such a conclusion gives
reason for pause. Marcuse's argument certainly appears to be
plausible. The opposition is caught within a web of extremes. It
must either adhere to the rules of the established framework and
be defeated or, refusing to compromise, adopt the only available

radical strategy and be defeated. Once again, however, we find Marcuse offering an analysis leading relentlessly to the separation of the critical opposition from the mass of society. Earlier it was the proposal for an educational dictatorship that obscured the real prospects for influencing a political practice beyond the organizational frontiers of a minority. Here, the strategy of violence further divides the left from its prospective allies. The political and theoretical implications are striking. If the New Left had adopted these strategies it would have placed insurmountable obstacles between it and those groups that, together with the left, comprise Marcuse's historical agent of social transformation. Marcuse's strategies systematically widen the distance between subjective and objective factors. His theoretical conception of revolution waits upon a viable practice—but both wait upon a new conception of subjectivity.

On a few occasions Marcuse appears to qualify the scenario depicting the unhappy future of the opposition. According to Marcuse's analysis a definite sequence of events is to be anticipated, ending in the defeat and isolation of the left. Perhaps, however, the opposition can avoid this fate or, to be precise, avoid defeat. This is implied by Marcuse when he discusses violent revolution—not strategies leading to revolution—*by a minority* and its *justification*. Such discussions, in other words, implicitly view violent revolution as though it could become a reality if a minority chose to will it.

Two examples are outstanding. In his examination of the defense of Gracchus Babeuf before the High Court of Vendôme, Marcuse argues that Babeuf's justification for acts of "extreme civil disobedience" was based on the principle that the established government was not legitimate because it did not allow for the satisfaction of the people's true interests and needs. Babeuf's subversion was not aimed at the government exclusively, for the people wrongly accepted these institutions as legitimate. Consequently,

> because the people for whom the revolution is to be made are deceived, hostile, or apathetic, it will be a revolution by a minority, that means, it will involve the Terror—against the enemies of the revolution who would presumably include the deceived and misled people in whose interest the revolution is to be carried through . . . If they do not spontaneously *act* as majority because they are "mis-

led" or kept in ignorance or deprived of the means to act effectively, the revolution — their revolution — must needs become the concern of the leadership: it must become a dictatorship for though not by the majority.[41]

It is important to remember the context of Marcuse's statement. He is discussing the justification for Babeuf's attempted part in the Reign of Terror. Yet, I believe there is no license involved in claiming that its meaning is intended to extend beyond this context. Actually, the statement invokes an argument that by now is quite familiar. Where the mass is nonrevolutionary, the revolution must assume but one course of action. In another place Marcuse concentrates on the justification for revolution without regard for any particular historical context. A sound defense for violence, he contends, rests upon a "historical calculus" that demonstrates that the revolution reduces the "sacrifices exacted from the living generations on behalf of the established society" and "the number of victims made in defense of this society in war and peace."[42]

By drawing attention to these few occasions where Marcuse embraces violence as the solution to the problem of changing social conditions, an important point can be made. All the evidence suggests that Marcuse's final position on violence is ambivalent. While his strategic analysis viewed violence as a necessary evil, violence clearly left the opposition paralyzed. Inadvertently or deliberately, it is difficult to say, Marcuse proved violence to be an inappropriate means of achieving revolutionary aims. New strategies must be sought. Where this view is altered, though implicitly, and violence is approved for its strategic effectiveness, an ambivalence in Marcuse's position toward violence becomes apparent.

It is here that a deeper and more serious problem arises: who are the violent minorities? Marcuse would answer as he has always. It is the left, which means an organization and in the best of circumstances an alliance of all groups decisive to social transformation. But terms such as "minority," "leadership," "dictatorship," and "tribunal" are open to other interpretations — perhaps to that of terrorism. Could a violent minority be a terrorist minority? Lamentably, such an interpretation is intelligible though not plausible when the corpus of Marcuse's writings on revolution is reviewed. Nevertheless, it would be a simple matter to turn an attack on terrorism into an attack on Marcuse's theory, even though his theory, as I have indicated, for the most part illustrates the folly, on pain of paralysis, of any violent opposition. Thus, it is no surprise when in the aftermath of terrorist activities in West Germany, Marcuse feels obligated, and perhaps pressured, to declare unambiguously his attitude toward terrorism.

> In taking a position towards terrorism in West Germany, the Left must first ask itself two questions: Do terrorist actions contribute to the weakening of capitalism? Are these actions justified in view of the demands of revolutionary morality? To both questions I must answer in the negative.[43]

Not all of Marcuse's strategies are as problematic as those of violence and the proposed counteradministration. At times he seems concerned to prescribe rather definite limits to the types of practices in which an opposition should engage if its aim is to attract popular support. Marcuse is unaware of a possible conflict, for it is apparent that these limits call into question his other proposed strategies.

For two reasons, Marcuse argues, the left must choose its language carefully. First, long-standing ideological and political conflicts between the communist and Western worlds have discredited all versions of socialism. At the same time, the history of communism implicitly ties the socialist idea to the violation of human rights and freedoms and to the crimes of totalitarianism. To avoid incrimination and intimidating and alienating its public, the left must conscientiously distinguish itself from modern socialist regimes. A critique of their practices should be incorporated as a left strategy. An important argument, it seems not to have occurred to Marcuse that violence and educational dictatorship would reproduce the practices characteristic of the societies he would have the left critique.

Second, the theoretical discourse of socialism must be discarded by the left opposition. Marcuse warns that "if you say to anyone in the United States today, 'What we want is socialism and the expropriation of private property in the means of production and collective control,' then people run away from you."[44] Marcuse does not mean by this that the opposition should substitute ordinary language for the language of traditional

Marxist theory. On the contrary, the terms of the opposition also must break the hold of the established universe of discourse on the individual. What language can perform this dual function and where does it originate?

The New Sensibility

Figuratively speaking it is the language of Eros, and it originates with the student rebellion. For that reason student protest held a very special significance for Marcuse. Actually, its true impact on the author of *Eros and Civilization* hardly can be imagined. Libidinal rationality, the reality principle of a nonrepressive society, assumed new meaning in the wake of the moral-sexual qualities of the student revolt. In light of Marcuse's humanism, it is no surprise that he drew attention to the "humanitarian" accent of the student movement. No longer confined to a mere theoretical indictment of modern society, Marcuse's second dimension at last found a living, concrete, and political manifestation in the form of the counterculture. It is no accident that the *Essay on Liberation*, devoted to an examination of the student contribution to the New Left, begins with a chapter entitled "A Biological Foundation for Socialism?" Marcuse viewed the student rebellion as a practical verification of his anthropological foundation for critical theory. Returning to the anthropological themes of *Eros and Civilization, An Essay on Liberation* represents the libidinal impulse by the "new sensibility." Thus, Marcuse's moral turn to the left is prefigured in the earlier study. Neglecting the left would have been tantamount to casting off much of the work on Freud, the foundation supporting his theory of domination as well as his concept of emancipation.

All the qualities of Eros are displayed by the new sensibility. Its basic disposition is nonviolent in the broadest sense. It is opposed to poverty, toil, exploitation, aggression, the transformation of nature to satisfy repressive needs, the ugly creations and awesome seriousness of modern civilization. It celebrates the playful, the calm, the beautiful, the receptive faculties of man through which human relations and the relations of man and nature would be pacified. In these qualities is contained Marcuse's vision of a nonrepressive society, a socialist society qualitatively different from the established society. The new sensibility antici-

pates an individual who would be biologically incapable of tolerating the restraints historically imposed upon man's nature and
the ways of life that have grown out of these restraints.

True socialism, in other words, presupposes individuals who
have the "need" for a socialist society prior to its emergence. As
representatives of the new sensibility the students were already
such individuals. If the transition to socialism occurred within
the context of the new sensibility, the first phase of socialist construction could be shortened. It could dispense with repressive
practices introduced into socialist society for the purpose of re-
habilitating individuals who had internalized norms completely
hostile to a socialist way of life. In fact, Marcuse argues, the
transition to socialism must be accomplished by a "new type of
man,"[45] one who already has cultivated a new sensibility. If the
transitional needs were inherited from a repressive society, socialist planning could not avoid replacing technological domination with a form of domination equally virulent.

Marcuse's new sensibility is not entirely without difficulties,
for though opposed to violence it has one thing in common with
it. Its radical departure from the status quo makes it unlikely
that the new sensibility would attract support from those tied to
the production process. Here the privileged character of the student opposition surfaces. The counterculture flourished precisely because the students were removed from the larger culture
rooted in the process of mass consumption and production. The
qualitative difference of the new sensibility already was implicit
in the social and economic division of labor. And the radical dis-
juncture of experience within the division of labor both explains
and symbolizes the incompatability of the new sensibility and the
repressive sensibility necessary to the production and reproduction of society. The new sensibility constituted such a principled
threat to the established order that there was never a danger of
its assimilation. The system's elasticity reaches its threshold at
the point where it confronts Eros. But in this, the new sensibility's greatest strength, is its greatest weakness. The new sensibility was too radical to elicit any response but hostility from those
upon whom the left would have to depend in practice for a transition to a rational society to occur.

Now, however, we are in a position to cross the theoretical
bridge to *Counterrevolution and Revolt*. The important initial

step is to recognize a difference between the new sensibility, on the one hand, and Marcuse's proposed educational dictatorship and violence, on the other. Whereas the new sensibility is not primarily a form of calculated rebellion but is first and foremost an expression of human needs that only subsequently crystallize into more or less organized protest, counteradministration and violence are strategies designed to achieve revolutionary goals not formally rooted in the strategies themselves. An explanation of this difference also explains why Marcuse finally abandoned the theory of one-dimensionality.

Why is the new sensibility an authentic expression of human needs, and under what conditions are these needs asserted? The new sensibility derives from libidinal needs — universal human needs — that have undergone repression in the course of socialization into the social organization of production. Ideological structures internalized as individual belief systems enforce these repressions. When the rationality of the ideological structures begins to erode, much of the external social and the internal psychological pressure to maintain the repressions gradually is removed and the repressed needs are liberated as the new sensibility. But, since these (universal human) needs begin to surface when the rationality of ideological beliefs decay, because the ideologies basic to the operation of the social system *are shared by all its members*, there is an excellent chance that a far greater proportion of society's members than that represented by the students will experience the unfettering of repressed needs when the system of production and its cultural normative structures are weakened.

This argument captures the true significance of Marcuse's new sensibility. As an anthropologically grounded political practice — in other words, as a political practice grounded in human needs and not merely in a particular group occupying a privileged place in the social division of labor — the new sensibility represents not simply the needs of its student bearers but the needs of all members of society. And a political practice rooted in universal human needs is a potentially universal practice. Conditions that produce the new sensibility, such as the breakdown of ideological norms, also should produce on a much broader scale a comparable sensibility that Marcuse would be obliged to recognize by virtue of its libidinal, anthropological di-

mensions. When common needs are brought to common awareness, though not necessarily to the same degree of critical awareness, the subject of social transformation is no longer confined to
the student movement. And if the groups constituting this new
subject are also objective factors in the revolutionary process,
then the new subject is likewise a *historical* subject of change.

The new sensibility now becomes much more than a curiosity
in Marcuse's work. It is the theoretical link between *Eros and
Civilization* and *Counterrevolution and Revolt* which compelled
him to abandon *One-dimensional Man*. What we shall see presently is that in *Counterrevolution and Revolt* Marcuse has expanded his focus beyond the student movement to a consideration of a new sensibility prevailing among other groups within society, perhaps even among the mass!

Liberal Politics: The Road to Reunifying Theory and Practice

Counterrevolution and Revolt begins portentously. Surveying recent political developments in the West and in the Third World,
Marcuse declares that "the Western world has reached a new
stage of development: now, the defense of the capitalist system
requires the organization of counterrevolution at home and
abroad." As evidence he refers to the West's anticommunist mobilization in Indochina, Indonesia, Nigeria, the Congo, and the
Sudan, as well as to Western support of violent military suppression of national liberation movements in Latin America. Imperialism is in the process of worldwide counterinsurgency and reorganization. Internally, Western nations have been shaken by
widespread political instability. Restorative measures are political — technical-administrative rationality has ceased to be an effective means of containing and managing contradictions and
conflicts. Marcuse's examples are drawn largely from the United
States — the incidents at Kent State and Jackson State; the deaths
of black militant leaders Malcolm X, Martin Luther King, Fred
Hampton, and George Jackson; Nixon's policy of law and order
and his conservative appointments to the Supreme Court. Western political and military intervention in the Third World is explicitly counterrevolutionary; within Western nations measures
are preventive, counterrevolutionary in anticipation of increasing political unrest. Overall, the national and international ob-

jective of counterrevolution is to stave off a "world-historical revolution" that would critically undermine the stability and hegemony of capitalism.

Rather than focus on the extreme manifestations of political opposition and the reactions of the established institutions, however, Marcuse's analysis concentrates on a gradual but steady erosion of allegiance to the social system. The broad structural dimensions of the analysis are familiar. A new social basis of production emerges through the technological rationalization of the entire process of mass production and consumption. Radically different from the production process as it had appeared to Marx, a technologically extended means of production likewise extends the mass base for revolution. The intelligentsia is drawn into the process of developing and maintaining technical productivity, and the enormous growth of the "tertiary sector" (the production of services) recruits an army of salaried employees and transforms the middle classes into administrative functionaries and servants of capital. This new working class retains the objective relation to the productive process that Marx had attributed to the proletariat, but it is no longer the proletariat. The "universe of exploitation" has been enlarged by a "totality of machines—human, economic, political, military, educational."[46] Potentially, the opposition becomes the entire dependent mass, the working population as a whole.

Not only potentially, however, for now Marcuse makes a startling turn. The *technical* apparatus of production can be rationalized increasingly; indeed, the entire economic and political system can be organized and reorganized according to the developmental logic of technical reason. But at the highest stage of the rationalization of production and consumption—the consumer society—a threshold is reached beyond which the rationalization of the *social* system cannot proceed and at which point its rationalization actually is thrown into reverse. The objective contradictions of *advanced industrial society* enter into the consciousness of the individual. The subjective factor is revitalized— this time on a mass scale parallel to that of the productive base of exploitation.

It is important to emphasize that the contradictions upsetting the rationalization of the social system are those peculiar to advanced industrial society, that is, those issuing directly from the rationalization of consumption and production. Only after these new contradictions have had an impact upon the social system do those contradictions traditionally associated with capital — such as inflation and the decline in real wages, unemployment, and international monetary difficulties — and those resulting from threats to imperialist domination become salient. Marcuse offers an impressive list of the newer, more lethal contradictions — feelings of a loss of human dignity corresponding to the manipulation of human needs; an aversion to acquisitiveness (earlier noted as the disgust with the waste of the affluent society); an impatience with dull, arid merchandise; a hatred of servitude in the guise of technology, of deprivation in the guise of the good life, of the pollutions of technical progress. These and other contradictions provoke a variety of responses to the established institutions — deliberate inefficiency, absenteeism and sabotage of work at all levels of production, widespread hostility and indifference. The tendency toward massive disaffection is summarized best by this statement in *Counterrevolution and Revolt*: "The fetishism of the commodity world is wearing thin: people see the power structure behind the alleged technocracy and its blessings."[47] And the cause of this transparency? It is prosperity, not poverty. "It is the overwhelming *wealth* of capitalism," Marcuse argues, "which will bring about its collapse."[48]

Of course, these contradictions and their manifest discontents existed before they were discovered by Marcuse. As I have argued earlier, it was Marcuse and not the members of society who so totally succumbed to the fetishism of technical reason. What matters here, though, is that because and not in spite of its inherent dynamic, Marcuse's one-dimensional society, his "universe" of ordinary affairs, has now assumed a multidimensional and extra-ordinary character.

Why did Marcuse become sensitive to these discontents? As I have suggested, the answer is to be found in the particular interpretation he attached to them. For Marcuse, I believe, they became expressions writ large of his new sensibility. In *Counterrevolution and Revolt* they are referred to as "transcendent needs," needs created by technological rationalization as the artificial needs created by capital are emptied of content. And these needs are transcendent because they develop within the womb of a society whose institutions can neither meet nor even acknowledge them. For example,

- the dissatisfaction with tedious, unimaginative, fragmented work is expressed as the need to conceive and organize forms of labor that gratify personal needs for creativity;
- the glut of the affluent society sates the need for material acquisition, which in turn destroys the justification for tolerating an intensified struggle for existence. Out of this is born the desire for free time and the reduction, if not abolition, of competitive and aggressive relations between men, the sexes, and the generations;
- the quantitative improvements bought by the good life visibly entail an ever diminishing quality of life as nature is wasted and the environment polluted, restoring the need for beauty and inspiring a pacified attitude toward nature.

In each of these cases it appears to the individual that the very same technical resources and achievements that organized one form of life can be reorganized to prepare the conditions for a qualitatively different existence. Marcuse expresses this point by saying that "the contradiction between that which is and that which is possible and ought to be, penetrates, in very concrete forms, the mind of the dependent population."[49]

Thus, Marcuse's argument views technological rationalization as completely having run its historical course. The abstract norms of progress and productivity that promised a comfortable and happy existence are filled out by practices that are experienced negatively in a dual sense. Not only have the promises failed to materialize and unanticipated and grave consequences been ushered in, but a positive horizon of new possibilities has arisen. On these two accounts rationalization has destroyed the credibility of the normative structures that are the raison d'être of modern capitalism. "With this historical shift," Marcuse explains, "capitalism denies its legitimation to rule any longer the life of men and women."[50]

Has Marcuse's evaluation of technical reason changed? In a sense it has, for technological rationality is no longer presented as the effective means of domination that it had been in his previous work. But it is not that technics has ceased to be a new form of control. Its effectiveness as a form of domination has altered not because his understanding of technical reason has changed but rather because Marcuse's view of the subject has altered considerably. If the individual did not possess the capacities to resist technological rationalization, there could be no discussion of discontents and transcendent needs as new motives for revolutionary change. Quite clearly, Marcuse now has adopted a conception of a very complex subject. In *Counterrevolution and Revolt* the rationality of the subject, that is, many of his needs, capacities, and dispositions, is understood implicitly to be qualitatively different to some extent from the rationality of technics. Only with such an understanding could Marcuse discern an opposition between individual and society and, as we shall see next, reunite critical theory with political practice. In Marcuse's earlier work his conception of subjectivity did not recognize a qualitative difference. His theoretical analysis *began* one-dimensionally with the single dimension of technical reason, a purely structural rationality. Since within his theory the individual was already overwhelmed, because oversocialized, his analysis could do little more than demonstrate that social relations conformed to this single dimension. When, in *Counterrevolution and Revolt*, Marcuse moved from a theory of one-dimensional society, he also moved from a one-dimensional theory.

Marcuse's concept of the individual is now newly anchored between two extremes of subjectivity. It is neither the oversocialized, behaviorist subjectivity that sets no limits to the extent to which the individual can be shaped by society, nor the isolated critical subject who stoutly prevails against the forces of one-dimensionality to speak in the voice of Reason. More and less than these extremes, Marcuse's subject experiences discontents and aspires to radically new needs, which erode its allegiance to the system, but both the discontents and the needs are grasped with uncertainty. They remain vague. As such, the subject is *disposed* critically but is not yet a critical subject.

Marcuse describes the character of this individual as "unpolitical, diffuse, and unorganized."[51] The individual is distinguished by ambivalence. Unhappy but uncertain why and what to do about it, the subject under conditions of stress could become reactionary as well as radical. Worsening economic strains within society (the traditional contradictions of capital) and threats to imperialist domination could produce those conditions, which, combined with deepening popular discontents, could spur an escalation in the counterrevolution and a totalitarian mobilization of the dependent mass. But the other side of the ambivalence, the rational, progressive tendencies of the contradictions — Marcuse's transcendent needs — could be developed, too. This would require the intervention of the New Left.

What form would this intervention take? In this area significant advantages are derived from Marcuse's new concept of the subject. Suffering discontents, aspiring to new needs, partially disaffected from the established order, in an immediate sense this individual is already politically disposed. Not unpolitical, in other words, but "prepolitical," this subject is receptive to a clarification and elaboration of his disposition, receptive to discussion, debate, in short, to political discourse. Since the individual is already critically engaged, the aggressive posture of the left vis-à-vis the dependent mass is mitigated. Marcuse ceases to speak of educational dictatorship and counteradministration. The left and groups within the mass, such as the working class, meet each other from their respective bases, in terms of their own grievances and goals. Organization proceeds democratically and without the hierarchy structured according to a distinction between those who do and those who do not know. Because a critical disposition is no longer confined to an isolated minority, violence is exchanged for a politics of legitimate protest and participation. Marcuse now approves "a long march through the institutions" — "working against the established institutions while working in them."[52]

Within a year following the publication of *Counterrevolution and Revolt* the United States terminated its involvement in Southeast Asia. During that same period the New Left declined precipitously. As it appeared in Marcuse's 1972 study, the relation between theory and practice was designed to propel the left onto a new plane of political activity. Marcuse's greatly extended social basis of production and exploitation redefines the social basis of social change, and his richer, more complex notion of the individual at the same time redefines the objective factor of revolution, the dependent mass, as subjectively *disposed* to sweeping social transformation. Marcuse's theory offers a radical critique of the existing state of affairs, but the individual on whose behalf this critique is waged is not yet a radical subject. Rather, this individual is, according to Marcuse, discontented and more —precarious, uncertain, ambivalent, receptive to political discourse. Given such an individual, theory is obliged to draw Marcuse's conclusion, a conclusion, in fact, that Marcuse had first drawn in his early writings: theory and practice meet on the plane of radical criticism and a radicalized liberal politics.

Notes

1. See William Leiss, "Critical Theory and Its Future," *Political Theory*, 2, 3 (Beverly Hills: 1974), pp. 330-349.

2. Herbert Marcuse, "On the New Left," in *The New Left: A Documentary History*, edited by Massimo Teodori (New York: Bobbs-Merrill, 1969), p. 469; address presented on December 4, 1968, at the twentieth anniversary program at the Guardian, New York City.

3. Herbert Marcuse, "The Concept of Negation in the Dialectic," *Telos*, 8 (St. Louis: 1971), p. 130; originally published as "Zum Begriff der Negation in der Dialektik," *Filosoficky casopis*, 15, 3 (Prague: 1967), pp. 375-379.

4. "On the New Left,"p. 472 (italics added).

5. Herbert Marcuse, "The Problem of Violence and the Radical Opposition," *Five Lectures* (Boston: Beacon, 1970), p. 96; originally published as "Das Problem der Gewalt in der Opposition," in *Das Ende der Utopie* (West Berlin: Maikowski, 1967), pp. 47-54.

6. Herbert Marcuse, *An Essay on Liberation* (Boston: Beacon, 1969), p. 67.

7. Ibid., p. 51.

8. See Herbert Marcuse, *Revolution or Reform? A Confrontation*, Afterword by Franz Stark (Chicago: New University Press, 1976), p. 72; originally published as *Revolution oder Reform? Herbert Marcuse und Karl Popper*, Afterword by Franz Stark (Munich: Kosel, 1972). See also Herbert Marcuse, "Revolution aus Ekel," *Der Spiegel*, 31 (Hamburg: 1969), pp. 103-106.

9. See chapter six, p. 280.

10. Herbert Marcuse, "Freedom and the Historical Imperative," *Studies in Critical Philosophy* (Boston: Beacon, 1973), p. 219; originally published as "La Liberté et les impératifs de l'histoire," *La Liberté et l'ordre social* (Neuchâtel: la Baconnière, 1969), pp. 129-143.

11. Herbert Marcuse, "Liberation from the Affluent Society," in *To Free a Generation: The Dialectics of Liberation*, edited by David Cooper (Baltimore: Penguin, 1968), p. 183.

12. *An Essay on Liberation*, p. 53 (italics added).

13. Herbert Marcuse, "The Question of Revolution," *New Left Review*, 45 (London: 1967), p. 3; originally published as "Ist die Idee der Revolution eine Mystification?" *Kursbuch*, 9 (West Berlin: 1967), pp. 1-6.

14. "Liberation from the Affluent Society," p. 192.

15. See Herbert Marcuse, "Comes the Revolution: Reply to Marshall Berman's review of *One-dimensional Man*," *Partisan Review*, 32, 1 (New Brunswick: 1965), p. 159.

16. See chapter five, pp. 231-247.

17. See chapter six, pp. 277-280.

18. See chapter four, p. 143.

19. "The Problem of Violence," p. 84.

20. Ibid., pp. 83-84.

21. Herbert Marcuse, "Re-examination of the Concept of Revolution," *New Left Review*, 56 (London: 1969), p. 30.

22. "The Problem of Violence," p. 95.

23. Ibid., p. 84.

24. "Re-examination of the Concept of Revolution," p. 31.

25. Ibid., pp. 30-33; see also Herbert Marcuse, "The Inner Logic of American Policy in Vietnam," in *Teach-ins: U.S.A.*, edited by Louis Menashe and Ronald Radosh (New York: Praeger, 1967), p. 65.

26. Herbert Marcuse, "Karl Popper and the Problem of Historical Laws," *Studies in Critical Philosophy*, p. 201; originally published as "Notes on the Problem of Historical Laws," *Partisan Review*, 26, 1 (New Brunswick: 1959), pp. 117-129.

27. "Marcuse Defines His New Left Line," *New York Times Magazine* (October 27, 1968), p. 30.

28. Herbert Marcuse, "Ethics and Revolution," in *Ethics and Society*, edited by Richard T. De George (New York: Doubleday, Anchor Books, 1966), pp. 137-138.

29. Herbert Marcuse, "The End of Utopia," *Five Lectures* (Boston: Beacon, 1970), p. 76; originally published as "Das Ende der Utopie," *Das Ende der Utopie* (West Berlin: Maikowski, 1967), pp. 11-20.

30. Ibid.

31. *An Essay on Liberation*, p. 58.

32. "The Problem of Violence," p. 91.

33. According to Marcuse's theory of technological domination, the dramatic changes in both the structure of the family and the processes of socialization discussed in the last chapter began to occur in the period between the two world wars. See "The Obsolescence of the Freudian Concept of Man," *Five Lectures* (Boston: Beacon, 1970), p. 46; originally presented as an address entitled "The Obsolescence of Psychoanalysis," at the annual meeting of the American Political Sci-

ence Association, 1963, but first published as "Das Veralten der Psychoanalyse," *Kultur und Gesellschaft*, 2 (Frankfurt: Suhrkamp, 1965), pp. 85-106. Calculations based upon Marcuse's theory indicate that the generations of the 1950s and 1960s should have been the first generations of one-dimensional progeny and consequently those *least* capable of rebellion and psychological resistance to advanced industrial society.

34. "On the New Left," p. 469.

35. "The Problem of Violence," p. 92.

36. "Liberation from the Affluent Society," pp. 190-191.

37. "The Problem of Violence," pp. 90, 106.

38. *An Essay on Liberation*, p. 68.

39. Ibid., p. 69.

40. Ibid., p. 68.

41. Herbert Marcuse, "Thoughts on the Defense of Gracchus Babeuf," in *The Defense of Gracchus Babeuf*, edited by John Anthony Scott (Amherst: University of Massachusetts Press, 1967), pp. 102-103.

42. "Ethics and Revolution," p. 140.

43. Herbert Marcuse, "Murder Is Not a Political Weapon," *New German Critique*, 12 (Milwaukee: 1977), p. 7; originally published as "Mord darf keine Waffe der Politik sein," *Die Zeit*, 39 (Hamburg: 1977), pp. 41-42. In a discussion with Peter Merseberger, Marcuse acknowledged that his proposals for violence can be interpreted in ways other than those he intends. "*Merseburger*: In principle, however, you still condone a positive terror, one that would be able to liberate repressive society from some repression. *Marcuse*: I would not call that terror. I approve of any movement, any possibility, that would reduce or perhaps even eliminate the prevailing terror and the prevailing oppression. *Merseburger*: If necessary, by means of terror? *Marcuse*: If necessary, yes. But then one would have to specify very precisely the meaning of 'necessary.' We see it is very easy for me to get trapped in these matters." "Gespräch mit Peter Merseburger: Herbert Marcuse und die prophetische Tradition," in *Weltfrieden und Revolution*, edited by Hans-Eckehard Bahr (Hamburg: Rowolt, 1968), pp. 295-296.

44. "The Problem of Violence," p. 98.

45. Marcuse argues that "we have here and today a historically new situation. The technological and scientific development of production has achieved a stage in which this new man has ceased to be a matter of mere speculation . . . A new type of man has become possible whose life and whose instincts—I would lay stress on the instincts—are no longer determined by what Max Weber called 'inner-worldly asceti-

cism' or by what we call the Judeo-Christian work ethic, the ethic of renunciation and of business." "Professoren als Staats-Regenten?" *Der Spiegel*, 35 (Hamburg: 1967), pp. 115–116.

46. Herbert Marcuse, *Counterrevolution and Revolt* (Boston: Beacon, 1972), p. 13.

47. Ibid., p. 21.

48. Ibid., p. 7.

49. Ibid., p. 21.

50. Ibid., p. 30.

51. Ibid., pp. 23, 25.

52. Ibid., p. 55.

EIGHT

The Aesthetic Dimension and the Second Dimension

> From the nature of art as it is usually conceived according to the single category of appearance and beauty, the tragic cannot honestly be deduced at all.
>
> Nietzsche, *The Birth of Tragedy*

IN *COUNTERREVOLUTION AND REVOLT* Marcuse was speaking directly to the New Left. His teachings, specifically the analysis of advanced industrial society and the merging of radical theoretical criticism and liberal politics, went unnoticed or unheeded. In the wake of the New Left's decline, Marcuse eventually returned to the earlier theory of technological domination and one-dimensional society. But he did not immediately abandon his optimistic appraisal of the tendencies toward new political developments. Rather, at first he held fast to the arguments of *Counterrevolution and Revolt*.

Continuity was preserved through a series of short essays written between 1972 and 1975.[1] In each Marcuse maintains that within the constellation of decaying social, economic, and political processes of advanced industrial society lie the possibilities for historical change—if only they would be developed through political organization. In one of these essays there is something of an urgent and imploring tone. Marcuse insists emphatically that it is false to speak of the miscarriage or failure (*Scheitern*) of the New Left.[2] But only through organization can the movement, lying dormant within the womb of the established society, form the alliances instrumental to effecting change.

324

And the politics of organizational practice, Marcuse emphasizes throughout these essays, should conform to liberal strategies. Radical theory and liberal politics, of course, would not constitute a perfect unity between theory and practice. Such a unity is never accomplished even under the most revolutionary circumstances. Theory, by its very nature, Marcuse explains, always contains within it an essential conflict or tension with practice.[3] Theory's task is continually to project new possibilities for transformation and to identify new obstacles to these possibilities. Practice, therefore, must constantly be redefined to accord with theoretical revisions. And in the present era, Marcuse continues to argue, theory demonstrates that liberal strategies are best suited to push toward the realization of projected theoretical aims and beyond the recognized barriers to those aims. Now, real progress can be made. Advanced industrial society is not, as it had been, so tightly integrated that the inevitable result is its decline into barbarism. As Marcuse says, "The necessity of Socialism again confronts the necessity of Fascism. The classical alternative 'Socialism or Barbarism' is more current today than ever before."[4]

Not all of the New Left was resting quietly after its wartime encounter with the establishment. During this brief period, when Marcuse's ambition seems to have been to move and inspire the left by instructing it about its political potential, he also focused on what in 1974 he claimed was "perhaps the most important and potentially the most radical political movement that we have" — the movement for women's liberation.[5]

Marcuse's interest in the women's liberation movement was spurred for precisely the same reason that he was attracted to the New Left. The women's movement, perhaps far more than the New Left, was the living expression of the new sensibility. Women's liberation would be human liberation because the social order that would adhere to feminist principles would also adhere to a new reality principle. Feminine characteristics are those of Eros and, as such, correspond to the truest potentialities for a socialist society. For Marcuse, "feminist socialism" represented the antithesis of the performance principle, the emancipation of the senses and the intellect from the rationality of domination, "creative receptivity versus repressive productivity." Feminist socialism would release the female element, libido, as a power in the

rebuilding of all social institutions.[6] Before the feminist movement could move to this higher stage of emancipatory politics,
however, the equality of women was the first objective and the
absolute prerequisite for liberation. "Only as an equal economic
and political subject," Marcuse declared, "can the woman claim
a leading role in the radical reconstruction of society." Here,
once again, Marcuse remains within the theoretical framework
of a radical critique of society while proposing liberal political
practice as a means eventually to secure the influence required
for organizing on an expanded scale.

The essays written during the years following *Counterrevolution and Revolt* mark the conclusion of Marcuse's attempt to define a new relationship between theory and practice. As we shall
see in this chapter, in his final work, *The Aesthetic Dimension*,
Marcuse returns to earlier theoretical convictions and appears to
hold them more strongly than ever. Certainly, Marcuse never alters his vision of socialism. Libidinal rationality is still socialism's
guiding principle. But Eros is no longer entrusted to the vicissitudes of political practice, no longer vested in the erstwhile politics of the New Left's new sensibility. Eros finds a new and sublimated refuge in art.

Art for the Sake of Theory

It may be surprising that Marcuse's last work is devoted *exclusively* to aesthetics. In the final pages of the discussion we shall
discover why Marcuse concentrates his theoretical energies on art
and why, in light of his return to the theory of technological
domination, this development is not unusual in the least. But at
this point in the analysis of Marcuse's critical theory, it will most
definitely come as a surprise to learn that his last work brought
Marcuse back full circle to the subject with which he began his
career over fifty years earlier.

In the curriculum vitae attached to his doctoral dissertation,
Marcuse offers this interesting biographical note.

> After my discharge [from the military] in the winter of 1918, I stud-
> ied for four semesters in Berlin and four semesters in Freiburg on a
> regular basis. I first pursued German studies (*Germanistik*) and
> then modern German literary history became my major field and
> philosophy and political economy my minor subjects.[7]

But Marcuse's dissertation, *The German Artist Novel (Der deutsche Künstlerroman)*, completed in 1922 for his doctoral degree awarded the following year from the University of Freiburg, can hardly be considered a study of art for art's sake. It is primarily a work in social theory. The theoretical framework of Marcuse's investigation is erected predominantly from Hegel's *Aesthetics* and from two works by George Lukács, *The Soul and the Forms* and *The Theory of the Novel*. *The German Artist Novel* is of an enormous length, as complex as it is long, and by any standards a contribution to a general sociological theory of aesthetics. It is clearly deserving of an examination in itself. While such a project cannot be undertaken within the scope of this study on Marcuse, the central thesis of his dissertation can be described and in this way *The German Artist Novel* as a whole can be related to Marcuse's subsequent critical and aesthetic theory.

In his dissertation, Marcuse argues that there are two fundamental relationships that the artist can have with society; each depends upon the nature of the social order in which the artist lives and works. A society can be homogeneous, meaning that all its economic, social, political, and cultural sectors mesh harmoniously because they are bound together tightly and unified spiritually by a single set of norms. Consequently, the life of an entire society is uniformly expressed through a common spiritual ethos. When such societies have prevailed historically, in his work the artist simply mirrors the nation's spirit and reflects the nation's entire life. The artist, in other words, like all other members of the society, shares the common ethic and is merely an extension of the consciousness of the whole, having no independent perspective. More important, this perfect unity between the ideas portrayed in art and the idea that permeates all aspects of existence fulfills the artist's need to present an aesthetic vision of a spiritually unified social life.

Modern societies, however, dating roughly from the time of Luther, are characterized by an absence of unity. This breakdown of a uniform social spirit occurs with the development of classes, the division of society into new social strata, professions, and so forth, and with the cultural complexity that follows in the path of this development. Under these conditions, when a unified form of life is disrupted, an opposition arises between art and life (social existence). The artist becomes separated from the surrounding world as his recognition of a shattered cultural unity forces him to an awareness that there is no universal social spirit through which he can establish an identity. The artist's separation compels him to define himself as a subject, individual, or personality in relation to the antagonistic parts of his society. As Marcuse puts it, the artist now "awakens into self-consciousness." As society's various aspects become objects of the artist's work, nothing in the society satisfies the artist's need to portray a unified vision of social life. Art can only reproduce the fragmentation of culture. The artist novel expresses this alienation of the artist from society. In the novellas of Thomas Mann, the artist's self-consciousness of his separation and of the missing universal spirit in his work reaches its most intense expression. At this stage in the progress of the artist novel, the artist passes beyond a self-consciousness of his opposition to society. He attempts to reunify art and life by depicting a higher, more rational idea of a unified spiritual existence through a new aesthetic form.

Throughout Marcuse's writings, this conceptual framework guides his analysis of the relationship between art and society. Homogeneous, well-integrated societies produce art that conforms to established norms. Art cannot escape the iron cage of social life. Inherently antagonistic social orders, on the other hand, give birth to artistic works that do not reflect the dominant ideology but are independent of and oppose it. Art thrives on the basis of such conflict for it is driven to make strides toward an aesthetic conception of a rational social order that would develop the progressive dimensions of the antagonisms without becoming divided internally. In this chapter, it will be seen that Marcuse finally views advanced industrial society as a homogeneous social order in which art mirrors social values and flatters social institutions. He then looks back to an earlier stage of capitalism during which social antagonisms produced an art with an aesthetic vision of an order that would develop its historical possibilities for a universal community that meets the needs for freedom and fulfillment of all individuals.

Marcuse completed his dissertation on an optimistic note. The struggle of the bourgeois artist to create an aesthetic form that would reunify art and life is symbolic of a real historical struggle—"A piece of human history becomes visible behind the literary-historical problems: the struggle of the German man for the new community."[8] Marcuse meant, of course, that the individual in postwar Germany was struggling for a socialist community. In 1922, Marcuse could not have imagined that the community that was to emerge was to be Fascist totalitarianism. Against its Fascist perversion, the idea of the true human community remained guarded by bourgeois art. Several decades and another war were to pass before Marcuse would write *The Aesthetic Dimension*. In this work bourgeois art is still charged with guarding the socialist vision. But on this occasion Marcuse did not argue that it is a vision that the individual of advanced industrial society is struggling to achieve.

Critical and Uncritical Elements of Art

It will be recalled from an earlier discussion of Marcuse's essay "The Affirmative Character of Culture" that the concept affirmative culture denotes those dimensions of the intellectual and spiritual world, such as art, philosophy, and religion, that are held to be intrinsically higher and more valuable than interests that contribute directly to earning a living.[9] Culture articulates, albeit in many different forms, ideals expressive of hopes, desires, and aspirations that generate a tension between the world of mind and spirit and the sphere of necessary labor. The cultural universe is decidedly optimistic in that it expresses the ideas of beauty, pleasure, harmony, virtue, forgiveness and love, truth and justice. Culture protects notions of happiness as attainable ideals. In so doing, the realm of culture assumes critical qualities. By sustaining the idea of a better life, it implicitly indicts society for its lassitude in fulfilling the promises of affirmative culture.

But unlike religion and philosophy, art is unique in its loyalty to the ideals of affirmative culture. Religion sacrifices human happiness in the here and now by reserving it for an afterlife, thus fostering a worldly stoicism. Philosophy, too, relinquished its claim to an ideal of happiness halfway through the modern era. Only Marxism, Marcuse argues, "takes seriously the concern for happiness and fights for its realization in history."[10] Insofar as they accept the established social order as a legitimate means for achieving human happiness, other post-Idealist philosophical systems, such as utilitarianism, positivism, and existentialism, betray the belief in an ideal conception of felicity. After Hegel, Marcuse contends, philosophy compromised the "critical distance" from society that had been a distinct feature of philosophical idealism.

For Marcuse, therefore, the value of art lies precisely in its uncompromising allegiance to a critical distance from the norms and institutions of the prevailing society. How is this unique critical function of art to be explained?

First, by virtue of aesthetic form, art possesses a remote and eccentric language that contrasts sharply with ordinary discourse. Through art, particular human experiences are removed from their historical and social context and are universalized as a realm of potential experience for all mankind. In other words, particular experiences are given a new form as *universal* human potentialities. At the same time, universal potentiality takes on a meaning quite different from that assigned to "potential" by ordinary language. The realm of possibility is subjected to the play and fancy of the aesthetic imagination that prescribes its own rules. Art permits deeds, exploits, and achievements to transpire according to wishes, dreams, and desires that are left unfulfilled in reality. Not only does art represent experience as universal, but universal potentialities are re-presented as *realized*. Consequently, art introduces a qualitatively different content to social life by preserving the image and memory of an alternative truth, the truth of fulfillment. It is with its image of a radically different social reality that art functions as a transcendent mode of thought and as the conscience of society constantly reminding it of a higher purpose.

Second, and most important, the progressive characteristics of art are not restricted to its transcendent nature. Whereas the transcendent function of art lies in its ability to serve as a vehicle for fantastic creations and re-creations of historical experience and derives from art's being a language of fulfillment, the idea of future happiness is also linked, Marcuse argues, to an actual *experience* of gratification provided by art. Beauty is a quality that has pertained to all forms of art traditionally. The normal response to the beautiful is a peculiar sublimated gratification that might be crudely described as a synthesis of sensuous and intellectual pleasure — rapture perhaps. Marcuse is suggesting that the critical disposition of art is intimately associated with the pleasure giving qualities of beauty, an association that binds together truth and beauty, future and present, the promise of gratification and its realization in a single moment. The enjoyment, musing, and contemplation of art breeds pleasure, delight, and happiness in such a way that the truth of art, fulfillment, is momentarily experienced. Marcuse expresses this point by saying that

> if the individual is ever to come under the power of the ideal to the extent of believing that his concrete longings and needs are to be found in it — found moreover in a state of fulfillment and gratification, then the ideal must give the illusion of granting present satisfaction. It is this illusory reality that neither philosophy nor religion can attain. Only art achieves it — in the medium of beauty.[11]

Beauty emerges as the decisive element of aesthetic form.

Further examination reveals that the critical traits of art are more than counterbalanced by its conservative tendencies. It is here that the affirmative character of art is encountered. This can be understood in several ways.

First, although art presents an ideal of future happiness and the individual even experiences this ideal through the pleasurable response to beauty, beyond this art is ineffectual. It does not, indeed cannot, by virtue of its being art, transform the ideal into the real, temporary into permanent gratification. The social universe remains intact, coextensive with an aesthetic universe that can offer only an ideal image and a fleeting experience of its antithesis. This is what Marcuse means when he argues that the promise for a felicitous existence upheld by art is an illusion.

Next, by transforming the aesthetic promise of lasting fulfillment into an experience of momentary satisfaction, beauty "pacifies rebellious desire." The temporary uplifting that art provides may certainly instruct the individual about the repressive nature of his everyday existence. But the pleasurable respite that art affords could intensify the individual's dissatisfaction with society only to accentuate his attachment to the pleasures of art at the expense of any critical appraisal of social conditions responsible for his discontents.

Last, the aesthetic experience is intensely personal, tending further to isolate the individual socially and increase his powerlessness.

To summarize, Marcuse's "Affirmative Character of Culture" stresses that an inner freedom must suffice through art. In light of its purely *formal* presentation of alternatives to the established social order, and through happiness and pleasure that is merely compensatory for that which is denied by repressive institutions, art implicitly acknowledges the impossibility of external fulfillment. Marcuse submits, however, that at the very least art sustains a private sphere that until recently has been safe from the exigencies of labor and from social and political manipulation.

Art for the Sake of Authoritarianism

FOR THE SAKE OF FASCISM

Within the context of Fascist politics the nature of this inner freedom takes on an added significance for Marcuse. His contention that the affirmative, pleasure giving qualities of art prevail over its critical function is directed toward associating the individual's inner spiritual freedom with his instinctual makeup and the role of the pleasure principle. In brief, Marcuse is extremely interested in the soulful and passionate nature of the aesthetic response. Fascism is able to utilize those same instinctual desires normally sublimated in the response to works of art. Under fascism, the inner spiritual realm, having its basis in the instinctual wishes, is externalized and finds pleasurable expression in mass culture. Marcuse argues, for example, that the "festivals and celebrations of the authoritarian state, its parades, its physiognomy, and the speeches of its leaders are all addressed to the soul. They go to the heart, even when their intent is power."[12] Art appears to have an indirect relation to the mass psychology of fascism, or to what Marcuse referred to earlier as the "total mobilization" of the individual.[13] Whereas the individual's experiences of art remove him critically from the requisites of social order, Fascist authoritarianism is able to eliminate the alienating effects of art by exploiting the emotive content of the inner realm of spiritual freedom.

FOR THE SAKE OF SOVIET MARXISM

What Marcuse had believed in 1937 to be a distinctive trait of fascism, that is, its tendency to eliminate critical forms of transcendent discourse, of which art is a singular illustration, is elevated in his later work to the status of a dynamic and defining characteristic of modern authoritarian regimes. In *Soviet Marxism* we find the same phenomenon explored, although the cultural mechanics are quite different.

The Soviet proclamation that communism has realized universal emancipation does not erase the reality of oppression and deprivation. And these ideological claims become even more inflated in an effort to conceal the real possibilities at hand for freedom and the reorganization of production relations created through the development of technology. But the Soviet people cannot know of these possibilities unless they have access to a form of political or cultural discourse that is critical of the organization of Soviet society. As Marcuse puts it, "There is a need for ideological transcendence beyond the repressive [Soviet] reality."[14] Because the totalitarian state suppresses all political opposition that would challenge its authority to define the objectives of technological progress, Marcuse argues that "the ideological sphere which is remotest from the reality (art, philosophy), *precisely because of its remoteness*, becomes the last refuge for the opposition to this order."[15]

Soviet ideological disputes, for example, the state against philosophy, the state against art, therefore operate at a high level of abstraction. This, of course, is the implication of "remote." By "remoteness" Marcuse has two characteristics in mind. He is referring to the extent to which a form of thought, or cultural language, appears to be unrelated to the practical affairs of organized social life. Also, this term pertains to the nature of the specialized vocabularies of cultural discourse used to express ideas that cannot be expressed in ordinary language. The abstractness of a specialized language makes it difficult to manipulate, because abstract concepts cannot be precisely translated into political terms. Being remote in both of these senses, philosophy and art always pose the danger that some critical meaning will escape the ideological coercion and disrupt the stability of totalitarian society. This explains why the authoritarian state invests so much energy in overseeing the work of philosophers and artists.

Nevertheless, Marcuse declares, the critical spirit of philosophy has been broken through the coercive measures of the Soviet apparatus. Metaphysics must progress in line with the constraints of dialectical materialism, itself subject to constant reinterpretation. And the threat of suppression forces Soviet dialecticians to overcome any temptation to resist the vicissitudes of Marxist "orthodoxy." Ethical philosophy has been "transformed into a pragmatic system of rules and standards of behavior [and] has become an integral part of state policy."[16] All other philosophical trends that would eventually threaten the Soviet system are disproved and disapproved of. The remaining battlefield for ideological contention becomes art.

Realism is the officially sanctioned art form within the Soviet Union. Realism, however, is a potentially critical aesthetic methodology. If art truly reflected reality, the work of art would boldly contradict theoretical interpretations of the prevailing socialist reality by Soviet ideologues. For this reason, realism must necessarily acquiesce in a manner after that of philosophy. Realism assumes an illusory or magical character to the extent to which it succumbs to the technical operational rationality of Soviet Marxism, which demands the false or unreal presentation of the real. Through art, the reality of deprivation is transformed into a "reality" of fulfillment, the reality of oppression glorified as the "reality" of freedom.

The development of Soviet realism was originally intended to perform a dual function. It was meant to purge the elements and influences of Western formalism from Soviet art. Formalism, as was noted above and shortly to be considered further, maintains that beauty is the universal quality of all art and represents the ideal of human happiness as a goal to be realized at some future time. Instead, Soviet realism would "objectively reflect" the *achievement* of the ideal in Soviet society. After 1917, Marcuse explains, Soviet realism asserted that the "Bolshevik Revolution has created the [social and political] basis for the translation" of socialist ideals into reality.[17]

But Marcuse contends, provisionally at least, that the Soviet attack on its formalists was destined to fail. It is in the very nature of formalism to forge new languages, artistic forms, that can master the reality that is the object of art. Form must always contain rules and symbols quite different from those of social reality if the latter is to be dramatically transfigured through art. The more that political coercion impinges on artistic form, the more does the form of art become abstract and surrealistic in an attempt to escape the operational terms of Soviet realism. The sole end of artistic enterprise then becomes the creation of forms that by virtue of their abstract character make political retranslation impossible. Not only is formalism therefore deeply committed to the ideal of freedom, but the form of the commitment places this ideal beyond the manipulative reach of the state. Marcuse holds out the possibility, however, that formalism may one day be forced to submit to increasingly effective totalitarian constraints. Within the Soviet Union, "even 'formalistic' and 'abstract' elements may still become reconcilable with conformist enjoyment. In its societal function, art shares the growing impotence of individual autonomy and cognition."[18]

FOR THE SAKE OF ADVANCED INDUSTRIAL SOCIETY

By this point in the discussion, certain themes have begun to emerge from Marcuse's approach to aesthetics. Artistic form appears to be the single most important critical element of art. Its critical function is preserved unless some social and political dynamic, such as we encountered in Marcuse's analysis of fascism, is used to manipulate the emotive basis of art or if political pressures are brought to bear, as they have been in the Soviet Union, which would eventually subdue artistic form and paralyze its critical disposition. The argument Marcuse pursues in *One-dimensional Man* is quite similar to those of "The Affirmative Character of Culture" and *Soviet Marxism*. Art is the final refuge for criticism but is jeopardized by practices threatening to coordinate the critical dimension of art with the norms of the established order. In this work, as far as art is the concern, Marcuse's analysis is focused on Western advanced industrial societies. The type of authoritarianism described, however, includes many of the characteristics of Fascist and Soviet totalitarianism.

Though the attack on art within Western advanced industrial society is noncoercive, it is more effective than its German and Soviet counterparts. In the West, artistic enterprise occurs within a tolerant societal framework. Art is permitted its own truths and may proceed on its own terms, but its norms are unfamiliar, strange, and meaningless for that very reason. Whereas the Soviet political system is a less socially and economically integrated society than those in the advanced West, which means that many of its sectors would be highly receptive to the critical and transcendent qualities of art, the extent of socioeconomic integration in Western advanced industrial society tends to make it impervious to the ideals that art represents.

The contentment of those who live and work in advanced industrial society not only contributes to the lack of impact and the impotence of art by creating an apathetic public but also nurtures ignorance of art's meaning and purpose. And in a society where all cultural and material artifacts are reduced to the commodity form, the only art produced will speak to the repressive needs and interests of the common man. Art must necessarily incorporate the value attributed to it by a society bent exclusively on increasing affluence. The result is that the ideals of art are assimilated by a nonidealistic reality. Art, Marcuse contends, "is brought down from the sublimated realm of the soul or the spirit or the inner man, and translated into operational terms and problems."[19]

Marcuse indulges in a periodic optimism when he endeavors to revive an aesthetic that tenaciously clings to a critical function by continuing to portray an order different from that which the individual most intimately experiences. He turns to the art of the pretechnological era, which forcefully expressed a real antagonism between the aesthetic and the social universe. At that time art projected an infinitely more pleasant reality than even the most privileged experienced. A genuine material basis for contrast permeated the existence of each individual, who was naturally receptive to the alluring and seductive images of dreamlike poetic visions. Marcuse recognizes the anachronistic character of the art of a pretechnological culture and dwells on it not for the sake of nostalgia but in order to recapture what he believes to be the suppressed possibilities of a technological society. The fantasies of a pretechnological era could become a modern reality principle; its art links its past with our present and future. The beauty of traditional art would stimulate the recollection of deeply repressed desires for a higher gratification. Once again, the truth function of art is based upon its relation to unconscious life processes. Are there other critical dimensions to traditional art?

Marcuse also praises the outrageous and eccentric figures who were the legendary heroes of much great traditional art. He explains his admiration for the Don Juans and Fausts, who, in spite of the social order's refusal to permit their real-life counterparts to violate social taboos, are acclaimed in art for their refusal to obey the moral constraints of social order in their quest for a life and experience guided by a transvaluation of values. They are progressive forces in a social milieu that secretly envied their attempts to realize unfulfilled longings, while it openly and hypocritically condemned their arrogance, irony, insolent mockery, and self-righteous egoism, which, if in any other form than art, would breed havoc, disorder, and confusion in a stable world that relies on obedience to other standards for reward and punishment. Technological society, on the other hand, smugly ignores the unproductive romanticism of these figures of a pretechnological culture. Indeed, it is the antihero of pretechnological society who has become the modern hero — the politician, military man, and police official who secure the system's continued ability to deliver the goods, a system whose satisfaction has made obsolete the aesthetic ideals of a bygone era. And what has become of the heroes born in a feudal and early industrial age? Where they have survived in the art of the present, they have been transfigured; "they are no longer images of another way of life but rather freaks or types of the same life, serving as an affirmation rather than negation of the established order."[20]

Technological society invalidates the ideals of traditional art in another significant way. The sociohistorical basis of pretechnological art played a decisive role in its formation. The content of traditional art, as opposed to its form (beauty), derived many of its norms from the politically and economically advantaged social classes. It is these social and political freedoms that the present societies have realized and in many instances surpassed through democratization and modernization. Traditional art, then, is critically meaningful only in its most *abstract* dimensions, as form or beauty, as the promise of happiness.

Additional and perhaps more sophisticated reasons exist that explain how the images of conventional art have been subverted by the achievements of the modern era. The pristine world of nature, once providing not only the imagery for the work of art but the model upon which the concepts of form and beauty had been based, has been invaded by the noise and pollution of industrial progress. Nature, whose simple realistic portrayal constituted the representation of the ideal of beauty, has been purged of those qualities that made it ideal. Marcuse expresses this change by saying that "when cities and highways and National Parks replace the villages, valleys and forests; when motor boats race over the lakes and planes cut through the skies—then these areas lose their character as a qualitatively different reality, as areas of contradiction."[21]

Advanced industrial society further prevails over the critical power of art in a way that becomes visible when the relationship among art, beauty, pleasurable satisfaction, and sublimation is underscored. For Marcuse, art allows for sublimation of the libidinal drives in two ways. First, the form of the oeuvre, as beauty, is a sublimated expression of the artist's need for libidinal gratification.[22] Form, in a sense, suspends, in the art work, the libidinal element. Eros appears as beauty. Second, the pleasure generated through the aesthetic response, the appreciation and experience of form and beauty, is sublimated gratification. Artistic creativity and the response to art, therefore, are both sublimated outlets for repressed erotic drives. Insofar as aspects of art seem to be related to Eros and its sublimation, technological society's ability to modify its performance principle to expand the social use of unsublimated libido, thus diminishing the social necessity for its repression, would contribute to the subversion of the emotive reservoir from which art draws its critical power. At this point, the discussion is returned to Marcuse's concept of repressive desublimation.[23]

Mechanization has eliminated many forms of traditional labor that utilized aggressive instincts and required the repression of erotic drives. As Marcuse says, technology has " 'saved' libido, the energy of the Life Instincts," but Eros is then exploited as unsublimated sexuality and becomes a positive force in the work world. Sexuality is given a market and promoted as exchange value in the form of clothing, faddish styles, sexy office women, sexy office men, the new levity and licentiousness attached to "swinging," and so forth. The intermingling of sexuality and the business world makes work pleasurable and even desirable. And as long as labor is pleasurable, it will be subject to control and progress in the interest of technological rationality. "Pleasure, thus adjusted, generates submission," Marcuse explains.[24] Unsublimated drives, instincts that were previously repressed, now serve the interests of political oppression. Thus, sexual liberation, as a mode of repressive desublimation, contributes to the erosion of art and the aesthetic experience by reducing the need for the repression and sublimation of Eros. The seriousness with which Marcuse approaches this phenomenon is indicated by his implicit willingness to sanction the continued repression of Eros in place of its unsublimated but socially useful exploitation.

Repressive desublimation contributes to the erosion of the critical power of art in a second way. Contemporary literature, film, and popular music openly and profitably exploit the sexual revolution and in so doing affirm rather than contradict the prevailing culture. If the cultural sphere that traditionally maintained a critical stance toward society now takes the perverse form of desublimation and presents *it* as the ideal (Marcuse refers to "O'Neill's alcoholics and Faulkner's savages," *Streetcar Named Desire*, *Lolita*, and so on), the repressive social reality acquires a legitimacy and authority denied it by conventional art. By capitulating to one-dimensional thought and by encouraging one-dimensional behavior by celebrating its obscene and pornographic aspects — in effect, by desublimating the aesthetic form and eliminating beauty from the art work — art directly contributes to authoritarianism. And by aesthetically encouraging repressively desublimated modes of expression, art helps to bring about its own demise by further undermining the sublimation necessary for an authentic aesthetic experience.

Last, the critical disposition of art is compromised in still one other way. Marcuse suggests that the affirmative character of contemporary art may also be indicative of changes in that most essential aesthetic faculty, the imagination. In *Eros and Civilization* Marcuse argued that the realm of freedom could be defined as the "free play of the faculties." The unfettered imagination is committed to a truth that opposes the repressive rationality of the performance principle. An emancipated imagination would pacify existence by restoring the pure form of nature and by releasing human nature from the domination of technical reason.

In the modern age, however, Marcuse contends that the achievements of technological society merge the powers of the imagination with the productivity of science. Imagination is now harnessed to technological rationality, bent to its values, designs, and objectives. Marcuse explains, for example, that the

> imagination has not remained immune to the process of reification. We are possessed by our images . . . Rational is the imagination which can become the *a priori* of the reconstruction and redirection of the productive apparatus toward a pacified existence, a life without fear. And this can never be the imagination of those who are possessed by the images of domination and death.[25]

Art for the Sake of Freedom

It is evident that form is a concept indispensable to Marcuse's critical theory, and although he uses this term frequently and unsystematically the following usages can be identified: (1) art as the sublimated form of fantasy or the imagination, the articulation of needs and desires repressed at an unconscious level of existence; (2) beauty as the universal form of art; (3) various historical art forms, broadly conceived as pretechnological and technological art; (4) and reality as the perverse form of art, which pertains to the desublimation of the aesthetic form, the erosion of the critical dimension of art as a critical dimension of experience, and the release of unsublimated drives into a society that provides repressive modes of gratification. There is a final conception of form that must now be considered: art as the form of reality! By this Marcuse means that art would be abolished as a sublimated refuge for Eros and that reality would become subject to the play of the imagination, reshaped according to the rationality of the libidinal instincts.

This last notion of form corresponds roughly to the second dimension in *Eros and Civilization*, where Marcuse is preoccupied with the shape that the social universe would assume if repressed libidinal drives were permitted to become the dominant social drives. Relying on his interpretation of Freud's metapsychological theory, Marcuse in *Eros and Civilization* considered what radical changes in social relations must proceed from the nonrepressive translation of Eros into a new reality principle. Here we are now considering the manner in which art is doubly related to the second dimension—first, as the sublimated expression of Eros, from which it derives its critical power, and, second, as the potential form of reality. Since art is constituted as the sublimated expression of erotic drives, art, the aesthetic dimension, can throw additional light on the characteristics of the second dimension.

An exclusively functional theory of artistic form views it as an organizational device. Tones, colors, images of objects, and so forth, are made to conform to an objective framework of some sort that imposes order on disorderly, random elements. Beauty seems to derive from form's ability to master and organize reality. Marcuse gives depth to the functional notion of form by establishing its psychological basis. Matter, Marcuse argues, "comes to rest within the limits of accomplishment and fulfillment" established by form. Form eliminates movement, tension, aggressiveness, and violence; thus, "narcissistic Eros, [the] primary stage of all erotic and aesthetic energy, [which] seeks above all tranquility,"[26] is gratified. Through art, sublimated gratification of repressed drives yields pleasure, and pleasure is dynamically related to the experience of the beautiful. Art, particularly as regards the concept of form, is a potential dimension of reality in that it represents the satisfaction of unfulfilled biological and instinctual needs. It is fitting, therefore, that in its form as art Marcuse's realm of freedom would be termed the aesthetic dimension, as the term "aesthetic" applies to (artistic) beauty and biological sensibility. This sensibility, moreover, carries political and normative connotations in that it suggests a biological basis for a new mode of existence defined by qualitatively different social and political relationships.

If this aesthetic sensibility of freedom and fulfillment, which has found a sublimated though limited expression in art, could be translated into practice without being perverted as it is in an authoritarian society, then "beauty will find a new embodiment when it no longer is represented as real [artistic] illusion but, instead, expresses reality and joy in reality."[27] Art would then have no purpose or function. The end of art would mark the beginning of the second dimension.

This idea appears in *One-dimensional Man* as the concept of "aesthetic reduction." The essential dynamic of advanced industrial society is its ability to expand the realm of socially necessary labor through the artificial creation of needs and through a quantitative extension of the goods and services that society must produce in order to sustain itself. This quantitative extension of the productive apparatus is the decisive factor in the determination of the aggressive and destructive form of man's relationship to man and nature. Consequently, Marcuse concludes that "qualitative change seems to presuppose a *quantitative* change in the advanced standard of living, namely, reduction of overdevelopment."[28] This reduction of overdevelopment is an aesthetic reduction because it is precisely the libidinal sensibility sublimated in art that would pacify existence and thus tame aggression and constantly decrease surplus labor and production. The aesthetic reduction would be possible only in a society that did not compel the sublimation of the aesthetic sensibility in art.

But Marcuse's claims for the powers of the libidinal sensibility are not based merely upon Freud's theory of the instincts. Marcuse argues that a libidinal rationality is at work in art itself. In other words, Marcuse wants to demonstrate an interesting parallel between the dynamics of instinctual behavior in the social sphere and the vicissitudes of the instincts in the aesthetic sphere. Instinctual processes enter into the art work and actually determine the nature of the relationship between artistic form and content. This notion is very clearly illustrated by Marcuse in *An Essay on Liberation.*

> The aesthetic necessity of art supersedes the terrible necessity of reality, sublimates its pain and pleasure; the blind suffering and cruelty of nature (and of the "nature" of man) assume meaning and end—"poetic justice." The horror of the crucifixion is purified by the beautiful face of Jesus dominating the beautiful composition, the horror of politics by the beautiful verse of Racine, the horror of farewell forever by the *Lied von der Erde*. And in this aesthetic universe, joy and fulfillment find their proper place alongside pain and death.[29]

Marcuse's analysis, of course, is double-edged. He is pointing to what he refers to as the "internal ambivalence of art" reflected in the "reconciling" power of the aesthetic form. Aesthetic form, as Marcuse more frequently expresses it, is affirmative and progressive. In other words, art certainly portrays inequality, injustice, adversity, and misfortune. But the indictment of the social order made through such artistic contents is canceled as the anguish conveyed is transfigured through its beautiful appearance. Beauty reconciles us to oppression by making it pleasurable.

Yet, it is the progressive side of art's ambivalence that is most important to Marcuse. The aesthetic dynamic that Marcuse has uncovered, a sort of aesthetic alchemy whereby the agony and distress of reality are magically transformed into pleasure, is actually Eros, true to its biological and instinctual form, harnessing aggression. Since the artistic metamorphosis of pain into pleasure occurs through the form of art, which is rooted in the imagination expressive of libidinal needs, art provides an unusual insight into the form of a social existence that has ceased to require the renunciation of libidinal drives. The interaction of artistic form and content is demonstrable of the natural relationship of the libidinal and aggressive instincts. It thus anticipates a radically different basis for social organization. In art, Eros masters aggression the way that it would in a society that did not demand the repression of Eros. This is precisely Marcuse's argument when he explains that "as desired object, the beautiful pertains to the domain of the primary instincts, Eros and Thanatos. The mythos links the adversaries: pleasure and terror. Beauty has the power to check aggression: it forbids and immobilizes the aggressor."[30] With this, it is a simple matter to grasp the meaning of Marcuse's assertion that "the aesthetic dimension can serve as a sort of gauge for a free society." And finally, when Marcuse declares that "The Way of Truth passes through the realm of the Beautiful," he has not merely borrowed a metaphor from classical German aesthetics; he has summarized his theory of a second dimension of freedom, happiness, and fulfillment.

Bourgeois Art as the Final Refuge for Criticism

Without a doubt, Marcuse's aesthetics is a decisive aspect of his critical theory. The truth of art lies exclusively in the aesthetic form. Form is the expression of beauty and Eros. Through form we regain knowledge of a higher freedom whose sovereignty is reaffirmed in the ascendancy of form over content each time a new work of art is created and at each moment a literary, musical, or poetic work is experienced. Within the art work artistic content suffers the defeat that is the "imagined" and "fantastic" fate of the real oppression that it portrays. In art, the revolution is always victorious. Is the transcendent form still characteristic of modern art and, if not, what sort of art continues to embrace form as the aesthetic means for representing a new dimension of human experience?

Modern art is conformist. It sacrifices the truth of the aesthetic dimension by transforming art into a language and experience that affirms and supports the established social order. Form, modern art contends, is a deadly obstacle to the artist's search for an aesthetic presentation of modern civilization that will display its horrors and spiritual poverty. Form lies — as beauty it only re-forms the object of art, conceals its real properties, and opposes the artist's effort to make them transparent. Modern art also wants to democratize art, render its meaning accessible to the ordinary individual, who, unlike the members of privileged socioeconomic groups, is not equipped to grasp the significance of art. Form would unnecessarily complicate art by introducing an unbridgeable separation between the world of art and the world of everyday affairs. Modern art dispenses with traditional aesthetic form in order to communicate the terrible form of existence. But in its desublimation or destruction of form, Marcuse argues, against its intentions modern art is not radicalized. As form disappears from art, art's critical disposition and the aesthetic dimension recede in proportion. Art is assimilated into the fabric of one-dimensional society. "If we look at this historical element in art," Marcuse explains, "we would have to say that the crisis of art today is only part of the general crisis of the political and moral opposition to our society, of its inability to define, name and communicate the goals of the opposition."[31]

This argument is also made forcefully in *Counterrevolution and Revolt*. In this work, as well, Marcuse accuses Marxist aesthetics of committing the same error as modern art. Marxist aesthetics opposes all formalism in favor of a realistic depiction of the material conditions of the working class. But Marcuse insists that art must sever all connections with Marx's revolutionary agent. He dismisses the possibility of a Western socialist art that envisions the working class as the vehicle for radical change by saying that "where the proletariat is non-revolutionary, revolutionary literature will *not* be proletarian literature."[32]

Where modern art and Marxist aesthetics fail, Marcuse contends, bourgeois art succeeds. Bougeois art, he exclaims, "opens the established reality to another dimension: that of possible liberation."[33] It is thus the art of an *earlier* stage of capitalism that becomes critical of the art and social organization of its most advanced stage. And how does Marcuse account for the critical power of bourgeois art? His explanation, and his crucial distinction between the art of the bourgeois era, modern and Marxist art, is best summarized, perhaps, when Marcuse declares that

> there is no work of art which does not break its affirmative stance by the "power of the negative," which does not, in its very structure, evoke the words, the images, the music of another reality, of another order repelled by the existing one and yet [literally] alive in memory and anticipation, alive in what happens to men and women, and in their rebellion against it. Where this tension between affirmation and negation, between pleasure and sorrow, higher and material culture no longer prevails, where the work no longer sustains the dialectical unity of what is and what can (and ought to) be, art has lost its truth, has lost itself. And precisely in the aesthetic form are this tension, and the critical, negating, transcending qualities of bourgeois art — its antibourgeois qualities. To recapture and transform them, to save them from expulsion must be one of the tasks of the cultural revolution.[34]

By preserving aesthetic form, bourgeois art continues to represent the aesthetic dimension and thus to anticipate the second dimension. The socialist future depends on safeguarding the images of the bourgeois past from the domination of the present. Bourgeois art is not art for art's sake but art for the sake of Eros and freedom.

As we saw in the preceding chapter, *Counterrevolution and Revolt* is distinguished in a significant way from Marcuse's earlier writings on one-dimensional society. By virtue of the contradictions arising from technological rationalization and those traditionally associated with capital, the stability, legitimacy, and social integration of advanced industrial society was in a process of deterioration. On the wave of these stresses and strains an opposition, and a potentially revolutionary opposition, was being born that could effectively challenge the established order if a liberal politics informed its organizational strategies. This argument is carried an interesting step further by Marcuse's claims regarding the critical function of bourgeois art. As is clearly indicated by his final remark in the passage just cited, it must be one of the tasks of the opposition to recapture and save from extinction the transcendent qualities of bourgeois art. The vision of a free society that such art embodies would serve both as a practical inspiration and as a theoretical guide for a gradually expanding political opposition. Most important, according to the arguments of *Counterrevolution and Revolt*, there exists both an opposition that could seize upon and politicize the progressive aesthetic achievements of the bourgeois past *and* a critically disposed individual to whom such a radical appeal would be meaningful. What must be emphasized is that it is only through a living opposition that the dead art of the past becomes animate and an oppositional force. Without an existing opposition, bourgeois art remains buried and its critical powers remain buried with it.

In his final book, *The Permanence of Art: Against Any Particular Marxist Aesthetics (Die Permanenz der Kunst: Wider eine bestimmte Marxistische Aesthetik)*, translated from the German as *The Aesthetic Dimension: Toward a Critique of Marxist Aesthetics*, Marcuse departs from the optimism of *Counterrevolution and Revolt* and returns to the theory of technological domination and one-dimensional society. The new work retains Marcuse's aesthetic theory unchanged. Marcuse's critique of Marxist aesthetics and modern art, the theory of the critical function of aesthetic form and its affirmative characteristics, the relation of form and beauty to Eros, the imagination, and the pleasure principle, and bourgeois art as the apotheosis of the aesthetic representation of freedom and fulfillment — in short, all the arguments scattered through the many works discussed in this chapter are collected into *The Aesthetic Dimension*. But it is Marcuse's return to his earlier theoretical convictions that is most significant.

In *The Aesthetic Dimension* the focus is exclusively on art. The discussion no longer proceeds within the context of an analysis of the deterioration of social order and the emergence of an opposition in advanced industrial society. The central argument of *Counterrevolution and Revolt* has been discarded. Once again, critical theory is without practice. Not only the revolutionary class subject but also the critically disposed individual subject have ceased to be a source of political resistance and political change. Bourgeois art is the only remaining sphere of criticism in a society wherein all forms of political and cultural discourse have bowed to the domination of technical reason.

> The encounter with the truth of art happens in the estranging language and images which make perceptible, visible, and audible that which is no longer, or not yet, perceived, said, and heard in everyday life.[35]

But if the message of art is no longer, or not yet, heard by a critical subject, to whom can bourgeois art appeal? Marcuse answers by saying that "in the present, the subject to which authentic art appeals is socially anonymous . . ."[36] Now, in a one-dimensional society, critical theory alone possesses knowledge of the past and through it knowledge of the future. Marcuse made this very point forty years earlier, in fact, when, in the midst of fascism, he turned to restore the truth of critical theory from the ruin and crisis to which it had been brought.

> More and more, the [bourgeois] culture that was to have been abolished [through revolution] recedes into the past. Overlaid by an actuality in which the complete sacrifice of the individual has become a pervasive and almost unquestioned fact of life, that culture has vanished to the point where studying and comprehending it is no longer a matter of spiteful pride, but of sorrow. Critical theory must concern itself to a hitherto unknown extent with the past — precisely insofar as it is concerned with the future.[37]

Bourgeois art can appeal to no one, save a socially anonymous subject. Its passing is mourned only by the critical spirit that knows of the truth locked securely away within the aesthetic dimension. Who will inherit the truth sheltered by critical theory when it, following after bourgeois culture, slips silently and invisibly into the past?

Notes

1. The essays have been collected in Herbert Marcuse, *Zeit-Messungen* (Frankfurt: Suhrkamp, 1975). The first, "Marxismus und Feminismus," was originally published as "Marxism and Feminism," *Women's Studies*, 2, 3 (Old Westbury: 1974), pp. 279-288; "Theorie und Praxis" was published in *Zeit-Messungen* for the first time; "Scheitern

der Neuen Linken?" was presented in April 1975 at the University of California, Irvine; the German translation is an expanded text of this address, which to my knowledge has not been published in English.

2. "Scheitern der Neuen Linken?" p. 42.

3. "Theorie und Praxis," p. 21.

4. "Scheitern der Neuen Linken?" p. 48.

5. "Marxism and Feminism," p. 279; all references to this article are to the original English publication.

6. Ibid., pp. 282-283, 285, for Marcuse's equation of the feminine with the libidinal.

7. Herbert Marcuse, *Der deutsche Künstlerroman, Schriften*, 1 (Frankfurt: Suhrkamp, 1978); the copy cited in this chapter is a microfilm of the original text of the dissertation obtained at Smith College, Northampton, Massachusetts.

8. *Der deutsche Künstlerroman*, p. 454.

9. See chapter two, pp. 55-57.

10. Herbert Marcuse, "The Affirmative Character of Culture," *Negations: Essays in Critical Theory* (Boston: Beacon, 1968), p. 100; originally published as "Über den affirmativen Charakter der Kultur," *Zeitschrift für Sozialforschung*, 6, 1 (Paris: 1937), pp. 54-94.

11. Ibid., p. 119.

12. Ibid., p. 127.

13. See chapter two, p. 57.

14. Herbert Marcuse, *Soviet Marxism: A Critical Analysis* (New York: Random House, Vintage Books, 1961), p. 112.

15. Ibid., p. 110 (italics added).

16. Ibid., p. 113.

17. Ibid., p. 115.

18. Ibid., p. 120.

19. Herbert Marcuse, *One-dimensional Man: Studies in the Ideology of Advanced Industrial Society* (Boston: Beacon, 1964), pp. 57-58.

20. Ibid., p. 59.

21. Ibid., p. 66.

22. See Sigmund Freud, "Formulations Regarding the Two Principles in Mental Functioning" (1911), *Collected Papers*, 4 (New York: Basic Books, 1959), p. 19. And Marcuse, speaking through the authority of Freud's theory, argues that "in the artistic Forms, repressed instinctual, biological needs find their representation." "Art in the One-dimensional Society," in *Radical Perspectives in the Arts*, edited by Lee Baxandall (Baltimore: Penguin, 1972), p. 60; this essay was published originally in *Arts Magazine* (New York: May 1967), pp. 26-31.

23. See chapter five, pp. 255-257.

24. *One-dimensional Man*, p. 75.

25. Ibid., p. 250.

26. "Art in the One-dimensional Society," pp. 59-60.

27. "The Affirmative Character of Culture," p. 131; see also Herbert Marcuse, "Art as Form of Reality," *New Left Review*, 74 (London: 1972), pp. 51-58.

28. *One-dimensional Man*, p. 242. In advanced industrial society the opposite tendency prevails—"quantitative progress absorbs the qualitative difference between possible freedom and existing freedoms." "Die Zukunft der Kunst: Die Gesellschaft als Kunstwerk," *Neues Forum*, 14, 167-168 (Vienna: 1967), p. 865.

29. Herbert Marcuse, *An Essay on Liberation* (Boston: Beacon, 1969), p. 44.

30. Ibid., p. 26.

31. "Art in the One-dimensional Society," pp. 54-55.

32. Herbert Marcuse, *Counterrevolution and Revolt* (Boston: Beacon, 1972), p. 125.

33. Ibid., p. 87.

34. Ibid., pp. 92-93.

35. Herbert Marcuse, *The Aesthetic Dimension: Toward a Critique of Marxist Aesthetics* (Boston: Beacon, 1978), p. 72; originally published as *Die Permanenz der Kunst: Wider eine bestimmte Marxistische Aesthetik* (Munich: Carl Hanser, 1977).

36. Ibid., p. 32.

37. Herbert Marcuse, "Philosophy and Critical Theory," *Negations*, p. 158; originally published as "Philosophie und kritische Theorie," *Zeitschrift für Sozialforschung*, 6, 3 (Paris: 1937), pp. 625-647.

The Imaginary Witness

> It is not the portrayal of reality as hell on earth but
> the slick challenge to break out of it that is suspect.
> If there is anyone today to whom we can pass the re-
> sponsibilities for the message, we bequeath it not to
> the "masses," and not to the individual (who is
> powerless), but to an imaginary witness—lest it per-
> ish with us.
>
> Max Horkheimer and Theodor W. Adorno,
> *Dialectic of Enlightenment*

COMPOSED FROM THE depths of despair, an obituary for the idea
of a way of life not realized and for the theory that had given it
refuge, these words were written, Horkheimer and Adorno tell
us, "when the end of the Nazi terror was within sight."[1] Though
I would venture to say that it is not, whether this statement is descriptive of their later work cannot be considered in this study.
With the exception of his New Left period, it is undoubtedly the
position that aptly characterizes Marcuse's work as it evolved after 1933. In the end Marcuse leaves us not only with a society
without opposition but finally with a society even without the
idea of opposition. All members of the social order, all forms of
thought, are so totally identified with its ideology that there
would not be the merest shred of independence that must survive
if an authentic concept of criticism is to be part of a human vocabulary. The whole of advanced industrial society is untrue,
but the closed circle of ideological meaning that defines its boundaries includes neither individuals who could grasp the meaning
of such an assertion nor concepts that would make the assertion
possible. Critical theory, its knowledge of the society and of its

alternatives, becomes the property of an imaginary witness, of an individual who no longer exists. The imaginary witness, however, is the mournful and melancholy legacy of a critical spirit born from the horrors of fascism.

Before Marcuse's social theory acquired the rationalistic cast in reaction to fascism that predetermined its neglect of the individual, through the theory of historicity the individual had become the new foundation upon which Marcuse placed the Marxist theory of revolution. Ideology could obstruct the emergence of class consciousness but not the insights of working-class individuals, insights that Marcuse viewed as the embryos of a class informed interpretation of social existence. As "subjectively" both individual and class at the same time, the individual was a viable political entity. Once this was established theoretically, what was needed was a political practice that would draw the individual toward a sharper definition of the extraordinary meaning implicit in his insightful but ordinary understanding of social life.

To exemplify the political practice of "concrete philosophy," Marcuse called forth Socrates, Plato, and Kierkegaard, not the leaders of a past revolution. His point, however implicit, was clear. If Marxist theory were to take seriously its understanding of the impact of ideology upon the minds of the members of the working class, then its concept of class consciousness would be an inflated criterion for radical activity that both exaggerated and disregarded the real potentialities for radical action. There could be neither the possibility of a sudden leap or breakthrough from ideological to "correct" thinking nor the possibility that until such a time the individual would be completely dominated by ideology. With class as the exclusive determinant of radical action, a radical theory that embraced these possibilities both underestimated and overestimated the ideological pressures that bound the individual to society: underestimated, because no new conditions can abruptly and completely displace the ideology that pervades the experience that shapes the individual; overestimated, because this theory overlooks the fact that this experience includes other elements that enable the individual to penetrate the ideological veil concealing the forces that mold him.

Such a theory, therefore, was not at all radical. In the name of revolution it displayed an ignorance of the real limits and possibilities of radical action and thus could never grasp action's real preconditions. Only a theory that recognizes the effects of reification and realizes that the structure concealed by ideology generates insights that transcend appearances can be a radical theory. Such a theory is radical because it recognizes that the individual is necessarily ambivalent. By grasping the individual's plight Marcuse's theory discovered that insight can become knowledge and disposition opposition only through a politics of engagement and discourse. Liberal politics surfaced as an authentic radical politics, liberal theory as a theory of revolution. Marcuse's project did not liberalize radicalism but radicalized liberalism. The position that Marcuse arrives at with *Counterrevolution and Revolt* returns to his early project and in a precise way expresses this radicalization of liberal political practice.

Among contemporary variants of critical theory there is presently little work that in its basic theoretical and practical objectives and conception of the individual resembles Marcuse's project. There are signs, however, that the broad based intentions of Marcuse's early writings also animate some recent developments, particularly in the area of interpretive social theory.[2] An example of the research conducted in interpretive theory is William Connolly's study, *Appearance and Reality in Politics*.[3] Without attempting a detailed exposition of Connolly's rich and complex work, I want to draw attention to certain aspects that establish it as a counterpart to Marcuse's early project.

Drawing initially upon the results of Richard Sennett and Jonathan Cobb's *Hidden Injuries of Class*,[4] Connolly focuses upon the set of beliefs through which the worker justifies his acceptance of the work routines and authoritarian controls that are fundamental to his everyday existence in industrial society. The worker's tolerance of these harsh practices is motivated by an "ideology of sacrifice." Through his willingness to sacrifice to improve his children's opportunities for social mobility, the worker can claim the respect of his family, which in turn lends dignity to his life activity and provides him with self-esteem and a personal identity.

Because the worker's identity is largely rooted in his sacrifice, the ideology of sacrifice serves as the basis from which he interprets the meaning and significance of events within the social order. Connolly explains, for instance, that the worker's sacrificial orientation to work and family helps to condition his reaction to welfare recipients and student dissidents.

> If the welfare recipient claims that unemployment is created by structural causes rather than by the personal defects of the recipient, the worker's very possession of a job may appear to be more a matter of luck than self-discipline and desert. If the recipient calls for higher levels of support the worker's own sacrifice may begin to look foolish . . . If radicals treat equality of opportunity as a fraud they unwittingly undermine the worker's hopes for his children's future and render his sacrifice fruitless.

The claims of welfare recipients and radicals threaten the worker by calling into question the rationality of his sacrifice. If the worker were to acknowledge the validity of their claims, his own claim to respect would be lost and his identity would collapse. So much rests upon the ideology of sacrifice that it constrains the worker to deny the truth of such challenges. The worker responds defensively. If the self-esteem and personal identity attached to this ideology are to be secured, the worker must react by insisting that those "who challenge it in various ways are either irresponsible or indulge themselves in utopian dreams."

But as conservative as the worker's reaction to the challenges of the welfare recipient and radical appears to be, it also contains and conceals a far less conservative disposition. Connolly suggests that while the worker's reaction does identify differences between the conduct of these groups and that of the worker, it also magnifies these differences and distorts the motives of these constituencies. Within the worker's inflated characterizations of the attitudes and beliefs of these groups can be detected an effort to suppress inner doubts on the part of the worker about the point of his sacrifice and the truth of the ideology sustaining it.

> The tendency of the accusers to accentuate differences between their own behavior and that of the accused, and to suppress awareness of the real grievances felt by these constituencies, protected a disorienting discrepancy within themselves between the beliefs and aspirations appropriate to the roles they play and their declining allegiance to those beliefs and aspirations.

And not only in the worker's inflated response can doubt and disaffection be discerned. It is a fair assumption that the worker is sufficiently intelligent to know that his own economic security is not guaranteed; that he could become unemployed would lead him not only to empathize but perhaps also to identify with the welfare recipient and be tempted to share his perspective on and interpretation of the social system.

An important question now arises: what would this disposition look like if, no longer constrained by the ideology of sacrifice, it became the explicit standpoint from which the worker would newly interpret, that is, reinterpret, social life? Connolly offers the following description. Workers, he submits, would begin

> to externalize a range of doubts that had been internalized. They may begin to probe previously suppressed questions about the legitimacy of a system which, as they now see it, requires them to seek dignity in such undignified ways. Perhaps they will begin to locate themselves within the same class as many of those formerly accused of freeloading, to see the accused and themselves as members of a subordinate class which reaps the fewest rewards, receives insufficient space to carve out a dignified life, and is called upon to bear the largest sacrifices when the larger economy is under pressure. The reinterpretation will reconstitute political alliances and cleavages; it will politicize grievances previously relegated to a non- or semi-political status such as the right to a job, class inequality, and the social preconditions of self-respect. The diminished sense of individual agency accompanying the demise of the ideology of sacrifice will be offset, at least initially and to some degree, by the enhanced sense of the working class as a potential agent of collective change. It ushers in the liberal moment.

It is important to bear in mind that this portrayal of the worker's reinterpretation deliberately exaggerates the beliefs and political orientations implicit in the disposition subordinate to the ideology of sacrifice. By exaggerating the implicit dimensions of the disposition it is possible clearly to ascertain the extent to which it involves a direct challenge to the ideology of sacrifice and hence why it remains suppressed and undeveloped within the established social system.

Connolly refers to the reinterpretation as a liberal moment because it does not entail a *commitment* to reconstitute the society's basic institutions, such as the welfare state, the structure of consumption and profit, the market system, and so forth. In fact, it would be exceedingly difficult for the worker to shift from a liberal orientation to a commitment to sweeping institutional transformation. If the worker's disposition were to escape the constraints of the ideology of sacrifice and be expressed as a liberal reinterpretation of social life, these new beliefs and attitudes would then be threatened by constraints of a structural nature. Connolly argues that the interdependence and intermeshing of societal institutions "creates an institutional structure terribly resistant to serious reconstitution." Overwhelmed by the complexity of the institutional structure, insofar as reforms presuppose massive institutional changes, the liberal reinterpretation and its sense of collective agency may dissipate and perhaps recede into the old ideology of sacrifice. In short, the liberal moment is "inherently unstable" and "prone to invalidation."

This brief summary of a few aspects of Connolly's *Appearance and Reality in Politics* has had to pass over interesting elements and important moves in just one of the arguments of the study. Nevertheless, it can be appreciated that Connolly is exploring territory similar to that mapped out by Marcuse's early work, though with this important difference. Connolly's arguments unfold within the framework of an interpretive theory that incorporates an ideological and a structural dimension. Here lies the significance I wish to attach to Connolly's study. Interpretive theory provides the theoretical foundation for the existence of a politically active, radically disposed subject, while the ideological and structural factors offer an explanation for the inhibition of the disposition. Whether or not Connolly's and other such investigations will withstand critical analysis largely depends upon the further development of an interpretive theory with ideological and structural moments, now in its formative stages.

Yet, although the status of interpretive theory cannot be considered at this time, its significance, from the standpoint of Marcuse's early work and as it is apparent in Connolly's study, should be drawn out and emphasized. Like that of Marcuse, Connolly's individual is disposed to radical activity though constrained from pursuing it. The liberal moment is constrained first by the ideology of sacrifice and then, if expressed, would be constrained by the logic of institutional structures. By pressuring dispositions to remain implicit dimensions of thought and action, ideological and structural constraints shape an "ambivalent" individual who, at a conscious level deeper than that of the dominant ideology of sacrifice, is receptive to radical change. Connolly also considers the question pertaining to the conditions under which the disposition to radical activity actually would begin to surface. Ultimately, however, he is sympathetic to the view emerging from Marcuse's early writings, a view that would be supported and elaborated through interpretive theory and that begins to draw out the latter's political implications. An important test for determining whether ideological and structural constraints would prevail over subordinate and critical dispositions is a *practical political* immersion in the social existence of the individual — Marcuse's "public act."[5] Practice, not theory, gives life to hidden dispositions and by so doing clearly *grasps* faintly glowing attitudes that in their inarticulate form necessarily appear to analysis to have little chance to survive the deadening weight of ideology. Theory can only pose the question that practice alone can answer.

What is the cost of ignoring Marcuse's early project, in effect, of ignoring the significance of hidden though radical political dispositions of the individual? To answer this question theory must decide to what extent the conditions of modern society resemble those that characterized the period in which Marcuse's project was developed. At that time, Marcuse appears to have sensed that neglecting the theoretical and practical imperatives that he gave expression to in his early work would seal the fate if not of his society then of the socialist alternative to it. In retrospect, there may be reason to believe that his sense was correct. When Marcuse became a victim of fascism, the promise and implications of his early writings fell victim, too. If the significance of his project goes unheeded, if it is conceived as a "slick challenge" to break out of the existing state of affairs, does the danger also exist that a fate similar to Marcuse's fate, to the fate of his work and of the society to which he belonged, could come to pass today?

Notes

1. Max Horkheimer and Theodor W. Adorno, *Dialectic of Enlightenment* (New York: Herder and Herder, 1972), p. ix.
2. An excellent introduction to interpretive theory is Brian Fay, *Social Theory and Political Practice* (London: George Allen & Unwin,

1977). Charles Taylor's "Interpretation and the Sciences of Man," *Review of Metaphysics*, 25, 3 (Haverford: 1971), pp. 4-51, is the acknowledged text for the principles of interpretive theory.

3. William E. Connolly, *Appearance and Reality in Politics* (New York: Cambridge University Press, 1981). Excerpts are with the permission of the author; all quotations from the third chapter. Pagination unavailable at the publication date of *The Imaginary Witness*.

4. Richard Sennett and Jonathan Cobb, *The Hidden Injuries of Class* (New York: Random House, Vintage Books, 1973), especially pp. 51-188.

5. See chapter one, pp. 28-37.

Bibliography

Works by Herbert Marcuse

The following listing is based both upon bibliographies dated October 1968 and March 1972 that I received from Herbert Marcuse and upon my own research. I have listed all works published after 1972 and those published before that date but omitted from the 1968 and 1972 bibliographies prepared by Marcuse. To the best of my knowledge, the bibliography produced here is the most complete that has been published to date.

Marcuse's works are listed chronologically. Satisfactory English translations are noted. Major works by Herbert Marcuse have been translated into one or more of the following languages: Catalan, Czech, Danish, Dutch, English, Finnish, French, German, Greek, Hebrew, Italian, Japanese, Norwegian, Polish, Portuguese, Serbo-Croatian, Korean, Spanish, Swedish, and Turkish.

COLLECTED WORKS

Suhrkamp Verlag is in the process of publishing Marcuse's collected works. Thus far, the following volumes have appeared.

Schriften, 1: *Der deutsche Künstlerroman* [and] *Frühe Aufsätze* (Frankfurt: Suhrkamp, 1978), 594 pages. Part 1: *Der deutsche Künstlerroman*. Part 2: *Frühe Aufsätze*: "Beiträge zu einer Phänomenologie des Historischen Materialismus" (1928); "Über konkrete Philosophie" (1929); "Zum Problem der Dialektik I und II" (1930–1931); "Transzendentaler Marxismus?" (1930); "Das Problem der geschichtlichen Wirklichkeit" (1931); "Zur Auseinandersetzung mit Hans Freyers *Soziologie als Wirklichkeitswissenschaft*" (1931); "Neue Quellen zur Grundlegung des Historischen Materialismus" (1932); and "Über die philosophischen Grundlagen des wirtschaftswissenschaftlichen Arbeitsbegriffs" (1933).

Schriften, 3: *Aufsätze aus der Zeitschrift für Sozialforschung, 1934–1941* (Frankfurt: Suhrkamp, 1979), 320 pages. "Der Kampf gegen den Liberalismus in der totalitären Staatsauffassung" (1934); "Zum Begriff des Wesens" (1936); "Studie über Autorität und Familie," first published in 1936 as "Theoretische Entwürfe über Autorität und Familie: Ideengeschichtlicher Teil"; "Über den affirmativen Charakter der Kultur" (1937); "Philosophie und kritische Theorie" (1937); "Zur Kritik des Hedonismus" (1938); and "Einige gesellschaftliche Folgen moderner Technologie" (1941). As indicated in an editorial note, although not published in the *Zeitschrift für Sozialforschung*, "Theoretische Entwürfe über Autorität und Familie: Ideengeschichtlicher Teil," retitled by the editors "Studie über Autorität und Familie," is included in this volume because of its relevance to the arguments of the essays it accompanies and because it belongs to the same period. Published in *Studies in Philosophy and Social Science [Zeitschrift für Sozialforschung]*, "An Introduction to Hegel's Philosophy" (1940) is excluded from this collection because it is an early version of the Introduction to *Reason and Revolution: Hegel and the Rise of Social Theory* (1941), pp. 3–29, which will be published as a separate volume of the collected works. Also excluded but without explanation, "Autorität und Familie in der deutschen Soziologie bis 1933" (1936) apparently was not considered pertinent to these essays or to the collected works generally. This omission seems to me unfortunate.

Schriften, 5: *Triebstruktur und Gesellschaft: Ein philosophischer Beitrag zu Sigmund Freud*, translated by Marianne von Eckhardt-Jaffe (Frankfurt: Suhrkamp, 1979), 232 pages. This volume is a translation of *Eros and Civilization: A Philosophical Inquiry into Freud* (Boston: Beacon, 1955).

1922

Der deutsche Künstlerroman, 454 pages. Dissertation completed in 1922 for the doctoral degree awarded the following year from the University of Freiburg. Published in Herbert Marcuse, *Schriften*, 1 (Frankfurt: Suhrkamp, 1978). The copy used for this study was a microfilm of the original text of the dissertation obtained at Smith College, Northampton, Massachusetts.

1925

Schiller-Bibliographie unter Benutzung der Trömelschen Schiller-Bibliothek (Berlin: S. Martin Fraenkel, 1925), 137 pages.

1928

"Beiträge zu einer Phänomenologie des Historischen Materialismus." *Philosophische Hefte*, 1, 1 (Berlin: 1928), pp. 45–68. English trans-

lation, "Contributions to a Phenomenology of Historical Materialism," *Telos*, 4 (St. Louis: 1969), pp. 3-34.

1929

"Besprechung von Karl Vorländer: *Karl Marx, sein Leben und sein
Werk.*" *Die Gesellschaft*, 6 (part 2), 8 (Berlin: 1929), pp. 186-189.
Über konkrete Philosophie." *Archiv für Sozialwissenschaft und Sozialpolitik*, 62 (Tübingen: 1929), pp. 111-128.
"Zur Wahrheitsproblematik der soziologischen Methode: Karl Mannheim, *Ideologie und Utopie.*" *Die Gesellschaft*, 6 (part 2), 10 (Berlin: 1929), pp. 356-369.

1930

"Besprechung von H. Noack: *Geschichte und System der Philosophie.*" *Philosophische Hefte*, 2, 2 (Berlin: 1930), pp. 91-96.
"Transzendentaler Marxismus?" *Die Gesellschaft*, 7 (part 2), 10 (Berlin: 1930), pp. 304-326.
"Zum Problem der Dialektik" (part 1). *Die Gesellschaft*, 7 (part 1), 1
(Berlin: 1930), pp. 15-30. English translation, "On the Problem of
the Dialectic," *Telos*, 27 (St. Louis: 1976), pp. 12-24.

1931

"Das Problem der geschichtlichen Wirklichkeit: Wilhelm Dilthey."
Die Gesellschaft, 8 (part 1), 4 (Berlin: 1931), pp. 350-367.
"Zum Problem der Dialektik" (part 2). *Die Gesellschaft*, 8 (part 2), 12
(Berlin: 1931), pp. 541-557. English translation, "On the Problem
of the Dialectic," *Telos*, 27 (St. Louis: 1976), pp. 24-39.
"Zur Auseinandersetzung mit Hans Freyers *Soziologie als Wirklich-
keitswissenschaft.*" *Philosophische Hefte*, 3, 1-2 (Berlin: 1931),
pp. 83-91.
"Zur Kritik der Soziologie." *Die Gesellschaft*, 8 (part 2), 9 (Berlin:
1931), pp. 270-280.

1932

"Besprechung von Heinz Heimsoeth: *Die Errungenschaften des deutschen Idealismus.*" *Deutsche Literaturzeitung*, 53, 43 (Berlin:
1932), pp. 2024-2029.
*Hegels Ontologie und die Grundlegung einer Theorie der Geschicht-
lichkeit* (Frankfurt: V. Klosterman, 1932), 368 pages. Second and
third editions were published by Klosterman in 1968 and 1975, respectively.
"Neue Quellen zur Grundlegung des Historischen Materialismus." *Die
Gesellschaft*, 9 (Part 2), 8 (Berlin: 1932), pp. 136-174. English

translation, "The Foundation of Historical Materialism," *Studies in Critical Philosophy* (Boston: Beacon, 1973), pp. 1–48.

1933

"Philosophie des Scheiterns: Karl Jaspers Werk." *Unterhaltungsblatt der Vossischen Zeitung*, 339 (December 14, 1933).

"Über die philosophischen Grundlagen des wirtschaftswissenschaftlichen Arbeitsbegriffs." *Archiv für Sozialwissenschaft und Sozialpolitik*, 69 (Tübingen: 1933), pp. 257–292. English translation, "On the Philosophical Foundation of the Concept of Labor in Economics," *Telos*, 16 (St. Louis: 1973), pp. 9–37.

1934

"Besprechung von Herbert Wacker: *Das Verhältnis des jungen Hegel zu Kant*." *Deutsche Literaturzeitung*, 55, 14 (Berlin: 1934), pp. 629–630.

"Der Kampf gegen den Liberalismus in der totalitären Staatsauffassung." *Zeitschrift für Sozialforschung*, 3, 2 (Paris: 1934), pp. 161–195. English translation, "The Struggle against Liberalism in the Totalitarian View of the State," *Negations: Essays in Critical Theory* (Boston: Beacon, 1968), pp. 3–42.

1936

"Autorität und Familie in der deutschen Soziologie bis 1933." *Studien über Autorität und Familie* (Paris: Félix Alcan, 1936), pp. 737–752.

"Theoretische Entwürfe über Autorität und Familie: Ideengeschichtlicher Teil." *Studien über Autorität und Familie* (Paris: Félix Alcan, 1936), pp. 136–228. English translation, "A Study on Authority," *Studies in Critical Philosophy* (Boston: Beacon, 1973), pp. 49–156.

"Zum Begriff des Wesens." *Zeitschrift für Sozialforschung*, 5, 1 (Paris: 1936), pp. 1–39. English translation, "The Concept of Essence," *Negations: Essays in Critical Theory* (Boston: Beacon, 1968), pp. 43–87.

1937

"Philosophie und kritische Theorie." *Zeitschrift für Sozialforschung*, 6, 3 (Paris: 1937), pp. 625–647. English translation, "Philosophy and Critical Theory," *Negations: Essays in Critical Theory* (Boston: Beacon, 1968), pp. 134–158.

"Über den affirmativen Charakter der Kultur." *Zeitschrift für Sozialforschung*, 6, 1 (Paris: 1937), pp. 54–94. English translation, "The

Affirmative Character of Culture," *Negations: Essays in Critical Theory* (Boston: Beacon, 1968), pp. 88-133.

1938

"Zur Kritik des Hedonismus." *Zeitschrift für Sozialforschung*, 7, 1-2 (Paris: 1938), pp. 55-89. English translation, "On Hedonism," *Negations: Essays in Critical Theory* (Boston: Beacon, 1968), pp. 159-200.

1939

"Besprechung von *International Encyclopaedia of Unified Science.*" *Zeitschrift für Sozialforschung*, 8, 1-2 (Paris: 1939), pp. 228-232.
"Besprechung von John Dewey: *Logic: The Theory of Inquiry.*" *Zeitschrift für Sozialforschung*, 8, 1-2 (Paris: 1939), pp. 221-228.

1940

"An Introduction to Hegel's Philosophy." *Studies in Philosophy and Social Science* [*Zeitschrift für Sozialforschung*], 8, 3 (New York: 1940), pp. 394-412. An early publication of the Introduction to *Reason and Revolution: Hegel and the Rise of Social Theory* (New York: Oxford University Press, 1941), pp. 3-29.

1941

"A Rejoinder to Karl Löwith's Review of *Reason and Revolution.*" *Philosophy and Phenomenological Research*, 2, 4 (Buffalo: 1941-1942), pp. 564-565.
Reason and Revolution: Hegel and the Rise of Social Theory (New York: Oxford University Press, 1941), 431 pages. Second edition with Supplementary Epilogue (New York: Humanities, 1954), 439 pages. Paperbound edition, with new preface, "A Note on Dialectic" (Boston: Beacon, 1960), 431 pages.
"Review of Frye, Albert Myrton and Albert William Levi, *Rational Belief: An Introduction to Logic*; Ushenko, Andrew Paul, *The Problems of Logic*; Wood, Ledger, *The Analysis of Knowledge.*" *Studies in Philosophy and Social Science* [*Zeitschrift für Sozialforschung*], 9, 3 (New York: 1941), pp. 487-490.
"Review of Gilson, E., *Dante et la philosophie.*" *Studies in Philosophy and Social Science* [*Zeitschrift für Sozialforschung*], 9, 3 (New York: 1941), pp. 512-513.
"Review of Mises, Richard v., *Kleines Lehrbuch des Positivismus;* Russell, Bertrand, *An Inquiry into Meaning and Truth.*" *Studies in Philosophy and Social Science* [*Zeitschrift für Sozialforschung*], 9, 3 (New York: 1941), pp. 483-486.

"Review of Perry, Ralph Burton, . . . *Shall Not Perish from the Earth.*" *Studies in Philosophy and Social Science [Zeitschrift für Sozialforschung]*, 9, 3 (New York: 1941), p. 531.

"Review of Trinkhaus, Charles Edward, *Adversity's Noblemen: The Italian Humanists on Happiness.*" *Studies in Philosophy and Social Science [Zeitschrift für Sozialforschung]*, 9, 3 (New York: 1941), pp. 513-514.

"Review of Walton, Albert, *The Fundamentals of Industrial Psychology*; Britt, Stuart Henderson, *Social Psychology of Modern Life*; Brennen, Robert Edward, *Thomistic Psychology.*" *Studies in Philosophy and Social Science [Zeitschrift für Sozialforschung]*, 9, 3 (New York: 1941), pp. 500-501.

"Some Social Implications of Modern Technology." *Studies in Philosophy and Social Science [Zeitschrift für Sozialforschung]*, 9, 3 (New York: 1941), pp. 414-439.

1948

"Existentialism: Remarks on Jean-Paul Sartre's *L'Etre et le néant.*" *Philosophy and Phenomenological Research*, 8, 3 (Buffalo: 1948), pp. 309-336. Republished, with a Postscript in German, as "Existentialismus," *Kultur und Gesellschaft*, 2 (Frankfurt: Suhrkamp, 1965), pp. 49-84. Reprinted in English, with the Postscript translated, as "Sartre's Existentialism," *Studies in Critical Philosophy* (Boston: Beacon, 1973), pp. 159-190 (the English reprint contains errors and omits most of the last paragraph of the original essay; this paragraph contains interesting comments on Heidegger's philosophy). Also excerpted as "Sartre, Historical Materialism, and Philosophy," in *Existentialism versus Marxism*, edited by George Novack (New York: Dell, Delta Books, 1966), pp. 165-205.

1949

"Lord Acton: Essays on Freedom and Power." *American Historical Review*, 54, 3 (Richmond: 1949), pp. 557-559.

"Review of Georg Lucács': *Goethe un seine Zeit.*" *Philosophy and Phenomenological Research*, 11, 1(Buffalo:1949), pp. 142-144.

1954

"Dialectic and Logic since the War." In *Continuity and Change in Russian and Soviet Thought*, edited by Ernest J. Simmons (Cambridge: Harvard University Press, 1955), pp. 347-358.

"Recent Literature on Communism." *World Politics*, 6, 4 (New York: 1954), pp. 515-525.

1955

Eros and Civilization: A Philosophical Inquiry into Freud (Boston: Beacon, 1955), 277 pages. Paperbound edition, with new Preface (New York: Random House, Vintage Books, 1962), 256 pages. Hardbound edition, with "Political Preface 1966" (Boston: Beacon, 1966), 277 pages. Paperbound edition, with "Political Preface 1966" (Boston: Beacon, 1974), 277 pages.

"Eros and Culture." *Cambridge Review*, 1, 3 (Cambridge: 1955), pp. 107-123.

"The Social Implications of Freudian 'Revisionism.' " *Dissent*, 2, 3 (New York: 1955), pp. 221-240. Reprinted as the Epilogue to *Eros and Civilization: A Philosophical Inquiry into Freud* (Boston: Beacon, 1955) and in *Voices of Dissent* (New York: Grove, 1958), pp. 293-312.

1956

"A Reply to Erich Fromm." *Dissent*, 3, 1 (New York: 1956), pp. 79-81.

"La Théorie des instincts et la socialization." *La Table ronde*, 108 (Paris: 1956), pp. 97-110.

1957

"Die Idee des Fortschritts im Lichte der Psychoanalyse." *Freud in der Gegenwart: Ein Vortragszyklus der Universitäten Frankfurt und Heidelberg zum hundersten Geburtstag, Frankfurter Beiträge zur Soziologie*, 6 (Frankfurt: 1957), pp. 425-441. First presented as an address in German in Frankfurt and Heidelberg, July 1956. English translation, "Progress and Freud's Theory of Instincts," *Five Lectures* (Boston: Beacon, 1970), pp. 28-43.

Preface to Franz Neumann, *The Democratic and Authoritarian State* (New York: Free Press, 1957), pp. vii-x.

"Theory and Therapy in Freud." *Nation*, 185 (New York: 1957), pp. 200-202.

"Trieblehre und Freiheit." *Freud in der Gegenwart: Ein Vortragszyklus der Universitäten Frankfurt und Heidelberg zum hundersten Geburtstag, Frankfurter Beiträge zur Soziologie*, 6 (Frankfurt: 1957), pp. 401-424. First presented as an address in German in Frankfurt and Heidelberg, July 1956. English translation, "Freedom and Freud's Theory of Instincts," *Five Lectures* (Boston: Beacon, 1970), pp. 1-27.

1958

Preface to Raya Dunayevskaya, *Marxism and Freedom* (New York: Bookman, 1958), pp. 7-12. Omitted from later editions.
Soviet Marxism: A Critical Analysis (New York: Columbia University Press, 1958), 271 pages. Paperbound edition, with new Preface (New York: Random House, Vintage Books, 1961), 256 pages.

1959

"Notes on the Problem of Historical Laws." *Partisan Review*, 26, 1 (New Brunswick: 1959), pp. 117-129. Reprinted as "Karl Popper and the Problem of Historical Laws," *Studies in Critical Philosophy* (Boston: Beacon, 1973), pp. 193-208.
"The Ideology of Death." In *The Meaning of Death*, edited by Herman Feifel (New York: McGraw-Hill, 1959), pp. 64-76.

1960

"De l'ontologie à la technologie: les tendences de la société industrielle." *Arguments*, 4, 18 (Paris: 1960), pp. 54-59.

1961

"Language and Technological Society." *Dissent*, 8, 1 (New York: 1961), pp. 66-74.

1962

"Emanzipation der Frau in der repressiven Gesellschaft: Ein Gespräch mit Herbert Marcuse und Peter Furth." *Das Argument*, 23 (West Berlin: 1962), pp. 2-12.
"Idéologie et société industrielle avancée." *Méditations*, 5 (Paris: 1962), pp. 57-71.

1963

"Dynamismes de la société industrielle." *Annales*, 18, 5 (Paris: 1963), pp. 906-933.
"Zur Stellung des Denkens heute." In *Zeugnisse: Theodor W. Adorno zum 60. Geburtstag*, under the sponsorship of the Institut für Sozialforschung and edited by Max Horkheimer (Frankfurt: Europäische, 1963), pp. 45-49.

1964

"Industrialisierung und Kapitalismus." *Max Weber und die Soziologie huete* (Tübingen: J. C. B. Mohr [Paul Siebeck], 1964), pp. 161-180. English translation, "Industrialization and Capitalism," *New*

Left Review, 30 (London: 1965), pp. 3-17. Revised as "Industrialisierung und Kapitalismus im Werk Max Webers," *Kultur und Gesellschaft*, 2 (Frankfurt: Suhrkamp, 1965), pp. 107-129. English translation of the revision, "Industrialization and Capitalism in the Work of Max Weber," *Negations: Essays in Critical Theory* (Boston: Beacon, 1968), pp. 201-226.

One-dimensional Man: Studies in the Ideology of Advanced Industrial Society (Boston: Beacon, 1964), 260 pages.

"World without Logos." *Bulletin of the Atomic Scientists*, 20 (Chicago: 1964), pp. 25-26.

1965

"A Tribute to Paul A. Baran." *Monthly Review*, 16, 11 (New York: 1965), pp. 114-115.

"Comes the Revolution: Reply to Marshall Berman's Review of *One-dimensional Man*." *Partisan Review*, 32, 1 (New Brunswick: 1965), pp. 159-160.

"Der Einfluss der deutschen Emigration auf das amerikanische Geistesleben: Philosophie und Soziologie." *Jahrbuch für Amerikastudien*, 10 (Heidelberg: Carl Winter Universitätsverlag, 1965), pp. 27-33.

"Einige Streitfragen." *Praxis*, 1, 2-3 (Zagreb: 1965), pp. 377-379.

Epilogue to Karl Marx, *Der 18. Brumaire des Louis Bonaparte* (Frankfurt: Insel, 1965), pp. 143-150. English translation, "Epilogue to the New German Edition of Marx's *18th Brumaire of Louis Napoleon*," *Radical America*, 3, 4 (Cambridge: 1969), pp. 55-59.

Epilogue to Walter Benjamin, *Zur Kritik der Gewalt und andere Aufsätze* (Frankfurt: Suhrkamp, 1965), pp. 95-106.

Kultur und Gesellschaft, 1 (Frankfurt: Suhrkamp, 1965), 180 pages. Contents: "Der Kampf gegen den Liberalismus in der totalitären Staatsauffassung" (1934); "Über den affirmativen Charakter der Kultur" (1937); Philosophie und kritische Theorie" (1937); and "Zur Kritik des Hedonismus" (1938).

Kultur und Gesellschaft, 2 (Frankfurt: Suhrkamp, 1965), 184 pages. Contents: Über die philosophischen Grundlagen des wirtschaftswissenshaftlichen Arbeitsbegriffs" (1933); "Existentialismus" (1948); "Das Veralten der Psychoanalyse," German translation of "The Obsolescence of Psychoanalysis," an address presented at the annual meeting of the American Political Science Association, 1963, and published in English as "The Obsolescence of the Freudian Concept of Man," *Five Lectures* (Boston: Beacon, 1970), pp. 44-61; "Industrialisierung und Kapitalismus im Werk Max Webers" (revised from 1964); "Ethik und Revolution," first published in this anthology but originally an address in English presented at the University of Kansas in 1964 and subsequently published in English as "Ethics and Revolution," in *Ethics and Society*, edited by Richard T. De George (New York: Doubleday, 1966), pp. 133-147; "Bemerkungen zu einer Neubestimmung der Kultur," German translation of "Remarks on a Redefinition of Culture," *Daedalus*, 94, 1 (Cambridge: 1965), pp. 190-207.

"On Science and Phenomenology." In *Boston Studies in the Philosophy of Science*, 2, edited by Robert Cohen and Marx W. Wartofsky (New York: Humanities, 1965), pp. 279-290. Address presented at the Boston Colloquium for the Philosophy of Science, February 13, 1964.

"Perspektiven des Sozialismus in der entwickelten Industriegesellschaft." *Praxis*, 1, 2-3 (Zagreb: 1965), pp. 260-270. Address presented at Korcula, Yugoslavia, summer 1964. English translation, "Socialism in the Developed Countries," *International Socialist Journal*, 2, 8 (Rome: 1965), pp. 139-151.

"Remarks on a Redefinition of Culture." *Daedalus*, 94, 1 (Cambridge: 1965), pp. 190-207. Reprinted in *Science and Culture*, edited by Gerald Holton (Boston: Houghton Mifflin, 1965), pp. 218-235. This collection was republished (Boston: Beacon, 1967).

"Repressive Tolerance." *A Critique of Pure Tolerance* (Boston: Beacon, 1965), pp. 81-117. A Postscript was added to the 1968 edition, pp. 117-123.

"Socialist Humanism?" In *Socialist Humanism*, edited by Erich Fromm (New York: Doubleday, 1965), pp. 107-117.

"Statement on Vietnam." *Partisan Review*, 32, 4 (New Brunswick: 1965), pp. 646-649.

"The Problem of Social Change in the Technological Society." In *Le Développement social*, edited by Raymond Aron and Bert F. Hoselitz (Paris: Mouton, 1965), pp. 139-160. Volume printed for limited distribution. Address presented to a UNESCO symposium on social development, May 1961.

1966

"Ethics and Revolution." In *Ethics and Society*, edited by Richard T. De George (New York: Doubleday, Anchor Books, 1966), pp. 133-147. First published in *Kultur und Gesellschaft*, 2 (Frankfurt: Suhrkamp, 1965).

"Role of Conflict in Human Evolution: Discussion." In *Conflict in Society*, edited by Anthony de Reuck and Julie Knight (London: Ciba Foundation, 1966), pp. 36-59. Participants: Marcuse, Kenneth E. Boulding, Karl W. Deutsch, Anatol Rapoport, and others.

"Sommes-nous déjà des hommes?" *Partisans*, 28 (Paris: 1966), pp. 21-29.

"The Individual in the 'Great Society:' Rhetoric and Reality" (part 1). *Alternatives*, 1, 1 (San Diego: 1966), pp. 14-20.

"The Individual in the 'Great Society' "(part 2). *Alternatives*, 1, 2 (San Diego: 1966), pp. 29-35. Parts 1 and 2 reprinted in *A Great Society?* edited by Bertram M. Gross (New York: Basic Books, 1966), pp. 58-80.

"Vietnam: Analyse eines Exemples." *Neues Kritik*, 36-37 (Frankfurt: 1966), pp. 30-40.

"Zur Geschichte der Dialektik." *Sowjetsystem und Demokratische Gesellschaft*, 1 (Freiburg: 1966), pp. 1192-1211.

1967

"Aggressivität in der gegenwärtigen Industriegesellschaft." *Die Neue Rundschau*, 78, 1 (Frankfurt: 1967), pp. 7-21. English translation, "Aggressiveness in Advanced Industrial Society," *Negations: Essays in Critical Theory* (Boston: Beacon,), pp. 248-268.

"Art in the One-dimensional Society." *Arts Magazine* (New York: May 1967), pp. 26-31. Based on an address given at the School of Visual Arts in New York City, March 8, 1967. Reprinted in *Radical Perspectives in the Arts*, edited by Lee Baxandall (Baltimore: Penguin, 1972), pp. 53-67.

Das Ende der Utopie (West Berlin: Maikowski, 1967), 151 pages. "Das Ende der Utopie" and "Das Problem der Gewalt in der Opposition" were presented at the Free University of Berlin in 1967. Translated into English as "The End of Utopia" and "The Problem of Violence and the Radical Opposition," *Five Lectures* (Boston: Beacon, 1970), pp. 62-69 and 83-94, respectively. Questions and discussion following each address have been published in full in the German edition and abridged in the English edition.

"Die Zukunft der Kunst: Die Gesellschaft als Kunstwerk." *Neues Forum*, 14, 167-168 (Vienna: 1967), pp. 863-866.

"Ist die Idee der Revolution eine Mystifikation?" *Kursbuch*, 9 (West Berlin: 1967), pp. 1-6. English translation, "The Question of Revolution," *New Left Review*, 45 (London: 1967), pp. 3-7. Reprinted as "On Revolution: An Interview," in *Student Power*, edited by Alexander Cockburn and Robin Blackburn (Baltimore: Penguin, 1969), pp. 367-372.

"Love Mystified: A Critique of Norman O. Brown." *Commentary*, 43, 2 (New York: 1967), pp. 71-75. A review of Brown's *Love's Body*. Reprinted in *Negations: Essays in Critical Theory* (Boston: Beacon, 1968), pp. 227-243, and in *Sources*, edited by Theodore Roszak

(New York: Harper & Row, 1972), pp. 434-455.

"On Changing the World: A Reply to Karl Miller." *Monthly Review*, 19, 5 (New York: 1967), pp. 42-48.

"Professoren als Staats-Regenten?" *Der Spiegel*, 35 (Hamburg: 1967), pp. 112-118.

"The Inner Logic of American Policy in Vietnam." In *Teach-Ins: U.S.A.*, edited by Louis Menashe and Ronald Radosh (New York: Praeger, 1967), pp. 64-67. Address presented at the University of California, Los Angeles, March 25, 1966.

"The Obsolescence of Marxism." In *Marx and the Western World*, edited by Nikolaus Lobkowicz (Notre Dame: University of Notre Dame Press, 1967), pp. 409-417.

"The Responsibility of Science." In *The Responsibility of Power: Historical Essays in Honor of Hajo Holborn*, edited by L. Krieger and F. Stern (New York: Doubleday, 1967), pp. 439-444.

"Thoughts on the Defense of Gracchus Babeuf." In *The Defense of Gracchus Babeuf*, edited by John Anthony Scott (Amherst: University of Massachusetts Press, 1967), pp. 96-105.

"Zum Begriff der Negation in der Dialektik." *Filosoficky casopis*, 15, 3 (Prague: 1967), pp. 375-379. English translation, "The Concept of Negation in the Dialectic," *Telos*, 8 (St. Louis: 1971), pp. 130-132.

1968

"Credo nel progresso, nella scienza, nella tecnologia ma usati al servizio dell'uomo." *Tempo* (Milan: July 2, 1968), pp. 16-23.

"Gespräch mit Peter Merseburger: Herbert Marcuse und die prophetische Tradition." In *Weltfrieden und Revolution*, edited by Hans-Eckehard Bahr (Hamburg: Rowolt, 1968), pp. 291-307. A discussion on October 23, 1967.

"L'Express va plus loin avec Herbert Marcuse." *L'Express* (Paris: September 23, 1968), pp. 54-62.

"Liberation from the Affluent Society." In *To Free a Generation: The Dialectics of Liberation*, edited by David Cooper (Baltimore: Penguin, 1968), pp. 175-192. This volume has been republished (New York: Collier, 1970).

"Marcuse Defines His New Left Line." *New York Times Magazine* (New York: October 27, 1968), pp. 29-109.

Negations: Essays in Critical Theory (Boston: Beacon, 1968), 290 pages. Contents: "The Struggle against Liberalism in the Totalitarian View of the State" (1934); "The Concept of Essence" (1936); "The Affirmative Character of Culture" (1937); "Philosophy and Critical Theory" (1937); "On Hedonism" (1938); "Industrialization and Capitalism in the Work of Max Weber" (1964); "Love Mystified: A Critique of Norman O. Brown" (1967); "Aggressiveness in Advanced Industrial Society" (1967).

Psychoanalyse und Politik (Frankfurt: Europäische, 1968), 78 pages. Contents: "Trieblehre und Freiheit" (1957); "Die Idee des Fortschritts im Licht der Psychoanalyse" (1957); "Das Ende der Utopie" (1967); and "Das Problem der Gewalt in der Opposition" (1967).

"Varieties of Humanism." *Center Magazine*, 1, 5 (Santa Barbara: 1968), pp. 12–15.

1969

An Essay on Liberation (Boston: Beacon, 1969), 91 pages.

Ideen zu einer kritischen Theorie der Gesellschaft (Frankfurt: Suhrkamp, 1969), 191 pages. Contents: "Neue Quellen zur Grundlegung des Historischen Materialismus" (1932); "Studie über Autorität und Familie," first published in 1936 as "Theoretische Entwürfe über Autorität und Familie: Ideengeschichtlicher Teil"; "Das Individuum in der 'Great Society'" (parts 1 and 2) (1966); and "Zum Begriff der Negation in der Dialektik" (1967).

"La Liberté et les impératifs de l'histoire." *La Liberté et l'ordre social* (Neuchâtel: la Baconnière, 1969), pp. 129–143. English original, "Freedom and the Historical Imperative," *Studies in Critical Philosophy* (Boston: Beacon, 1973), pp. 211–223. An address presented in English in 1969, though first published in French that year.

"Nicht einfach zerstören." *Neues Forum*, 16, 188–189 (Vienna: 1969), pp. 485–488.

"On the New Left." In *The New Left: A Documentary History*, edited by Massimo Teodori (New York: Bobbs-Merrill, 1969), pp. 468–473. An address presented on December 4, 1968, at the twentieth anniversary program at the Guardian, New York City.

"Re-examination of the Concept of Revolution." *New Left Review*, 56 (London: 1969), pp. 27–34.

"Revolution aus Ekel." *Der Spiegel*, 31 (Hamburg: 1969), pp. 103–106.

"Revolution 1969." *Neues Forum*, 16, 181 (Vienna: 1969), pp. 26–29.

"Revolutionary Subject and Self-government." *Praxis*, 5, 1–2 (Zagreb: 1969), pp. 326–329.

"Student Protest Is Nonviolent Next to the Society Itself." *New York Times Magazine* (New York: May 4, 1969), p. 137.

"The Realm of Freedom and the Realm of Necessity: A Reconsideration." *Praxis*, 5, 1–2 (Zagreb: 1969), pp. 20–25.

"The Relevance of Reality." In *American Philosophical Association: Proceedings and Addresses, 1968–1969* (College Park: 1969), pp. 39–50. Extended version of Marcuse's presidential address at the annual meeting of the Pacific division of the American Philosophical Association, March 28, 1969.

1970

Five Lectures (Boston: Beacon, 1970), 108 pages. Contents: "Freedom and Freud's Theory of Instincts" (1957); "Progress and Freud's Theory of Instincts" (1957); "The Obsolescence of the Freudian Concept of Man," originally "The Obsolescence of Psychoanalysis," presented as an address to the annual meeting of the American Political Science Association, 1963, but first published in German as "Das Veralten der Psychoanalyse" (1965); "The End of Utopia" (1967); and "The Problem of Violence and the Radical Opposition" (1967).

"Humanismus-gibt's den noch?" *Neues Forum*, 17, 196 (Vienna: 1970), pp. 349-353.

"Marxism and the New Humanity: An Unfinished Revolution." In *Marxism and Radical Religion: Essays toward a Revolutionary Humanism*, edited by John C. Raines and Thomas Dean (Philadelphia: Temple University Press, 1970), pp. 3-10.

"USA: Organisationsfrage und revolutionäres Subjekt." *Kursbuch*, 22 (West Berlin: 1970), pp. 45-60. Reprinted in *Zeit-Messungen* (Frankfurt: Suhrkamp, 1975), pp. 51-69.

1971

"Charles Reich as Revolutionary Ostrich." In *The Con III Controversy*, edited by Philip Nobile (New York: Pocket Books, 1971), pp. 15-17.

"Conversation with Sam Keen and John Raser." *Psychology Today*, 4, 9 (Del Mar: February 1971), pp. 35-66.

"Dear Angela; letter." *Ramparts*, 9 (Berkeley: February 1971), p. 22.

"The Movement in a New Era of Repression: An Assessment." *Berkeley Journal of Sociology*, 16 (Berkeley: 1971-1972), pp. 1-14. Address presented at the University of California, Berkeley, February 3, 1971.

1972

Counterrevolution and Revolt (Boston: Beacon, 1972), 138 pages.

"Art as Form of Reality." *New Left Review*, 74 (London: 1972), pp. 51-58.

Revolution oder Reform? Herbert Marcuse und Karl Popper. Afterword by Franz Stark (Munich: Kosel, 1972), 48 pages. English translation, *Revolution or Reform? A Confrontation*. Afterword by Franz Stark (Chicago: New University Press, 1976), 111 pages.

1973

Studies in Critical Philosophy (Boston: Beacon, 1973), 227 pages. Contents: "The Foundation of Historical Materialism" (1932); "A Study on Authority" (1936); "Sartre's Existentialism" (1948); "Karl Popper and the Problem of Historical Laws" (1959); and "Freedom and the Historical Imperative" (1969).

"When Law and Morality Stand in the Way." *Society*, 10, 6 (New Brunswick: 1973), pp. 23-24.

1974

"Marxism and Feminism." *Women's Studies*, 2, 3 (Old Westbury: 1974), pp. 279-288. Reprinted as "Socialist Feminism: The Hard Core of the Dream," *Edcentric* (Eugene: November 1974), pp. 7-47. German translation, "Marxismus und Feminismus," *Zeit-Messungen* (Frankfurt: Suhrkamp, 1975), pp. 9-20.

1975

"Dialogue: Marcuse-Millet." *Off Our Backs*, 5, 7 (Washington, D.C.: 1975), pp. 20-21. A secondhand account of Marcuse's presentation.

Zeit-Messungen (Frankfurt: Suhrkamp, 1975), 69 pages. Contents: "Marxismus und Feminismus" (1974); "Theorie und Praxis" (1975); "Scheitern der Neuen Linken?" (1975); and "USA: Organisationsfrage und revolutionäres Subjekt" (1970).

1976

"Ist eine Welt ohne Angst möglich?" *Der Spiegel*, 37 (Hamburg: 1976), p. 199.

Revolution or Reform? A Confrontation. Afterword by Franz Stark (Chicago: New University Press, 1976), 111 pages. Translated from *Revolution oder Reform? Herbert Marcuse und Karl Popper.* Afterword by Franz Stark (Munich: Kosel, 1972).

1977

Die Permanenz der Kunst: Wider eine bestimmte Marxistische Aesthetik (Munich: Carl Hanser, 1977), 78 pages. Revised and translated into English as *The Aesthetic Dimension: Toward a Critique of Marxist Aesthetics* (Boston: Beacon, 1978), 88 pages.

"Heidegger's Politics: An Interview with Frederick Olafson." *Graduate Faculty Philosophy Journal*, 6, 1 (New York: 1977), pp. 28-40. Taken from the transcript of a film presented at a conference on the philosophy of Martin Heidegger, sponsored by the Department of Philosophy at the University of California, San Diego, May 4, 1974.

"Mord darf keine Waffe der Politik sein." *Die Zeit*, 39 (Hamburg: 1977), pp. 41-42. English translation, "Murder Is Not a Political Weapon," *New German Critique*, 12 (Milwaukee: 1977), pp. 7-8.

1978

Gespräche mit Herbert Marcuse (Frankfurt: Suhrkamp, 1978), 153 pages.
The Aesthetic Dimension: Toward a Critique of Marxist Aesthetics (Boston: Beacon, 1978), 88 pages. Revised from *Die Permanenz der Kunst: Wider eine bestimmte Marxistische Aesthetik* (Munich: Carl Hanser, 1977).

1979 AND LATE UNPUBLISHED AND UNFINISHED WORKS

"The Reification of the Proletariat." *Canadian Journal of Political and Social Theory*, 3, 1 (Winnipeg: 1979), pp. 20-23.
Review of Bahro, Rudolph, *Die Alternative*. Unpublished.
"Cognition and Aesthetics." Unpublished and unfinished.

Secondary Works on Herbert Marcuse

ABEL, L. "Seven Heroes of the New Left." *New York Times Magazine* (New York: May 5, 1968), pp. 30-31 and continued on later pages.
ABOSCH, HEINZ. "Marcuses englischer Rückzug." *Deutsche Zeitschrift für europäisches Denken*, 27, 10 (Stuttgart: 1973), pp. 984-988.
ABOU, S. "H. Marcuse ou le procès de la société contemporaine." *Travaux et jours*, 31 (Beirut: 1969), pp. 67-91.
ACHINGER, GERHARD. "Marcuse und die Deutschen: Eine Diagnose der deutschen Krankheit 1968." *Österreichische Lehrerzeitung: Organ der Lehrerschaft in der Österreichischen Volkspartei*, 24, 5 (Vienna: 1968), pp. 20-21.
AGGER, BEN. "Marcuse and Habermas on New Science." *Polity*, 9, 2 (Amherst: 1976), pp. 158-181.
AHLERS, ROLF. "Is Technology Intrinsically Repressive?" *Continuum*, 8, 1 (Chicago: 1970), pp. 111-122.
_____. "Technologie und Wissenschaft bei Heidegger und Marcuse." *Zeitschrift für philosophische Forschung*, 25 (Meisenheim am Glan: 1971), pp. 575-590.
ALBRECHT, HERBERT. *Deutsche Philosophie Heute: Probleme, Texte, Denker* (Bremen: Carl Shunemann, 1969).
ALLINSON, ROBERT E. "The Role of the Artist as Marxist Artist in Prerevolutionary Society." *Journal of the West Virginia Philosophical Society*, 12 (West Virginia: 1977), pp. 10-12.

AMBACHER, MICHEL. *Marcuse et la critique de la civilisation américaine* (Paris: Aubier, 1969).

ANDRÉ-STÉPHANE. *L'Univers contestationnaire: etude psychanalytique* (Paris: Payot, 1969).

ANDREW, EDWARD. "Work and Freedom in Marcuse and Marx." *Canadian Journal of Political Science*, 3, 2 (Toronto: 1970), pp. 241–256.

———. "A Reply to William Leiss, 'Technological Rationality: Notes on Work and Freedom in Marcuse and Marx.'" *Canadian Journal of Political Science*, 4, 3 (Toronto: 1971), pp. 400–404.

ANSHEN, RUTH NANDA. "Authority and Power: Erich Fromm and Herbert Marcuse." *Journal of Social Philosophy*, 5 (Augusta: 1974), pp. 1–8.

ARNASON, JOHANN PALL. *Von Marcuse zu Marx: Prolegomena zu einer dialektischen Anthropologie* (Neuwied: Luchterhand, 1971).

ARVON, HENRI. *Le Gauchisme* (Paris: Presses universitaires de France, 1974).

AXELROD, SIDNEY. "On Some Uses of Psychoanalysis." *Journal of the American Psychoanalytic Association*, 8, 1 (New York: 1960), pp. 175–218.

BAHR, HANS-DIETER. *Kritik der "politischen Technologie": Eine Auseinandersetzung mit Herbert Marcuse und Jürgen Habermas* (Frankfurt: Europäische, 1970).

BARTIG, HANS-FRIEDRICH. *Herbert Marcuses utopische Wirkung* (Hanover: Niedersächs Landeszentrale für politische Bildung, 1971).

BATTCOCK, GREGORY (ed.). *Marcuse and Anti-Art: Aesthetics for Rebellion* (New York: Dutton, 1973).

BAUERMANN, ROLF, AND HANS-JOCHEN RÖTSCHER. "Zur Ideologie der 'Neuen Linken.'" *Deutsche Zeitschrift für Philosophie*, 18 (East Berlin: 1970), pp. 282–304.

———. *Zur Kritik "kritischer Theorie der 'Frankfurter Schule'"* (Halle: Martin-Luther Universität, 1971).

BAYER, OSWALD. "Marcuses Kritik an Luthers Freiheitsbegriff." *Zeitschrift für Theologie und Kirche*, 4 (Tübingen: 1970), pp. 459–478.

BEDAU, HUGO ADAM. "Revolutionary Theory, Revolutionary Nonviolence, and Revolutionary Rights." *Philosophy in Context*, 5 (Cleveland: 1975), pp. 67–78.

BEIRHAERT, LOUIS. "Vers une civilisation non repressive? Marcuse et Freud." *Etudes*, 329 (Paris: 1968), pp. 131–135.

BENOIST, JEAN-MARIE. "Marcuse, un *Aufklärer* contre les lumières." *Critique*, 24, 258 (Paris: 1968), pp. 943–964.

BERKI, R. N. "Notes on Marcuse and the Idea of Tolerance." In *Dissent and Disorder: Essays in Social Theory*, edited by B. Parekh (Toronto: W.U.S. of Canada, 1971), pp. 53-59.

_____. "Marcuse and the Crisis of the New Radicalism: From Politics to Religion?" *Journal of Politics*, 34, 1 (Gainesville: 1972), pp. 56-92.

BERL, EMMANUEL. "En lisant Marcuse." *Preuves*, 18, 211 (Paris: 1968), pp. 84-89.

BERMAN, MARSHALL. "Theory and Practice." *Partisan Review*, 31, 4 (New Brunswick: 1964), pp. 617-626.

BERNSTEIN, RICHARD J. "Herbert Marcuse: An Immanent Critique." *Social Theory and Practice*, 1 (Florida: 1971), pp. 97-111.

BESSONOV, B. N. "Le Sens social de l'interprétation de la dialectique hégélienne par H. Marcuse" [in Russian]. *Filosofskie nauki*, 4 (Moscow: 1976), pp. 88-97.

BEYER, WILHELM R. *Die Sünden der Frankfurter Schule: Ein Beitrag zur Kritik der "kritischen Theorie"* (West Berlin: Akademie, 1971).

BLAKELEY, T. "Some Recent Soviet Works on Marcuse and the Frankfurt School." *Studies in Soviet Thought*, 13 (Fribourg: 1973), pp. 158-159.

BLANCO, LUIS. *Marcuse* (Algorta: Zero, 1971).

BLOCH, ERNST. "Diskussion mit Herbert Marcuse." *Praxis*, 5, 1-2 (Zagreb: 1969), pp. 323-325.

BONTEMPO, CHARLES J. (ed.). *The Owl of Minerva* (New York: McGraw-Hill, 1975).

BORGOSZ, JOZEF. "Herbert Marcuse's 'Homo Novus' as an Expression of the Crisis of the Consumption-Orientated Personality Model." *Dialectics and Humanism*, 1, 1 (Warsaw: 1974), pp. 163-171.

BOTTOMORE, T. B. *Marxist Sociology* (London: Macmillan, 1975).

BOUDIER, C. STRUYKER. "Alienation and Liberation: Evil and Redemption in the Thought of Sartre and Marcuse." *Man and World: An International Philosophical Review*, 6, 2 (The Hague: 1973), pp. 115-141.

BOURDET, YVON. "L'Espoir des sans espoir: une critique de Marcuse." *L'Homme et la société*, 9 (Paris: 1968), pp. 131-139.

BRAYBROOK, DAVID. "Marcuse's Merits." *Transaction*, 6, 11 (Fulton: 1969), pp. 51-54.

BREINES, PAUL (ed.). *Critical Interruptions: New Left Perspectives on Herbert Marcuse* (New York: Herder and Herder, 1972).

BREUER, STEFAN. *Die Krise der Revolutionstheorie: Negative Vergesellschaftung und Arbeitsmetaphysik bei Herbert Marcuse* (Frankfurt: Syndikat, 1977).

BRONNER, STEPHEN ERIC. "Art and Utopia: The Marcusean Perspective." *Politics and Society*, 3, 2 (Washington, D.C.: 1973), pp. 129-161.

BURNHAM, J. "Sock It to Us, Herbert." *National Review*, 20, 46 (New York: 1968), p. 1158.

BYKHOVSKII, B. "Marcusism against Marxism: A Critique of Uncritical Criticism." *Philosophy and Phenomenological Research*, 30, 2 (Buffalo: 1969), pp. 203-218.

CALLAHAN, D. "Dissent on Marcuse." *Commonweal*, 87 (New York: 1968), p. 551 and continued on later pages.

CAMMARANO, LEONARDO. "La rivoluzione come bene di consumo." *Rivista di studi crociani*, 7 (Naples: 1970), pp. 219-231.

CANTONI, REMO. "L'antropologia immaginaria di Marcuse." *Rivista di filosofia*, 60, 3 (Turin: 1969), pp. 243-288.

CARANDINI, G. "La dimensione di Marcuse: note al saggio 'uomo a una dimensione." *Quaderni di sociologia*, 17, 4 (Turin: 1968), pp. 327-369.

CASINI, PAOLO. "L'eclissi della scienza." *Rivista di filosofia*, 61, 3 (Turin: 1970), pp. 239-262.

CASTELLET, JOSÉ M. *Lectura de Marcuse* (Barcelona: Ediciones 62, 1969).

CERTEAU, MICHEL DE. "Savoir et société: une 'inquiétude nouvelle', de Marcuse à mai 68." *Esprit*, 36, 10 (Paris: 1968), pp. 292-312.

CERULLO, MARGARET. "Marcuse and Feminism." *Telos*, 41 (St. Louis: 1979), pp. 185-186.

CHAZAUD, D'JACQUES. *Les Contestations actuelles de la psychanalyse* (Toulouse: Privat, 1974).

CHIRPAZ, FRANCOIS. "Aliénation et utopie" [Herbert Marcuse]. *Esprit*, 37, 1 (Paris: 1969), pp. 74-88.

CIAFRÈ, GIUSEPPE. "Uno studio italiano su Herbert Marcuse." *Logos*, 1 (Naples: 1972), pp. 118-128.

CIARDO, MANLIO. "Infinità dell'universo o infinità della storia?" *Rivista di studi crociani*, 7 (Naples: 1970), pp. 420-436.

———. "L'antitecnocrate Marcuse profeta di tirannidi tecnocratiche." *Rivista di studi crociani*, 8 (Naples: 1971), pp. 178-183.

CLAIR, ANDRÉ. "Une Philosophie de la nature." *Esprit*, 37, 1 (Paris: 1969), pp. 51-73.

CLECAK, PETER. "Marcuse: Ferment of Hope." *Nation*, 208 (New York: 1969), pp. 765-768.

CLÉMENT, MARCEL. *Le Communisme face à Dieu, Marx, Mao, Marcuse* (Paris: Nouvelles editions latines, 1968).

COHEN, ALAIN J. *Marcuse, le scénario freudo-marxien* (Paris: Editions universitaires, 1974).

COHEN, JERRY. "Critical Theory: The Philosophy of Marcuse." *New*

Left Review, 57 (London: 1969), pp. 35-51.

COHEN, MARSHALL. "Norman Vincent Peale of the Left." *Atlantic*, 223 (Boston: 1969), pp. 108-110.

COLLETTI, LUCIO. "Von Hegel zu Marcuse." *Alternative*, 13, 72-73 (West Berlin: 1970), pp. 129-148.

CRANSTON, MAURICE. "Herbert Marcuse." *Encounter*, 32, 3 (London: 1969), pp. 38-50.

DE BODOYA, J. *Marcuse y el socialismo: el socialismo imposible* (Madrid: Paraninfo, 1970).

DECKE, G. "Die theoretische Basis von Marcuses Geschichtsphilosophie und Gesellschaftstheorie: Freuds Psychoanalytische Anthropologie als Marxismus-Ersatz?" *Zeitschrift für evangelische Ethik*, 12 (Gütersloh: 1968), pp. 372-384.

DE FEO, NICOLA M. "Ragione e rivoluzione nel pensiero dialettico" [Herbert Marcuse]. *Aut Aut*, 99 (Milan: 1967), pp. 49-76.

DELAUNAY, VADIM. "Marcuse." *Esprit*, 9 (Paris: 1977), pp. 20-28.

DELBEZ, LOUIS. *La Pensée politique allemande* (Paris: R. Pichon et R. Durand-Auzias, 1974).

DELBO, CHARLOTTE. *La Théorie et la pratique: dialogue imaginaire mais non tout à fait apocryphe entre Herbert Marcuse et Henri Lefebvre* (Paris: Anthropos, 1969).

DEMICHEL, FRANCINE. *La Psychanalyse en politique* (Paris: Presses universitaires de France, 1974).

DEMO, PEDRO. *Herrschaft und Geschichte: Zur politischen Gesellschaftstheorie Freyers und Marcuses* (Meisenheim am Glan: A. Hain, 1973).

DE PAZ, ALFREDO. *La dialettica dell'estetica: saggio sul pensiero estetico di Herbert Marcuse* (Bologna: Ponte nuovo, 1972).

DESJARDINS, RENÉ. *Le Souvenir de Dieu: recherche avec Saint Augustin* (Paris: Beauchesne, 1975).

DESPOTOPOULOS, CONSTANTIN. "Une Critique de la société industrielle avancée." *Archives de philosophie du droit*, 14 (Paris: 1969), pp. 97-118.

DEVITIS, JOSEPH L. "Marcuse on Education: Social Critique and Social Control." *Educational Theory*, 24, 3 (Urbana: 1974), pp. 259-268.

_____. "Mannheim and Marcuse: Social Control in Reconstruction and Revolution." *Southwestern Journal of Philosophy*, 6 (Norman: 1975), pp. 129-141.

Die Frankfurter Schule im Licht des Marxismus: Zur Kritik der Philosophie und Soziologie von Horkheimer, Adorno, Marcuse, und Habermas (East Berlin: Akademie, 1971).

DOMENACH, JEAN-MARIE. *Le Sauvage et l'ordinateur* (Paris: Seuil, 1976).

DORIA, FRANCISCO A. *Marcuse: vida e obra* (Rio de Janeiro: Jose Alvaro, 1969).

DRUCKMAN, MASON. *Community and Purpose in America* (New York: McGraw-Hill, 1971), especially pp. 353-401.

DUCLOW, DONALD. "Herbert Marcuse and 'Happy Consciousness.' " *Liberation*, 14, 7 (New York: 1969), pp. 7-15.

DWORKIN, GERALD. "Non-neutral Principles." *Journal of Philosophy*, 71, 14 (New York: 1974), pp. 491-506.

EASLEA, BRIAN. *Liberation and the Aims of Science: An Essay on Obstacles to the Building of a Beautiful World* (Princeton: Rowman and Littlefield, 1974).

EICKELSCHULTE, DIETMAR. "Ein Pseudoprophet und seine Schüler: Die Westliche 'neue Linke' in Östlichem Licht." *Wissenschaftlicher Dienst Südosteuropa*, 17, 5-6 (Munich: 1968), pp. 98-99.

_____. "Revolution und Ethik bei Herbert Marcuse." *Lebendiges Zeugnis*, 1-2 (Paderhorn: 1972), pp. 83-100.

EICKHOFF, FRIEDRICH-WILHELM. "Über Herbert Marcuses Freud-rezeption." *Wege zum Menschen: Monatsschrift für Seelsorge, Psychotherapie, und Erziehung*, 24, 8-9 (Göttingen: 1972), pp. 281-289.

EIDELBERG, PAUL. "The Temptation of Herbert Marcuse." *Review of Politics*, 31, 4 (Notre Dame: 1969), pp. 442-458.

ENGEL, DAVID E. "Response to Professor Richard LaBrecque." *Philosophy of Education: Proceedings of the Twenty-eighth Annual Meeting* (Edwardsville: 1972), pp. 270-274.

ENGLEHARDT, HARTMUT. "Aesthetik als Politik! Zu Herbert Marcuses letztem Buch." *Die Neue Rundschau*, 84, 4 (Frankfurt: 1973), pp. 730-737.

ESCHOTADO, ANTONIO. "La obra de Herbert Marcuse." *Revista de occidente*, 71 (Madrid: 1969), pp. 129-159.

_____. *Marcuse: utopia y razón* (Madrid: Alianza, 1969).

FAGONE, VIRGILIO. "La filosofia ad una dimensione di Herbert Marcuse." *La civiltà cattolica*, 119, 3 (Rome: 1968), pp. 26-40.

_____. "La critica della ragione tecnica nella filosofia di Marcuse." *La civiltà cattolica*, 121, 2 (Rome: 1970), pp. 340-353.

FAHRMANN, HELMUT. "Eindimensionales und zweidimensionales Denken: Herbert Marcuse und die Tradition." *Neue Sammlung: Göttinger Blätter für Kultur und Erziehung*, 11, 3 (Göttingen: 1971), pp. 273-290.

FARGANIS, SONDRA. "Liberty: Two Perspectives on the Women's Movement." *Ethics: An International Journal of Social, Political, and Legal Philosophy*, 88, 1 (Chicago: 1977), pp. 62-73.

FAUSTO, GIANFRANCESCHI. *Teología eléctrica: ensayo sobre signos de los tiempos* (Madrid: Prensa española, 1973).

FEDOSEEV, P. I. "Le Problème du social et du biologique en philosophie et en sociologie" [in Russian]. *Voprosy filosofii*, 3 (Moscow: 1976), pp. 56-74.

FERGUSON, THOMAS. "An Interview: Herbert Marcuse's 'On the Question of Reform or Revolution,' Introductory Note." *Listening*, 8 (River Forest: 1973), pp. 86-93.

FERNÁNDEZ, RODRIGO. "Marcuse: posibilidad y concreción." *Revista de filosofía de la Universidad de Costa Rica*, 12 (Costa Rica: 1974), pp. 59-70.

FINGARETTE, HERBERT. "Eros and Utopia." *Review of Metaphysics*, 10, 4 (New Haven: 1957), pp. 660-665.

FISCHER, GEORGE (ed.). *The Revival of American Socialism: Selected Papers of the Socialist Scholars Conference* (New York: Oxford University Press, 1971), especially pp. 244-321.

FLAY, JOSEPH C. "Alienation and the Status Quo." *Man and World: An International Philosophical Review*, 2, 2 (Indiana: 1969), pp. 248-262.

FOYACA, M. "El pensamiento revolucionario de Marcuse: última formulación." *Revista de fomento social*, 24, 95 (Madrid: 1969), pp. 307-315.

FRANCOVICH, GUILLERMO. *El estructuralismo: Lévi-Strauss, Foucault, Marx, Sartre, Marcuse, McLuhan* (Buenos Aires: Plus ultra, 1973).

FRANKLIN, MITCHELL. "The Irony of the Beautiful Soul of Herbert Marcuse." *Telos*, 6 (St. Louis: 1970), pp. 3-35.

FREMSTAD, J. "Marcuse: The Dialectics of Hopelessness." *Western Political Quarterly*, 30, 1 (Salt Lake City: 1977), pp. 80-92.

FRIEDENBERG, EDGAR Z. "UNITRUTH One Dimensional Man." *Commentary*, 37, 4 (New York: 1964), pp. 83-85.

FROMM, ERICH. "The Human Implications of Instinctivistic 'Radicalism.'" *Dissent*, 2, 4 (New York: 1955), pp. 342-349.

FRY, JOHN. *Marcuse: Dilemma and Liberation* (Stockholm: Almquist & Wiksell International, 1974).

GABRIEL, OSCAR. "Thesen zur Universalität der Herrschaft in der industriellen Gesellschaft: Anmerkung zu einer Schlüssel-Kategorie der Gesellschaftsanalyse Herbert Marcuses." Ph.D. dissertation, University of Hamburg, 1975.

GEISLER, U., AND H. SEIDEL. "Die romantische Kapitalismuskritik und der utopische Sozialismusbegriff Herbert Marcuses." *Deutsche Zeitschrift für Philosophie*, 17 (East Berlin: 1969), pp. 409-421.

GIRALDI, GIOVANNI. "Il vero Marcuse." *Sistematica*, 1 (Milan: 1968), pp. 111-113.

GLAESER, BERNHARD. "Arbeit und Freiheit bei Herbert Marcuse." *Zeitschrift für philosophische Forschung*, 24 (Meisenheim am Glan: 1970), pp. 589-596.

GLASER, KURT. "Marcuse and the German New Left." *National Review*, 20, 26 (New York: 1968), pp. 649-654.

GOLD, H. "California Left: Mao, Marx, et Marcuse." *Saturday Evening Post*, 241, 21 (Indianapolis: 1968), pp. 56-59.

GOLDMANN, LUCIEN. "Das Denken Herbert Marcuse." *Soziale Welt*, 20, 3 (Göttingen: 1969), pp. 257-273.

GORZ, ANDRE. "Call for Intellectual Subversion." *Nation*, 198 (New York: 1964), pp. 534-537.

GRAUBARD, ALLEN YEHUDA. "One-dimensional Pessimism." *Dissent*, 15, 3 (New York: 1968), pp. 216-228.

_____. "The Political Position of Herbert Marcuse." Ph.D. dissertation, Harvard University, 1970.

GREEMAN, RICHARD. "A Critical Re-examination of Herbert Marcuse's Works." *New Politics*, 6, 4 (New York: 1967), pp. 12-23.

GRIFFIOEN, L. "Negatieve filosofie en kritische theorie (Marcuse over Hegel en Marx)." *Philosophia Reformata*, 34 (Kampen: 1969), pp. 101-120; summary, pp. 120-121.

GROUTT, J. "Marcuse and Goodwin Tangle at Temple." *Commonweal*, 90, 10 (New York: 1969), pp. 279-280.

GUGGENBERGER, BERND. "Psychoanalyse und Weltflucht: Die Selbstzerstörung des marcuseschen Revolutionsgedankens." *Frankfurter Hefte: Zeitschrift für Kultur und Politik*, 28, 9 (Neuwied: 1973), pp. 615-621.

HABERMAS, JÜRGEN. "Technology and Science as 'Ideology.' " *Toward a Rational Society* (Boston: Beacon, 1970), pp. 81-122.

_____. *Philosophisch-politische Profile* [Herbert Marcuse and others] (Frankfurt: Suhrkamp, 1971).

_____ (ed.). *Antworten auf Herbert Marcuse* (Frankfurt: Suhrkamp, 1968).

HACKER, ANDREW. "Philosopher of the New Left." *New York Times Book Review* (New York: March 10, 1968), pp. 1-37.

HEARN, THOMAS. "On Tolerance." *Southern Journal of Philosophy*, 8 (Memphis: 1970), pp. 223-232.

HEIN, HILDE. "Aesthetic Consciousness: The Ground of Political Experience." *Journal of Aesthetics and Art Criticism*, 35, 2 (Cleveland: 1976), pp. 143-152.

HELMS, HANS G. "Linksradikalismus unter Monopolkapitalistischen." *Deutsche Zeitschrift für Philosophie*, 17, 10 (East Berlin: 1969), pp. 1180-1209.

HERMANN, KAI. *Die Revolte der Studenten* (Hamburg: Christian Wegner, 1967).

"Hilfe von Arbeitslosen." *Der Spiegel*, 25 (Hamburg: 1967), pp. 103-104.

HINDERY, R. "Marcuse's Eroticized Man." *Christian Century*, 87 (Chicago: 1970), pp. 136–138.

HINTON, J. M. "Linguistic Philosophy, Empiricism, and the Left." *Philosophy*, 48, 186 (London: 1973), pp. 381–385.

HOCHHUTH, ROLF. "Der alte Mythos vom 'neun' Menschen." *Club Voltaire*, 4 (Munich: 1970), pp. 112–144.

HOEFNAGELS, H. "Marcuse." *Streven*, 22 (Amsterdam: 1968–1969), pp. 126–135.

HOFFMAN, ROBERT. "Marcuse's One-dimensional Vision." *Philosophy of the Social Sciences*, 2 (Toronto: 1972), pp. 43–59.

HOFSTRA, SJOERD. *Over universiteit: Marcuse en rationaliteit* (Leiden: E. J. Brill, 1969).

HOLSHEY, HELMUT. "Psychoanalyse und Gesellschaft: Der Beitrag Herbert Marcuses." *Psyche*, 24 (Heidelberg: 1970), pp. 188–207.

HOLZ, HANS-HEINZ. "Philosophie als Interpretation." *Alternative*, 56–57 (West Berlin: 1967), pp. 235–243.

_____. *Utopie und Anarchismus: Zur Kritik der kritischen Theorie Herbert Marcuses* (Cologne: Pahl-Rugenstein, 1968).

_____. *Die abenteuerliche Rebellion: Bürgerliche Protestbewegungen in der Philosophie—Stirner, Nietzsche, Sartre, Marcuse, Neue Linke* (Neuwied: Luchterhand, 1976).

HOROSZ, WILLIAM. *The Crisis of Responsibility* (Norman: University of Oklahoma Press, 1975).

HOROWITZ, DAVID. "One-dimensional Society?" *International Socialist Journal*, 4 (Milan: 1967), pp. 811–830.

HOROWITZ, GAD. *Repression: Basic and Surplus Repression in Psychoanalytic Theory—Freud, Reich, and Marcuse* (Toronto: University of Toronto Press, 1977), especially pp. 179–214.

HOROWITZ, MICHAEL. "Portrait of the Marxist as an Old Trooper." *Playboy*, 17, 9 (Chicago: 1970), pp. 175–232.

HOWE, I. "Herbert Marcuse or Milovan Djilas." *Harper's*, 239, 1430 (New York: 1969), p. 84 and continued on later pages.

ISRAEL, JARED, AND WILLIAM RUSSEL. "Herbert Marcuse and His Philosophy of Copout." *Progressive Labor*, 6, 5 (New York: 1968), pp. 59–72.

JACOBY, RUSSELL. "Marcuse and the New Academics: A Note on Style." *Telos*, 5 (St. Louis: 1970), pp. 188–190.

JANICAUD, DOMINIQUE. "Marcuse hors de la mode." *Les Etudes philosophiques*, 24, 2 (Paris: 1969), pp. 159–171.

JANSOHN, HEINZ. *Herbert Marcuse: Philosophisch Grundlagen seiner Gesellschaftskritik* (Bonn: Bouvier, 1971).

JAY, MARTIN. "The *Institut für Sozialforschung* and the Origins of Critical Sociology." *Human Factor: Journal of the Graduate Sociology Student Union, Columbia University*, 8 (New York: 1969), pp. 6–18.

_____. "Metapolitics of Utopianism." *Dissent*, 17, 4 (New York: 1970), pp. 342–350.

_____. "The Frankfurt School in Exile." *Perspectives in American History*, 6 (Cambridge: 1972), pp. 339–385.

_____. "The Frankfurt School's Critique of Marxist Humanism." *Social Research*, 39, 2 (New York: 1972), pp. 285–305.

_____. *The Dialectical Imagination: A History of the Frankfurt School and the Institute of Social Research, 1923–1950* (Boston: Little, Brown, 1973).

JOHNSON, PAUL J. "Human Dignity and Marcuse's Erotopia." *Philosophy Forum*, 10 (DeKalb: 1971), pp. 293–303.

JONES, RICHARD M. "The Return of the Un-repressed." *American Imago*, 15, 2 (Boston: 1958), pp. 175–180.

KALTENBRUNNER, GERD-KLAUS. "Der Denker Herbert Marcuse, I: Revolutionärer Eros." *Merkur*, 21, 11 (Munich: 1967), pp. 1080–1084.

_____. "Vorbild oder Verführer? Über den politischen Einfluss der Philosophie Herbert Marcuses." *Wort und Wahrheit*, 25, 1 (Freiburg: 1970), pp. 46–50.

KATEB, GEORGE. "The Political Thought of Herbert Marcuse." *Commentary*, 49, 1 (New York: 1970), pp. 48–63.

KATZ, BARRY M. "New Sources of Marcuse's Aesthetics." *New German Critique*, 17 (Milwaukee: 1979), pp. 176–188.

KAUFMAN, ARNOLD S. "Democracy and the Paradox of Want-Satisfaction." *Personalist*, 52 (Los Angeles: 1971), pp. 186–215.

KEENAN, BRIAN. "The Power of Negative Thinking." *Dialogue: Canadian Philosophical Review*, 10 (Kingston: 1971), pp. 317–331.

KELLNER, DOUGLAS. "Introduction to 'On the Philosophical Foundation of the Concept of Labor.' " *Telos*, 16 (St. Louis: 1973), pp. 2–8.

_____. "Critical Theory, Democracy, and Human Rights." *New Political Science*, 1 (New York: 1979), pp. 12–18.

KEOHANE, NANNERL O. "Communication and Tolerance: A Commentary on the Tinder and Wolff Papers." *Polity*, 6, 4 (Amherst: 1974), pp. 480–487.

KETTLER, DAVID. "Alienation and Negativity." In *Contemporary Political Philosophy*, edited by K. R. Minogue and A. de Crespigny (New York: Dodd, Mead, 1975), pp. 1–48.

KING, RICHARD. *The Party of Eros: Radical Social Thought and the Realm of Freedom* (Chapel Hill: University of North Carolina Press, 1972).

KLIBANSKY, RAYMOND (ed.). *Contemporary Philosophy: A Survey, 4: Ethics, Aesthetics, Law, Religion, Politics, Historical and Dialectical Materialism* (Florence: La nuova italia, 1971).

KOLAKOWSKI, LESZEK. *Main Currents of Marxism: Its Origin, Growth, and Dissolution, The Breakdown*, translated by P. S. Falla (Oxford: Clarendon, 1978), especially pp. 396-420.

KORF, GERTRAUD. *Ausbruch aus dem "Gehäuse der Hörigkeit?" Kritik der Kulturtheorien Max Webers und Herbert Marcuses* (East Berlin: Akademie, 1971).

KRISTOL, I. "The Improbable Guru of Surrealistic Politics." *Fortune*, 80 (Chicago: 1969), p. 191 and continued on later pages.

KRONBERGER, F. "Notes sur *Eros et civilisation* de Herbert Marcuse." *Bulletin de psychologie*, 22, 3-4 (Brussels: 1968), pp. 37-39.

KUNZLI, ARNOLD. *Über Marx hinaus: Beiträge zur Ideologiekritik* (Freiburg: Reinbach, 1969), especially pp. 190-201.

LABRECQUE, RICHARD. "The Relevance of Marcuse to Human Development." *Philosophy of Education: Proceeedings of the Twenty-eighth Annual Meeting* (Edwardsville: 1972), pp. 256-269.

_____. "What Is to Be Done? Pragmatism at the Crossroads." *Studies in Philosophy and Education*, 8, 3 (Edwardsville: 1974), pp. 183- 201.

LACROIX, JEAN. *Le Désir et les désirs* (Paris: Presses universitaires de France, 1975).

LANDES, JOAN B. "Marcuse's Feminist Dimension." *Telos*, 41 (St. Louis: 1979), pp. 158-165.

LANDMANN, M. "Critiques of Reason from Max Weber to Ernst Bloch." *Telos*, 29 (St. Louis: 1976), pp. 187-198.

LAPLANCHE, JEAN. "Notes sur Marcuse et la psychanalyse." *La Nef*, 26, 36 (Paris: 1969), pp. 111-138.

LA POINTE, FRANÇOIS. "Herbert Marcuse: A Bibliographic Essay." *Journal of the British Society for Phenomenology*, 4 (Manchester: 1973), pp. 191-194.

_____, AND CLAIRE LA POINTE. "Herbert Marcuse and His Critics: A Bibliographic Essay." *International Studies in Philosophy*, 7 (Binghamton: 1975), pp. 183-196.

LAURENT, JACQUES. *Lettre ouverte aux étudiants* (Paris: Albin Michel, 1969).

LAWYER, TOM. " 'Basic Marcuse' Sprachhilfe für den Umgang mit 'Fortschrittlichen.' " *Civitas: Monatsschrift des Schweizerischen Studentenvereins*, 25, 11 (Immensee: 1970), pp. 973-975.

LEE, DONALD. "The Concept of Necessity: Marx and Marcuse." *Southwestern Journal of Philosophy*, 6 (Norman: 1975), pp. 47-53.

"Legion vs. Marcuse." *Nation*, 207 (New York: 1968), p. 421.

LEISS, WILLIAM. "Technological Rationality: Notes on 'Work and Freedom in Marcuse and Marx.' " *Canadian Journal of Political Science*, 4, 3 (Toronto: 1971), pp. 398-400.

_____. *The Domination of Nature* (New York: Braziller, 1972), especially pp. 199-212.

_____. "The Problem of Man and Nature in the Work of the Frankfurt School." *Philosophy of the Social Sciences*, 5 (Aberdeen: 1975), pp. 163-172.

_____. "Critical Theory and Its Future." *Political Theory*, 2, 3 (Beverly Hills: 1974), pp. 330-349.

LELLI, MARCELLO. "Marcuse e i cecoslovacchi: note su lavoro e tecnologia." *La critica sociologica*, 111, 10 (Rome: 1969), pp. 136-148.

LICHTHEIM, GEORGE. *From Marx to Hegel* (New York: Seabury, 1974).

LIPP, WOLFGANG. "Apparat und Gewalt: Über Herbert Marcuse." *Soziale Welt*, 20, 3 (Göttingen: 1969), pp. 274-303.

LIPSHIRES, SIDNEY. "Philosophy and Empiricism: Herbert Marcuse Encounters Behavorial Science." *Sociologia*, 6, 2 (Rome: 1972), pp. 7-24.

_____. *Herbert Marcuse: From Marx to Freud and Beyond* (Cambridge: Schenkman, 1974).

LÓPEZ CALERA, N. M. "Filosofía de la negación y crítica social en Herbert Marcuse." *Revista de estudios políticos*, 167 (Madrid: 1969), pp. 69-101.

LOUBET DEL BAYLE, JEAN-LOUIS. "Herbert Marcuse, prophète du 'Grand refus.' " *Revue: littérature, histoire, arts, et science des deux mondes*, 1 (Paris: 1970), pp. 84-107.

LUTZ, ROLLAND RAY, JR. "The 'New Left' of Restoration Germany." *Journal of the History of Ideas*, 31, 2 (New York: 1970), pp. 235-252.

"Macht des Negativen." *Der Spiegel*, 30 (Hamburg: 1967), pp. 97-98.

MACINTYRE, ALASDAIR. "Modern Society: An End to Revolt?" *Dissent*, 12, 2 (New York: 1965), pp. 239-244.

_____. "Herbert Marcuse: From Marxism to Pessimism." *Survey*, 62 (London: 1967), pp. 38-44.

_____. *Herbert Marcuse: An Exposition and a Polemic* (New York: Viking, 1970).

MANFREDI, MARIO. "Marcuse e l'antropologia freudiana." *Annali della Facoltà di lettere e filosofia*, 15 (Bari: 1972), pp. 217-240.

MARABINI, JEAN. *Marcuse et McLuhan et la nouvelle révolution mondiale* (Tours: Mame, 1973).

"Marcuse: Cop-Out or Cop?" *Progressive Labor*, 6, 6 (New York: 1969), pp. 61-66.

MARGIOTTA, UMBERTO. "Ragione e realtà nella filosofia occidentale: I. Kant e Herbert Marcuse." *Aquinas*, 14 (Rome: 1971), pp. 290-306.

MARÍN MORALES, J. A. "La intersección Marx-Freud vista por Herbert Marcuse y Norman Brown." *Arbor*, 93, 363 (Madrid: 1976), pp. 79-96.

MARKS, ROBERT W. *The Meaning of Marcuse* (New York: Ballantine, 1970).

MARSCH, WOLF-DIETER. *Philosophie im Schatten Gottes: Bloch, Camus, Fichte, Hegel, H. Marcuse, Schleiermacher* (Gütersloh: Gütersloher, 1973).

MARTÍN, AMÉRICO. *Marcuse y Venezuela: se aburguesa la clase obrera en Venezuela* (Caracas: Cuadernos Rocinante, 1969).

MASSET, PIERRE. *La Pensée de Herbert Marcuse* (Toulouse: Privat, 1969).

MATTICK, PAUL. *Critique of Marcuse: One-dimensional Man in Class Society* (New York: Herder and Herder, 1972).

MATZ, ULRICH. *Zur Theorie des demokratischen Verfassungsstaates und der Revolution* (Munich: K. Alber, 1975).

MAURER, REINHART. "Der Angewandte Heidegger: Herbert Marcuse und das akademische Proletariat." *Philosophisches Jahr der Gorresgesellschaft*, 77, 2 (Freiburg: 1970), pp. 238-259.

_____. *Revolution und Kehre* (Frankfurt: Suhrkamp, 1975).

MAURER, WILHELM. *Autorität in Freiheit: Zu Marcuses Angriff auf Luthers Freiheitslehre* (Stuttgart: Calwer, 1970).

MAZZETTI, ROBERTO. *Herbert Marcuse o una filosofia-storia del nostro tempo (I nostri problemi)* (Salerno: Beta, 1973).

McINNES, NEIL. *The Western Marxists* (New York: Library Press, 1972), especially pp. 142-168.

MENÉNDEZ UREÑA, ENRIQUE. "La teoría crítica de escuela Frankfurt." *Pensamiento*, 29 (Madrid: 1973), pp. 175-194.

MERQUIOR, JOSÉ GUILHERME. *Arte e sociedade en Marcuse, Adorno, e Benjamin: ensaio crítico sobre a escola neohegeliana de Frankfurt* (Rio de Janeiro: Tempo brasiliero, 1969).

MIDDLETON, RICHARD. "Cage and the Meta-Freudians." *British Journal of Aesthetics*, 12 (London: 1972), pp. 228-243.

MILLER, KARL. "The Point Is Still to Change It." *Monthly Review*, 19, 2 (New York: 1967), pp. 49-57.

MITCHELL, ARTHUR. *The Major Works of Herbert Marcuse: A Critical Commentary* (New York: Monarch, 1975).

MONTGOMERY, J. W. "Marcuse." *Christianity Today*, 14 (Washington, D.C.: 1970), p. 47.

MOORE, JOHN. "Freud, Marx, and Tomorrow." *Kinesis*, 4 (Carbondale: 1971), pp. 31-41.

MORRA, GIANFRANCO. "Marcuse e i sovietici." *Ethica*, 8 (Forlí: 1969), pp. 153-155.

MOUSSEAU, JACQUES, AND PIERRE-FRANÇOIS (eds.). *L'Inconscient de Freud aux techniques de groupe* (Paris: Rete-C.E.P.L., 1976).

NICOLAS, ANDRÉ. *Herbert Marcuse ou la quête d'un univers transprométhéen* (Paris: Seghers, 1969).

_____. *Wilhelm Reich ou la révolution radicale* (Paris: Seghers, 1972).

NIELSON, KAI. "On the Choice between Reform and Revolution." *Inquiry*, 14 (Oslo: 1971), pp. 271-295.

NIN DE CARDONA, JOSÉ. MARÍA. *Herbert Marcuse* (Madrid: Instituto Reus, 1972).

NUZZACO, FRANCESCO. *Herbert Marcuse: filosofo dei nostri tempi* (Rome: Picar, 1969).

OLÉRON, PIERRE. "Le Behaviorisme en question." *Revue philosophique de la France et de l'étranger*, 161, 4 (Paris: 1971), pp. 417-434.

O'NEIL, JOHN (ed.). *On Critical Theory* (New York: Seabury, 1976); see the essays by O'Neil, Ben Agger, Shierry Weber, Paul Piccone, and H. T. Wilson.

ORIOL ANGUERA, ANTONIO. *Para entender a Marcuse* (Mexico City: Trillas, 1970).

OROZ RETA, JOSÉ. "La postura filosófica de Marcuse entre Freud y Marx." *Crisis*, 18 (Madrid: 1971), pp. 53-61.

PALMIER, JEAN MICHEL. *Sur Marcuse* (Paris: Union générale d'éditions, 1968).

_____. *Présentation d'Herbert Marcuse* (Paris: Union générale d'éditions, 1969).

_____. *Herbert Marcuse et la nouvelle gauche* (Paris: P. Belfond, 1973).

PAREKH, B. "Utopianism and Manichaeism: A Critique of Marcuse's Theory of Revolution." *Social Research*, 39, 4 (New York: 1972), pp. 622-651.

PASQUALOTTO, GIANGIORGIO. *Teoria come utopia: studi sulla scuola di Francoforte (Marcuse, Adorno, Horkheimer)* (Verona: Bertani, 1974).

PERETZ, M. "Herbert Marcuse: Beyond Technological Reason." *Yale Review*, 57 (New Haven: 1968), pp. 518-527.

PERLINI, TITO. *Che cosa ha veramente detto Marcuse?* (Rome: Ubaldini, 1968).

PEROTTINO, SERGE. *Roger Garaudy et le marxisme du XXᵉ siècle* (Paris: Seghers, 1969).

PERROUX, FRANÇOIS. *François Perroux interroge Herbert Marcuse . . . 'qui réspond'* (Paris: Aubier-Montaigne: 1969).

PEZZIMENTI, ROCCO. "Marcuse and the Young Dissenters." *Rassegna di scienze filosofiche*, 29 (Naples: 1976), pp. 115-135.

PICCONE, PAUL. "Phenomenological Marxism." *Telos*, 9 (St. Louis: 1971), pp. 3-31.

_____, AND ALEXANDER DELFINI. "Marcuse's Heideggerian Marxism." *Telos*, 6 (St. Louis: 1970), pp. 36-46.

PLEBE, ARMANDO. "Attualità e invecchiamento di Marcuse." *Logos*, 1,

2 (Naples: 1969), pp. 328-342.

PLESSNER, HELMUTH. "Homo absconditus." *Merkur*, 23, 11 (Munich: 1969), pp. 989-998.

POHIER, JACQUES. "Eindimensionalität des Christentums: Zum Thema Marcuse und der eindimensionale Mensch." *Consilium: Internationale Zeitschrift für Theologie*, 7, 5 (Mainz: 1971), pp. 324-330.

POPPI, ANTONINO. "Analisi del discorso morale di Herbert Marcuse." *Studia patavina*, 18 (Padua: 1971), pp. 612-647.

PROTO, MARIO. *Introduzione a Marcuse* (Manduria: Lacaita, 1968).

RATNER, CARL. "Totalitarianism and Individualism in Psychology." *Telos*, 7 (St. Louis: 1971), pp. 50-72.

READ, HERBERT. "El arte como segunda realidad." *Convivium*, 26 (Barcelona: 1968), pp. 81-90.

_____. "Società e arte irrazionale Herbert Marcuse." *Comunitá*, 24, 161-162 (Milan: 1970), pp. 131-140.

REBOUL, OLIVIER. "La Pensée politique de Comte et de Hegel." *Dialogue: Canadian Philosophical Review*, 9 (Kingston: 1970), pp. 181-202.

REINISH, LEONHARD (ed.). *Permanente Revolution von Marx bis Marcuse* (Munich: Callwey, 1969).

RHODES, JAMES M. "Pleasure and Reason: Marcuse's Idea of Freedom." *Interpretation*, 2, 2 (The Hague: 1971-1972), pp. 79-104.

RIEDEL, MANFRED. "Der Denker Herbert Marcuse, II: Die Philosophie der 'Weigerung.' " *Merkur*, 21, 11 (Munich: 1967), pp. 1084-1090.

RIGA, PETER J. "Herbert Marcuse et la critique sociale." *Justice dans le monde*, 11 (Louvain: 1969-1970), pp. 348-369.

ROBINSON, PAUL. *The Freudian Left: Wilhelm Reich, Geza Roheim, Herbert Marcuse* (New York: Harper & Row, Colophon Books, 1969).

ROCAMORA, PEDRO. "Herbert Marcuse y la crisis del hombre tecnológico." *Arbor*, 72 (Madrid: 1969), pp. 261-270.

RODI, FRITHJOF. *Provokation-Affirmation: Das Dilemma des kritischen Humanismus* (Stuttgart: W. Kohlhammer, 1970).

ROHRMOSER, GUNTER. *Das Elend der kritischen Theorie: Theodor W. Adorno, Herbert Marcuse, Jürgen Habermas* (Freiburg: Rombach, 1970).

_____. "Revolution, Philosophie, und Psychoanalyse bei Herbert Marcuse." *Universitas*, 28 (Stuttgart: 1973), pp. 405-410.

ROSZAK, THEODORE. *The Making of a Counter Culture* (New York: Doubleday, 1969), especially pp. 84-123.

ROTENSTREICH, NATHAN. "The Utopia of the Aesthetic Ethos." *Journal of Value Inquiry*, 5, 1 (The Hague: 1970), pp. 44-53.

Rovatti, Pier Aldo. "Esigenza di una costituzione soggettiva in Marcuse." *Aut Aut*, 100 (Milan: 1967), pp. 74-82.

_____. "Marcuse and *The Crisis of the European Sciences*." *Telos*, 2 (St. Louis: 1968), pp. 113-115.

_____. "Il comunismo nell'ultimo Marcuse." *Aut Aut*, 135 (Milan: 1973), pp. 81-85.

Ruprecht, Anthony Mark. "Marx and Marcuse: A Comparative Analysis of Their Revolutionary Theories." *Dialogue*, 17, 2-3 (Milwaukee: 1974-1975), pp. 51-57.

Rusconi, G. *La teoria critica della società* (Bologna: Il Mulino, 1970).

_____. "Marcuse e l'origine della 'Teoria critica della società,' 1928-1938." *Contributi dell'Instituto di filosofia*, 1 (Milan: 1970).

Sachsse, Hans. "Die Technik in der Sicht Herbert Marcuses und Martin Heideggers." *Proceedings of the Fifteenth World Congress of Philosophy*, 1 (Varna: 1973), pp. 371-375.

Sanovio, Piero. "La rivoluzione è sempre marxista?" *La fiera letteraria* (Rome: May 30, 1968), pp. 3-4.

Santinello, G. "La morale del pensiero negativo (Adorno, Horkheimer, Marcuse)." *Incontri culturali*, 3 (Rome: 1970), pp. 51-68.

Sauer, Ernst Friedrich. *Amerikanische Philosophen: Von d. Puritanern bis zu Herbert Marcuse* (St. Augustin: Kersting, 1977).

Schneider, Carl D. "Utopia and History: Herbert Marcuse and the Logic of Revolution." *Philosophy Today*, 12 (Ohio: 1968), pp. 236-245.

Schwab, George. "Legality and Illegality as Instruments of Revolutionaries in Their Quest for Power: Remarks Occasioned by the Outlook of Herbert Marcuse." *Interpretation*, 7 (The Hague: 1978), pp. 74-89.

Sedgewick, Peter. "Natural Science and Human Theory: A Critique of Marcuse." In *The Socialist Register*, edited by Ralph Miliband and John Saville (New York: Monthly Review Press, 1966), pp. 163-192.

Serrano Villafañe, Emilio. "A propósito de Marcuse." *Revista de estudios políticos*, 174 (Madrid: 1970), pp. 113-144.

Shapiro, Jeremy J. "From Marcuse to Habermas." *Continuum*, 8, 1 (Chicago: 1970), pp. 65-76.

_____. "The Dialectic of Theory and Practice in the Age of Technological Rationality: Herbert Marcuse and Jürgen Habermas." In *The Unknown Dimension: European Marxism since Lenin*, edited by Dick Howard and Karl Klare (New York: Basic Books, 1972), pp. 276-303.

_____. "Herbert Marcuse (1898-1979)." *Telos*, 41 (St. Louis: 1979), pp. 186-188.

SHMUELI, EFRAIM. "Contemporary Philosophical Theories and Their Relation to Science and Technology." *Philosophy in Context*, 4 (Cleveland: 1975), pp. 37-60.

SIGISMONDI, CARLO. *Marcuse e la società opulenta* (Rome: Cremonese, 1974).

SING, H. "Herbert Marcuse und die Freiheit." *Politische Studien*, 25, 213 (Munich: 1974), pp. 65-77.

SINGH, R. "A Comparative Study of the Philosophy of Friedrich Nietzsche and Herbert Marcuse." *Humanitas*, 3, 1 (Pretoria: 1975), pp. 93-95.

SIQUÁN, MIGUEL. "La vida y la obra de Herbert Marcuse." *Convivium*, 27 (Barcelona: 1968), pp. 89-101.

SLATER, IAN. "Orwell, Marcuse, and the Language of Politics." *Political Studies*, 23, 4 (London: 1975), pp. 459-474.

SLATER, PHIL. *Origin and Significance of the Frankfurt School: A Marxist Perspective* (London: Routledge & Kegan Paul, 1977), especially pp. 26-92.

SOLASSE, BERNARD. "La Démarche critique d'Herbert Marcuse ou un nouveau type de critique sociale." *Canadian Journal of Political Science*, 2, 4 (Toronto: 1969), pp. 448-470.

SPARROW, J. "Marcuse: The Gospel of Hate." *National Review*, 21 (New York: 1969), pp. 1068-1069.

SPITZ, DAVID. "Pure Tolerance: A Critique of Criticisms." *Dissent*, 13, 5 (New York: 1966), pp. 510-525.

____. "The Pleasures of Misunderstanding Freedom." *Dissent*, 13, 6 (New York: 1966), pp. 729-739.

____, AND PHILIP GREEN. "Again: Tolerance, Democracy, Pluralism — An Exchange." *Dissent*, 14, 3 (New York: 1967), pp. 368-373.

____, AND ROBERT PAUL WOLFF. "On Tolerance and Freedom." *Dissent*, 14, 1 (New York: 1967), pp. 95-98.

STEIGERWALD, ROBERT. "Osservazioni sulla dialettica in Herbert Marcuse." *Critica marxista*, 6, 3 (Rome: 1968), pp. 35-47.

____. "Dialektik und Klassenkampf bei Herbert Marcuse." *Deutsche Zeitschrift für Philosophie*, 17, 5 (East Berlin: 1969), pp. 601-606.

____. *Herbert Marcuses dritter Weg* (Cologne: Pahl-Rugenstein, 1969).

____. "Herbert Marcuse's 'Critical Theory.'" *Revolutionary World*, 11 (Amsterdam: 1975), pp. 240-248.

STERN, SOL. "The Metaphysics of Rebellion: On Herbert Marcuse." *Ramparts*, 6, 12 (San Francisco: 1968), pp. 55-60.

STEUERNAGEL, GERTRUDE A. *Political Philosophy as Therapy: Marcuse Reconsidered* (Westport: Greenwood, 1979).

STILLMAN, E. "Marcuse." *Horizon*, 11, 3 (New York: 1969), pp. 26-31.

STOCKMAN, N. "Habermas, Marcuse, and the *Aufhebung* of Science and Technology." *Philosophy of the Social Sciences*, 8, 1 (Aberdeen: 1978), pp. 15-35.

STOEV, STOJU G. "The Neofreudism of E. Fromm and H. Marcuse: A Critical Analysis." *Darshana International*, 15, 3 (Moradabad: 1975), pp. 31-38.

STOHS, MARK. "The Role of Hedonism in Marcuse's Early Thought." *Man and World: An International Philosophical Review*, 9, 4 (The Hague: 1976), pp. 325-341.

STRUHL, KARSTEN. "Marcuse's Search for the Revolutionary Agent." *Radical Philosophers' Newsjournal* (Somerville: Spring 1978), pp. 19-29.

SUMPER, DARÍO. *Sociología, historia, y teoría* (Bogota: Ediciones de la Universidad nacional, 1974).

TADIC, L. "Herbert Marcuse: Zwischen Wissenschaft und Utopie." *Praxis*, 8, 1-2 (Zagreb: 1972), pp. 141-168.

TESTA, ALDO. *Rivoluzione culturale e scuola dialogica: la dimensione marcusiana e il dialogo* (Bologna: Cappelli, 1969).

THERBORN, GÖRAN. "A Critique of the Frankfurt School." *New Left Review*, 63 (London: 1970), pp. 65-96.

TRAGTENBERG, MAURICIO. "O anti-Weber: Herbert Marcuse." *Revista brasileira de filosofía*, 21 (São Paulo: 1971), pp. 15-25.

ULLE, DIETER. "Notwendige Kritik der 'kritischen Theorie' [Herbert Marcuse, *Der eindimensionale Mensch* . . .]." *Deutsche Zeitschrift für Philosophie*, 16, 4 (East Berlin: 1968), pp. 483-489.

_____. *È rivoluzionaria la dottrina di Marcuse?* (Turin: Borla, 1969).

_____. "Kulturrevolution und Kunst: Bemerkungen zur kulturauffassung Herbert Marcuses." *Weimarer Beiträge: Zeitschrift für Literaturwissenschaft, Aesthetik, und Kulturtheorie*, 12 (East Berlin: 1973), pp. 93-104.

VALADIER, PAUL. "Modernité et critiques de la modernité." *Etudes*, 334 (Paris: 1972), pp. 361-376.

VAN DEN ENDEN, H. "Kultur- und Ideologiekritik bei den Neodialektikern, Adorno und Marcuse." *Philosophica Gandensia*, 9, 1 (Ghent: 1971), pp. 4-34.

VASCONCELOS, PERBOYRE. "Mensagem estética de Herbert Marcuse." *Convivium*, 8, 3 (São Paulo: 1969), pp. 202-210.

VELLILAMTHADAM, THOMAS. "Affluence versus Transcendence: A Reflection of Marcuse's Analysis of the Affluent Society." *Journal of Dharma*, 3 (Bangalore: 1978), pp. 45-52.

VERGEZ, ANDRÉ. *Marcuse* (Paris: Presses universitaires de France, 1970).

VERZILLO, ANNA. "La critica di Marcuse al formalismo scientifico." *Annali della Facoltà di lettere e filosofia*, 15 (Bari: 1972), pp. 385-411.

VIANO, C. A. "Marcuse o i rimorsi dell'hegelismo perduto." *Rivista di filosofia*, 59, 2 (Turin: 1968), pp. 149-183.

VILLARROEL, JESÚS. "Presupuestos de la revolución en Marcuse." *Studium*, 12 (Madrid: 1972), pp. 515-536.

VINCENT, JEAN-MARIE. *La Théorie critique de l'école de Francfort* (Paris: Galilée, 1976).

VIRCILLO, DOMENICO. "L'uomo a una dimensione di Marcuse e l'immaginario di Sartre." *Teoresi*, 27 (Catania: 1972), pp. 51-76.

VITIELLO, VINCENZO. "Scienza e tecnica nel pensiero di Heidegger." *Pensiero*, 18 (Rome: 1973), pp. 113-148.

VIVAS, ELISEO. *Contra Marcuse* (New York: Dell, Delta Books, 1971).

WALSH, J. L. "Why Marcuse Matters." *Commonweal*, 93, 1 (New York: 1970), pp. 21-25.

WALZER, MICHAEL. "On the Nature of Freedom." *Dissent*, 13, 6 (New York: 1966), pp. 725-728.

WEBER, HENRI. *Marxisme et conscience de classe* (Paris: Union générale d'éditions, 1975).

WELLMER, ALBRECHT. *Critical Theory of Society* (New York: Herder and Herder, 1971).

WETTERGREEN, JOHN ADAMS, JR. "Is Snobbery a Formal Value? Considering Life at the End of Modernity." *Western Political Quarterly*, 26, 1 (Salt Lake City: 1973), pp. 109-129.

WIATR, J. J. "Herbert Marcuse: Philosopher of a Lost Radicalism." *Science and Society*, 34, 3 (New York: 1970), pp. 319-330.

WIDMER, K. "Society as a Work of Art." *Nation*, 211 (New York: 1970), pp. 23-26.

WILDEN, ANTHONY. "Marcuse and the Freudian Model: Energy, Information, and *Phantasie*." *Salmagundi*, 10-11 (New York: 1969-1970), pp. 196-245.

WILLMS, BERNARD. *Revolution und Protest oder Glanz und Elend des bürgerlichen Subjekts Hobbes, Fichte, Hegel, Marx, Marcuse* (Stuttgart: W. Kolhammer, 1969).

WINTHROP, HENRY. "Variety of Meaning in the Concept of Decadence." *Philosophy and Phenomenological Research*, 31 (Buffalo: 1971), pp. 510-526.

WODDIS, JACK. *New Theories of Revolution: A Commentary on the Views of Frantz Fanon, Regis Debray, and Herbert Marcuse* (London: Lawrence and Wishart, 1972).

WOLFF, KURT, AND BARRINGTON MOORE, JR. (eds.). *The Critical Spirit: Essays in Honor of Herbert Marcuse* (Boston: Beacon, 1967).

WOLFF, ROBERT PAUL. "Marcuse's Theory of Toleration." *Polity*, 6, 4 (Amherst: 1974), pp. 469-480.

_____. "Herbert Marcuse: 1898-1979: A Personal Reminiscence." *Political Theory*, 8, 1 (Beverly Hills: 1980), pp. 5-8.

ZAHN, LOTHAR. "Herbert Marcuses Apotheose der Negation." *Philosophische Rundschau*, 16 (Tubingen: 1969), pp. 165-184.

ZAMOSHKIN, I. A., AND N. V. MOTROSHILOVA. "Is Marcuse's 'Critical Theory of Society' Critical?" *Soviet Studies in Philosophy*, 8, 1 (White Plains: 1969), pp. 45-66.

ZIMA, PIERRE VACLAV. *L'Ecole de Francfort* (Paris: Editions universitaires, 1974).

Index